BECOME A
BETTER PARENT

MATTHEW AMOS

ISBN:
978-0-692-13633-1

DEDICATION

Dedicated to my wife Gina and our children, Isla and Max.

A special dedication to our daughter, Emily, who is no longer with us.

I must mention Emily, who was tragically still born, as she plays such an important role in my life and always will. There is a saying in life after when something tragic happens along the lines of "Not a day goes by I don't think about…" Well I can honestly say that doesn't really apply to me in a sense, because I think about her all the time, not just once every day. My life will never be the same after what happened and I still very much struggle with it. All I can try to do is find strength and do positive things such as writing this book. So if there is anyone I would really like to dedicate this to, it would be Emily.

CONTENTS

CONTENTS CONT.

CONTENTS CONT.

CONTENTS CONT.

CONTENTS CONT.

ACKNOWLEDGMENTS

I would like to acknowledge my wife and children as much of the content in this book is based upon my real-life experiences of being a parent. This includes the good as well as the bad, mainly in terms of sharing things that have worked, and things which haven't. I would also like to acknowledge my parents Maggie and Colin, to whom I owe so much for everything they did for me growing up. Also my immediate as well as my extended family and friends who play a big part in my life. More generally, I would also like to acknowledge all of the parents that I interact with on a daily basis. Some I know, some I don't. In the case of those I don't I will share my observations, not judgments, throughout the many things I regularly see – again the good and the bad.

FOREWORD/INTRODUCTION

Dear Parent. You might be thinking, "so what is this book about"? Before I answer that, I want to make it very clear from the start that this is not a book written by a parent who thinks he is the perfect parent or proclaims to be anything close to it. I think we all know there is no such thing as the perfect parent, or person for that matter. But I'm sure it might also cross your mind to think what qualifies this guy to give advice on parenting? Well, other than being a parent myself, I will be the first to admit there's not an awful lot. I have no fancy title or a PhD and I haven't won any parenting awards. So although I might not be selling myself a great deal here, I simply wanted to write a book on parenting, from an everyday/here and now/real-world parent's perspective. So that's actually my sell to you as a reason for reading this, as I'm the first to admit I'm not the perfect parent and nowhere near the sort. I'm not saying or think that just because I'm writing a book on parenting makes me a perfect role model parent who has all the answers, as this is an admission that I'm far from it. I'm no expert on parenting but with something as unique as parenting, should we be always looking for a so called expert for advice? How about just listening to a parent who experiences similar things to you, knows the type of things you're going through, understands the challenges, knows how you feel? By writing this I'm not going to pretend to be something I'm not and so I think with such honesty, real parents in the real world will be able to relate to many of my thoughts, as well as the many things that I will address in this book. Anyway that's enough from me perhaps trying to justify why you should read on. Maybe just look at it this way – if there is something/anything in here that will help make you a better parent then surely that's worth it?

With this book, I simply want to share some of my experiences, advice and observations that I have learned to date. I will share what I want to call real world examples to which, I believe, many other parents out there go through similar if not the same type of experiences. Again, this is not designed to be a message from the expert, but if anyone can take some positive advice from what I have learned and observed so far, then I believe I have served a positive purpose for writing this book. I hope many, ranging from the new, to more experienced parents, can understand or relate to my thoughts in their own lives which in turn can help them in the real and fast paced world we live in. Not just that, I hope to reach the expectant parent on potentially new areas to think about which they may not have even considered. Above all, everything is written with a purpose of becoming a better parent.

I'm sure that there will be certain elements within this book that you may disagree with, but my intent is to, at least, provoke thought. We all know there are many different approaches and styles to parenting. But I'm sure where we all would agree and be on the same page is that we ultimately want what's best for our children. I'm sure that on a personal level, whilst stating the obvious, we want to be the best parents that we can possibly be. As I said at the beginning, there is no such thing as the perfect parent so to put a positive spin on this, as there is no end it does mean that there is endless room for us to improve and try to become better parents. The onus therefore is on us individually to seek that improvement, to take the responsibility to learn and develop, just as we do in say our professional careers as an example. When it comes to parenting, I think the saying "Learning on the Job" is perhaps ultimately most relevant as we experience new things all the time in which we have no past experience in dealing with.

We all lead/live different lives, live in different places and simply, are at different stages of our lives. You may be reading this as a new parent, expectant parent or even as a grandparent. In addition, you may have one child, 5 children or 10 children. I think you get my point here, so what I would say is that you have to look to apply my advice and consider it against your own unique set of circumstances. However, although we do lead different lives, I believe that parents today face many similar challenges which I will focus on throughout.

Another thing I would like to make clear from the start is that this is not a book for a new parent with crash course advice on how to change a diaper/nappy or anything like that. This book is more about looking to share my thoughts on parenting principles, addressing what I believe are some of the most important things in parenting, but are topics which don't necessarily or automatically come to mind when it comes to advice. Some of my advice stems from things that I think have worked well, from mistakes I have made, and also the good, bad and the sometimes ugly I have observed from other parents. I will also share or pass on what I believe to be good advice from which I have previously came across one way or another.

The chapters will also look at some more common things you will be familiar with but as stated, I would also like to think some of the chapters will provide many new things for you to consider. I would say this is not your conventional parenting book but ultimately you will make the call on that. These are my personal views and mine alone, so you may not agree with everything I have to say but in an age of political correctness, I still believe in the importance of expressing yourself as well as the benefit of debating issues when there are differences in opinion. I think it's important to be open to such differences, new ideas and views rather than be narrow or single minded by shutting anything out which remotely goes against your trail of thought. So all I would say to you when reading this is to be open minded and give some of my advice a try if you like the sound of it.

When I say be open minded, I mean don't be defensive about anything you read as it certainly isn't intended to be personal in anyway. I find it's very natural to become defensive or guarded when looking at parenting advice or your own children. It's easy to be sensitive and to take things to heart when it comes to you and your family, but I cannot emphasize enough that all of this is written with a specific goal/focus which is to become a better parent. So I repeat my advice is be open specifically bearing in mind the goal/focus of this book. Some of you may also be thinking why on earth would I want to hear from someone else telling me what I should and shouldn't do with my own kids? I get it and I say this because with myself included, when it comes to certain things you especially don't need anyone else telling you how to raise your own children. But I certainly would like to think this book is written in such a way where there is no telling involved. I don't pretend to have all the answers so the main thing is that the advice offered is based around sharing experiences and ideas. It's for you to consider and apply to your own circumstances so you then decide should you want to action something in anyway. So before I go any further, this is another point I want to make clear in that there is no telling from my part. I totally understand how personal parenting is and how important it is for parents to make their own decisions.

Speaking personally, I consider myself as open-minded in such a way where if someone gave me some constructive parenting advice which might go against something I currently think or I'm doing, I would consider it. I would consider it based on the fact it might give me the opportunity to improve or do something better. Essentially make me become a better parent one way or another! When I say consider it, it means just that, consider. It doesn't mean I will necessarily take on board everything or agree with every single bit of advice that comes my way. However, I believe that I'm open enough to think a little differently on something or change something I might be doing, if I determine on reflection/consideration that there is in fact a better way. Again it's about becoming a better parent. I don't think there can be too much time for things like stubbornness, single-mindedness or just generally being so set in your own ways to where you cover your eyes/ears or just switch off when there is a different point of view. So maybe also bear this in mind as you go through.

One of the main things that I hope gets across is that the language and advice offered in this book is something all parents can relate to, understand and can easily be taken on board should you choose to do so. Essentially I'm talking at the same level as you. This book is speaking parent to parent and will provide you with many ideas that you can easily and immediately look to put into action if you want to. I have come across a lot of parenting books and advice which use a lot of jargon and narrative which sounds almost text book like, searching for some form of idealistic approach. Not just that, you can read something which is offering advice with fancy words but sometimes you walk away and think, what is the advice here? Is it practical and can I apply it to my life? Am I being offered some actions that I can look to implement at home? Therefore my intent is to not give some ideological/fairy tale parenting advice which, when applied in the real world is not applicable after all. Or as I personally like to put it arty-farty advice which sounds like fluff and doesn't provide you with any specifics to take on board at all. In fact, I do want to acknowledge when it comes to parenting and children some things are a lot easier said than done. By recognizing the complexity of parenting and the day-to-day challenges, I think it's easier to talk at a level where other parents will quite simply get it.

I want to get across my thoughts from a real-world parent's point of view. I don't really want to label myself as an ordinary guy, or normal, or the modern day parent, but hopefully you understand where I am coming from with this type of generic description/label. Ultimately, I'm a regular guy with a wife and two kids which is my family to support. By providing some of my experiences and examples, I hope you can easily relate to what I'm saying and use it to good effect. Essentially what I'm saying is that all parents have to deal with the everyday hectic challenges of time constraints, limited resources, work commitments, stress, lack of energy, finances, multi-tasking, distractions and being pulled in each and every direction, only wishing for a few more hours in the day. I get that as parents the reality is we're always on the go whether its school, bills, work, chores, and activities on repeat. I also want to acknowledge something as a real world parent. This is not to be confused with moaning/complaining as I'm sure you're like me in that you love nothing more than being a parent. For all the love and joy it brings let's be honest being a parent brings such a wide range of emotions. This includes things like stress and worry and with the constant challenges/demands we face in our hectic lives, being a parent at times can be exhausting/draining where it can completely suck all the life out you.

My thoughts and advice are genuinely intended for all parents. Some may disagree, but I don't think the age of the parent is the key factor on who to listen to for parenting advice. I tend to think that, in this sense, age is just a number and we can all learn from each other. So, for those parents who are older/wiser, have more children than me and are more experienced when it comes to parenting, I also want to make very clear that I don't think I'm some sort of know-it-all. We are all at different stages in our life and come from all walks of life so this is my take on parenting so far with the intent of offering advice for anyone who wants to listen. So I think what I'm trying to get to is for you to consider my words rather than necessarily dismiss anything I have to say, given the fact that I'm still relatively new to parenting. That's not suggesting you will either but back to my point I do think to a certain degree age is just a number. I don't need to spell it out but just because someone may be older and has a lot more children doesn't necessarily mean that they're automatically a great parent. The opposite is also true so I think my advice to you reading this, is to look at what I have to say perhaps more objectively or in isolation and apply it to your own life/circumstances. This is not to say I'm right either so I repeat I will not ever pretend to be some form of Mr know-it-all on any parenting topic. As I said, be open to my advice and, whether you like it or not on any given area, so at the very least you can give it some further thought based on your own opinions/circumstances.

I will shortly introduce my family but as a father, I'm sure there might be the odd thing here and there in this book that might resonate more with other fathers. However, in the main this is advice for parents, both mum and dad, and so the point is that it's certainly not designed for just dads or just mothers for that matter. But ultimately you will be the judge of that. Really I want this to be as far-reaching as possible and no more so than with the new or expectant parents ready to start their new journey. I hope some of my thoughts help you consider some things that you may not have thought about or did not/have not necessarily come to your mind, even as or whilst you're preparing to be a parent.

At this time, it makes sense for me to introduce my family. I won't go into too much detail at this stage other than to share that I'm married to Gina and we have been married for almost 10 years. We have a daughter Isla who is currently 6 and a son Max who is our new-born. Our family would not be complete if I did not mention our other daughter Emily, who was tragically still-born. At this time, I don't really feel the need to explain any further about my family or go into detail about the love I have for them as it goes without saying.

I would like to close my opening remarks by saying that I'm so proud to be a father. I can now not imagine my life any other way. I'm sure this is something you can relate to as my wife and I have said before that it's almost strange to look back at a time before we had kids as it now seems as though it was in a previous life or a lifetime ago. Or to put it another way, we can't now imagine our lives any other way, without our children. Parenting is the most rewarding gift and it brings so many emotions along the way. So far I have already experienced varying degrees of highs and the lowest of lows and no doubt the ups and downs will only continue. I will repeat there is no such thing as the perfect parent but as it's the most important job for all mothers and fathers, my view is that all we can do is try and get better. With that, I think we have a responsibility to learn and get better because it's so important, although we might not necessarily always look at it this way. We will all have different goals and aspirations when it comes to our children. But a point I would like to reiterate, is that I think we would all agree that at the end of the day, we want what is best for our children. I hope some of my advice, thoughts, guidance and observations can benefit you in some way. I'm really hoping that you will take a lot out of reading this which helps you to become a better parent, which in my view is the most important job of all. I think it's best to admit that you're always learning. This is because it's then easier to be more human in that you will be open to advice, acknowledge your mistakes, where you learn from them rather than playing the blame game, making an excuse or dismissing responsibility.

I thank you in advance of reading this. Enjoy the read and I sincerely hope you can implement some of my advice to have a positive impact on your life as a parent and the lives of your children. In time you can then decide for yourself if you really have become a better parent.

1 SCHEDULE/PLANNING/TIME MANAGEMENT

There are many chapters in this book and I haven't really given them any order of priority other than this one. Schedule, planning and time management are, I believe, all linked together. What I believe becomes vital with parenting, is managing your own time as well your children's, as the term "time management" clearly suggests. I'm over-simplifying here, but the key is to really consider what you as the parent, as well as your child, do with your time. I'm sure time management as a term or concept and its importance, has been preached to you on many occasions whether it's in your professional or personal life. When it comes to parenting, I like to look at it as managing your priorities with your family and children and then ensuring time is allocated to your priorities. I say this because I know how life can sort of just get in the way of what's actually important to you. Hopefully this makes sense to you when I refer to time management when focusing on parenting, as I think it does need to be broken down a little further, rather than just saying time management in a broad sense. If you have your priorities set as a parent and manage your time around those then you have focus/structure and a purpose to your day. In essence you revolve your schedule/life around your priorities rather than the other way round where you try and fit in where you can the things that are most important to you. At face value it might appear to be a very subtle difference between the two, but the impact can potentially have a very significant difference over time.

Scheduling and planning are focused on the short-term future so that you have more control of your present. It might seem obvious advice but in the real world it's a lot easier said than done to be productive and do purposeful things each and every day, individually as a parent and also with your child/children. I want to make clear that I understand this challenge very clearly. However, I believe that having planning/scheduling as a primary focus, combined with good time management; you will be setting yourself up for success. Not just that, you will be putting you and your family in a good position to achieve things on a daily and then on a long-term basis. I don't want to give some text book or generic advice here by saying "form good habits to achieve your goals over time". What I'm saying is set yourself up just so you can do purposeful things every day. Or set up your child so they can do something which is of benefit to them so, in essence, you are all using your time wisely.

Parents frequently use sayings like "there are not enough hours in the day" or "the day has just run away with me". Yes, we all have days like this but let those days be more of the exception and not the everyday norm. That is why having a schedule/structure and planning ahead is key. Otherwise all too frequently the day will pass you by, everything will seem a bit of a blur, one day will roll into the next and, most frustratingly, you feel that you have not accomplished anything. I believe that if you don't plan ahead and essentially know what you have planned to set out to do, that is when your head can be easily put into a spin. I also tend to find if you're not organized, don't have things planned out in line with your priorities is when you feel like you're trying to do a hundred things at once and where it feels like you're always going at a hundred miles an hour. Not just that, you have all of the distractions/temptations and all of the other things going on around you, or that get thrown at you on a daily basis. That is the exact time that everything can become a blur and then the day gets away with you. This is when you are also more inclined to be lazy and choose an easy option rather than what is necessarily the best one. So there are implications. A simple example might be giving your child fast food over a healthy meal, or putting the TV on rather than you reading them a story, or playing outside with them. It's impossible to plan out every second of the day but you will know when your child will have some downtime so can you pre-plan to do something with them? In this book, I will focus on many simple everyday examples like this. It's doing things on your terms but not in any selfish kid of way. What I mean by that is it's all about taking back control of your day and ensuring that you have the opportunity to take action on the priorities you had already set out to do. So, with our basic example, can you look to move some things around in your day, so that you make sure you're able to read with your child before bed-time rather than have them sitting them in front of a show they may have already seen many times before?

I will repeat this on several occasions as I think it rings true that, for all the best planning in the world, life throws many things at you as a parent, so at times you will need to be flexible and adapt. It might seem a little contradictory in that, whilst I'm saying plan/structure and schedule your week, I'm also saying don't have it so stringent that you have to stick to it methodically. If something does come up see if you can move one of your other priorities and adjust your schedule accordingly. This way you will appreciate how much your schedule helps you as you will find a way of getting something done that is really important and that you have committed to doing that day or week.

I really hope this initial advice doesn't sound patronizing in anyway, as at first hand, it's really pointing out the obvious. I do see a lot of parents/families who are well organized with their children when it comes to getting ready for school, getting to school on time, and then picking them up from school – things like that. This, however, is a predetermined schedule which essentially you must look to follow as it's already set out for you. So I want to go deeper and look more specifically at those gaps during the day which are not pre-determined. What I'm referring to and suggesting that you pay close attention to, is the time that you ultimately have the responsibility for, to ensure that it's used most effectively/efficiently. It's looking at this time in a bit more detail and, by planning ahead, I believe that, with good choices, you can make an incredible difference to your child in the long-term with things like their health, nutrition, education, sporting activities or anything else you may identify of importance to you as a family.

My advice is to pay close attention to the time that you share with your children and the additional time your child has away from school/education. You might not always be with them because of work commitments as an obvious example but, by planning ahead, can you look to ensure your child will be doing something worthwhile? You may need to work with your spouse, partner, friends, and grandparents if this means taking them to practices, lessons and other such activities. Because, if you don't, this is when it's easy to fall into the trap when your children use this time by watching the same old shows, playing the same video games or playing on their cell phone. This is when it feels like one day rolls into the next without much being accomplished. My advice is to utilize the spare time your children have each and every day. Utilize it so that they are not doing the same thing for 6 months to a year which may be getting home from school, watching TV, playing a video game, playing on the cell phone and then going to bed. I admit I maybe over exaggerating here, but I just want to highlight the potential trap.

On the other hand it might seem very normal to some for their child to follow a similar routine. Hopefully this might make you consider that there could be a better use of that time? Utilize this time so they can learn and develop in something new and I think you will see the benefit of doing so over a period of time like 6 months to a year. This is where I believe that you, as the parent, come in and play such a key role. I feel that it's on the parent, particularly with younger children, to be proactive to ensure that their children will be doing something productive for their personal benefit. This book is about becoming a better parent so I think you will be doing just that by ensuring that your child is making positive use of their time.

This is a personal opinion, but I don't see enough parents really taking the time where they're giving full consideration to these "gaps" of time in the week ahead and as a result they end up taking things more day by day. This isn't a criticism either as it's so easy to do living as a real world parent. With so many things going on in the present moment, and other things whirling through your mind at times you may feel that just getting through, or surviving, the day is a success. It might be that you are so consumed with the present that you can't begin to think about what you, or your children, will be doing in a few days' time. But I really do think this type of feeling can at least start to be eradicated with some forward planning. This is so that you can start to make progress in areas which you value as a parent. On the same note, this will also enable you to apply more focus on what you feel is important both day-to-day and over a longer period of time for your child.

This book has many chapters which rely on you successfully planning ahead, and scheduling, so that you can do things like exercise and give healthy meals to your children. So more on that to follow, but I think you need to understand that planning/scheduling will become your friend in such hectic times in our fast paced world. This will enable you to have more control of your time and what you and your children are doing, or not doing. My suggestion to you is not to take things day by day, just take a little time at the start of each week to establish your priorities and then schedule/plan accordingly. We have all heard of the saying "make each day count" and, speaking personally, by establishing my priorities and planning ahead, my intention is always to do just that. Saying something like "make each and every day count" to me does sound more like an affirmation or some ideological slogan and I do want to talk as a real world parent. Let me make clear this is not about doing overelaborate things (I will give some personal examples shortly). Again I believe it's about keeping your priorities in check so that you and your children are doing things in line with those priorities. I'm not going to say each and every day, as I know it's not as simple/easy as that, but let's just say more often than not. So what I'm really trying to say is do your best so that the day, week or month doesn't pass you or your children by as I think this can easily happen. Like you I'm a real world parent so I won't deny that there are days when I don't get much done or, to put it another way, some days are just better, or more productive than others. As a parent life can throw so many things at you and unexpected events can also throw you off course. I don't know about you but I hate it when a day or two goes by and, for one reason or another, the days were unproductive and either I, my children, or family as a whole, did not get much done. So this is why I really recommend having that little bit of foresight, looking ahead a little, seeing the wood through the trees so to speak. Call it what you want but this is where I believe you come in and where you need to take that responsibility as parent so that you can ultimately look to make as the saying goes "each day count". This is for you as a parent and for your child so that life doesn't pass anyone by. I believe this concept also applies to us on an individual basis and on a personal level, so I will also look at this in forthcoming chapters.

There are many different methods and techniques out there related to scheduling/planning and time management. I will share mine with you shortly but my advice is to do what you know will work or that you know that you will action. If you don't like the way I do it that's fine, the concept is the most important thing. All I would say is to make the action simple and easy. You don't have to spend a lot of time to plan the week ahead and you certainly don't need to overcomplicate it either. Keep it simple and this will increase the likelihood that you will continue doing it and I'm sure you will quickly see the benefits of doing so.

My wife has a saying as she can be forgetful at times that she has "mum/baby brain". I know what she means and I don't know if it has caught on yet for dads but I definitely feel that I have "dad brain" at times – meaning there is so much swirling around in your mind that you can forget something you just set out to do only a moment ago. So I will share some simple advice that works for me and my wife and I think that works well. I must acknowledge this advice is certainly not rocket science or anything new for that matter which is why I actually think makes it all the better. It's simple and takes very little time. Therefore, it's very easy to do; it's just a matter of being disciplined to do the action each week and to plan ahead. So a simple example: we plan our meals for the week ahead on a Sunday and we know who is cooking on which day. This way we get all we need when we do the food shop and know we have planned out some healthy meals for the week.

Now I must pause and say this is an example that works for us. It's just that, an example. We are all different so again use it as a guide as to what works for you. This may be a bad example for some depending on what job you have and all the different activities you may do, but the main thing that I'm trying to highlight is that planning ahead helps us save time. I know some will say I don't know what I would want to eat in three days' time so why would I decide now? I get that too but, again, I'm trying to give real world parenting advice. So my view is that I would rather plan and get everything I need rather than have to go to the grocery store each and every day and then decide. I think the more you leave it to the last minute the more inclined you will be to pick up takeout food rather than cook. I'm all for things that save time so make something which will give left overs for the next day or make a batch that you can freeze for another time. Again, this is nothing new and I'm sure there are so many parents already doing this. I'm just highlighting a point relating to time management, scheduling and planning ahead as this is relevant in this instance and applied in a very basic form. This simple time-management technique which I would imagine that many parents use, essentially gives us back valuable time in our busy day/week whilst also ensuring we eat healthy food.

Another thing that works well for me is that I have a planner/calendar book which has a new week on each page and on each page the week is broken up into days of the week. For each day, I write down my three or four priorities that I want to get done for each day in the week ahead. I also try and schedule with a specific time in mind for that day. This is so that, again, I know ahead of time and can work around my various commitments for that day whether it's my job or something else. This allows me to stay focused, and these priorities are mainly personal which focus on me and my family/children. I find three or four is optimal as any more than that depending on what it is, may over-stretch yourself when you want it to be realistic/achievable. Sure there are days when I don't get it all done. I may roll something over, or another priority might come up, so I may need to adjust but being aware of my priorities still allows me to be in control even if it means having to reschedule something. I know myself that I will get it done. So, to give you some examples of my priorities I'm not referring to anything complicated it's more of the day-to-day actions which are achievable. So, one week my daughter may have an event at school on one day, so this will be listed as a priority for me to attend. I know this may need me to be flexible for some other things throughout the week so that I can be sure to show up. I may be working out on two or three of the days, scheduling my daughter to be at her golf/tennis practices or making sure that I call one of my relatives. In these examples it shows that I have priorities for myself and my children. A priority of mine is my health so I try to exercise. For my children a priority of mine is to give my daughter opportunity, so I plan and schedule her sports for the week ahead. This is a priority of mine using her spare time to plan and schedule something like sports as I think it is of benefit to her and is, quite frankly, a better use of time. This may be with coaches, myself or just the general co-ordination of who is available to take her where and when. It might need us to call on a grandparent to take her one day but again the importance of planning enables us to give that heads-up rather than a last minute call only to find they can't take her because they have something else on. That is the beauty of planning and being organized; you're not doing or asking people things on the spur of the moment. With life so hectic these days, it's seems almost impossible to do anything or for anyone to be available at the drop of a hat.

I really don't want to come across judgmental with what I'm about to say, I just want to point out observations I frequently see. For instance, I see many parents in a constant rush, chasing their tail so to speak, always in a hurry, showing up late or leaving everything to the last minute. I'm not saying that this never happens to us but I feel things like this can, at least, be reduced by better planning and organizing. So yes, there are times my wife and I are scrambling, rushing around, and late for something with our children. All I would say is that by planning, scheduling and being organized this is more of a rarity rather than something which happens all the time. My advice is to work with your spouse/partner and simply communicate, so that you're both on the same page with the schedule for the week and you know who's doing what. Because things are so hectic, I don't know about you, but I like having a schedule to work around so that as a family we're less inclined to try and do something on the fly or scramble around at the last minute to try and get somewhere. For example, if I suddenly asked my wife to take my daughter to her golf lesson on the day that it's planned, it becomes that more challenging. I suspect that most parents don't like something suddenly being asked of them so, again, by knowing in advance it's a lot easier to work around rather than try to fit in, and there is a difference between the two. I believe that when someone is rushed or constantly pushed for time the most appealing option in terms of what to do with time, is to choose the easiest one. But is the easy option ultimately good for you as a parent or for your child?

It works for me and going back to an earlier point you might be reading this thinking "why on earth would you need to write down and plan to call a relative or have that as a priority"? I get why it might seem a little strange to some, but for me, I know that if I plan on doing something I will do it and I won't forget. If I don't plan or schedule it, and although I won't do it purposely, I think there is a chance I may forget with my so called "dad/baby brain." For example, I call my Great Uncle in England every week and he cherishes the call and so do I. So something like this is a priority of mine and I would not intentionally forget to call him but it's easy to do as a parent, so this is why I plan ahead to ensure that I do it. Hopefully you understand now where I'm coming from. You won't all have a Great Uncle that lives overseas but, using this as an example, how often do you hear someone say something along the lines of: "I must give her/him a call and catch up".… "It's been too long since we last spoke"… "I have lost touch with"….? Again I'm bringing this back to planning ahead, scheduling and time management. You may mean to do something today, tomorrow, this week or sometime soon but, without trying to patronize/undermine, without planning or scheduling it does become difficult because you're more inclined to find yourself muddled in the present when you're getting pulled in many directions. Essentially there are just so many different things that kind of just get in the way. In those latest examples, I believe that it's not something that we deliberately do as it often dawns on us from nowhere that we should contact someone we have been meaning to for a long time. But if you plan/schedule at the start of the week and say to yourself "I'm going to call or visit my old friend/relative on Wednesday" then you're more likely to do it. If on Wednesday something happens out of the blue then you can adjust and do it on Thursday or Friday. Again, very common sense stuff but all the more likely to happen by planning ahead and being organized as best as you can realistically be. I'm just saying this because forward planning/scheduling and time management are things that really work for us. I won't pretend that every day goes according to plan and that I achieve everything I set out to. But it does keep me focused and keeps my priorities in check. It's so useful on those days which can start to get the best of you or when nothing seems to go your way.

You might also be thinking what does this example of connecting with a family or friend have to do with parenting? Well, I will touch on it more later in the book, but it means that although your children are no doubt your top priority, I believe that, at the same time, it doesn't mean that you forget about other people around you. I think my examples illustrate areas which are important to be a good parent both directly and indirectly. Take working out for example. This is very personal to me but it means I'm taking care of myself so I believe it has an indirect benefit. I think it indirectly makes me a better parent if I work out as I'm more likely to have more energy, and a more positive attitude/outlook which, in turn, will rub off on my wife and children. All I know is that I feel better about myself when I work out and stay in shape. I have a more positive outlook if I'm maintaining a healthy lifestyle in terms of what I eat and exercise. This follows the classic advice of your attitude and behavior being like a mirror to those around you where it has almost a domino effect on others – good or bad. Meaning, if you are upbeat and positive, others around you are more likely to demonstrate the same traits but, conversely, if you have a negative attitude then the opposite might well apply/be true. Taking my daughter to her practices and planning them in advance is a direct benefit as this directly and positively impacts the use of her time. When I'm available to take her this is time I really cherish and value which is why I establish it as a priority each and every week. Whereas something like reaching out to a loved one is more of an indirect benefit as I feel the value/positives of staying connected with loved ones. I feel the importance of these different things should not be downplayed in anyway as all carry some significance as a parent, especially to me. You may well have different priorities or things you think are more important to you, but the key to all this is to make sure you incorporate what really matters to you in your everyday life.

So doing something like planning your week ahead, looking at what you're going to eat or what you'll be doing each day is really quite a simple action. It only takes up a few minutes but, for me, the key part is just having the discipline to do something like this so you can take control. I will say it throughout this book that, as a real world parent, things will not regularly go to plan and you need to be in a position to adjust here and there. But then again, without having something to keep you focused is exactly when the day does run you rather than the other way around. This is not to say you will ever have that complete control of it but without your priorities being set ahead of time is when I think you're more likely to end up making bad choices. I think by having good planning you will then have a guide to help get you through the day/week to ensure what you're doing reflects your priorities or more simply what matters to you.

Whilst writing such a book I think it's very important for me to be open and honest throughout. I certainly won't pretend I have all the answers and have everything figured out. So focusing on the topic, generally speaking I do consider myself as very organized, I feel I have my priorities straight and look to ensure my time reflects such priorities. But with that do I have days where I don't accomplish anything? Do I have days that get the best of me? Do I still have days where I feel like it's running me rather than the other way around? The answer to such questions are yes, of course I still have days like this. Look perhaps a funny reality is if you don't fall from time to time, then maybe you're not living up to the life or have enough game as a real world parent. Jokes aside, all I would say that such days for me are now more of the exception rather than the everyday norm. But like I said, I certainly won't pretend that because I'm organized I tick everything off on my to do list each and every day. I know it doesn't work like that. I know that for the most organized parent in the real world, the constant daily challenges can throw so many different things at you. So there will be times when you're just flat out, exhausted and can do no more. This is certainly not about being hard on yourself when the inevitable will happen every now and then. All I'm saying or what I think is if you follow a similar approach to the advice in this chapter it's so much easier to get back up again after an off day. On the other hand, if you're not organized and your off days are the norm rather than the exception, then I'm sure it's a case of things will just spiral or continue to escalate out of control. It will be somewhat of a vicious cycle where you will feel like you're running around in circles or like your chasing your tail most if not all of the time.

I believe that we all want to lead good and healthy lifestyles and whilst we all may have different interpretation of the term "lifestyle", I personally think a good lifestyle is when you have some control of it. I feel it's important for you to have goals/priorities set out both personally as well as for your family/children. This will then help to shape your daily/weekly priorities to ensure you accomplish what is important to you. You then make good choices and I think this stems from being in a position to make those good choices by setting you and your family up for success, all by planning ahead of time. A key point with good planning/scheduling and time management is that, whilst you may not ever have complete control, you will at least have a lot more of it or feel more in control. I believe it's important for both parents and children to have an element of structure in their life. Either way and just to reiterate, that's when the old adage will ring true being either you run the day or it will run you! If the day runs you then I think you're more inclined to pick up bad habits, pay less attention to your health and what your children are actually doing in their spare time. Then, over a period of time, you may reflect and feel there may be a lack of progress or lack of accomplishment. I also think the opposite is true so take control by becoming a skillful planner/scheduler. By doing so, I think you, your children and your family as a whole, will not only see the benefits in the present but, perhaps, more importantly over a much longer period of time, helping you to become a better parent along the way.

2 CONTROL

The opening chapter leads quite nicely onto this one, looking at the term "control", whilst still keeping some focus on planning/scheduling and time management. It can certainly be debated, but my general view is that you have the responsibility of managing your children's time outside of school, be it where they sit and watch TV, play video games, play on their phone, or alternatively, learn how to play a new sport, practice on a current sport or an instrument as some simple examples. Now to stay on this for a moment and specifically focused on the word "control". Now I would imagine that most people would have somewhat of a negative image of a controlling parent. In another chapter, I will look at something similar with a description of a pushy parent, but in both cases I think the terms need to be put into context. Here we're considering time and what your child essentially does with their time. Like it or not, and you can use another word if you like, but as a parent I believe that you control what your child does with their time in direct and indirect ways. When I say "control" I mean it more in a positive way of being hands on rather than passive. And what I mean by being hands on is just making sure that your child is doing positive and productive things with their time on a regular or even daily basis. On the other hand, if you take more of a passive approach, then perhaps just be mindful more than anything that valuable time might be being wasted on an almost daily basis. And when I say time being wasted, I mean to consider whether your child could be doing something much better for their own benefit both in the short and long-term. If you think about it logically we have set bed-times and dinner times as examples for our children, which I suspect would be considered as normal. So when a parent is concerned with the time that their child goes to bed, I believe that the parent should be equally concerned with how they spend their spare time throughout the day. Essentially it's about understanding the importance of such free time and perhaps placing equal importance on it as, perhaps, you maybe do with other more structured things during a regular day. So my advice is to consider the term "control" in this context, but either way, as parents we have full responsibility for our children. I think when looked at in terms of responsibility, then the thought of being a controlling parent almost goes away, as it is our duty as parents to take charge.

So hopefully you will understand the point that I'm trying to make here, but one way or another, I think we have control of how our child uses their time. What I'm saying is to choose something which will have a positive impact on them. I do want to clarify my point when I say "control of time", as I believe it does depend on the child's age. However, thinking about it logically, until your child can drive, they're very dependent on you to take them places as they may not be able to get too far by themselves. To take it a step further by monetizing it, you as parents pay the bills so you control what you buy, whether it's those devices, TV subscriptions/plans, cell phone or on the other hand maybe those lessons in any given activity. I say you have control in circumstances like this but it also does come down to choice of whether you ultimately call the shots or not. Parents can easily relinquish control from a very early age to their children if they decide to do so or, to put it another way, allow for it to happen. My view is that this can begin to form some negative norms which are hard to reverse once they have become established. Not just that when your child is in "control" and is effectively making decisions from an early age as to what it is they do with things like spare time, then you lose that authority when you want them to follow your directions or maybe have them try something new.

All I'm saying is that I think you really need to play close consideration to how your child spends their time. You may not like the term "control", but I want to use it to emphasize the point. The way I see it, it's you, as the parent, who has that control and so it then comes down to your choices. If anything it's your responsibility so again see it in that sense rather than necessarily as controlling in anyway. You either plan out your child's week by ensuring that they're doing positive things outside of their education by signing them up for classes, sports, activities whilst also ensuring that they have allotted time for their homework. Play time is essential too, but I believe that, in order to make sure your child has good opportunities to develop, it just needs some good forward planning and scheduling to ensure that they're ultimately making the best use of their time. So hopefully you're beginning to understand the context of "control" with what I'm referring to in such instances. Think about it, and this isn't undermining children, but they won't necessarily be thinking along the lines of: "Am I making best use of my time doing this?" Or…"Could I be doing something better with my time" Or… "Am I doing something productive in my spare time?" Again it's more your responsibility as a parent to think like this.

Let me make clear that I'm also not suggesting that you should watch over them like a hawk, and you need to think about or manage every second of the day. This is far from the point that I'm trying to make. Let me give an example where you sign your child up to a soccer/football club (or any sports club) which may practice twice a week after school. You may not think of it in such a way, but essentially the way I see it is that by doing such a thing, you're having control in how they spend their time to a positive effect, as you're making the choice to sign them up. Of course, involve your child in the process as to what it is you're signing them up for. I think that if you don't have pre-planned activities like this (there are many, many more) you lose that control and structure. As I said, this is just one example and it certainly doesn't need for you to be shelling out money on instructor led classes all the time.

If your schedule permits as a parent, can you take your child out in your spare time to practice on their sport? Can you go and ride your bikes together? Another point I would like to clarify when I say "doing something productive", this is not about thinking of some off the wall or extravagant thing that you need to schedule each and every day. I believe that it's more about doing something relatively simple and easy to do which might actually seem to have little impact on the day itself. The impact is actually seen over time as a result of doing something productive to the point that it becomes almost a very positive habit. So a few examples, how about a kid playing basketball each day for a year? Or a kid practicing putting every day for 30 minutes? Or a kid playing the guitar or the drums each day? We all want good things for our children so think about it for yourself, would you agree that helping to ensure something like this happens is a good thing? Do you agree for this to happen the parent needs to take some form of control to ensure it does happen? To then look at this another way by sitting back, not taking such a hands on approach your child might have the "control" by choosing to do what he/she wants. I already said this and I'm not saying all kids will decide to do the following but I'm sure many, if given the choice, and if there is nothing planned for them after school, would decide after getting home to maybe watch some TV, play a video game or be glued to their cell phone as the most likely outcomes.

I repeat that you can't control what your child does every second of the day and I'm not thinking or suggesting for one minute that this is what you should do. That, in my view, is not good parenting and I'm sure something like the term "control freak" immediately comes to mind. So I want to make it abundantly clear that this is not about obsessing over what they're doing all of the time. But realize that you do have full responsibility for your child, so what I'm saying is to just take a little time at the beginning of each week to look at what your child will be doing. Looking at the examples I just gave regarding basketball, golf and a musical instrument - it could just be as simple as ensuring that such an activity is already structured into the day. Bringing it back to control, if you don't take the time to do this – who else will? Would things like this get done or actually happen if you don't take the lead or take it upon yourself? If you think about it you're only really looking at a window of something like 4-5 hours (if that) which I think, for most will be the time between when they get out of school and the time they go to bed. The benefit of this is that if your child is enrolled in activities, it will help you co-ordinate things like travel, when/what your child will be eating, things like that. It's about having that general understanding so that you are, as a family, doing positive things. It sounds a little cliché using buzzwords to say things like "making each day count" or "be productive." But essentially whether you use such a term or not, that is what you will be doing by having that control. Bringing it back to an earlier point, I personally hate it when we're not organized as a family and when we're up against it to get through the day, where it seems like nothing good has come from it. So I will keep coming back to the term "control" and the context here with the use of time, I like to consider it as something which will help you as it does for us. This is not about becoming a regimented parent or family, it's about setting yourself up for success each day. That is what I'm referring to with control, in that you take back some control so that you run the day as best you can, as to what works best for you and your family. Take control so that something good comes from each day. Again this doesn't have to be a major milestone achieved each and every day. Focus on the so called little things which eventually do become big things when accumulated over time.

For me, it's all about making good choices, and whilst all parents ultimately want to do the right thing or what is best for their children, this can be a challenge in the present moment. Think about it. Personally, I think this is because it might be easier/more beneficial to pick a negative choice (easier and more appealing) over a positive choice in the present if you're stressed, your head is in a spin and when the day is getting the best of you. All of which, I believe, can be helped with planning ahead. I stress the word "helped", as again, living in the real world, I will admit that this will not guarantee or mean that every day is now a great one where you get everything done on your to-do list and where everything falls into place oh so smoothly. So bear that in mind too, this exercise is about setting yourself up, or at least giving your and your family every chance of some success each day to the point that you feel as though you're achieving something or something good has come from it. When I say "achieving something" again I'm not talking about anything earth shattering, I mean more about having the satisfaction from something positive you've done that day – all related to your role as a parent and the impact you have/make on your children. Or, put it this way, again in the context/spirit of control; make sure that you do your part as a parent in the same way that you tell your child... "As long as you do your best." Do your best by taking responsibly for that spare time which your children have.

So hopefully, I suitably put the term "control" as a parent into context so that you can see where I'm coming from. This is not about being the stereotypical obsessive or controlling type. This is about life as a real parent where, at times, it can be a challenge to just get through the day. I will be the first to admit to the importance of giving your child an element of freedom and responsibility. But what makes parenting complex is that there is no simple answer to this either. It will depend on many factors, not least age, development, maturity and the environment in which they are raised. It's having that trust in them that they will use their time productively. Nothing is equal when it comes to children, not even those brought up in the same family, as there are so many variables. So I won't deny that the judgment of the parent is key too, using that parental instinct as to when you perhaps need to take control a little more or, on the other hand, give more license to your child when they're making good choices. These choices are something we will look at more in another chapter.

I purposely used the word "control" for this chapter, really to emphasize the responsibility that you have as a parent in how your child spends their time. I believe that if you understand the importance of your responsibility, then you're more likely to give a lot more consideration to what your child will be doing, where and when, on a daily basis. So don't be put off when I refer to "control" as I think that it's easier to perceive this as something actually negative. What I'm saying is to approach it, or look at it in another way, so that your main purpose is actually very positive in that you're looking to ensure that their spare time is used in a very good way. By taking such steps, I believe will help you become a better parent.

3 TAKE STOCK

Continuing with a similar theme for now, here is something I think all parents should do: take stock of how your child spends their time on a regular day. This again very much relates to the previous chapter and what was just discussed. But now this is about taking a step back and really understanding what your child does with their time. You may think that you know, but by taking this step back to really look at it, might prove to be a bit of an eye opener. Now don't be put off by this as I suggest that you keep it very simple. All I would do is spend no more than 5-10 minutes with a pen and paper writing it down. Also don't worry about it being done with pinpoint accuracy; this is purely something for awareness only. So round to the nearest half hour if you need to, until you allocate all 24 hours in the day. Another way of doing it is, essentially, in list form whereby you go from 0-24 and fill in the gaps. If anything you could even just figure it out in your head. I reiterate to keep it simple otherwise you may be put off doing it. We all know there are apps out there for everything these days. You could try and put a tag on your child, follow them round with a clip board and then log it online so that it produces some fancy charts, but as I said, I don't think any of this is necessary. Use your common sense. Half of it should be very easy to do as when you allocate sleep and school, this takes up the most part of your 24 hours on a typical weekday. The rest you fill in the gaps of what they do in terms of play, sports/activities, TV, video games, homework, social media, reading, dinner time, whatever it maybe.

Before I go on, I want to pause for a moment as I'm sure some of you may be reading this thinking; are you seriously suggesting I don't know what my child is doing on a daily basis? Let me make clear I'm not saying you need to do such a thing because there are so many parents these days oblivious to what is going on around them. I'm not saying that at all. This exercise is more about looking at the finer detail, perhaps just going that little step further to what we normally would. Of course as parents we know the main things our children are doing each day. Of course we know all the important things going on in their life. But let's not forget being a real world parent, life is demanding and there is no hiding from the fact we have so much going on. I think what I'm really saying is I'm sure you'll know what they're doing, but in some cases it's maybe more in a general/overall sense. If this is the case, this is just about looking at those gaps of time during the day, which might only be here and there. So essentially it's really getting that deeper understanding of what is done during those gaps of time each day.

As I said, this is something I advise purely for your awareness only and if anything, preventing ignorance. Although this is simple I do think it provides a level of detail, or that deeper dive that a parent needs rather than just generalizing each week day into something like school, homework, dinner, then bed. I'm not suggesting anything else as I think that it's important for parents to have a good idea as to how their child currently spends/uses their time. By you, yourself, spending a few minutes doing this, it allows you to be more aware/conscious/attentive. This then allows you to be responsive if you identify that actually, your child could be making better use of time by doing something else which is more beneficial to them. Let's look a little more on the example I just gave in generalizing each week day into something like school, homework, dinner, then bed. I'm sure you will know this and that is what I refer to having that general sense of what they're doing. But back to the point I just made there are still many gaps and a lot of time to fill in the day even when you factor these things in. So if anything this chapter is more concerned with taking stock of that so called "free time."

Hopefully doing something like this, if you choose to do so, will raise your attention, highlighting and then enabling you to give some more consideration to what your child is up to in that free time. That time may well be used very wisely, but then again you may think about whether they could or should be doing something different if you determine it's not. Of course and I repeat you will know the overall main things such as school, but by doing such a task you're now looking at it all and in just that little more detail. I will say it again that this isn't something that needs to be too technical. This certainly doesn't need some fancy gadget or some advanced formula to provide you data to analyze. Sure, not every day is the same and your child may do different things from one day to another. For instance, they might have soccer on a Monday and baseball on a Wednesday, which is why I suggest that you group sports & activities generally speaking together. Keep it simple and again use some common sense, you're purely being more observant here. Related to this, I think this might be something you can look to do once every six months. Of course things change, but again this is all about once in a while taking stock of what your child is up to. The only exception I would say needs some additional consideration is doing the same thing, but this time looking at weekends and summer holidays rather than just weekdays.

Let's start with weekends. I think it's a good idea to pick a day on the weekend and look to do a similar exercise. The main reason being that you obviously have a lot more hours in the day to fill in as your child will not be at school. For this, I recommend that you stick to the same approach of keeping it simple and following a similar method. This time I acknowledge that it may be a little harder to do as one weekend can greatly/vastly differ to the next with what you're doing. So in this case, I would once more highlight that you use your common sense. You might not have a "typical" Saturday or Sunday, but you could try and look at this more as to how you as a family spend your time when you're all together, rather than necessarily in isolation of just looking at your child. This continues to be for your awareness, so in this instance it may make sense to do this a couple of times depending on how much your weekends actually differ. What I would also say is that this is something you should definitely consider doing during summer vacation/holidays. Take out your true week or two of actual vacation time but, again, do this as a one-time thing on a regular summer day to see what your child is really up to. This also isn't about spying or checking up on them it's all purely for your understanding.

The key messages: Don't be ignorant and don't downplay the importance of free time in any way! Look, we all live busy lives as parents – I get it! If it's a case where, at times, you're only with them for minutes rather than hours on some days particularly when you're working, my view is that it's not enough just to ask them if they've had a good day without knowing what they really did. You need to have that understanding. I don't know about your kids, but sometimes if I ask my daughter what she has been up to, I don't get a lot back other than maybe a few words. But your child explaining their day isn't the issue here, it's about you as a parent taking a step back to see what they actually did that day or have planned out for the next. Referring to a key point from the previous chapter, this isn't about being a controlling parent, but more about taking that responsibility.

At the crux of it all is really to look at how they spend their time between when they get out of school and when they go to bed. One of the main reasons for doing this is to determine if valuable time is being wasted. You obviously have to factor in things like dinner time or homework. My views here are leading down an obvious path in that I think that it's on you as a parent to determine, in this free time that they have, what they're actually doing. My advice is place as much importance on this free time as you do with say with time at school or dinner time or bed-time. Before you say anything, I want to make a point that I don't think this is the case for all, but I do see that it's easy to fall into a trap of your child being glued to their cell phone or TV during these free hours. Such behavior can quickly become the norm and when a child develops habits which when you determine are unwanted habits, it becomes a lot harder for them to reverse.

Let's recap a little before I move on, I don't suggest you having a long list of tasks to do here. I just think that a little distinction is required as to what your child will be doing as it will obviously vary from a weekday to a weekend and also on a day during the summer break. So look at this maybe once every six months, looking at a weekday when your child is in school and then pick a day on the weekend to do something similar. The only addition is then to do this over the summer break/holiday when school is out and your child has a lot more free time. I reiterate, keep it simple as this should only take a few minutes. By all means involve your child in the process to also help to create some self-awareness for themselves. They may well see that they're spending too much time doing something in one particular area.

One more time, keep this exercise simple. I think that by doing this will allow you to become more mindful, which in turn will allow you to have a mindset shift, where you take action if you then determine that your child is spending too much time in one area. It might be your child spends way too much time watching TV or playing video games, but on the other hand it also works both ways. In some instances, it might be that your child actually spends too much time studying, has little or no playtime, or they might be playing a sport too much. By taking stock, I believe that it will give you the awareness that you need. We talk about finding balance in the modern day world, but this is not so much about finding a perfect balance between everything because, again, that's just not living in the real world. But what something like this does is perhaps highlight an area that may be neglected. As in the example I just gave, it could be that your child spends all of their spare time studying and playing sports. This may sound great, but you may determine that they also just need some time every now and then to just play with their friends outside or some basic downtime to actually take it easy once in a while. So it might help you identify some important things they're actually missing out on.

I think something simple like this allows you to be more reflective and it might be that you ask yourself questions about what would benefit your child rather than what will necessarily entertain your child and keep them quiet? I think that such questions are key, particularly during summer break where, in our case, our child is essentially off for 3 months – that is a long time! So I believe that it's key for my wife and I to look at what our child will be up to over the summer. The key may well be for it to be fun, but I think you can still plan fun things which will benefit your child rather than just keeping them entertained for a few hours doing something like putting on some movies. Some form of balance is key to it all, but not to the point where you are concerned about dividing everything up equally, where you're checking/ticking every box. You don't have to have it so structured, but at the same time, if you don't plan your trip away, activities, studying, pool days/beach days, sports you might say at the end of it all "where did the summer go?" If that happens you may end up with that feeling of regret that you really didn't do anything with your family and more importantly, your child didn't really get up to much where an opportunity was missed for them to further develop in something. I don't know about you and maybe I'm the odd one out when it comes to this, but when I see time has been wasted, I see it as a missed opportunity. Not in a drastic sense like missing out on a once in a lifetime opportunity, but just more of having a feeling we could have done something better. That is where I feel the responsibility as a parent as I think it's on me to ensure my children and us as a family, are doing meaningful things. Again nothing necessarily new, off the wall, grand/spectacular, deep or spiritual, just making the best use of time, day-to-day. There will be more to follow specifically on this topic of summer vacation/holiday time in a later chapter.

I will quickly add a point here that I acknowledge that all families have different budgets which can determine some of the things that you do, but don't let that be an excuse. There is still so much you can do and plan out and there are plenty of free activities like a trip to the park, a visit to the library, a visit to the playground, kicking/throwing a ball around or arranging sports activities with friends or just simply playing outside – kids will amaze you with what they can get up to. But not just looking at summer I think we all have regular feelings such as, "Where did that week go?" or "Where did the past few months go?" or "We're already half way through the year?" Time does fly, so again, this all comes back to looking to make the best use of it as a parent, specifically focusing on what your child does theirs.

I really recommend you do something like this so your child isn't wasting valuable time day after day. It might not even be as much as looking at it in such a way to see if time is being wasted, but maybe just consider could they doing something different? Could they be doing something different which would be a far better use of time? I think you can only really answer this question by taking stock, gaining that full understanding on how they currently spend/use all of their time. I'm talking as a real world parent so I'm not thinking about anything off the wall or crazy here. A few ideas, but how about substituting some TV time for reading? Doing a little more study? Scheduling regular personal practice time for their given sport or activity? Instead of sticking on a movie can you take them to the park or encourage them to play some ball games outside? It could be a simple as playing catch! Can you introduce/expose your child to something new (like a sport) and see if they like it instead of them being on some form of a device? Again nothing extravagant. To give you a specific example to where I live in Florida, there seems to be a basketball court close to or in every neighborhood/community. So in my case, why not take my child and introduce her to the sport and go play it for a little while? I really do recommend that you speak to your child and ask them about ideas related to things like this. As well as suggesting, you can also ask them for ideas related to the things which they enjoy and like to do or alternatively would like to try. You might find out they could easily do more of something which they want to do which will at the same time benefit them. In some cases you may need to take the lead as it just might be that your child doesn't know they could be doing this/that instead – especially if it's something new or something that have never been exposed/introduced to before! There also might be more of a dependence on you as the parent if they're reliant on you to take them somewhere, but if you can find the time my advice is do it. So here, it might just be a case of planning it, to again make better use of time, so that your child is doing that more beneficial thing whatever it may be.

By taking stock you're really taking that additional step of wanting to know and learn what your child is up to. It all adds to playing that active and not passive role as a parent. More importantly, by taking stock, I think that it can open your eyes to areas which might be working well, but also to areas which you as a family, parent or the child themselves can improve on. Or to put it another way, identify how you can make better use of time. By being self-aware as a parent you can then be in a much better positon to take those positive actions and respond for the benefit of your child. This book is about being a better parent. I think a very basic, but essential fundamental part of that is ensuring that you place great emphasis on, as well as understanding the importance of what your child does with their time. It might seem when kids are young that they have an endless amount of free time. So why not use that wisely? I think it's your responsibility as the parent to think in such a way as I think it's a lot harder for children to have that perspective/foresight and maybe it will be too little, too late when they do. The previous chapter focused more on taking that responsibility/control whereas this chapter has been more focused on ensuring that you actually have that understanding. This is so that you're then in a better position to act after assuming that full responsibility. Remember all of this is for the benefit of your child, utilizing their time day after day. So combining the two whereby you're taking that full responsibility and then acting on it in this area after gaining that understanding, I believe will help you become a better parent. Let's not forget your scheduling/planning/time management is key which was also discussed in the opening chapter, which hopefully shows how all of these elements are linked together and are all just as important as the next.

4 CHOICES

When I'm referring to "choice" in this chapter, the focus is on how much freedom that you give your child or children to have choices in many different areas. I think that it is something to which a parent should pay close attention to and give a lot of thought. So let me explain a little as what I think requires close consideration is how much leeway you give your child. I would be the first to admit that there is no "one size fits all" answer here. It very much depends on your own individual circumstances and, I think, most importantly, the age and maturity of your child. It's only natural for them to decide things for themselves as they get older and, as they begin to have more responsibilities, so they can also develop their independence. This very much relates to aspects in the opening chapters when looking at the term "control". I'm sure that there is plenty of parenting advice out there which supports the notion of giving your child choices. I'm sure that it follows this up by saying something like it empowers them to make decisions and increases their own personal responsibility. That is what I would call ideal world advice to a degree, but, in the real world, if this is the case then I think that you, as a parent, need to pay close attention to determine whether they're actually making good choices? It's all well and good to give them freedom but don't forget that you have the ultimate responsibility and you need to determine whether they're making smart choices if you do, or decide to, go with such an approach. Again, speaking rather generically, you have to find what works best for you. It's obviously not necessarily best to let your child decide everything, but you don't want to be running some form of dictatorship either where your child can't or doesn't know how to decide anything for themselves. It may well be that you do give your child the opportunity to make a lot of decisions for themselves. By doing so you may find that they do make good choices and so such a process helps them to mature - essentially creating a win-win situation. Again being real-world parents we all know that this is a lot easier said than done. In addition, you also have to factor in, and allow for them to make those mistakes without coming down too hard on them, as I think mistakes are fundamental to growing/improving in something/anything.

So what choices am I referring to? I want to make clear that these choices are not around things like learning, where I think there is a great benefit of letting kids figure things out for themselves. I'm looking more at those big and small everyday type choices/decisions. I will start off with so called small ones. A very/general example, at the end of the day, when everyone is ready for something to eat for dinner, do you let your child decide, or do you make the call on what everyone eats for dinner? If you already have something prepared in advance then you're essentially deciding what they eat. This is because they have no choice or control over what you put on the table and therefore you indirectly decide on whether it's a meal full of good nutrition or not. This is why pre-planning is key. If you let your child decide and they go with some French fries or a bag of chips and a soda as that is satisfying enough for them in the moment, then clearly letting them decide is the wrong thing to do. Now I'm not saying that you need to be super healthy and juicing with all kinds of fruit and veg. All families love a pizza night every now and then and I would say don't necessarily be too strict when at a restaurant or eating out either. Again there must be balance between every now and then, and all of the time.

I will refer to some old sayings throughout the book and I like the one "give them an inch and they will take a mile." I think this applies to a lot of people and especially children. I think close attention needs to be made, as if too much leeway is given and your child starts to make poor choices, then there is a danger that they will form unwanted habits. We all know that those habits are then hard to break - especially when they're now calling the shots and act as if they're the boss, if you know what I mean? The example provided is fairly basic but I think it's good for parents to reflect on what their child has a say in and what they don't. You can then assess whether you need to be more assertive and take back more control in certain situations.

Shifting gear a little to give you a specific example with my daughter looking at choice, where she absolutely hated swimming classes when we first introduced her to them. Living in Florida we're fortunate to have nice weather year round and there are many pools to which we have access including her grandparents and there is also a shared facility in our community. So we felt it was very important for her to have lessons, purely from a safety point of view more than anything. We were not looking at it any more than that other than maybe an added bonus of being able to enjoy quality time as a family together at a pool – we were not looking in terms of developing her into a competitive swimmer. Overall, it must have taken a good year (12-16 months) for her to start to enjoy swimming. She sometimes cried when she knew she had a lesson but my wife and I persevered through it, again purely for safety reasons. When I say cry it was hysterical crying at times when she would dread going. Today, she cannot get enough of the pool where she loves to swim, jump in and out of the pool and, if we would let her, she would probably play in there all day long. Her love, attitude, name it what you will towards swimming made a complete transformation/full circle change in just over a year. In the moment a year might seem like a long time but, given her age, it's nothing and the sometimes painful process has definitely been worthwhile as we can now enjoy great pool days. The process was slow, even tedious at times, and progress was so gradual that there were even moments when we thought she was taking one step forward but two steps back. However, in the end like I said, it was all worth it. A point I would stress is that it all needs to be within boundaries and age appropriate, as my child in this case was not jumping in at the deep end so to speak with swimming in those early stages. It was a very gradual process. So, before anyone jumps to conclusions when I say she was hysterical crying, it had nothing to do with her being asked/forced to do anything not applicable to a beginner swimmer. She just didn't like things like water splashing in her face or getting her hair wet – little things like that. At the time, it was like the world was coming to an end if a bit of water splashed on her face!

So back to choices being the theme of this chapter. In those early days, if we had given our daughter the choice to learn to swim or not she would have said no every time. In essence we made her go and when it comes to child safety, I don't think many people would argue with the reasons why we persisted with it. As I said, we now enjoy the benefits of doing this by having nice afternoons at the pool and we get joy in seeing how much fun our child has. In addition, she has also made many friends at our community pool. But again to emphasize the earlier point, she would have initially decided not to go if we had given her the choice. So as parents, we took control of this situation. At no point was our daughter involved in deciding whether or not she would go, by us giving her any choice. However, we did highlight the importance of doing so throughout, to try and help her understand why we were still sending her to lessons.

I think this is a good example as safety comes into the reasoning and when child safety comes into play, people can somewhat excuse a "pushy parent" for being persistent. But what about other things where safety is not involved? Children stop playing sports or playing an instrument as other examples all of the time. But why? Who is making the call here? Are they quitting? Is their reasoning acceptable? I think these are all good questions to ask. I think a parent then needs to ask themselves whether they should allow this to happen if their child is ultimately deciding to stop doing something and, as an alternative insist that he/she keeps going and perseveres like we did with swimming! Some kids jump from one activity to the other without really giving one a good go. I highlight that there will be times when the decision is perfectly legitimate. It might be a bad group, poor coaching, bad facilities/environment or something like that. However, in such cases it might well just require a change of scenery rather than just stop playing all together. There also might be a time when a child has given something a real good go, done their best, but it's something that is just not right for them and that's ok too. But back to our swimming example it took more or less one whole year for my daughter to go from completely hating something to completely loving it through a combination of things but, ultimately, a key part was our persistence as parents – we were making the choice and not our daughter. From an early age a child may not perhaps understand the long-term importance of not giving up or persevering in something to get to that point where you really start to enjoy it. Only parents can really have that long-term outlook on deciding what will be best for their child. So it might mean having to put up with challenges in the short-term to then enjoy the many long-term benefits something could ultimately bring – again like our swimming example.

I want to focus more on those scenarios where someone might quit when it gets a little harder, tougher, or more demanding and requires more effort. Do you allow your child to stop something if they're frustrated by short-term results? I will keep going back to the swimming example as a lot of these things came into play early on. From hating it, being scared, frustrated, to name a few of the feelings my daughter had, we eventually saw our child break through barriers and then it all becomes worthwhile. This all may sound a little over-the-top, but by doing this you can at least highlight the importance of not giving up on something, as our child understood the process and can be proud of what she achieved. There were no medals, prizes or certificates this was just simply persevering or to use more of an everyday term, grinding it out.

To further emphasize the point let's look at another example, being school. Our daughter is 6 and is only in her first year of elementary school. In the main she loves it but already there have been days where she says something along the lines of "I don't want to go to school today". I'm sure many of you reading this have, or will experience this at one time or another. The reason I make this point is that hopefully it will strike a chord in that, even when your child might say such a thing, you don't even contemplate them missing school – they just go no matter what and no matter how much they moan or whine about it. So my advice is to consider having a similar response for other things which might not be deemed as vital as school/education or your child's safety. What about when practice/lessons for a sport or activity is involved? I mentioned it earlier that there are kids out there who need no encouragement to play a sport for example, and would play all day long if they could. But I feel that the reality is that there are many times when it doesn't play out like this. There may be times when your child might have had a little setback, or is frustrated, so they don't want to practice as hard. Or their confidence might be a little low. There can be many reasons why your child might not want to do an activity in the present moment. This is why I think that, for the most part, it will be very rare to have such a smooth path where you as a parent won't have to ever deal with ongoing challenges/issues. Maybe, like school, because they go typically 5 days a week, and if they play a sport or activity roughly 3-5 days a week as well, granted this just might be a reason why kids don't want to do it once in a while. But going back to the root of advice looking at choice, when going through a challenging time with your child who may no longer want to do something or quit, then maybe consider applying the same reaction as in my swimming and school examples. In these cases where child's safety and education come into play, I'm sure that it would not cross a parent's mind to let their child quit, give up or not go. So all I'm saying is to consider applying this same logic to your child's sport or activity (or anything related to this) so that there is no contemplation of quitting when the going gets a little tough. Hopefully you can see it all comes down to choice.

I refer to sports throughout the book as I do have a big passion for sports. I think experiences for children in sports help develop some key positive behaviors which become applicable in many other key areas like education and overall attitude. So back to choices, I will provide another example which I see in many kids of all ages. I hear parents often say things like "we want out children to decide what they want to do" or "we want them to find their passion". Again my response here is rather broad-brush as individual circumstances differ so vastly but, speaking generally, I wouldn't flat out reject or criticize such an approach for a child, but I would however question it. I would question the point and say that it's all well and good, but is the parent providing opportunities for their children to try or expose them to different things? My response is that if you went this way, then parents still need to be very much hands-on in the process, essentially providing opportunities for the child to find their passion so they can decide what it is that they want to keep doing. Specifically looking at choice, if your child goes to a dance class or music class or basketball clinic and after two or three times they say that they don't like it and they don't want to go anymore, do you let them make that call? I would question that decision as you don't want to make it easy for them to quit anything. When starting something new it takes time to adjust no matter what age, although in my experience I do find it comes more natural to children at a younger age to just get on with it and get to grips with things.

I'm sure that you would all agree that parents want their child to have a passion for something – to essentially find their passion. The subject of finding a passion for your child could possibly warrant a book in itself. I think that opinions will differ significantly in this area. The reality is I don't think that there is a simple answer or method. Sure, there are examples out there when a child may naturally have a love for something and the passion evolves very naturally by itself; in essence there is no real need for much interference, direction or even support. They practice and work hard when no one else is watching! This is obviously a somewhat perfect scenario, but I would imagine that such cases would be exception rather than norm. When I say "interference", again using both ends of the spectrum that can have extreme behaviors and in this case I'm referring to the parental behavior. Meaning whatever your child has a passion for whether it is arts, sports, education, whatever; I believe there will never be a case where a child fulfils their potential seamlessly. We all know that part of the process, and what comes with the territory in life, are ups and downs, failure and rejection, and no doubt times when they may want to give something up and quit. That may well be the point when some positive "interference" is required and again it comes back to choice. Do you let your child quit or give up on something the moment that it gets hard or when something doesn't go their way? It keeps coming back to choice and parents play such a pivotal role in choice and sometimes you may have to take back some control. No two children are the same so it's not easy to make general assumptions and this is where you as a parent need to use your own instinct of what is right for your child. Developing a passion for something is an area that I will look at in a lot greater detail later in the book. However, I wanted to also raise it in this chapter in line with the theme of "choice", as I believe that the choices we make as parents are perhaps the most important factor when considering something like this. Your child may well decide and make the "choice" to quit something, but don't forget it will also be your "choice" if you allow for it to happen.

As I said, I will continue to look at passions later in the book. For something very much in the present, with an example of where your choice comes into play, it might be dealing with something simple such as the weather conditions. It might be too hot, too cold, really windy, rainy outside. We seem to have it all in Florida and, obviously, for most of the year it's on the warmer side. But wherever you are in the world you have to deal with some unpleasant conditions at times and that still brings it back to choice. Or to put it another way wherever you are in the world, I think you will agree that you will never have "perfect" conditions most of the time. So looking at something like the weather and if you let your child have the choice on doing something when it's not "perfect conditions"; do you let your child have the say and if they take an easy way out, do you go along with it? Or do you give them the choice and if they take the easy route do you then insist that they continue? Or do you not give them an option at all and encourage them to get on with it if they start to moan a little? Throughout the book, I frequently provide clarity on such points. So in this instance before the health and safety inspectors come looking for me, I'm not saying that you should make your child stay out and play in hurricane force winds, or in a tropical rainstorm/thunderstorm, or dangerously hot/cold weather - again some common sense comes into play. But what I'm saying is not to let your child take the easy option in the moment and that comes with choice. My view on it, and you may disagree, is that a little rain or cold doesn't hurt anyone. Just because it's cold outside doesn't mean that your child is going to get the flu for example. Sure, there are many variables, an obvious one being the type of activity and you have to factor in the age of the child too, things like that, I get it! But again this is where you as the parent perhaps in the present moment need to take a longer term perspective. It's a big world out there which can be unforgiving at times. So if you don't let your child do that extra soccer practice because it's too cold or rainy, my view is that it will do no good as the time will eventually come when they do have to play a game in the cold/rain.

As I said, I live in Florida and I often smile when the temperature drops a little or there is some rain as I see parents freak out and it's like the world is coming to an end, which is taking it to the extreme the other way. I will provide a specific example with my daughter who plays tennis and as I said in Florida it's hot virtually all year round. So there are times when, in the moment she might not want to play because it might be a little warm, but that is the time I don't provide a choice for her and there is no option other than to say "let's go". Then, as soon as we get out there and into it and she is having fun, it's all worth it. That is the time I might choose for us to jump in our community pool to cool off afterwards so we have a really fun couple of hours playing outside, doing something really meaningful.

I will give another recent example when it was quite windy for my daughter's tennis lesson, but certainly nothing extreme. Her coach said that some parents had cancelled their lessons that day because of the wind. Look, at the end of the day, as parents, we have the right to make such choices. It is hard for me to not come across as being critical or judgmental here, but all I would do is question such an approach. Is it the case where it is the parent who actually doesn't want to be out in the wind but the child couldn't care less? I think that to have credibility with anything you need to consider all angles by considering different points of view, which is why I say that I would just question such an approach. So I'm certainly not saying that I'm right in what I think. But with this standalone example, I do have difficulty seeing any benefit in cancelling a child's practice just because it's windy out, other than it's just not as pleasant to be outside compared to when there is no/less wind. So, like with so many other areas in this book, my advice is to give an example like this consideration for yourself and you decide. It all comes back to choice so maybe the best approach is to look at it from the point of view being "What is actually best for my child?"

It can all be so subtle that it doesn't need you to act like some super strict parent; you can just do things with subtleties that make your child get on with things without giving them a choice. Let's go back to the beginning of my tennis example with my daughter. With it being a little hot outside it might be easy for me to say shall we go out and play? My daughter, given the option, may have said something along the lines of "can I stay in and watch a show on TV as it's too hot out". Even for me, as a parent, at the time this looks like a good option, as putting myself in the moment; it's hot outside so I could always put a TV show on for her. I can take some time to chill out in our nice air conditioned home. I want to make the point here that it's equally as important too for parents not to take an easy way out. So the most likely outcome if we decided to stay at home would be that my daughter would have watched some form of cartoon and I would have probably gone on the couch and just looked at my cell phone for an hour or so. Sure we can always do something different indoors and interact and I'm not saying that we could not have done something positive, such as reading, or something like that. I'm just trying to demonstrate that you're sometimes faced with an easy option or a hard one. I will leave it for you to decide which one would be best in the long-term. When looked at it this way it may seem a "no-brainer" as to what choice you make. When I just said a choice between the easy or the hard one, thinking about this a little more, it's not actually hard for me to go out and play with my daughter it just requires more effort – that's really all it is. In cases like this you should be mindful as to whether this will start to form a good or bad habit? We all face choices day by day like this one and I think that we can all relate to something like working out. In the moment there are times when the last thing we might want to do is work out and we just want to chill and watch our favorite series. But, again, if we start to frequently take that easy choice then it will begin to form an unwanted habit which then may creep into other areas of your life. On the other hand, if you take the harder choice in the moment like working out or going out in the heat then that forms another kind of habit in the long-run. That's my view anyway. Again, the subtle choices we make have such a gradual impact that we only see the benefits in the long-run. As a parent, I'm so proud when I look back at old videos of my daughter playing sports, because it shows how her dedication and our commitment as parents to our child, pays off in the long-run. This is evident as; even looking back at a video from just a few months ago we could see such good improvement/progress now in the present moment. This improvement has been made possible by a number of factors not least, playing during the many times when it has been a little hot/humid/sticky/muggy call it what you want, outside. So, in this example here when I say subtle approach in relation to choice, I actually remove it just by being more assertive. That kind of "Let's-go" attitude where it's just getting on with it. I think what sometimes makes it harder is when we actually bring choice into play in the present moment in simple things like this. I mean this in a way where you end up weighing up the best option like staying in against going out in the heat or wind, where in your own mind you're going through the pros and cons. When this happens the easy choice then becomes that more tempting, like staying in rather than going out in the wind/rain/cold/heat or whatever it may be.

In this chapter, I may have gone a long winded way to get to the main point, but hopefully you now see it. Sometimes as a parent you have to take back control and limit the choices or say that a child has to just stick at something. I'm sure many of you can relate to the saying of "grinding it out". Be persistent and give it a good go. Understand that progress can be very slow and there may be times when you feel that your child may be getting nowhere in the process of learning something new. You might say this is perfectly normal and I love one of the rules in my daughters classroom at school which is applicable here which is "It's ok to make mistakes." The easy trap to fall into is to expect instant results, success, and rapid progress with little effort/time. Applying common sense, this is just flat out unrealistic. I think if you understand this and are all-in, whereby you're committed for the long-haul, then the choice element doesn't even come into play in terms of quitting. Already speaking from experience, children go through phases and there will be some things you will just have to deal with and ride out.

So keep going in the short-term when no doubt you as the parent, as well as your child, will experience the many but expected frustrations we all go through at times – like our swimming example. I just mentioned that some phases you may just need to ride out because through such challenges you may even question: Why are we even doing this? Also, the problem with a negative phase is that you may well know your child is going through one, but there no clue on how long it will last. Again I'm talking to you as a real world parent and so I say the reality is there will be times when you will be frustrated – even to the point where giving up, quitting or no longer doing this/that anymore does cross you or your child's mind. It's sometimes easier said than done to have everything in perspective during your mini highs and lows of going through such a process. You may even understand in the moment that in the grand scheme of things a negative experience has little or no significance. However, I think we all come to understand that anything related to our child does carry significance and so it's easy to get caught up in the moment. But my advice to you will still remain in that you to stay the course so to speak. Otherwise you fall into a danger of going round and round in circles – that is if your child has too much choice and starts to go with the easy option of deciding when to stop doing or giving up on something. If they try soccer one month and don't like it and then try track and field the next and then basketball the month after, the child isn't really committing to anything. Progress is so gradual and very much a slow burn process. Sure, some kids instantly take to something but for others it may take a while for them to really start enjoying it and seeing progress – again I will refer to my daughter for whom it took over a year for her to start to enjoy swimming! I'm not trying to take any credit here, but I do want to make the point that I believe it was our choices as parents, which ultimately played a key part in helping her to get to such a point.

To round this chapter up: as a parent we can look at choices in many different ways. I said in the chapter that it's important to look at both the big and smaller choices, but this chapter was really looking more at who makes decisions on choices, you as the parent, or your child? Again it's hard to look at in a broad way because this is not about an either/or in that it's you or your child who makes all the choices. Clearly there are times when a parent needs to take control and there are other times when it's much better for a child to make a choice/decision. You also need to consider if your child is making choices in certain areas, whether they're simply making good or bad ones. Mistakes are of course ok, this is more about looking at times when your child might quit or no longer wants to do something or might go with that easy option. I provided examples like education and safety which I'm sure are somewhat of an non-negotiable so all I'm saying is to maybe think about whether this more assertive approach can and should be applied to other things. This is because choice doesn't really then come into play, as there's no deliberating. I do want to repeat a point and make clear that this is not about being a commanding parent where you don't let your child have a say in anything. In can be subtle to where you're just firm and have a somewhat, let's get on with it/keep going, attitude when you start to hear a little whining, moaning or excuses. I don't know about you but I think that, with so many things in parenting, there is no simple answer and there is no exception here. Sometimes as parents we really do know what is best for our kids, even when faced with some resistance from them. My view is that a parent can be assertive in a positive way and sometimes it makes it a whole lot easier if your child understands that they don't actually have a say in the matter – like the school and swimming example! So sometimes that choice element is actually removed or taken out of the equation when given that long-term perspective. Either way, I hope you have come to the conclusion that your many different choices will play such a determining factor in becoming a better parent.

5 PUSHY PARENT

In this chapter, I want to give closer thought to the term "pushy parent". It's a term that we all hear from time to time these days and, personally, I think that it's a label which is frequently used without full consideration or understanding. I also think that many of you would agree that, in these modern times, if you were to be described as a pushy parent you might be offended because I tend to believe it has quite a negative connotation. It's simply a label but I believe that it needs to be put into some form of context. For example, if you look up the word "pushy" and other words with a similar meaning, you may come across "assertive" and also "aggressive" amongst other words. Both are at completely different ends of the spectrum as, generally speaking, "assertive" tends to be positive, whilst "aggressive" can be negative certainly in the context of parenting. That is why I think the term "pushy parent" needs to be put into context. I'm not denying that people can take it to the extreme and be forceful with their children, but on the other hand there are plenty of parents who are assertive with their children. So if that is the case they're, as the saying goes, being a pushy parent – but in a positive way. Therefore, just looking at the description alone, in both ways you could be described as a pushy parent. My suggestion to you is to consider this and think about how it is your responsibility to be at the positive end of the scale and be assertive with your child. If people want to label you as a "pushy parent" for being so; well as far as I'm concerned sobeit!

I want to stay with the term "pushy parent", but as an aside I think there are many other different sayings or descriptions of parents that I think need to be put into context and not just generically labelled. Just like the example I previously used in the chapter on Control and being a "controlling parent." Another example and a similar one might be describing a parent or a child as being "disciplined". Now some might think as "disciplined" being someone quite hard or strict which might be at the one end of the spectrum, to stick with that analogy, but at at the other end you can associate discipline with being organized/meticulous/methodical. Hopefully you see where I'm coming from now and like the adage "don't judge a book by its cover" when you hear of someone being labeled in a certain way. Hopefully this opens your eyes a little as to how, actually, being a pushy parent, or a disciplined parent, or a disciplined child can actually be something really positive, as long as it is indeed on the positive side of that spectrum.

In my opinion, there are many things in parenting where there is a fine line and this is a perfect example. The problem is that the "fine-line" is such a grey area, and is certainly not black and white. To make it even more complex the "fine-line" will differ from parent to parent and is actually more of a personal view than a collective one. When does a parent go too far or not far enough? Although there is no "one size fits all" answer here either, my advice to you is consider this for yourself in many different areas relating to your children and parenting. Also things like the maturity and the current skill level of your child in a certain area are some additional things for you to consider – as to what is appropriate in relation to how far your child should be "pushed". Only you can really answer for your own circumstances, but my advice is still ask yourself such questions and be honest with yourself if you have been too pushy, or have gone too far, and therefore crossed that line. Alternatively it might be that a parent isn't "pushy" enough, whereby the child essentially has free reign to do as they please. The tolerance of your child is also another variable. A similar term for a pushy parent is a demanding one. But, again, putting it into context there may be nothing wrong with asking a lot of your children, having high expectations for them. But I repeat it's a fine line as to identifying the point at which you are asking/demanding too much. Where is the point when your expectations go from realistic to unrealistic? I think this is something which is more specific case by case but nonetheless my suggestion is to ask yourself as well as ponder such questions so that you don't cross this imaginary line, which you may well need to determine and set for yourself.

Let's put it into context in the real world. Some parents may want to make sure their child stays on top of their homework, does extra practice at a sport, arrange for some additional 1:1 time with a coach to help them improve etc. Essentially doing some more of something for their overall benefit. So would you say that is being assertive or forceful/aggressive? Of course on the other hand, if a parent is being overly aggressive, being somewhat of a bully with their child, that is the other extreme and clearly not the way to go. What I'm trying to demonstrate in this example is how the label of a "pushy parent" can really be looked at in two different ways but in most cases people only tend to associate it with the negative one.

So if your prefer the description or sound of it, give yourself the label of an "assertive parent" and take an active role in what your child does. If you see that they could do with some help in certain areas, then encourage them to do more and work at it with them so they can keep on improving, little by little. At the same time if your child is developing a passion for something and excelling, then encourage it. Over time I think most parents will come to identify that to get positive results, it's not rocket science, it's simpler than that. In my view it comes down to practice and hard work. We all know that our kids are not perfect so there will no doubt be times when they might slack off, not give their best, or not show the best attitude. There is a time and a place for everything so, in this moment, do you let it slide or do you decide to be a little more "pushy"? There is no need to take it to extremes but there may be times when you simply might need to get on top of things so, again, does that make you a "pushy parent"? You maybe someone who has been called a "pushy parent" in the past but only you can be the judge here. You may also have observed another parent and thought to yourself that they are, or have referred to them as being a "pushy parent". If this is the case I'm not necessarily saying that you're wrong, but given this explanation and putting it into a little more context, you may well reflect a little differently? You will know yourself when you are being assertive or if you're being a little too forceful, so obviously you need to make sure that you're on the assertive side. Then it won't bother you in the slightest if someone labels you as a "pushy parent" without them knowing the full story. Take it as a compliment in that case if you're being nothing more than assertive.

We all want what is best for our children but that is just a grand, bold statement. It requires action from both the child, and you as the parent. You cannot wait for things to happen. You can't expect your child to get better at something if they won't/don't work at it and if you don't work at it with them by helping them out in any way you can. My view is that there will be times when you will need to push your children but I believe this can still be done in a positive way. Sometimes when a parent appropriately pushes their child, I think it actually shows how much they really believe in them. Let's remember that children are completely reliant on parents at a young age to take them to those lessons, practices, take that time on the evening to take them to something instead of staying home – we all have a choice. You can describe it in so many ways other than being pushy or assertive. If you think about it as parents we are there to assist, facilitate, help, enable, support – I think that is enough descriptive words for now and there are many more. Hopefully you get the idea!

Therefore, my suggestion to you is to be an assertive parent as it's your responsibility. To be frank with you, no one else will care for your child as much as you do. No one else will make sure they do that extra practice or take them to that 1:1, or help them to stay on track. No one else will constantly or continually push your child in a positive way for your child's overall benefit. Of course there are teachers and coaches out there who do care and can play a key role, but I personally think it all comes back to the parents, as it's the parents that have the ultimate responsibility to positively push their children – both day-to-day and perhaps more importantly for the long-run. Also as a parent no one knows your children better than you do, so you need to recognize all of those subtle little clues they give off and how to react to them in a positive way. As your child gets older they will no doubt need to assume more responsibility and take such positive actions upon themselves. However, and particularly in the formative years, I think it's down to the parents to instill important lifelong principles, simple ones such as hard work, dedication, discipline and practice. Again children won't necessarily have that long-term understanding or perspective on the importance of persisting or not giving up, where you see something through by sticking at it. Therefore, as the parent you may need to step in every once in a while to continue to push them as it might be only you that can have that more long-term outlook. So next time your hear the saying, or hear someone described as a "pushy parent", take a step back and look at the situation and give full consideration by putting it into context. You may well find that the parents who positively push their children have positive results in the long-run. To bring all this back to becoming a better parent, I believe if you do figure out a way to positively push your child, then you will be doing just that.

6 GRANDPARENTS

Grandparents are definitely worthy of a chapter when it comes to a book on experience and advice on parenting. I recognize that everyone's circumstances are different insofar that some kids might not have all of their grandparents living, or it might be more complicated than that where some parents no longer see or speak to their parents. What I'm going to again emphasize here is that all things are not equal, but I will share with you my experiences to date after our daughter was born and, hopefully, you can relate to some of my thoughts in your own personal circumstances.

Firstly we're fortunate to have all four grandparents living, and both my wife and I have great relationships with our immediate parents. What is unique in our case is that, as I'm originally from the UK, my parents still live in England whilst my wife's parents live closer by in what is now our hometown of Rockledge, Florida. As an aside, and a very long story cut short, I was born and raised in Birmingham, England and I went to University in the USA where I met my wife. After we graduated we moved to England and lived there for six and a half years at which point we decided to move back to the USA. During that time in the UK, our daughter, Isla, was born and she was just shy of her third birthday when we made the move to America.

Back to the grandparents. Whilst I currently cannot know the feeling, but I hope to have someday, is the deep love that grandparents have for their grandchildren in a way which must be so unique in seeing your own child now raising one of their own. One key thing I think to remember is that you as parents and they as grandparents only want what is best for your child. So always try to remember that key point.

With their new love and affection, involve them as much as you can, allowing them to see your children regularly and often. Essentially, cherish this time if you're lucky enough to still have your parents with you. It's not only special for them to be with your child, it's special for you to share the experience with them too. Not just with our parents, I see it all the time with other grandparents, that with their new love and excitement, especially in the beginning, they naturally want to spoil your child. As your child grows older this may well continue, and when they're together your "rules" may be much more relaxed, for example when they're alone with your child, or when they're sleeping over. My suggestion here, and what I have learned, is to embrace this to a degree and don't get caught up too much if they treat them to something, or allow them to have an extra bowl of ice cream, or stay up a little later – there are many more examples but I'm sure you know what I mean. Of course in life moderation with all good things is key so perhaps have a friendly word if you think that things are getting out of control, with too many toys being one example. The last thing you want is for your child to expect something every time they see their grandparents or be ungrateful when they do treat them. The point I'm trying to get to is that you should give grandparents some freedom and you shouldn't give them a rule book of things they need to follow. It's only natural for some of your rules to be a bit more relaxed to put it lightly, when your child is with them. I'm sure they will remind you that they have been around the block many more times than you and that they know what they're doing having raised kids (you) themselves! No doubt you will roll your eyes when they tell you this but let's face it they have a point.

So my advice is don't be that parent that has such a strict set of rules or a step by step list that you try to enforce under someone else's roof. I have to be honest I see or hear this type of thing a lot these days. Yes, they're with your child, but I really don't see any benefit with such an approach. Not only do I think it's not the way to go but I also think it's a sure fire way to create tension and have differences with your parents or in-laws. Give them that element of freedom because, if a you as the parent start to nitpick on everything, it will only cause stress and anxiety on both ends. The reason I highlight such a point is that we don't live in a perfect world and everything is not always rosy. I know of many parents who don't have a great relationship with the parents or in-laws and quite often because of minor issues. It's over silly little things where the stem or root cause is actually the parents trying to control everything they're doing. The hard reality is that your parents won't be around forever so don't waste energy or the valuable time you have over differences which are insignificant. If you have to let some things go, then let them go. You may be thinking "wow, this all sounds a little extreme", but I know that there are grandparents out there who would love to see more of their grandchildren and don't because of strained relationships. I also know of some grandparents who don't actually get to see their grandchildren at all.

I have said that I will be honest with you throughout and there is no exception here. So do my parents or in-laws occasionally do something with my daughter which might go against something we've been working on? Do they occasional do something which gets on my nerves, under my skin or I find a little annoying/irritating? Of course they do, but what I think my wife and I are good at is being fairly relaxed about it. We generally don't make a big deal of things that don't need to be made a big deal of. We also certainly don't have rules when it comes to seeing or being with our child and what they can and can't do. When I say that, I know it also work both ways. I'm sure there are times when my parents or in-laws may feel like they need to bite their tongue, they're treading on egg shells a little or we do something that may rub them up the wrong way. The reality is that with the day-to-day stresses that we all face, we might butt heads from time to time, or disagree on something, but again, it all goes back to the most important thing in that everyone wants what's best for the child. Staying with "what's best", that's why it's so important for grandparents to be active with their grandchildren because, speaking from my experience with my daughter, she loves spending time with both sets of grandparents. They're different types of relationships so she would be missing out on something extremely valuable if they weren't as active as they are in her life. Everyone's family circumstances are different so I do have to generalize here. I know of many parents who, for whatever reason, seem to limit contact with grandparents, or others where the relationship has broken down completely. Reasons will no doubt vary but I just find it to be a huge shame when I hear that it has got to that point for some. Look I'm no counsellor but if it has got to a point where relationships are shall we say strained, maybe try to bring it back to consider what's best for your child so any differences can at least be put to one side.

So my advice is simply to involve them. Of course you need time alone as a family but why not plan a vacation once a year together or a weekend away? You will create some great memories. Another bit of advice when it comes to grandparents is to share. Share videos and pictures of your child all day long with them as I know ours love to receive them. We live in an age where people are constantly uploading/posting pictures of their kids to social media. With that, be sure to send those photos/videos to grandparents before you upload anything onto any social media profile if they don't already have one. I will be blunt in that they will be much more interested in seeing them than your "online" friends.

I think what is also relevant to mention with grandparents is the question of finances. I will share with you that our parents, whilst they're not on the Forbes money list by any stretch of the imagination, are, shall we say, comfortable. Again I know that this won't apply to everyone as circumstances will differ, but if you're fortunate enough that your grandparents are able to help out a little, then don't be too proud to accept. Let them help as I know that, in our case, they really want to and it really does help us. So what am I talking about here? Again, and looking at extremes, I'm not talking about them paying your rent or mortgage every month but, as in our case our daughter who plays golf and tennis, both of our parents offer to pay for lessons here and there. Or it might be a case where she needs a new pair of tennis shoes and they offer to buy them. Here again there is balance that it's not all the time but every now and then. I would say don't be too proud to always say "no" but, at the other end of the scale don't expect them to always pay or become anywhere near entitled. But if they can and want to, let them pay for these type of things once in a while if they offer as it most certainly helps – just make sure you're gracious and let them know how much you appreciate it. The same sort of thing applies when they want to look after your child for the night or have a sleepover – let them, and be grateful. Again, with balance, you will know when you may be asking a bit too much, so it's really from time to time. I know this is a little vague and non-specific, but I think you can work it out for yourself.

So to end with my thoughts and advice with grandparents, I will simply reiterate some of the points I have already made. If you're fortunate enough to have some, if not all, living and you maintain a great relationship with them, involve them as much as you can with your child. I promise that you won't regret it. Again, applying some common sense, this doesn't mean them living or being with you 24/7, but if your child has a play, dance show, tournament, match, you name it….my view is be sure to invite them too. Look I will close this chapter by again speaking as a real world parent by saying that no matter how good your relationship is with your parents, you will no doubt have indifferences or get under each other's skin from time to time. All I would say is don't let things like this ever get in the way. Let grandparents be active and play a big part in your child's life, which I believe is all linked to becoming a better parent.

7 NON-NEGOTIABLE

Now I'm not going to pretend the concept of something being "non-negotiable" is some new idea or new advice that I'm passing along. The notion is commonly used these days in relation to a lot of personal development advice as a way to make positive changes for the better in an attempt to form new positive habits. The term "non-negotiable" is rather self-explanatory but, for those who may not be familiar with the idea used in practice, I will give some examples of how I perceive the way that it's best used. It might be a person who is looking to lose some weight and get back into shape, so a "non-negotiable" might be no more fried food, no more ice cream, no more cake or that they must walk a minimum of two miles a day. When it becomes non-negotiable then you simply have to do, or in some cases not do, a particular action, no excuses and no if, buts or maybes. I think the food example provides the best illustration as someone may have a non-negotiable of "no more dessert". When that individual is then out for dinner or at a party and offered some cake it might be easy to say "well go on then, just for tonight as I have been good all week". But the beauty of a "non-negotiable" is that there is now debate in your mind, no pondering, it is just a flat out "no" because you can't.

Hopefully this presents the idea, and I'm not really sure if there is an advised best number to have, but I think less is really more and it might only be one or two. That way it's more simple, realistic and you're more than likely to follow through and be committed. If it's a list of 10 different things, then suddenly it all becomes a bit diluted and hard to succeed in my opinion. My view is that you want to set yourself up for success.

So what does this have to do with parenting? I will now look to specifically apply this advice to parenting with the aim of making you a better parent.

So why not have a "non-negotiable" when it comes to your family or your role as a parent? I'm not sure if the notion of a "non-negotiable" has been looked at too deeply when it comes to positive parenting? I have come across some advice which tends to focus on rules and disciplines for the kid such as having no devices at the dinner table, but I'm not really thinking of that when it comes to a "non-negotiable". I'm thinking of things such as reading your child a story every night, sharing 30 minutes of play time each day with each other, doing arts & crafts, playing an instrument, playing a board game, dancing, singing, playing a particular sport and so on. These are just some examples and ideas, but this is where you have the opportunity to use your imagination as you know your child better than anyone. So what could you do each day which you know will greatly benefit them and bring you closer together?

Hopefully some unique ideas immediately come to mind, but I suggest that you keep it positive and not related to breaking rules or for disciplining your child. I suppose it can be used in that way for zero tolerance of an unwanted behavior or action, but see this as doing something progressive. My suggestion is that put your own spin on it, for example have one "non-negotiable" and do it for a week and then select another one for the next, and so on. Then you will have 52 different positive "non negotiables" throughout the year. Using my earlier thoughts, you could maybe start week one reading a book every night to your child, and then your next non-negotiable might be playing throw/catch each night for 30 minutes for a week. It could even be as simple as having a "non-negotiable" of providing more encouragement, giving your child the biggest hug and kiss each day and letting them know how much you love them and how proud of them you are. I believe that such simple actions work best and are ones that are realistic, meaning that you know you can do them and, as a consequence, you're more likely to follow through.

You may not like some of my examples or necessarily agree with doing a new one each week and that's fine, tailor it to what works for you. It might be you have a "non-negotiable" for a month and then find a new one, or just have one for the entire year, again it's a question of whatever works for you. Hopefully I have demonstrated how you can use this to have a positive impact on your child's life and your life as a parent. I think that it keeps you focused and you will naturally want to continue with it when you see the beneficial effects that it has. Let's just look at one of the examples a little more where a non-negotiable might be to read your child a bed-time story each night. Or alternatively, have your child read to you depending on their age – I'm speaking more in relation to my circumstances, given we have a 6 year old. So like with many other things in this book, apply the principle specifically to your own circumstances! Either way, the benefit of this is that when the time arrives nothing else matters. No matter what else is going on or has happened during the day, you will know you have this dedicated time which in this case is reading with your child. If your phone rings you ignore it, put it on silent for 30 minutes and be fully present. The beauty of something like a non-negotiable in this instance is that it's all about you and your child. You know where and when to be each day, if you choose something like this. The only thing I would say is that being a real world parent, do something you know you can actually commit to, mainly with what your work schedule permits. You will know yourself what is realistic and what isn't. But in saying that something like this could be used for your benefit, if say it does make you more disciplined in leaving the office on time each day, so that you will then be at home with your family.

I did mention to keep it constructive, specifically with your child, but maybe also consider a "non-negotiable" to correct an unwanted behavior or action, specifically to you as a parent. I will give you an example in that sometimes my wife and I might disagree with something in front of our child. To describe it, we sometime clash a little like the stereotypical "old-married couple". Whilst we should try and cut this out all together we did agree that we should no longer do this in front of our children. Not only does it upset our daughter, but it's sets a bad example. So we have a "non-negotiable" of no longer arguing in front of our children. Hopefully you appreciate my honesty here, whilst I'm very much happily married, again I'm talking to you as a real parent in the real world. I'm not going to write this and pretend that we're some perfect couple or family. I think the reality is whether you acknowledge it or not a lot of couples clash, bicker, argue and butt heads so to speak not in any malicious kind of way, but I would imagine it's common for couples to disagree on things regularly. Look the reality is, raising a family is very demanding/challenging/testing where at times it can take its toll, despite all of the joys it does bring. Not just that, I believe that, sometimes as parents, we can take things out on the ones we love. It might be a work related matter that we're stressed about and then a minor thing at home can send us over the edge, so to speak. So back to the theme of this chapter by applying a "non-negotiable" to an unwanted response or behavior I again think this will help make you become a better parent. I also think a lot of the advice in this book is focused on gradual and small improvements you can make and this is an example here. This isn't about a quick fix, or looking to have an instant impact by doing some one time deal which requires loads of effort. Something like this really requires your commitment more day-to-day, to then see the real benefits which are realized over time.

My suggestion to you is to give it a try, give it a go, and I think you will see how the process naturally evolves. More importantly you should see the positive effect that it has and I have no doubt that you will experience more fulfilment as a parent by committing to doing something positive each and every day. As parents we have all had days where it has run away with us, we have lost track of time and have that feeling of not really accomplishing anything. There will be more days like this in the future, hopefully as the exception rather than the norm, when you have control of your day with good forward planning. But either way, by having one or two positive parenting "non negotiables" it won't necessarily stop you having a bad day, but at least you will have the assurance that you will still do something which is extremely important to you as a parent and your child because you have to; it's non-negotiable!

8 WE ALL LIVE IN A BUBBLE

I didn't really notice this so much before I became a parent, but I soon realized how, as a parent, you begin to live in your own bubble and this is something I very much notice in other parents too. What do I mean by this? I'm not saying that this only relates to parents, it can relate to anyone but, as a parent, I'm sure you can appreciate how quickly your life becomes consumed. Parenthood is life changing and it certainly takes some adjusting to - there is no hiding from that! You have total responsibility for another person and this is multiplied depending on how many children you have. So with the demands and challenges of modern day parenting, some days can seem a bit of a blur and you can lose sense of what is going on outside of your immediate family which is what I'm referring to as your "bubble."

Everyone is busy these days whether you're a parent or not, but my suggestion here is to not become so self-consumed, thinking everything is all about you and your child – whereby essentially you forget about or neglect anything outside of your "bubble." There is nothing wrong with being extremely proud as a parent and you and your family will always be priority number one, there is no denying that either. There is also certainly nothing wrong about putting your family first. So what am I getting at? The point that I'm trying to make is that, although your child/children is/are your first priority, don't forget your other loved ones. I'm not really referring to your spouse either here and suggesting that you take a regular date night. What I'm getting at is not to forget things like your parents birthday, staying in touch and making effort with close friends, sending birthday cards/gifts/messages or Christmas messages to loved ones, keeping up with a regular call to an elderly relative which they cherish. I could go on and on with examples. My view is that becoming a parent shouldn't mean that these types of things become less important and you can now avoid making that regular phone call, because you have the excuse that you're now just too busy. I see this all the time with parents and even within my own immediate family. We're all human and things can get the best of us at times and we might innocently forget something important. So I'm not saying be overly hard on yourself if this happens, but what I'm saying is that you should not just forget your friends/family/loved ones outside of your immediate bubble. Don't lose touch with a lifelong friend saying you don't have the time or energy as, in my view that is just a really bad excuse.

I mentioned at the beginning of the book that I call my Great Uncle in England once a week. This is important to me and is a priority of mine. So in my own way, doing something like this helps me not to be so consumed in my own bubble. I think it's a simple example, I will be the first to admit a phone call is not by any means overstretching myself and that I should give myself a huge pat on the back for doing this. At the same time, I think I could be easily forgiven if I forget to call or I now only call once in a while – say every few months. We're so thankful to have Max our new born with us and I'm sure you can appreciate having a new baby means we have a lot more going on. But I just don't want to use that excuse or take that easy way out. He would understand if I didn't call as much, but why should I stop doing this as much as I used to? Let's be honest we're all busy, we all have so many different things going on, but despite that I find there is always time, if you take the time if you know what I mean? This is my simple example and hopefully you can apply and relate to this in some way. If you can, my advice is not to forget or neglect something/someone which is of importance to you where you become so consumed in your own bubble. In some cases, I don't think this is even intentional for some so I don't want to throw out there how people can be selfish or so self-centered, although that can happen too. I mean it more to where you just sometimes may need to slow down, take a step back, or just be a little more mindful of other things going on around you – so you don't miss out or forget things of importance.

Now let's look at something like being late. Let's face it; the reality is that it takes a long time to get ready, and a lot longer to get out the house as a parent. It's a challenge in itself at times. You get your foot out of the door only to realize, when you are half way down the street, that you have forgotten something. Or it might be that you're ready to leave when nature calls for your child and, not only do you have to change their diaper but maybe their entire outfit. At one time or another we have all been running a little late to something – I think we all get it. However, the point is and bringing it back to your bubble personally, I think it can be excused from time to time, but my advice is not to think that the world suddenly revolves around you and your children now that you're a parent. I don't want to sound harsh here, but my point is really not to use your children as an excuse all the time. Being late is just one example but if you always blame being late on your kids, then I personally think that you're too consumed in your own bubble. Our lives differ in so many ways but as parents we all face the same challenge of meeting appointments on time when our children are making it difficult to even get out the door. My advice is not to think that certain rules only apply to you and not to others when we all face a similar challenge in that respect.

Staying with the thought that using your kids as a way out or excuse is not the way to go, I think that you will find that if you continue to do this without understanding or appreciating the world going on around you then you will soon be found out. I don't mean this in an offensive way, but I just mean that people will more or less come to the conclusion that it's now all about you. So my suggestion is not to miss out on a wedding, for example, because you can't travel with your kids which is essentially using them as your excuse for not attending. The reason I say not to use them as an excuse is because so many parents manage just fine and do get to those important occasions with their kids. My experience with some parents I know is that they're also the first to be offended when someone does not make an effort with them, or when someone says they can't get to their event/party. All things are not equal, but I have figured out that if you don't take interest or make an effort with anyone else then chances are that they won't make that effort with you, so don't get upset if/when that happens.

I will touch on this a little more, but it all comes back to the fact that the world doesn't revolve around you or your kids. So don't suddenly expect people to cater to your needs or have an expectation for people to drop everything they're doing for your benefit. My advice is don't ask for the timings of something to change so it can fit around your routine or your baby's nap time. My advice is don't be all high maintenance with all kinds of requests/demands involving a group of people at something like a party because I think for one-off type occasions we can all make the odd exception - even if you're regularly strict with something or so set in your ways. Again this might sound a bit harsh I know, but be honest do you know of someone like that? Someone so caught up in their own world without taking the time to consider anything outside of it. Even with something like this there can be somewhat of a fine line because look, we may all need someone to make the odd allowance or excuse us for something from time to time. I guess I will bring it back to the point to say that sometimes and in certain situations/circumstances you really do have to understand or realize that it's not all about you. I think that best sums it up really.

As this chapter is titled, We all live in a bubble; I must say I'm not trying to burst anyone's "bubble" with what I just said. I just want to share a few home truths more than anything and how sometimes it's necessary to be considerate of others as well as other things going on around you. In a weird kind of way, I actually think it makes you a better parent when you get that it's not all about you. I mean this in a sense that you don't get caught up with everything, or make something simple overly important or complicated, or that you just don't make a big/huge deal about everything. I think by just being a bit more humble naturally makes you more relaxed to things going on around you and you're not on edge with anything which affects you in some way.

I said at the beginning of the chapter that becoming a parent is life changing and I think that every parent would agree on that. So whilst I admit I'm going to be pointing out the obvious here essentially repeating what I just said, this means your life changes after becoming a parent. I think as your life changes so do you. This is not looking at whether you change for the better, it's just saying at face value you will change as a person, because of such a life changing event, which is becoming a parent. I don't really want to go any deeper with this as I'm sure some might even oppose this view. I'm not really meaning that your core life principles, values, or beliefs will change (although they might); I just mean it more in relation to your lifestyle. Immediately your priorities change and your life goes in a different direction. To put a light spin on this I'm sure most parents have said at one point something along the lines of "I can't party like I used to." But to bring this back to the theme of the chapter where my advice is to not get so caught up in your own bubble, I will admit and want to at least acknowledge that I believe we actually do change as people when we become parents, as a result of our life changing. It can be as simple as looking at it as with our changing lifestyles, like the simple example I just gave, where late night partying quickly becomes a thing of the past – for me anyway. So I think it's a good thing to understand and acknowledge this rather than shut it down with a response along the lines of "I'm still the same old me." I actually think we all live in our own bubble whether we're a parent or not, but as we're referring to parenting, I think this gets somewhat amplified/intensified when we do become a parent. So what I'm really trying to get to is that although our lives and lifestyles change and we do as a result of it, where we get even more consumed in our own bubble, my advice is don't take it to the extreme. I'm also not suggesting it's only negative things/changes that can happen. I just want to highlight this as another area for you to consider so that you don't gradually start to forget about very important areas that were once a big part of your life before becoming a parent. Because that's the point you don't overnight suddenly stop or neglect something. It might be much more gradual than that to where you then completely lose touch with someone over a period of time, referring to one of my earlier examples. But as I keep saying your life/lifestyle does change, so if anything I think it's important to understand this, to ensure your priorities remain in line. I highlight all of this because I think there is a potential trap which I have been referring to as a bubble, to where you end up getting so caught up in your own little world, almost forgetting about anything outside of it.

With family and friends, I do acknowledge that it needs to be somewhat of a two way street and that effort needs to be reciprocated. What I'm not getting at is petty behavior, where it's always 1-for-1, where it's like everything needs to equal out. There is nothing wrong in being a super proud parent and I think new parents have a tendency to want to show their child off to the world and again, go for it. However, be mindful of your close friends and family who may also have children of a similar age. Be sure you that you take the time and make an effort with other people and their children – don't expect the traffic to be one way which I see in some people. It's not all about you and it's not all about them either. What I'm getting at though is that if you're the one making all of the effort with a family member or friend with nothing back in return then maybe that's worth looking at. As I said before, things in life are not always equal, so I'm not saying you need to create a chart monitoring how much effort someone is making with you, or that you even need to be stubborn and not call someone because you called them last time and it's their turn to call you. But I think we all know the people who really care, and will always be there for us, whether it be a close friend, brother, sister etc.

I have to admit there are people I'm not as close with anymore because I didn't really feel the love if you know what I mean? I have had the experience where I felt like I was always the one to reach out but it was a one way street or I felt I didn't get support at a time when I really needed it. So as some relationships go I think it gets to the point where it can't be just one person trying to initiate contact or when you understand for yourself that person isn't really there for you in your hour of need. I don't think it's being stubborn either. In my case I haven't fallen out with anyone or it's not like I would never take their call, it's just I no longer make that same level of effort. The ultimate point I'm trying to make is to continue those extremely worthwhile relationships. If they really are true friends or loved ones they will understand more than anyone that you now have other priorities. This book is about becoming a better parent so simply relating the concept to this chapter; I would say that it's important for you not to shut out others around you. I don't mean that in a malicious kind of way either, more in a sense where you just don't take as much notice to what else is happening around you. You may well not be in touch with someone as often as before, or have as much free time on your hands but, again, this isn't to say that you can now forget other people or things going on outside your own "bubble." I keep saying this book is about becoming a better parent and I think there are so many ways in which you can do this. I think this area is a really important one and if anything it's not focused at all on your children, as this advice is actually saying not to become so fixated on just your kids/family, which I refer to as your bubble. But, I really feel if you have perspective and take time outside of your own little world, then this will only add to you becoming a better parent, mainly because you will feel so much better for doing so. Only you can tell for yourself your current position, so my advice is be honest about it and determine if you do need to take more time with others – or more time out of your own bubble. If you do then I think you will be able to understand for yourself if you think it does help you to become a better parent in that overall sense.

9 ROUTINE AND EVERYTHING STEP BY STEP

This may seem somewhat of a slight contradiction to my opening advice on what I believe is the most important thing when it comes to parenting. Let me explain, and this advice is mainly aimed at parents who have younger children or babies/new-born's, although some aspects may apply to all. Of course for those expectant parents, or for those of you thinking of, or having, another child, this is something to maybe consider. That is the question of having a routine. Now I'm all for a routine for a child, particularly infants and you will hear the word "routine" a thousand times with a new-born and the importance of getting them into one. This relates to my opening chapter on the importance of structure and planning, but the key difference here is that I believe that you still need to be flexible and in a position to adapt/improvise.

When our daughter was born we initially tried to keep to a very strict routine, but experience taught us that being so inflexible doesn't work and actually causes more stress/tension, resulting in a negative effect. We had frustrations, like many others no doubt, such as our daughter not napping as normal or not sleeping as she normally would because her routine was disrupted. There were then times when we were almost trying to force her to have a nap when she just didn't want one. But after a while we decided it was best not to let the routine get the better of us. That didn't mean we didn't try and stick to one, but we were just less stringent about it. In other words, we didn't act as though it was the end of the world if our routine was off or affected on any given day.

I see it all the time with parents, whether it's from family members, friends and other parents in general, that they really try too hard to stick to a routine. Whether it's that they can't go to that party because it will interfere with nap time, or they ask to change the time of an event to fit in with their child's schedule. My view on things like this is fairly blunt and emphasizes what was in the last chapter, in that you're not the only parent in the world and the world does not revolve around you and your child. I'm saying that you should try and maintain a routine but, if for a day you can't stick to your routine; don't think that, referring to my earlier point, the world is coming to an end. In addition to that, don't overreact either if it will take a day or two to get back on track with your routine, if you had to steer from it, as that will inevitably happen. You will soon get back into the swing of things.

You may disagree, and I'm not meaning to cause any offense here as I know a lot of parents who are overly strict about a routine. I'm speaking from experience, and it didn't work for us to be like this so I'm merely sharing that with you. As I said, I actually think it caused more stress and tension when we did try and stick to something so methodically. We would bicker and argue about it until eventually we decided to cool off the strict routine and took more of a relaxed approach. I do want to reiterate that we did still try and work to a routine; we just did not let it consume us.

What I'm saying is, every now and then, don't miss out on something you want to do, or a place where you want to go, or turn down an invite just because it doesn't fit with your routine/schedule. On the other hand, don't be selfish either and ask everyone to change their plans just so you can do something which works around your routine/schedule. You may get away with a one-off but, trust me; it will start to annoy people if you become so self-centered. We all are self-centered to a degree (some more so than others) and nothing is more important than our child but it can't always be about you.

I know of similar examples where parents have to ensure the same routine is followed, no matter where they are. Personally I think that's taking it to the extreme and that is being too inflexible. I don't know about you but if I'm on a vacation or even if it's a Saturday night, the last thing I want to worry about is a routine where it's like you have to meet a deadline. Stick to a schedule, but acknowledge the reality that you need to be flexible and adapt/improvise, as otherwise it will not be sustainable as no two days are the same. Think about it the modern day, fast-paced, call it what you want, world we live in. The reality is that it's almost impossible to perfectly follow a routine day in, day out.

I actually think it's quite easy for a parent to fall into a trap of taking everything to the extreme. At the root of it is love and just trying to do everything right by their child. Again every parent has the right to do what they think's best and with certain things parents may well have to find that something out for themselves. Speaking personally, I think as your learn on the job so to speak, you do become more relaxed with things and I particularly think this is true with our second child. I mean this in a way of not getting so caught up with everything. Essentially I think we're not making such a big deal of everyday things which we may have done more so with our first child. Speaking more generally I think it's easy for parents to have tendency to overdo it at times. I don't want to sit here and say something really condescending like my advice is just to chill out a little more. But the everyday things I'm referring to are things like smothering your child's hand with hand sanitizer just because they've touched something, or caking on sunscreen just for stepping outside, or not ever letting them go out in the rain, soaking your child with bug spray when they're playing out, or no one dare make a sound because the baby is asleep – it's things like this where I think it can get a little out of control.

Before I move on maybe this will bring a smile to your face with the point I just made? It's in relation to not making a sound when a baby or child is asleep. We've had this with both of our children more so when they were babies. It has been when they've been put down for a nap and we've tried so hard not to make a noise and the tiniest of sounds woke them. On the other hand there have been times when they're flat out, but there was a place we needed to be/go, so we needed to wake them up. I tend to find at those times is when the loudest drill in the world would not have even made them flinch and they would continue snoring away. I say this as this has frequently happened only to make a point that sometimes it kind of just works out that way, where everything doesn't go to plan or as you might hope. Not by where nothing ever works the way you intended, nothing ever goes your way or like the world is against you. I also think it's easy to perhaps try a little too hard at times, where you might try and force something rather than let it happen – this is where I tend to find the stress kicks in. But I think being a parent that's just the way it goes sometimes where simple types of things like this happen; where your child won't nap when you really want them to and they will nap all day long when you need to be somewhere or someplace. I also think this proves the point somewhat where although you may think you have the perfect routine going it's not going to work like clockwork every single day. I personally think living in the real world you need to be in a position to adapt/improvise or be flexible because as we know and as said before, no two days are the same. I just say all this so you don't get overly worked up when it doesn't work out the way you like, because I tend to think you'll find it will happen all a little too often!

Now I'm sure some might get carried away with some of my earlier points. So before anyone does that and just for the record, I think it's important for kids to put on sunscreen, wash/sanitize their hands and even use good old bug spray etc. My advice is just not to go overboard because when I see other parents taking things to the extreme, I don't know what it is but they just seem so worked up or stressed out. As a result they freak out over such little/minor things or pretty much everything. I refer back to times when we took some things to the extreme and the same applied – we were on edge most of the time. As I said it's easy for me to say don't get all worked up over something or don't make a big deal of things. I say this because let's face it; anything related to our child is a big deal. I think if you told a parent they need to relax or chill out a little, to put it lightly, I don't think they would take kindly to it at all. But I say all this because if you're a parent that is a little on edge at times, snappy, stressed or might overreact over little things, the best thing may be just to be honest and acknowledge it. If you do that then you don't need me or anyone else advising you on how to respond. I think you will work it out for yourself, if you do admit that there are times when you can take things to the extreme. Maybe you will learn like I did where perhaps initially I was trying a little too hard, trying to do the right things all of the time. It almost becomes to where it's like mistakes are never allowed, but I think you soon find out that's just unrealistic. Look as parents, whether you like to admit it or not, I think we all make a ton of mistakes. So not only is it unrealistic, I think it also adds pressure on you and maybe you then try and force certain things. The way I see it, parents have enough on their plate so for me, it doesn't make sense to add any additional pressure and certainly not with the little/everyday things.

Going back to looking specifically at routine, you actually tend to find that parents become more lenient when their child is sick for example; when they might have a cold or something like that. In this instance they're more understanding if their routine is affected. So be the same if your routine is off because you went to a family party or were invited to an event, or your child had a sleepover or anything similar to this. Another thing somewhat related to this is trying to do everything step by step and by the book so to speak. This is something we tried to do early on with our daughter, but we soon realized it wasn't for us and didn't work. Sometimes it's a case of learning as you go and figuring out what works for you. We just found that when we did try to do everything perfectly, like the routine, it just caused more anxiety and really, you start to put a bit too much pressure on yourself. I think the point here is that you can read the text book and try to follow things but there comes a point at which you also need to use your own parenting intuition/judgment – again looking at what works best for you.

I will give another real life example which we did and I know of other parents who do something similar all the time. You may have someone looking after your child. So along with your 20 bags of things you bring and leave with them is also a list of instructions for your child. We have all been there and seen/done it before. We know this is not a short list either, it's a long one of step by step instructions of what to do, what not to do, and the exact time it should be done. We have done it and I'm not criticizing anyone else who does this or has done it before either, because I won't be surprised if this applies to most, if not all parents, at one point or another. At the root of it, whether it be following a routine or doing everything by the book, is simply love for your child and it's only natural for the parent in this instance to ensure that their child is being cared for. I'm not actually saying that you shouldn't give any details of what your child may need because that friend, aunt or cousin may need it. All I'm really saying is to maybe relax/chill-out a little and don't worry/stress if everything isn't always followed, step by step, like some form of military operation. I mentioned this before, that if you leave your child in the capable hands of grandparents they will politely remind you that they raised you with no issues so you need not worry and, at the end of the day, they're right. Like the routine, just make sure that you don't go to the extreme when someone does look after your child; let's remember that they're doing you the favor! So don't hold them to account when you get home by checking every last detail to ensure everything was followed step by step to your liking. Don't take it to the extreme that, if they went to bed an hour later than normal which means they got less sleep, that you no longer allow your child to stay at your grandparent's house again because they didn't follow your directions.

Bed-time is an obvious example where I think parents try to stick to their rule book and become rigid in their day-to-day routine. This book is about advice; it's certainly not for me or anybody else to tell you what time your kids should go to bed. My advice is really for more of those one-off, or once in a while things. If there is a wedding, family party or it may even just be that Saturday night every now, don't go crazy about sticking to your child's bedtime/routine. My suggestion on these occasions would be to let it go, every once in a while. Staying with bed-time for a minute, again this can cause stress in a sense where, for example, if your child's bedtime is 8pm but it's now 8.10pm the world is now coming to an end! You might end up shouting at your child or your spouse/partner, because they should be in bed by now. The way I see it, every day is not the same so if you're home late yourself and running a little behind, don't feel pressured to try and stick to the regular bedtime where you're racing against the clock. My advice is that if it needs to be pushed back 30 minutes, then do it to take that pressure off yourself so it's not that catastrophe that it's made out to be when it's 5 or 10 minutes past bedtime. I'm just saying that if you try and stick to such a strict routine then at times it will feel as if you are racing against the clock to make it. I also think that it doesn't really allow for common sense things like this, where it would make sense for your kids to go to bed a little later than normal. It might not be ideal but it certainly wouldn't be the end of the world. So my advice is that if you do really like a routine then stick to it, but at least apply some common sense when needed to allow for some form of flexibility.

There may be instances when you may go against the so called rule book, and that's ok too. A specific example with our daughter is that she occasionally asks to sleep between us in our bed. Now I admit we don't make a habit of this but every now and then we let her. This probably goes against standard parenting advice of letting your child sleep with you but, like I said, this is something we do very occasionally. And, to be honest, there is nothing better than my little girl getting cozy between us. I just use this as example to illustrate that you need not try too hard to follow your daily routine or the textbook of parenting. I think it will end up driving yourself crazy, so just give yourself some leeway and I think you will find that things become less stressful. To give an analogy I think we have all heard someone referred to as being "book-smart" but may lack some common sense in the real world. Or it may be that person knows the text book answer but can't practically apply or action it in practice. Hopefully this analogy makes sense to you as I think it does have relevance to parenting. You can have a "book-smart" parent or someone who can talk a good game but sometimes you might just have to apply some common sense to a situation. All of our lives and circumstances are unique in their own right, so as the parent you will know more than anyone what might be best for your child in a certain situation – even it that sometimes means going against any parenting manual.

Diet is another area where I see parents being very strict in trying to follow a regime. I will specifically look at Diet with its own chapter later in the book. There I will focus more on the importance of scheduling, but here I want to stay on this notion of looking to follow something so strictly as it were. There is nothing wrong with that either, in wanting your child to have a healthy balanced diet, I place great importance on it myself – plus we all know of the saying "you are what you eat!" I also understand that children have allergies too, so there are genuine reasons for being strict with diet if this is the case. However, speaking more generally, if your child doesn't have an allergy to any food my advice would be to definitely place high importance on what your child eats, but don't let it take over to the extent that it becomes an obsession. I've seen this at times in public settings where it might be a wedding, birthday party, restaurant or a general gathering and parents make a big issue about the food their child will be eating. At the end of the day parents are free to do what they want so this isn't really a criticism, but its more advice in a way to reconsider such an approach because personally, I would find it exhausting. To try and keep track of exactly what your child eats by reading every label it can become somewhat of a fixation. I just think that if you become so preoccupied in a certain area, then you might waste time and energy or neglect something else of importance in another. I think that, with parenting, some things can be over complicated and I think diet is one of them. Personally I'm not concerned that my child doesn't eat everything organic, as a general example. I think it's easy to over-think when, in reality, common sense should prevail. With food, stick to a healthy balanced diet and, of course, ensure that fruit and vegetables are part of it. But, at the same time, if occasionally my child has something which would be deemed a little unhealthy, whether it be at a birthday party or get together, that's ok too. Or to put it another way, I just won't make a big/huge deal of it. I certainly wouldn't ask for anyone to make any special allowances unless there was an important reason like an allergy.

Hopefully you get the point that I'm trying to make in this chapter. To summarize: Don't take things to the extreme where it becomes an obsession or a big drama to try and follow some form of perfect routine or doing everything by the book as it were. I will say it one more time that this is in my view, not living in the real world. So you don't misunderstand, let me make clear I think routines are good. I think my main advice is that, as a parent, you do need to be in a position to be flexible and adjust things here and there depending on a specific situation. Don't get to the point where a routine takes over your life and prevents you doing those everyday things. You may probably find you become less stressed, tense and anxious if you can learn to let things go sooner rather than later if your routine is affected in some way because, sure enough, it will be. And guess what; if you're less stressed, tense and anxious, then surely you will be a better parent for it?

10 TOYS, REWARDS, RECOGNITION & GIFTS

When it comes to Toys, Rewards, & Gifts this is an area that you can maybe learn from one of the mistakes that I made as a parent. It doesn't instantly strike home, but I recently realized that my child had drawers and drawers of toys, so many that it's impossible to keep track of and she certainly couldn't play with them all at once. So I instantly came to the understanding/conclusion that my child had way too many. I came to this realization when my daughter was looking for one of her toys, but we couldn't find it because she had so many that it was lost in the crowd - not to the extreme of looking for a needle in a haystack, but at the same time not too far-off! As with many things that I refer to in different chapters in the book, the process is so gradual over time and then someday that realization hits you from nowhere. Of course a gradual process can result in positive outcomes, but in this case I think it's a negative one. The reason I say negative is that, first and foremost and in a practical way, so many toys are not utilized or played with at all. In some cases it's not even intentional. It might just be that, because she has so many, some are put in a drawer somewhere and are then just forgotten about. Also, and more generally speaking, kids grow out of things so quickly and move onto something else.

It's a gradual thing really where the toys build up over time and you suddenly realize that there isn't enough storage space for them all. So for this to happen, I have to take responsibility as the parent. I do have to say my daughter is well mannered and shows sincere thanks when she is given a gift but, like anything, you can maybe have too much of a good thing. I certainly don't want to get to a stage where my child would become entitled or show a lack of appreciation and these are just some of the danger traps when they get too much. It's something you have to try and manage. It's easy to buy your child a toy but you have to question yourself sometimes as to why they're getting it? Are you just getting more of the same, if you know what I mean? Am I rewarding them with something? Do they deserve a treat? Is it going to end up in a drawer after 5 minutes? More on this to follow.

Back to my daughters collection of toys. There is such a wide range as it's a mixture of purchases from us, family, friends as well as hand me downs from other generous people. Of course there are practical solutions when you identify this, with an obvious one being that your child can learn to share and give some toys to other children who are less fortunate. When you realize that you child has too many toys you cannot help but think of kids out there who don't have any and, as a parent, you really want your child to understand how fortunate they actually are.

Something else to consider is to maybe get rid of a used/old toy every time your child gets a new one. But rather than focus on the practical solutions at this time, I think that it's important to look at the root cause and actual prevention – essentially being proactive instead of reactive. Now I don't want to be a complete kill joy - I'm certainly not saying that you should never buy a toy for your child. I don't know what it is about seeing the look on your child's face when you give them a surprise. It may only last a few moments but still it's very special and should be cherished which is, in fact, even more of a reason to do it sparingly. No doubt family and friends will get something for your child every now and then if they have not seen them in a while so what I'm not saying is to refuse them or come across ungrateful in anyway, far from it. Really this is about focusing on what you buy for your child as in our case the majority of toys in our house have been purchased at one point by us, be it from birthdays/Christmas or even those impulse buys in the stores/shops.

In our case when I say our child has too many toys, I don't mean anything necessarily too grand or overly expensive. It's stuff like little figurines, gadgets, gizmos, soft toys and other little things like that. You can't help think that it's a waste and that your hard earned money could have been put to better use. For want of a better word, and being brutally honest, the vast majority of stuff can now best be described as "junk". You soon realize how quickly your child's favorite toy character can change from show to show. At the time something for a few dollars won't seem much, but as in our case when it's multiplied to the tens if not hundreds then it does add up to a lot of money. The issue of child commercials and advertising in stores can be debated all day long but really, as I already alluded to, it does come down to the discipline or restraint of the parents. It's so easy to give in as we have done many times but what I'm saying is to give this area the consideration it deserves. In our case the build-up of toys is something that steadily happened over time and something I suppose we never really paid close attention to, until we were running out of closet or storage space in our own home! The main one with our daughter being soft toys (cuddly toys) where she has so many on her bed and in different storage drawers in our home.

So, in terms of discipline, set yourself limits of how many toys you buy and I would pay more attention to those potential impulse buys at stores rather than necessarily for a birthday or Christmas. For birthdays and Christmas, I would also say not to go overboard, more so when children are so young that they don't even know or understand what they're really getting anyway. How often do you see a young child playing with an inexpensive or simple toy rather than the grand or expensive array of gifts they might have been given at one time on a birthday or a Christmas? I remember my mum saying something as a kid when I got all these gifts for Christmas and the only one I kept playing with was a little soccer ball which cost very little. You may want to splash out on your child's first birthday or Christmas, I get it, but talking from experience the fact that our child could not even comprehend what was going on you may want to delay any huge expense. I'm not saying no toys entirely as I think all children should have the pleasure to play with toys but do pay close attention to the amount your child has in those early stages in particular as, trust me, the amount quickly builds up without you knowing. As I said earlier, kids also have a habit of quickly moving onto the next thing before you know it. I think if you become more disciplined and controlled it will make the occasion when you do surprise your child with something that extra bit special.

Specifically with birthdays and Christmas, I actually think that as parents we have a tendency to overcomplicate it, overdo it or overthink it. I mean it in the sense that we can almost add pressure to it. We might think we have to get a certain thing, or buy a certain amount of things, hold a huge party or spend a set amount of money. It can also create a level of anxiety or stress, particularly at Christmas, when you have so much going on anyway that you now have a lot more on your day-to-day to do list. It was funny in a kind of way when I recently went to my daughter's friend's birthday party. It was at a climbing activity center and, don't get me wrong, the girls had a great time but I have a rough idea of the cost and it was certainly not cheap. The reason I say this because at the end of the party the girls seemed to have the most fun when they were in a small room together with balloons where they were just throwing them around. There was so much laughter, giggles and fun – they were just running around and having a good time. So just consider it because when I say we can overcomplicate things I mean it in a way where we feel the need sometimes to make a grand gesture, by doing something which is expensive, just because it's our child's birthday. But in this example the girls could have had as much, if not more fun, at a playground where they could just play together. I don't think children, particularly the younger ones, pay too much attention to the cost of something. We were also talking generally and the friend I was talking to said something in a joking way like "next year I will just get balloons and do it at home." We got talking more about gifts in general and he said his son still has unopened or unused toys that he had bought for him at Christmas. The fact is that the same applies to my daughter in that I'm aware that she got some gifts from last Christmas that she may have only touched once or twice, if at all. You cannot help but think it's just a huge waste.

With something like this it's so tempting in the moment to want to give things to your child which they want now, go all-out so to speak and it's not very natural in that moment to have a long-term outlook. This may be your first child so you want to go "all-out." But all I'm saying is to try and get a little perspective. Ask yourself: Will they remember this gift this time next year? Will your child not only remember what you got them, will they still be using it? Kids grow and mature at a rapid rate and you quickly realize this when you have something like a yard sale and you're now looking to sell a previously prized possession for some loose change. I'm really not trying to be a buzz-kill here and this is certainly not about never being able to treat your child to something. My advice is just to, at least, consider this from time to time as, to be honest, I would have certainly have previously benefitted from such guidance.

In my daughter's case, to provide a more specific example of what she has in excess are soft toys (cuddly toys) and clothes as well as shoes. I also think she has too many books, but I'm sure some might say you can't have enough books so I won't focus too much on that other than to say be realistic. Realistic in the sense of your child's reading level and how many books they can physically read bearing in mind everything else they have going on. It might be great to have a huge selection of choice but be mindful that collection could turn into another buildup of things which get lost with everything else. Maybe the good old library card is the way to go in that you get a few books and when you're done you exchange them for a few more. Although I was just looking mainly at toys, I do think the same principles very much apply with clothes and shoes. I'm not going to do a separate chapter looking at clothes as speaking personally, I will be repeating many of the points I just made, but I at least want to bring it up before I go any further. Similar to that of toys in that I'm fully aware that there are so many children in this world who don't have many clothes let alone a closet full. In our daughters case again it was a gradual build up until it suddenly hits you that she has far too many. As with toys, the build-up was a result of our purchases as parents and the generosity of family and friends. We have given a lot of our daughters clothes away as hand me downs or to good causes but my advice to you is consider what I'm saying to prevent it where the amount of clothes for a child becomes too much. This is not about closet space or storage space if anything it's about preventing waste through nonuse. In our case the money used to buy clothes for our daughter could have been spent/allocated in a much better way. Speaking very generically but based on experience, I would limit the amount of costumes you buy for your kid as in our case they have been the very much one-off/one-time use items. When I say costumes again speaking generically, I mean princess type costumes for girls and I'm guessing it might be similar for boys with action type figures. Ultimately we can debate the issue of excess toys and clothes all day long, but I think there is no doubt as parents we have to take responsibility for this. My advice to you is not let it get to such a point if you're fortunate enough to have a network of family and friends who get things for your child. Typically it's at Christmas time or with birthdays, so if any of this relates to you in some way if you know your child doesn't need any more toys or clothes, then you can politely let people know that if they ask you if there is something/anything they can get for your child. Applying the notion of prevention is better than cure in this case, take my advice on board and don't go overboard with toys and clothes however tempting it maybe.

For those parents reading this with a new born or perhaps expecting their first child I think it's important to have a specific mention to you as I think the temptation is to overdo it that much more with your first child – and I'm not just talking about toys or clothes here it could be anything! Like in other areas of the book where I have offered ideas, I'm really not trying to be a buzz kill/party pooper or say you have to think practically with every decision. I get it you will be so excited like any new or expecting parent, I'm definitely not trying to quash/dampen that, but at least think about what I'm saying so it doesn't get out of control so to speak. For new parents I think it really is a minefield where anything and everything gets thrown at you from car seats to strollers – I know of parents who have multiple strollers to the point where they almost have one for every day of the week! I'm sure parents sometimes feel the need to splash out or get the most expensive thing as that must be the best and you only want the best for your child. It's very easy to quickly spend a small fortune on all the things you think you may need, so I guess what I'm trying to say is not to always act on impulse. Of course you need things like a car seat or a crib, but without trying to come across as a complete cheap skate my advice is don't feel the need to always go for the most expensive thing. Secondly and speaking personally there are many things we got that we thought we may need and in the end were way under-utilized. So try and learn from my experience/lesson and I think that goes back to trying to at least cut out some of those impulse buys – again no matter how tempting they may be.

Looking now at rewards, we have a reward chart for our daughter which I think is fairly common place for most families these days. Ours is fairly simple in that there is a list of different tasks/to do's, and each day we place a sticker on the chart if any have been completed. When the chart is complete our child gets a reward of her choice. In addition, and as a follow on from what I have previously said, my wife and I now do a lot better in no longer doing those impulse buys or just getting or giving our daughter something for no justifiable reason. This is why I really like the concept as it works for us. Now as I said this is somewhat related because I'm not necessarily saying that you should have a reward chart for your child – I personally think that they're useful for developing some good habits and discipline which has happened in our case, but I'm sure there are parents out there who don't agree or feel the need for them. As I said, in our case it works, but there are many different things you can do or try. But for those who do have a behavioral chart or have something similar or more generally speaking if there is ever a time to reward your child my advice is why not do it with an activity/experience?

This is something we recently changed for our daughter's behavioral chart, once she had completed it, and I think it's something we've all benefited from. We end up doing something together and our child gets the same if not more enjoyment by experiencing something rather than just getting some sort of toy. Memories are not only so much more valuable, but they last much longer than a short lived gratification of getting a material object. It's also great to share an experience as a family. Now I'm not talking anything way too extravagant here, it could be a game of putt putt/crazy golf, a trip to the local theatre/movies, an in-door play place, zoo, museum etc. So why not consider this? In my daughter's case before we made the change, she was almost conditioned to think she will get a toy after completing her reward chart. That is what she wanted so we used to let her pick one out. Whilst in the moment she had that excitement and joy of getting one, I would have to say that the feeling is very short-lived. Comparing this to an experience your child can begin to appreciate different things. By doing such a thing it also encourages you as a family to try something new or go to a local place you may never have considered going before. A win-win all round.

Now I also think it works so much better in that when she sees that her hard work has paid off she is rewarded with an experience and ultimately it is something we all enjoy. So I recommend that you consider sharing many experiences where you can store many happy memories rather than storing a load of toys which end up in a storage box cluttering up your house. I think experiences are worth so much more than anything material. It's also a great feeling as it has often been the case with our daughter that she will kind of randomly bring up in a conversation… "remember when we did this/that" – "it was so much fun"… "can we do it again?"

I now want to touch more on the point that I mentioned and referred to at the beginning of this chapter. That is actually considering what you're recognizing in your child and thereby rewarding. As a parent, I think it's really important to look at what you're rewarding your child for; as it reflects the expectations you set as a family for your child/children. This is very simplistic advice and glaringly obvious but I say it because parents, including myself, can easily treat or give something to their child for no reason at all. Now at first hand there may seem nothing wrong with that providing it's more of a one-off, but we all know there are some kids who come to expect a toy every time they go to the stores and I believe most if not all would agree that isn't' desirable – not only does that develop entitlement but it also hits your wallet too!

Advice I like to try and follow is to reward effort and hard work if you're going to reward your child with something. As previously mentioned my wife and I recognized that we were previously buying too many things for our daughter and in a sense were rewarding her for no real reason. We are now seeing the benefit of changing our approach by stopping those impulse buys and having that mindset shift of thinking more about what we're actually rewarding. Now we recognize effort and hard work in important areas for our daughter and reward her now with an experience instead of a toy. So this goes back to you considering what are you actually rewarding? What expectations are you setting for your children? Are you rewarding things or behaviors which should actually be a given? I like the notion of rewarding effort in children as this begins to instill life valued principles that you do have to work at something to get better and you don't get something for nothing. Going back to my general advice, this does obviously have to be age specific to your child. I think a good illustration is looking at school as it's very easy to look at a grade or test result and base recognition/reward on that. Of course you're not going to reward your child for every grade, but I'm just using the example to make a point in this instance. Perhaps this is where praise/recognition of your child plays a greater role than any reward as well. The point being that if your child has worked extremely hard and studied, putting in a lot of effort and maybe gets a C grade, then my view is that effort should be rewarded. Another point to make is that reward does not have to be an experience, tangible or material object, as just said it can be as simple as your praise and genuine pride in their work ethic.

There is so much out there now on human performance (children and adults) that shows that people can excel and achieve great things in the long-term if they focus on hard work/effort/practice to make those small, even tiny, improvements in the short-term. Essentially focusing on the process instead of the result/outcome because, by focusing on the process with hard work/effort/practice with a desire to constantly seek that improvement, in the long-term the results will tend to take care of themselves. There is nothing new, but I do recommend learning more about this as like I said, there is so much already out there on this concept. I know this is rather a long winded way of saying that hard work should be rewarded but my advice to you is to do it and my belief is that you can start to do this at an early age. In our case we're already seeing the benefit and as parents it's principles like this that we value and want our children to understand for themselves. I personally want my daughter to develop the understanding whether it's learning how to read, to ride her bike on two wheels, to improve at her sports that it requires a lot of effort and practice – essentially a lot of hard work. Therefore as a parent, I don't become frustrated if it does take my child a bit longer than other kids to ride that bike, as the main thing is that she is putting in a lot of effort to do so something which makes me proud. At the same time I think this approach will help to reduce frustration in the kids themselves when performing something so they stick at it as they will soon find out that you don't always get things right first time. As a result, this method can work with simple to complex tasks. I can't remember where I heard it but I love the saying "progress not perfection" as that helps with the concept of continuous improvement. I think this style helps as kids are all at different levels with many different things. Not every parent has that stud or standout athlete or that straight A student and I think by now we all know that's ok. So, by actually rewarding the level or effort, hard work and practice, I believe that you will see the long-term benefits of doing so. Every child is unique to where they're currently at, so this way they can be rewarded and recognized for something, provided that it is really deserved.

So we have looked at toys, how your child is rewarded/recognized and, in the final part of the chapter I want to touch on the subject of gifts for your children. When I say gifts, this bit of advice is something to consider not at what you get/give your child but actually what others do. This advice comes with a note of caution as I would only consider using it very sparingly and only when appropriate with someone you're very close to like your parents (grandparents) where you can comfortably ask them anything. What am I referring to? Well there will be times particularly at Christmas and birthdays when, for example, your parents (grandparents) might ask "what can we get them?" or "what do they need" or "is there a particular toy they want?" Using the advice of an experience over something material, in this case why not ask for something that the child can experience? I don't need to provide an endless list of examples here and I don't mean something overly extravagant like a family vacation, I'm talking about things like tickets to a concert, show, sports game whatever you're all into…I think you get the idea. In some cases I think it also benefits others if you give them something specific, as people do have a hard time of knowing what to get. They might think will he/she like this? Is this the right size? Will someone else have already got this? And so on. So like I said if anything you might be doing someone a favor by asking for something like a specific experience as let's face it, buying/getting gifts at times can be a hassle. I mean this more of knowing exactly what to get where you can end up sometimes getting something for the sake of it. As an alternative to consider to an experience, although it's an experience of some sort, is asking for something you think will benefit your child. How about golf lessons? Piano lessons? Tennis lessons? I think your grandparents will have great joy in doing something like this as, potentially; it will be the start of a gift for a lifetime if they develop a passion for something. I will touch on this in greater detail in the next chapter in relation to giving the gift of opportunity. All I'm saying is to maybe think outside the box a little when someone close to you actually asks you what to get your child. This isn't about taking advantage, but just being more practical/creative if anything by looking to ensure a gift is actually utilized or made the most of, whatever it may be.

Another thing I would like to throw out there for you to consider is looking to set up some form of investment account for your child. Maybe this topic warrants a lot more consideration in a book on parenting advice, but I will add a disclaimer that I'm certainly no financial advisor. All I would say however is that I have been the beneficial recipient of some form of custodial account which my late grandparents actually set up for me when I was born. The way it was set up, I was not able to touch the fund until I was 21. So over the course of time it made a steady return and the money was put to great use as it was put towards the deposit for our first house. Now I know funds can lose money, there are no guarantees and what I do know as a modern day parent is that disposable income isn't hard to come by. But there are so many tools available today which make it so convenient for you, if you're in a fortunate position, whereby you can set one up for your child. You can also set up auto payments from your account each month so, after something is set up, you don't actual need to think about it other than maybe checking in on your fund choice every once in a while to look at progress. It doesn't necessarily need to be a big sum of money each month either, it's saving what you can and being disciplined about it. The way I see it is that when my kids are 18 I want to try and help them with getting a car or when they're 21 helping with that deposit on a house. The counter argument to this is that kids are too reliant on their parents to give and they become entitled etc. Personally I don't see it that way, my parents and grandparents have always looked to help me but in no way and at any time did I become entitled or expect handouts. I'm also really appreciative of what they have done for me. There is so much more to it than that and it obviously has a lot to do with overall upbringing on not being entitled but being extremely grateful for anything that is given to you. So essentially I want to do the same for my kids that my parents and grandparents did for me. I just simply want to be in a position whereby I can help/support, I don't want to hand it all on a plate to my children - I'm certainly mindful of that. For me I just want to be in a position to support them, certainly when they're making the transition to adulthood down the line.

Sometimes I think that, as parents we do need to have that long-term perspective although it's very easy to always be in the moment taking life day by day. But bringing this bit of advice back to toys, I think if you have some form of fund established then I think you will be in a better positon to look at what you buy your child – essentially you might think twice. Look I get it in the moment putting $20 into a fund which your child can't touch for many years is not as tempting as buying them a toy in the present moment. But maybe think of it this way when your child is 21, will you or they remember that toy? My advice to you is consider it because if the market is on your side then money has an almost magical way of compounding over time. As the saying goes "money makes money". To reiterate, I'm no financial advisor, there are high risk and low risk funds and obviously markets will be somewhat cyclical, but I know many who have benefited from something like this being established in their childhood. But by having such a long-term fund you don't really need to be fixated with any short-term swings. If you do your research I think you can find something conservative if you prefer a safe approach and I think your research will find that, historically, you will gain over the long-run.

To wrap up this section on the fund, I will bring it back to the advice that I just gave in respect of grandparents. I know that circumstances are different and that some kids might not even have grandparents. But what I do know is that there are many grandparents out there who want to get their grandchildren something big – if they can afford it of course. My advice to you is have that adult conversation, sure it might be an experience over a toy, but it might also be talking about setting up a long-term fund for your child. I keep saying that circumstances differ so this advice applies to me and I'm fortunate that I can have such conversations with both sets of grandparents. I must highlight I would not dream of having such a conversation with anyone else as I don't think it would be appropriate. For example, I wouldn't ask my sister to set up a fund however if one was already established it does actually make it easier for future gifts. If your child receives money from friends and relatives you can easily transfer it into their fund/account. Anyway that is enough financial talk for now. The main thing is that I wanted to put this bit of advice out there as another thing for you to at least consider. If you have things like auto payments set up, then grandparents might offer or could contribute on a weekly/monthly basis rather than buying that toy or object which has that short-term benefit. Again, this is still not to say that grandparents, or anyone else for that matter, can never get your child a gift like a toy or some form of clothing. All I'm trying to do is to encourage you to consider, from time to time, more of a long-term perspective rather than a short-term one. Grandparents are a good example as I think they naturally want to give, or shall we say spoil, their grandchild/grandchildren a little from time to time. If that is the case why not actually give it some thought and look at something which could be of real benefit for your child?

It goes without saying that as a real-world parent you have to pay close attention to how you spend your disposable income. But, whilst this is obvious, I know I still have much to work on in this area. Take all of my daughters toys for example, and I have no idea of the dollar value of them all combined for what we paid, but what I do know is that it will be tidy sum. As parents I think it's natural to want to get things for your children. Problem is when some of the things you look at have little value to your child, then you come to the realization that, at times, like it or not, you have essentially thrown money away. Like I've said, I'm no financial advisor but all I would say is that it's certainly worth your while to sit down, in my case with my wife, and everyone now and then look at how you're spending your money. We can improve but we are now paying a lot more attention to it so we are at least making some improvements/adjustments. The more I think about it there is little excuse these days as bank statements now provide at your fingertips a breakdown of how you spend your money each month and where it all goes. There is actually little effort required other than to have the discipline to take what actually is a small amount of time to look at such statements and have a conversation as a family. By doing so again, you just become a lot more aware so the next time you're at the store you will certainly, at least, think twice about what you're buying for your kid. In addition, you can also give a little more consideration to determine if your child really needs it. I think with such an approach this will help to prevent a case like ours where we have ended up with too many toys and clothes for our daughter.

So to conclude this chapter, I would say not to begrudge your child toys and if they're fortunate to have them just be disciplined as to how often you buy and then pay regular attention to the amount in your household. Try and sometimes to look at it more on a practical level, because I think you will be surprised how swiftly things can build up and as a result toys/games can quickly become under-utilized to where it just becomes a waste. As an alternative, and something that I have learned and which I would fully recommend is to consider buying experiences over toys or some other material object, especially when your child already has enough to enjoy. Also consider what you're rewarding and recognizing in your children before you get that toy or experience as a way to develop important lifelong principles. A final point is to consider taking advantage of those really close to you, who are generous with your children, by talking/discussing something like this with them. So I certainly don't mean it where you take advantage in a moocher/freeloader way either. It's about considering what people like grandparents get your children when you know that they want to get something, will do so anyway and will even at times ask you what to get. So when I say take advantage, do so by taking the time to think a little creatively, talk openly about it and use your imagination to ultimately benefit your child. By thinking in such a way and by taking this kind of approach, I believe will be another way in helping you to become a better parent.

11 GIFT OF OPPORTUNITY

This chapter relates to many of the points I just made, but I think the importance warrants more and specific focus. How many times have you heard someone say that "all kids need is a chance in life"? I believe that the gift of opportunity is all about giving your child a chance in something; anything come to think of it. Other common sayings that parents frequently use are "I want my child to have everything that I didn't have growing up" or something else to the effect "I would do anything for my kids." My advice to you as a parent is to consider those opportunities that you're currently giving your child or could give them in the future. When I hear a saying like the one I just referred to about wanting a child to have everything the parent didn't have growing up, I can't help but think that this have/have not is concerned more with material objects. I also think that you have to strongly admire a parent striving for this, if this is the case, but it's also important for the parent to consider whether what they're striving for, for their child, will actually be of benefit to them – or of long-term benefit?

I will provide a real life example and this does relate to the previous chapter on toys. As I am writing this Christmas has just passed and my daughter had many different things from clothes, toys, and experiences as presents. But on Christmas day itself she had all these new games to play with but what did she want to do? She wanted to play Hide and Seek (Hide and Go Seek for the American reader) and musical chairs. It's kind of funny if you think about it really and it's all very innocent on her part. Point is, kids get over things very quickly. I mean that in a way that they may quickly get over that "must have" toy and also I think they will soon get over it if you actually didn't get them that "must have" toy. So I really don't think that, as a parent, you do need to go all out for Christmas or birthdays even though it's very tempting. My advice to you is to consider giving your child an opportunity gift rather than a toy or a game. So what do I mean? Well how about signing up for a block of golf lessons, tennis lessons, piano lessons, guitar lessons, surf lessons, dance or singing lessons? Or it could be something like a golf or tennis membership. As I said earlier it can be anything really. The main thing is you're giving your kids a chance to experience something they have not experienced before.

Children, particularly at an early age like my daughter who is now 6, don't know what's out there yet and it's impossible for them to know. They don't know of all the different offerings/programs available to kids so it's on you as the parent to find out and give/expose your child those different opportunities. They're completely reliant on you to take them to and from places and to organize/schedule accordingly. Think about it another way, where a child may not ask to do something because they don't even know it's out there. Therefore it does require a parent to do some research and be proactive. How do most kids really start out with anything? I'm generalizing here, but most of the time it requires a parent or guardian to introduce them to something. This is not rocket science I know, but the key point I want to come back to is to question whether you're currently giving your child opportunities or enough opportunities? Are you that parent who gives your child a lot for their birthday and Christmas at a considerable financial expense? If so then I'm saying to consider giving the gift of opportunity instead. A key point is that this obviously is not confined just to Christmas or birthdays, but the reason I want to highlight it at these times is because, as parents we can often go a little overboard/all-out. I think it can actually be a little overwhelming for a child to get too many toys or there even might be times when they get the same thing twice. So with a little more thought you may well come to the conclusion that your child might be better off by being exposed to something else like a new experience.

This is a personal point of view, but I think a child is much better off being gifted some tennis lessons, surf lessons or horse riding lessons for example. These types of gifts are giving your child a chance and an opportunity. You're also giving your child the gift of experiences so don't underestimate or downplay the importance of that either. Sure a child might say that they want or prefer a toy to doing something like tennis lessons, but if they have not played or tried it before then they cannot know whether they will actually enjoy it or not. I suppose the challenge/difficulty is to see past the need for some form of instant gratification that something like a toy may bring because your child may not get and you may not see the same type of satisfaction from a slip that says you got them a block of lessons in something. It's for you as the parent and for your child to find out so if you do face any push back be supportive and encourage them to try a new activity. The benefit or joy if you like will be felt more long-term, but I think it will be more than worth it for all concerned. This, I believe, is then giving your child things you didn't have growing up if you weren't exposed to new experiences/opportunities. This is doing something really positive for your kids as you're providing them with all the opportunities that you can, given your own resources. This is when you are fulfilling those grand statements made at the opening of this chapter. I keep referring to the point that it can be anything and I believe this. I think you probably have figured out that, as a family, we have a passion for sports and there are so many sports to choose from these days. Offerings may vary depending on where you live in the world but no doubt with enough research you will find multiple options to consider. Although there are many sports it doesn't have to be a sport. I have already given the example of learning a musical instrument or it could be something art related, a language, fashion, travel, singing, dance, acting, modelling, academics, I could go on and on. I have been referring to introducing your child to something new but the same applies to something in which they're already developing an interest. If your child likes being out in the water and is developing a passion for surfing why not give the gift of some private surfing lessons? If your child loves to sing why not get them some lessons with a qualified instructor?

Another common saying that you hear parents tell their children is something along the lines of: "You can be anything you want to be." Now this is not a direct criticism of such a statement but I do think it's somewhat ideological. I think that, as parents, if you give this message to your children then make sure that you can back this up by providing opportunities for your child. This means exposing them to new things, giving them the resources that they need and doing all you can to set them up for success. Sure there are rags to riches stories out there and many other stories when people make it to the top with little help from their parents. I'm not denying it can't be done as there is plenty of proof out there. However, I'm more inclined to look at realities and as I will mention later there will always be exceptions to the rule. My belief or advice is not to do everything for your child, but to support them in any way that you can in giving them opportunities so this increases their chances of them being "anything they want to be". If you don't expose your kids to new things how will they know what's out there? So my view is that, if you believe that your child can be anything they want to be, then back it up by doing your part and all you can to support/help/guide. Essentially, give them the gift of opportunities.

I want to look at this a little more before I move on, briefly looking at opportunity along with talent. The reason for this is that sometimes I think they're perceived to be something external or more specifically given, where in this case, given to your child. A parent might think all my kid needs is an opportunity in something. But who is going to give that to them? The reality is no one is going to magically appear and give your child a once in a lifetime opportunity. I think it's on the parents to look to make things happen particularly with providing the initial opportunity whereby it might be introducing your child to something. I think it's on the parents to take that initiative and responsibility to make things happen. That's when I think you might be presented with what I call those external opportunities where it might be someone asks your child to try-out for a certain team – things like that. Point I'm really trying to get to is things like that don't just happen on their own.

I also want to touch on talent in a similar way where I think it's seen as something that might be given to our child – either they're talented in something or they're not. I think the danger is where it almost becomes the end of the conversation if a child is deemed to be untalented in something. But I just don't see it that way. Sometimes you just have to earn the right which might not be exactly applicable with what I'm saying here, but don't you have to really work at something to get really good? Does it not make sense that for a child to get really good in something they have to be given that specific opportunity to get really good? I hope I'm not confusing you here, but hopefully you can see where I'm coming from looking more now at time in regards to opportunity. So I think there are two parts here in that opportunity can be looked at in introducing your child to something new which they're never done before and then the opportunity in relation to time to allow for them to then develop. For this to happen I believe parents play perhaps the most crucial role almost to where the buck stops with them in some cases. Either it happens or it doesn't happen where either a parent gives up their time or they don't, they take their child to something or they don't, they sign them up or they don't. But are you really giving up time if you're giving your child the gift of opportunity? If you devote yourself and your time to giving your child an opportunity would that be something you never had growing up? Would this show you would do anything for your kids? Would it not show your child they can be anything they want to be by putting in the time and effort? It sounds so simplistic, but they need the opportunity of time to put in the time and effort. Perhaps the biggest gift a parent can give their child above all is their time over any object? I'm perhaps straying a little, but a child does need a parent or guardian to give their time to sign them up for something, to take them, to continually take them, to work with them outside of regular practices, to schedule, to travel and the many other things that fall on the parent which children are reliant on their parents to do – it all takes time. What I'm saying is that you're giving your child opportunity if you do all of this and the many other things. You're taking the responsibility and you're making things happen and not waiting for something to happen. You're giving them opportunity!

Before I look to close out this chapter, like I will do with others, let me clarify some of the points I made so that there is no misunderstanding. I'm not saying that you should now never get a birthday/Christmas gift/toy, as they should now all be replaced with things like lessons in a sport or activity. My advice is use common sense by looking at or considering the concept. Generally speaking, what I'm saying is if you do have a tendency to splurge a little on such occasions, then maybe just cut-back even a fraction on that and do something as outlined in this chapter. My advice would be to at least give it a try and see for yourself. There are, no doubt, many parents out there who do provide endless opportunities for their children, but at the same time there are many that don't and perhaps not intentionally either. So my advice to you is to consider this the next time you might be splurging out on your child. Sure it might be that your child says that they want something in particular, but this is where you need to come in as the parent and look at it a bit more logically or objectively. This isn't to say my view is right either, that is just it, it's my view, but my advice is to at least consider it. Consider giving your child opportunities that you never had rather than material things that you never had. If you want your kids to have everything you didn't as a child, consider what that want is, and what you're actually wanting to give them. If you're willing to do anything for your child consider what you're actually doing for them. I think this is simple and common sense advice and things for you to think about, which is why I like it. Linked to all of this is your time as a parent. Giving your child opportunity might just be as simple as devoting time to allow/give your child the opportunity to develop in something. Without your time, the opportunity might just end right there for your child. I hope this at least gets you thinking a little more creatively on what you can do for your child – remember it's all with a purpose of becoming a better parent. You never know, that opportunity gift you give your child may turn into a gift that will last a lifetime.

12 BE PRESENT

This advice is fairly common place these days but, for what it's worth, I will give my take on being present and in the moment when it comes to parenting. I will start this chapter by sharing with you observations that I see on a weekly basis. My daughter attends a weekly golf clinic for kids every Saturday morning. She loves to go; it's fun and enjoyable for all the children. The clinic lasts for 1 hour and during that hour, without exaggeration, whenever I glance and see the other parents in attendance, I would say around half of them are on their cell phones at any given moment. Sometimes there is a full-house where they're all on their phones at the same time. What are they doing? My guess is that the majority are on a social media site looking at the latest timeline or feed. There are even occasions when I've seen new kids a little out of control and the coaches could do with some parental assistance or intervention, but the parent is simply oblivious to what is going on and you see their finger scrolling up/down on their cell phone. Essentially the parent's body is present physically, but in terms of the mind, they're a million miles away. This is something I see all the time so this isn't even opinion, it's fact, based on what I see. Parents talk about "being there" for their children, but in cases like this they're nowhere near to being there/present.

I also see similar things when I take my daughter to a playground, as another simple example, where the kids are playing, but the parent or parents are on their cell phone/s. I'm sure you have also seen this before and there are other instances when I have seen it at swimming pools, vacations, kids birthday parties, I could go on and on. As a parent you may have done this before and in some cases I genuinely think it has become a habit for some people where they automatically grab their phone and go on auto pilot.

I do think the term being present does need to be put into context and considered specifically in relation to parenting. We hear the term itself so much these days, but think about what it really means to you? For me, well, I'll start with what I think it's not. Being present isn't being in the same room with your child/family, whilst you're sitting on your phone or sticking on some TV show where you all end up being in your own little world. Yes you can say/argue you're with or spending time with your child, but the reality is you're just going through the motions. I don't want to give some form of superficial explanation of what I think it is either, trying to overthink it all. We've all heard of the importance of spending quality time together, so I won't try and give a textbook definition of what I think being present means, rather I would encourage you to consider what spending quality time with your kids should really look like? This is about how you are day-to-day without having to act, do or be anything out of the ordinary. Quality time is not just about doing big or fancy things. Quality time together may just mean putting everything else on hold when you're talking with or listening to your child. I really think being present contributes to having that quality time with your children/family, again more on a day-to-day basis.

Back to the golf class and using this as an example to look at in more detail. Would you not agree that, for an hour, a parent could just put their phone away, be present and enjoy watching their child play? Why not observe the coaches and see if you can learn a thing or two that you can reinforce in your own time? Pay close attention to your child's emotions and see if they are genuinely enjoying the experience. Similarly when you go to a playground with your child you might only be there for 30 minutes so my advice to you is to take it all in. Take it all in so that you remember the finer details and you will be amazed at the things that touch you through observing and interacting with your child; their laugh, their smile or the unique things that children say. I think some may have the mentality that, whilst their child is with a coach, they consider this to be their free time, to switch off and go on their phone. My advice however, is not to consider this as switch off time, if anything it should be switch on time, to really focus on what your child is doing – by being present.

Why not listen to the lifelong advice of living in the moment? This advice is nothing new, but I would advise you to take it on board. I think we all get the importance of living in the moment, but we don't do or practice it enough. I'll say it throughout with similar sayings like "live in the moment" that sometimes we think to only apply this concept to something deemed perhaps significant or really important – more of a one-off. What I'm saying to become a better parent, apply the same concept of living in the moment more day-to-day and for more everyday things. That is my take on being present and in the moment. I actually find distractions to be rather stressful and when you're not present mentally, I think everything just then becomes a blur and that more importantly; you may miss out on something very special with your child. Why not try switching your phone off/on silent when you're with your child? I know some will say that you always need a phone on you these days for safety and in case of an emergency. I wouldn't argue against that, but if you're going out as a family, then maybe take just one phone and have it for that purpose only.

Don't think this is a tirade against cell phones and although it's safe to say I'm not the biggest fan of social media, I'm not really looking to debate this right now. There are also many other things that can take your mind away from being present. All I'm saying is that my suggestion to you is to put all distractions/temptations away when your child is doing something important. It could be anything; soccer practice, tennis practice, basketball practice and so on. It doesn't have to be a sport it could be music or theatre – anything. It might only be that they have practice or play once or twice a week for an hour each time, so give them your full attention which they deserve. In a previous chapter, I talked about the importance of not living in a bubble. But to go against that slightly here with something like your child's activity, this is the exact time when you should be in your own bubble with them. Nothing else should really matter, so you're then in a position to be fully present.

It doesn't have to be an activity either, it could be greeting your child when you get home from work, at the dinner table or listening to your child tell you about their favorite part of the day. I'm sure you've seen it before when a child is talking to their parent, but the parent is on their phone and I don't know how to explain it other than it's as if the child is being completely shut out. Again my advice to you is be present and take everything in where in essence you're "living in the moment". Hopefully you get the idea with what I mean by that. In such cases you're not acting out of the ordinary or doing something new/different. It's so much simpler than that where you're actually removing all of the noise around you so that you can just be there for your child. For longer periods, I think the same principle applies when you go away on a trip or on vacation - don't waste this truly valuable time on distractions. There are distractions other than a cell phone or a social media site, but I believe these are the most common from my observations of parents and people in modern times and in general everyday life. I have been guilty of it in the past, where I may have got distracted by a text or I was checking email or the score of a ball-game.

These are simple examples of very common traps to fall into. But I get frustrated when I'm so easily distracted, so it takes practice to actually switch off from devices and distractions/temptations, so that it can actually form a really positive habit when you're with your children. So I'm not saying that you shouldn't check the score or that text or even the latest timeline on social media. What I'm saying is that you can do it at a later time when there are far less important things going on or when you do have some time to yourself.

I want to give this point real emphasis to help demonstrate how meaningless it is to be consumed by something like the latest timeline on your phone. Obviously this doesn't apply to everyone, but I think you're in denial if you don't think that you see a lot of parents who seem more focused on their phone rather than interacting with their kids these days. I'm originally from the UK and there is a saying; today's newspaper headlines will be tomorrow's fish and chip paper...or something to that effect! Now interpret this how you like, but the way I see it is that it basically means that what might be of importance to look at today will be meaningless tomorrow. Think about it, would you want to read a newspaper from a year ago? Bringing it to the modern day, would you be interested in a looking at a timeline or feed on your phone from yesterday, last week, last month or even a year ago? People seem so consumed with what is going on in the present and what other people are doing but, to give it some perspective, no one will care to read or look at the same thing in say a week's time or even the next day. Hopefully you see the point I'm trying to make is that many parents give attention to things which actually have very little value or meaning. Again, I may sound judgmental here and it's hard not to come across that way, but let's remember we're focused on something much more important which is becoming a better parent! In saying all this, I will be the first to admit I have been guilty of it too in the past, being distracted with something on my phone, when my attention should have been with my child – trust me it's not worth it.

I don't think I'm even calling people out here, it's just the reality of everyday life nowadays, so I think it's very relevant to highlight in such a book. People on their phones when they're walking, driving or even whilst talking to someone else are just becoming a social norm. So you don't misunderstand, this isn't a debate on social media or anything like that as this chapter just focuses on being present. This book focuses on you becoming a better parent so the two are linked in that, if you want to become a better parent then my advice to you is always try and "be present" when with your children. Clearly social media is not the only thing people might be engaging whilst on their phone, but let's be honest I think many are. Other examples are group chats, texting, reading celebrity gossip or just random videos. I've already held my hands up as I know I have done it in the past, where I must have spent an hour or so just going from random video to random video online, jumping from one to the other. I keep saying cell phones and technology are obviously not the only distractions that can prevent us from being present, but I think they're perhaps most relevant and certainly prove the point. I don't think anyone can really deny the impact they have on our day-to-day lives. But whether it's a device or not, the concept/notion of distraction very much applies in the same way where it has the same ending result of taking you away from being completely/entirely present.

Related to this, I'm sure you have all come across someone you know or are speaking with and have been impressed by their memory as they recall something so distinctly from a long time ago. They can tell a story giving the minutest detail from the date, time of day, the weather, the food, the smells in the air, what they or what a loved one was wearing. I'm not going to add too much more here as I'm sure some would say that some people just have better memories and mind capacity than others. That may well be true, but it might also be that they were so present in the moment at the time, which is actually why they remember the finer details. So again, practice this with your child. Try it with your child, be so present that you remember not just the big things like the winning shot in a game, but also the simple things like them singing/dancing along to a song, the look in their eye or a unique sound they make. Just know you'll be missing out on something, whatever it is they're doing, every time you're not truly present. Take it all in, consume everything from the experience, be so present that you will remember everything. When time goes by and you sometimes try to recall or remember something from the day and struggle, it might not be that you forgot, it might well be your mind was elsewhere. You may need to consider whether you were actually there? Sure, you may have been physically present, but your mind may have been focused on other things/distractions at the time. My advice is not to let this happen when you're with your children, you never know you may even become less forgetful when trying to recall something if you're actually more present in the moment.

I would like to reiterate that being present takes practice and whilst being on a phone is an obvious distraction, in some cases it might not be something physical or tangible that is distracting you, sometimes your mind may be elsewhere through stress as an example. It's something I have learned and looked to develop. What I find helps is consciously having a mind-set that, when your child is doing something important, it becomes the time that you're aware that you need to put everything aside and give your child the full attention they deserve. I referred to it earlier as noise around you, so although it might not always be practical to turn everything else off in the real world, to stay with this analogy, at least try and turn some of the other things down.

To touch on this point a little more as most of the distractions I have provided relate to the use of technology or a cell phone – so let's look at something else. I will give you an example of something my wife and I notice that each of us do and which we're trying to stop. It might be we're playing a board game with our daughter and then the dishwasher stops so one of us says that we will empty it so play without me for this one. Or it might be that the laundry is done in the dryer so my wife wants to fold and put it away. Point is as parents there is always something to do, we multi-task and really just want to be done with daily chores so they're out of the way. However, if you look at it essentially we have an endless list of things which recur whether it be laundry, preparing lunches, dishes and a lot of the day-to-day stuff like this. So when I say "be present" it's about putting all of this to one side for a moment or for a short period of time. Sure, it's nice to get it out the way or get something off your to-do list, but the way I see it, it's another distraction when you're playing with your child. To get around this, my wife says that she likes to just get out of the house at times so she can just give her full attention to our children – it might be as simple as going in the backyard. I think it takes real discipline to not let distractions in when they're all around us. As in my wife's case sometimes it works best to step outside to avoid those household distractions because it seems there is always a job that needs doing or more simply there is too much going on inside. Something I'm guilty of is at mealtime, as I love my food, I'm a very fast eater. My daughter on the other hand is rather slow, so when I'm finished, I might think it's ok that I can wash up whilst my wife sits with her. But really that is the time I should just leave it and sit with my family at the dinner table and enjoy that time. It's easier said than done and perhaps can't be done every day, but generally speaking, parents always seem to be in a rush, there is always something to do and sometimes we just need to slow down. So despite these everyday constants in our lives, I say slow down so we can be more present, as let's face it, something's can or will just have to wait when it comes to our kids - so we can then be truly present with them.

I also know how it is that, every so often, your head feels like it's spinning with all the little things you have to do, where it seems like it can be a race against the clock. But I have come to learn that the little mundane tasks can wait when it comes to play time or talking with your child about their day.

Even then, if you're doing something else like dishes, as in my case, you're not really fully focused on what they have to say. I love nothing more than to hear about my daughter's day at school (although I admit it's hard at times to get much out of her). Sometimes she will tell me about her day, but other times I will have to ask several questions. Whatever response I do get, it's funny to listen to the random things she comes out with about her friends or what makes her day. I personally think it does require practice and a conscious effort to be present to avoid distraction/s. But just know by doing this it puts you in a position where you can give your child what they really need, being you, the parent and your full attention! Ultimately be present when you're with your children, otherwise that time will just be wasted, because you won't in fact, be fully present at all. I think that if you take this advice on board you will notice the many benefits it will bring – for you and your child! At the same time in doing so, I believe it will no doubt make you become a better parent.

13 TECHNOLOGY, SOCIAL MEDIA & CELL PHONES

There are fundamental parenting principles which are timeless, but I think you also have to consider the generation in which children are raised. I'm sure the following comment will have many differences in opinion so without any hard evidence, and this is purely a presumption, my view is that raising a child today is a lot different to how it was say 25 years ago. I'm not saying it's harder or easier to bring up a child, but just different. I'm sure the same will be said in 25 years' time looking back on today.

A personal view is that technology plays such a big part in our lives now as parents. More than ever we're growing dependent on technology to function, which affects everyone and this is perhaps the main reason when I say I think it's different when bringing up a child today. This is because I believe it has, in so many ways, made such a direct and indirect impact on parenting and how we currently raise our children. You also have to consider the direct impact it has on as well as how it affects children's lives. Everything now moves at such a fast pace; we're always on the go, and rarely switch off. In turn, I also believe this has developed more and more people to become even more impatient. We're now almost conditioned to everything being available and ready now, in an instant. The ironic part of all this is that technological advances were originally supposed to provide us more free time as it's an enabler to do more in a shorter space of time. However, I think it has had the opposite effect and if anything it has just led to us wanting more and more. Perhaps new challenges that technology has brought to modern day parenting are distraction and temptation – as just discussed in the previous chapter. For all the benefits technology brings and ways in which it makes life simpler, it also results in a constant state of alert where it's hard to ever switch off or focus on just one thing at a time. So many things can grab our attention by distracting us from what we're currently doing or had our mind originally set on. As a result and with direct reference to the previous chapter, I think one of the biggest challenges for a parent today is actually being present and in the moment with their child and not allowing distractions/temptations in. My view is that technology has an equal and significant impact on the role of the parent as much as it does on the child. It's perhaps easy to assume or point the finger at children/youth today on how easy it is for them to be distracted/tempted by technology, where they're always glued to some form of device. I think the reality is those same distractions/temptations very much apply to parents who may arguably utilize it as much as, if not more, than children/teenagers/young-adults.

In many ways, I think it's very relevant to have a chapter on technology, social media and cell phones when it comes to parenting. Leading on from looking at being present and starting with social media, as it has become such a huge part of peoples' lives in general and this is reflected in how much time people physically spend on social media channels. I have to say that I'm not the biggest fan of social media, but this is not intended to be a discussion on its pros and cons, as I want to focus on its impact with regard to good parenting. However, I do find it rather ironic that the word social is used for online communication. If someone was to describe someone else as social, I would picture that person being in the presence of a group of people rather than on a computer or cell/mobile phone. I think more and more people are developing communication skills in how to interact online, but then lack the different communications skills required when interacting face to face with another person in person. We all well know that people have certain online friends that they might ignore or have an awkward interaction when they actually see them in person. I could go on, but that is maybe for another debate.

So specifically back to parenting, looking more at the impact social media has on it. I think there are many similar traits that parents share when on social media when it comes to their children. It's certainly interesting what people put out there. Some take it to the extreme and like to put their whole life on display, where I think you'll know what I mean when I say some share everything, as it really is everything! But for most they tend to post and share only the good stuff. In this case, are people just showing off? Do they need attention? Do they need some form of approval? For what reason are they doing it? Are they trying to portray a life or lifestyle they lead in a photo when the reality might be somewhat different? What is the real purpose of the online profile? These questions might seem a little sinister, I admit that and I'm playing devil's advocate a little here. But sometimes I think people in general although as we're just focused on parenting, parents should actually think about what it is they're doing and why they do it. What is the real motive or actually benefit? I say all this because if anything think of the amount of time and attention you give, which in turns takes it away from many other areas which most notably may be your own children. It might just well be that it prevents you from being fully present when you're together.

When it comes to social media I think you certainly or perhaps most importantly have to factor in time. I'm referring to the amount of time spent specifically on social media or your cell phone/tablet/device in general. It will obviously vary from person to person, but from what I see there are many people out there who spend a lot of their time on social media, or aimlessly surfing the web, or on their cell phone texting, whatever it maybe. Not just that, particularly with social media, people have multiple accounts/profiles with the many different sites/options/platforms out there. So in other words I see a lot of people out there including parents who practically live on their phone. This may offend the "PC (Politically Correct) Police", but I see so many cell phone parents today. They are permanently held in the palm of the hand and for some an interesting question to ask would be: Who or what gets more attention? Your children or your cell phone? Might seem a crazy question to answer and I can imagine many of the cell phone parents being extremely offended if they were even questioned about this. But I won't try and be politically correct in this instance, as this is about looking at something much more important which is becoming a better parent. I see it all the time all around me from the grocery store, playground, sports field, school, driving, restaurants - you name it where the phone is always out and in prime position. I think the finger can easily be pointed at the younger parents, but the reality is that I observe it from all generations. Again if you're offended in any way, I suggest you observe for yourself the world around you a little closer and then judge for yourself.

However, there is a distinction as I see the cell phone parent as being somewhat addicted to their phone whereas for many I acknowledge that the habit is less extreme. Now I'm not even trying to call anyone out here. If you love being on your phone and spending a lot of time on it, then go for it. It's your choice. But I will keep going back to the theme of this book and it's about becoming a better parent. I have also said throughout that a key part of being a good parent is the time and attention that you can give to your children, certainly when in their presence. So what I'm saying is that you can't have it both ways where you can be on your phone whilst still being really attentive when you're with your child. I personally think you have to pick one or the other and when it's put that way it's a no brainer of what to pick/choose. Do you know of a cell phone parent? Do you spend too much time on your phone? Who do you give more attention to? If you do happen to be on your phone too much when with your children this is an easy win for you to become a better parent. It doesn't mean you need to throw it away or delete your social media account. It just means put it all to one side when you're with your kids. As a real world parent, I'm not perfect by any means and I won't pretend I never have or won't use it again in the future when I'm with my family. But by being extremely mindful of this I would say that it's now very rare rather than common/normal that I would ever be on it when with my children. What I must say in this instance is that I'm not referring to moments such as really important phone calls or messages, I'm really referring to the rather aimless surfing and scrolling people do. Essentially those distractions! As I said, I don't think anyone should be in denial about this, as it's there for all to see these days.

Before we move on my advice is be honest with yourself here by asking this question: Am I a cell phone parent? I say be honest as no one is judging you here. The reality is no one really cares if you are or you aren't. I raise this however as this book is about becoming a better parent. Maybe look at it this way: Every time you check that social media post or timeline when with your child, you're picking someone else over them. Essentially you're saying they're more important than your child. You may think that is an extreme way of putting it, but when you're choosing your phone over your child aren't you doing/saying just that? I think it's almost become a social norm where it's not even thought of in such a way. I don't know maybe it's just me as I have gone about this enough already, but back to becoming a better parent, I also think it's important that we feel/consider this for ourselves. When I say feel, I'm not talking anything deep or spiritual, but just as simple as having that connection with our children in those everyday moments. If you're zoned out on your phone when your child is talking to you or when they're doing something then I think you'll be the one to miss out. Being more present, I think will make you a better parent, but in turn I think you will also feel a better one as well as more generally feel better about yourself. Don't get me wrong, I don't want to say something along the lines of how parents should always give that undivided attention, as again this book is about real world parenting and it's not always as simple as that. But all I'm trying to do is highlight that you don't allow/decide/choose to add to the challenge which already exists by allowing your attention to easily turn elsewhere. Elsewhere, being away from your children on your cell phone/social media or any other device for that matter.

Speaking more generally on cell phones and as I said, my blunt view is that I see so many parents living on their cell phone today. From what I see, it has become a reality where people live on their phones. If you're constantly on your phone how can you truly be present? It's an opinion of mine, but like I said I think it's there for all to see these days – the proof is visible just by observing others. It's almost as if the cell phone has become a body part as I see it always in the hand of someone or attached somewhere else on the body. The new one seems to be where it's always positioned in the back pocket where it's easy to pull out if not already in hand. It's out at every opportunity and immediately the parent is somewhere else. I can't tell you how many times I have seen kids trying to get their parents attention before the parent even responds because they're spaced out on their phone. I have also seen parents react with annoyance that their child has interrupted their cell phone time. Have you seen a parent walking their child with a stroller, but on their phone at the same time? Have you seen a parent so consumed by their phone that their child seems almost ignored? What about on a car journey where the other parent is the passenger, but they choose that time to be on their cell phone rather than interact with their child? I can hear the responses to that already where it might be well we're just sitting in a car, but I don't know, why don't you just have a conversation?

I'm not saying that someone should never go on their phone and this might seem a bit of a tirade against their use. I get it there are many benefits that cell phones, technology and even social media bring to people, so I know it's not all bad! But let me try and put it another way if you oppose some of my views or take offence to it. How often do you hear a parent say "family first"? Now we will all have our own interpretation of "family first", but for me it means putting your family and in this case your child/children, above everything else. So if a parent is on their phone whilst their child is playing a game with them or just simply talking to them – in these instances are they putting "family first" or "cell-phone first"? I think the saying "family first" should be applied not only just to the so called big things, but perhaps also to those seemingly little every day interactions – which are just as important? Do you agree with seeing it from this point of view? It might sound a little out there, but to paint the picture you often hear someone say "family first" when a loved one is sick, so they drop everything to take care of someone, and rightly so. At that point that loved one is the only thing that matters. But what I'm suggesting is that you don't just apply the "family first" mantra to major life situations. It might sound a little obscure bringing this topic back to cell phones/technology/social media, but the way I see it there are many people out there putting their "cell phone first" rather than "family first". Call me judgmental all you want but I think it's there for all to see. I'm reiterating that this book is about becoming a better parent, so I don't really want to tip-toe around this subject. So even if just a little bit of this applies to you then my advice is to consider putting that phone away when you're with your kids. It's worth repeating, this is focused on when you're with your kids, this is not as much concerned in your own downtime when say they're in bed and you have time to yourself. So don't choose a social media site over them and don't be so concerned with what other people are up to. Concentrate on your family! My view is that even if you improve on this a little you're becoming a better parent as you will be giving your children more direct and purposeful attention. Love and attention, I think you would all agree, is at the heart of good parenting regardless of whether you agree or disagree with some of the points in this chapter.

Before I go on, I would like to make clear that I'm not the perfect parent when it comes to this topic whereby I'm sitting on my pedestal judging the world. Have I been on my cell phone before when my child is talking to me, playing a game or just wanted to do something with me? Of course I have. I'm saying this because I'm not proud of it and how it really frustrates me if I have done so, after the fact. So I'm also sharing my previous frustrations with you as I'm not going to try and pretend I have never done such a thing. I'm not even going to pretend I'm perfect with it now where I will never ever do it again, but all I would say is that I have become a lot better in this area and continue to improve. I have improved to where it's an exception/slip rather than a norm because I'm that much more conscious of not doing it. So the way I see it, this helps me become a better parent. I have learned from my previous mistakes and frustrations as well as by observing others. Trust me it's so not worth being on your phone on something like social media when you're in the presence of your child because it takes away time/experience that you're having with them. Again I know and speak from personal experience.

When you see someone scrolling up and down on their phone they're completely oblivious to the world around them. No doubt it has become a habit or even somewhat of an addiction. We all know there are articles in the media that present the idea that, although you might be physically in a location, mentally you are elsewhere. Whilst writing this in the present, there was a perfect example of what I'm saying the last time I went to the playground with my child. I observed another parent who was literally on their phone the whole time and didn't even respond when their child called their name as they were completely oblivious to what was going on around them. I was once guilty of this in the past, so again I'm not trying to come across as being perfect as I too have done it before. What I'm acknowledging is how bad it actually is and the example in my case is actually quite embarrassing to admit. My daughter was playing hide and seek (hide and go seek) with another girl at the playground and I was so engrossed with my phone, probably checking the latest soccer scores, something like that. When I got out of my trance it was my daughter's turn to hide and she had actually stepped outside the playground for her hiding spot and whilst I immediately had the heart sinking moment, the other girl's mother was quick to tell me she was right there. So not only was I embarrassed, I was extremely annoyed with myself and also, in that moment, I had put my child's safety at risk by not giving her my full attention. Children must have that at playgrounds and in similar scenarios where they're vulnerable to falling over or hurting themselves and trust me, that last thing you want is for something to happen where you were miles away on your phone! That is something I have also witnessed where a child has slipped and bumped their head where the parent was just not paying any form of attention, even though they were sitting right there, as again in that instance the parent was engrossed with their phone. Look I know things just happen are you can't always prevent certain things, but what I'm saying is at least by aware of what is actually going on around you.

In this chapter as well as in the previous one (there is a lot of crossover), I already addressed the important of putting aside any distractions to be present in the moment. I think for many the biggest distraction can be social media sites or your phone in general. So my suggestion to you is that, at the very least, become more aware of your actions if this resonates in any way. It's become so automated how people walk around with the phone in their hand and then just scroll up and down on it. I also want to revert back to something I touched on at the start of the chapter and look a little more on the motive of having some form of online profile. Don't forget the reason I'm doing this is because this chapter and book as a whole is focused on becoming a better parent. I think by considering something like this can make you better, simply by giving you more time back and/or enabling you to give more attention to your children. From the outside looking in, it now almost seems an unofficial competition of who posts what and who looks better on their online profile. Or people purposely do something so they can take that picture to post, but surely that makes it artificial? So has social media just become more and more about attention seeking? Do people need that seal of approval from someone else? Do they need to be acknowledged in some way? Is this related to being social in anyway? Do people try and present or portray some form of perfect life or lifestyle? Call me cynical, but I'm sure there are people out there who plan out their posts and purposely go someplace or do a certain thing so they can post something to show off to their network of so-called friends. So you inevitably compare yourself, and that's what I mean when I say it almost appears just to be a platform to show off, boast or brag rather than actually connecting with people. I know one response to this might be that it allows for your family to see what you're all up to. But look the way I see it, there are many other ways/platforms of sending/sharing photos/videos with your true loved ones. I also say this because I think many people out there will be underwhelmed in how much actual interest others really take – especially for all the time, effort and attention it all takes.

In some cases people have "followers" that they don't even know so they're strangers and so the more and more you think of it the more and more bizarre it actually is. People are in your network that you rarely meet, speak to or even in some cases where you have never met and are never likely to meet either! I was a previous user of social networks and I believe that most, like me, were initially drawn into the benefit of being able to stay in touch with loved ones and friends that more easily – for want of a better word, being social. However, I just don't think people really use their profiles for this anymore – I think the motives are now quite frankly rather different. Again I'm not deluded either and as I said earlier, I know it's not all bad and that there are still benefits. But at the same time I do think it continues to move away from some of the fundamental concepts of communication/interaction. When I come across someone looking at a timeline it tends to be full of nonsense really; whether it be an advertisement, a strange video of something, or something else peculiar, what someone is eating, what they're trying to sell like it's some form of online garage sale or it could be promoting a product or a scheme someone wants their "friends" to sign up for and nothing whatsoever to do with being social with one of your friends. Think about it. Do you actually communicate online other than the odd "like" here and there? Are you actually getting in touch with someone to see how they're doing? Are you arranging to meet up? Are you really being social?

I understand a new theme these days is that people use their social media profiles to try and sell you things. My wife has social media profiles and often comments on how people friend request her who she doesn't really know or vaguely remembers. If/when she accepts, she soon realizes that the real and only reason for the request is for them to try and sell her products on the latest pyramid scheme. Or I also understand that people now post what they're eating for breakfast, lunch and dinner! I don't know about you, but for me and perhaps the irony to all this is that it could not be getting further away from the notion of being social? In my view, to give my precious time and energy is just not worth it because I just think there are more important things to do. Speaking personally, I just don't want to have to keep up with different social media profiles. Quite frankly I have far too much going on already and I just see it as a distraction and I can think of so many better ways in how to use time. The way I see it something would have to give if I kept up with such accounts/profiles. Again it all comes back to the use of time, so like it or not, I think it does have such a significant effect on parenting directly or indirectly, whichever way you look at it! What would have to give would be my time. That time could be playing with my kids, exercising, calling someone or just being fully present wherever I am. Of course I still stay connected with immediate family and close friends/love ones; call me old fashioned, but I prefer more of a personal touch when it comes to being "social".

I do admit that I'm now a bit of an outcast as I no longer have social profiles and one of the main reasons why I disconnected was that I just could not be bothered with it any more. So I guess I'm the equivalent of a modern day dinosaur! I previously felt I needed to almost monitor what people were up to; otherwise I would be out of touch yet, at the same time, it felt like a chore as I felt almost obliged to update my profile on a regular basis. One of the other main reasons that I came off social media was that my network as a whole was so extended and I didn't really interact socially with the majority of my online "friends". I'm aware that many, including myself at the time like to add people to essentially monitor (or shall I say spy) on them to see what they're up to these days – with actually no intention of ever sending a message. Back to an earlier point, I had friends online who, if I passed them in the street, would not stop and talk or would look the other way, so in the end I came to the conclusion that it was all rather pointless or just not worth it. I believe that when we search and scroll and continue to look at other peoples' lives, then this is a missed opportunity as we should be more concerned with what we're doing in our own lives. This becomes so much more important when we have children as the main thing it actually does, being glued to the phone, is take up your valuable time. You can even put the distraction of being on a cell phone/device and not being present to one side, and just consider the amount of time spent which you can never get back. I bet you will be surprised in how quickly it can all add up over the course of a day, week, month or year. The reason I continue to emphasize this is that for parents in particular, I do see how this time could be used so much more effectively by doing things with your children. It could be anything; riding a bike, going to a playground, going for a walk, playing catch, playing/practicing sports, reading, playing a board game - very simple things. Or like with other examples, this time could be spent doing something for yourself, like exercise.

To use an analogy with smoking and we all know the negative effects smoking has, not just health issues, but also financial ones. As a deterrent to smokers you often see illustrations of the money you can save over a long period of time which equates to something like a family vacation and hence the example makes a strong case for current smokers to consider quitting. Now to use a similar argument with general cell phone use along with social media, personally I believe that it can affect your health, but I will stick with the financial element (well sort of). We all know the saying that "time is money" so think of all the time (money) you could save over a period of 6 months to a year if you disconnected from a social platform or aimless online/web surfing (playing phone games, going on apps, checking scores/updates, endless group chats, taking selfies, watching random videos, watching a live ball game, watching game highlights, binge watching a TV series on your device, reading celebrity gossip, viewing reality shows – this list could go on and on)? I say this particularly with those who may have multiple accounts/profiles on different sites, but this isn't just about social media as there are so many more distractions/temptations that phones or technology brings as I just alluded to. It may not translate directly into a dollar value, but I think the value you would receive would be worth so much more than anything monetary. I think from a health point of view you would be less stressed, more focused and less distracted, but as a parent think of all the things you could now do instead with your children. Maybe I'm over-thinking some of this, but I just see so many parents on their phones when they're with their children. In addition to not being present, they're effectively choosing to be on their phone rather than doing something else, like simply playing/interacting with their child. So although all of this might not directly apply to you, I have seen it for myself that it does apply to a lot of parents out there.

It could be something like an hour a day you save, or get back, by disconnecting. Again this is not all just about social media. So I would say purposely and proactively use that time to think of something you could do instead with your child that could positively impact their life. By positively impacting the life of your child you will get all of the personal satisfaction in the world. You might then find that you enjoy not constantly checking in on your phone. I can imagine that some of my advice and views will divide opinion somewhat. That's ok, I'm not writing this for any approval, and the main thing I hope is that you will at the very least, give this some more consideration. Some might think I need to relax or calm down a little here and whilst that maybe true as I might be harping on a bit, think about a regular day for you. You don't have to work it out to the nearest second, but when you factor in things like school, work, sleep there is not actually a lot of time when you and your child will actually be together. So for me allowing a phone/tablet or any other technological device to take away even more of this very precious little time is, dare I say it, careless.

To focus a little more on cell phones in general, my suggestion to you is not to overkill the amount of photos and videos you take of your child. Now, before you throw this book out of the window with outrage at the thought, I'm certainly not saying that you shouldn't take a lot, as I was as guilty as anyone of literally taking another photo or video of my daughter doing almost anything. I mean anything and doing this all the time, to the point where I just had numerous videos/photos of essentially the same thing. I almost felt the need to do it to try and capture everything, but it got to the point where I was taking it to the extreme. I think we all know how often our cell phones pop-up with a message these days of insufficient storage space when we try and take another photo or video! I will share with you a travel analogy to illustrate the point. I once came across this advice in a magazine and I really liked it and I think it can be applied to what I'm trying to say here. The idea being that, at times, you don't take out a camera or phone to take pictures, even when you are exploring or visiting somewhere for the first time. This focuses on the distraction element of wanting to take that perfect picture and that becomes the focus rather than taking everything else in. As that is the focus you're then not fully enjoying the experience, by focusing or obsessing over that perfect shot. So, as tempting as it is to take a photo and video of everything with our children, using this advice it's saying to sometimes try and do something where you don't think about the need of capturing it all on your phone. I'm sure this has happened to you as it has to us many times when our son or daughter does something funny, but we miss it so we try and get them to do it again so we can take a video. I think even with something like this when trying to then force something makes it become unnatural. So I think the advice is saying to take it all in and enjoy the experience, storing some of those special memories in your mind rather than necessarily on a device. I will give you a specific example although it wasn't on a trip; it was at a Halloween community event we went to with friends/family. One of our friends who was with us was filming their child on their phone the whole time from coloring things in at the arts and crafts station to even videoing their kid waiting in line. I totally get how some parents want to try and capture everything, but I do think there comes a point when it all does become a little overkill. It becomes too much or over the top to the point where you're in distraction mode focusing more on filming rather than taking everything else in or more simply actually interacting/engaging with your child and the people around you. Hopefully you get my point as what I'm saying is not to take it to excess where you end up having hundreds and hundreds of pictures and videos of essentially the same thing. Try and go a place where you don't take a video or picture once in a while and just have 100% focus on your child/family and the experience. I think that is the main point really that you limit all distractions so that you're again completely present and can take everything in. You may get more enjoyment with your child/family that way?

One thing I haven't addressed in this chapter is deciding when you should get your child their first cell phone? Or do you even let them have one at all? It's too early for me to have to deal with this issue, but I think this certainly requires close consideration. Of course age is a factor - so do you just give in to peer pressure/social norms because most of the other kids have one and your child will be the odd one out? Do you have pressure from your children? Do you give in? I appreciate it's not an easy thing to deal with. Then there is the concern of things like cyber bullying and the general welfare of your child of the potential things they could be exposed to. Again I'm not saying it's all bad, but I don't think you can just ignore or deny some potential risks/dangers. Of course you have to factor in cost too. I can also see some parents saying that their child needs a phone for safety reasons. Well if that's the main reason do they have a basic "flip-phone" where they can make and receive calls? I keep saying it; the main issue I have with phones is the amount of time it consumes from everyday lives. This is not just parents or children of course, but this book is about parenting so this remains the focus. So you have to consider the time your child will, or already does, spend on their phone and ask whether that time could be better spent? Remember a very simple life lesson: time is precious. Your child's time is precious so should you as the parent let it be used on a phone? Again call me old-fashioned (bearing in mind that I'm now 33), but I can think of a million better things a child could do better with their time, rather than taking selfies, texting, playing games, watching videos or on social media. Let's be honest and cut the BS, this is what most kids (not all) are doing on their phones. Whatever it is they're doing on there you may sometimes have to ask is that of any real benefit to them? Especially if it takes up so much of their valuable time. As a parent you really do call the shots on this one even when you're pressured. To share a recent story my daughter was playing at the playground and she knows this girl who I think is roughly about 8 years old. She asked to play with her and she kindly said yes, but I noticed she did have a cell phone. She spent the whole time on it and my daughter kept on trying to get her attention to play before she eventually gave up. She even made an innocent comment later along the lines of: "why was she on the phone the whole time?" Now on reflection I'm not being judgmental or even critical of this situation in anyway, but as this book is about real world parenting, this is no doubt a real world issue. I'm sure most would agree it's a topic that deserves such close consideration even if you disagree with some of the other things I've had to say. I will admit it's not easy as society in general has become very dependent on technology and it plays such a big part of our everyday lives.

So to round this chapter up as I think I have gone on and on somewhat. I would suggest that you go back to your social media profiles and maybe consider a few things. Would you miss it if you disconnected? What are you really using it for? Will the latest news feed or gossip really matter in 1 week, 1 year, 10 years' time? I just think that, as parents, we should ask ourselves such basic questions, especially if it does consume a lot of your time. But this is where you need to be honest with yourself. I've said this isn't just about social media however, as there are many other distractions/temptations on a phone/device that can take time away from us or turn our attention elsewhere. There is no judgment, but again, bringing it back to the purpose of this book which is to make you a better parent, then some things may have to give in order for you to do so. Agree or disagree with what I have said, at least reflect for yourself and determine if even minor adjustments are needed for you to become a better parent. Speaking from experience, when I do put all distractions away, give my 100% focus and attention to my children with whatever I'm doing, that time is so much more enjoyable. Try it for yourself if anything of what I said in this chapter resonates with you. I think it's time for me to get off my soap box now and talk about something else!

14 EXERCISE

Exercise you may ask? Yes, exercise. This chapter is not directed at your children, although obviously it's important for them to be active, this is aimed specifically at you. Now you might be thinking: What does exercise have to do with being a better parent? Whilst I cannot provide extensive scientific research, and I'm not sure if anyone can really provide any concrete evidence on the matter, from my perspective/experience, I feel so much better for exercising and maintaining a healthy lifestyle. I'm aware that there are studies that prove the almost "drug like high" that you get after exercise, but I'm not going to go into that detail either. I would just like to highlight the fact that my self-esteem, confidence, attitude and outlook are so much better after I exercise, because I feel good about myself. Of course this then translates into my mood and therefore I believe that it does affect how I am as a parent, meaning I'm more likely to be patient, energetic, positive, optimistic or less stressed – things like that. I don't think you can underestimate the importance of feeling good about yourself. I also don't mean it from a vanity point of view. More than anything, I think it's important to stay in shape to help maintain a level of energy that is needed in our fast paced lives as parents. Or to put it another way, we need to be active just to give us a fighting chance of keeping up with our children with their bundles of energy.

Aside from your personal attitude there are so many other benefits that do not necessarily jump out. For example, you want to be in shape so that when your kid gets older you can run around with them, play sports, and teach them how to throw a ball or even coach a team. Not just that, looking way down the line and when you're in your 60s/70s/80s – won't you want to be active with your grandkids? Another point, and again I have no scientific evidence to provide to prove my point, if your children see you maintaining a healthy lifestyle, balanced diet, and generally taking care of yourself, then that has to at the very least improve the likelihood that they will do the same? I'm not reading too much into this but to give some examples when I'm doing some push-ups my daughter often comes up next to me or jumps on my back and we do some together. Or my wife might be doing a work-out video and she joins in trying to imitate her Mommy. I'm sure many of you can relate to this in some way if you're active. Essentially you're setting the example of your lifestyle, good or bad. We are, as parents, role models after all. How often do you hear a timeless parenting statement, something along the lines of how children are a reflection/mirror of their parents? This obviously applies to many different things, not just exercise, but surely the same principle can apply here? Look I know all circumstances are unique so this is perhaps another trivial point. But these aren't my words as this kind of advice is already out there and somewhat stood the test of time – so surely it's worth considering?

The hard thing about all of this is that being a parent, and for all the joy it brings, it does pull you in all sorts of directions resulting in the gift of time being extremely limited. So this is where it's so important to realize this but at the same time not use it as an excuse or any easy out. Excuses are great when we really don't feel like doing something, and parents can use the excuse of not having the time all day long after they have kids. But there is always some time. I will explain further in this chapter but essentially we can all spare 15-20 min each day to do something for ourselves. It requires the discipline of being committed to doing it each day. What I specifically like to do is plan ahead, reverting back to the opening chapter. Look at it this way: There are 1440 minutes in every day so surely you can spare 15-20 of those minutes say 3 or 4 days each week? Not to get all fancy on you here, but this means there are 10,080 minutes each week. If you were to do some exercise for 20 minutes 3 days a week that would take up 0.59% of your entire week. If it a push you make it 4 days a week then it would take up a whopping 0.79% of your week. To round a little that means you still have 99.2% available to you. Ok that's enough of numbers.

What I personally do, for example, at some point during the day (typically it's towards the end of it), I will identify a time for the following day when I will have some availability to do a little exercise. This may mean waking up earlier, but when you plan ahead and commit yourself I think you're so much more likely to do it. Again I will keep on saying it, as a parent living in the real world you have to be flexible and adapt so it's not always easy to stick to a regimented daily schedule but you get the idea. Call me finger pointing or judgmental all you want, but, referring back to the previous chapter (sorry!), I see so many parents these days mindlessly on their phone just switching off. I think we all know that in the majority of cases, they're on social media, group chats, texting, taking selfies, surfing the web etc. So my view is that if you have time to do that then you have time to exercise. That is not to say that you shouldn't go on social media or any specific site, but it may be more beneficial to substitute just some of that time to doing something positive, like exercising? I say this because I know a lot of parents would say that they don't have time to exercise or they're way too busy or they have way too much going on. Whilst all that is most likely true, do you still find time to aimlessly browse the internet or social media? Do you sit and play those games on your phone? Do you still binge watch a series on TV or the endless amount of the so called reality shows? If the answer is yes to such questions, then perhaps the harsh reality is that you do have the time.

Towards the end of the book I will look at examples like this where we have short-term choices which do have long-term consequences. In the short-term or the present moment it might be so much easier/tempting to jump on your phone or put on your favorite TV series when you finally get time to yourself. My suggestion here is try and avoid the easier option and do something which will benefit your health. Alternatively do some push-ups or exercises whilst you watch your favorite show. I know that in the moment it's so much more appealing just to "kick-back". Resist that short-term temptation as you only need to do something for 15 minutes or so. For me personally, sometimes the hardest part is just starting and overcoming that urge not to do anything. Once I get going, I actually enjoy it. It's just a matter of overcoming that initial hurdle. If you do this on a regular basis, then no doubt you will feel the value long-term. Not just that, but if you keep it up I think you will find that you will continue to gain motivation to continue on a regular basis as you will feel the benefit. In the short-term you will have the satisfaction of doing something for yourself so it's a win-win. So when you do finally kick-back, you will enjoy your relaxation even more.

So this chapter is aimed at YOU. Don't feel selfish about doing this. You could even say that it's selfish for you to do this, but remember that it's for an important reason, that reason being that it could be making you a better parent. I smile when I hear the term, and I have to say I hate it, but take some "Me-time" because really that is what it is. Let's not kid ourselves, so many parents "Me-time" is on their phone or device so my suggestion to you is to use your "Me-time" wisely. Trust me when it comes to the day you are playing catch with you kids let alone your grandkids, you will not remember the social media newsfeeds that seemed important at the time. In addition, when it comes to that time of the year when the swim-suit comes out, don't have the regret of not staying in shape. As a father we all know the saying "Dad-Bod." So another point and here you can call it a little egotistical or what you want, but when you go on vacation with your kids, and are on the beach, trust me you don't want to be wishing that you exercised more! Again I think I'm speaking here as a real world parent, looking at the reality of how we sometimes think/feel.

I have used this term a lot, but I consider myself a real-world parent, and, yes, there are days when I'm exhausted or darn right flat out and I just feel like doing nothing. Sometimes the last thing I want to do is go for a run or do some push-ups in the house but this is why having a schedule and being disciplined is key to ensure it gets done. I once came across a term for people with a busy lifestyle, aimed more at high profile executives where time is extremely limited, that their goal should be that of healthy maintenance. I have to say I really like that term or goal as I think it provides realism, particularly for parents. So I say these things but at the same time, I do understand that on certain days the last thing you will want to do is work out. As stated, I have regular days like this and I would be the first to admit when this happens I occasionally decide to crash and burn rather than run around the block. This chapter is not about beating yourself up in such times or being overly hard on yourself if you're not perfectly sticking to some strict workout schedule. Again we're real world parents so it all has to be realistic. If anything this chapter's advice is about making sure exercise and staying active is at the very least on your radar. It's so you build it into your weekly schedule when you can and placing importance/priority on it. I understand it might not be priority number 1, but I just think exercise is an area which can be easily neglected. If it's neglected for too long, it then suddenly becomes a lot harder to have the energy to reverse such a situation. I also get that sometimes we could do with a little extra motivation to stay in shape or get back into shape but why not have your kids as your motivation? Let them be the reason why you do keep an active/healthy lifestyle.

Now don't get me wrong, I would love to have the body of a Greek God or that of a movie star hunk in a lead role with a six pack rock abs and bulging muscles. To get to that requires dedication on a monumental scale, probably with two a day work outs, personal trainers, dieticians and, probably for the rich and famous, a personal cook that provides all of the healthy meals that are required to get into tip-top shape. But when you consider this, it's important to be realistic – that is why I really like the saying "healthy maintenance". Simplistically speaking this means that two-day sessions are not required and really it's doing 15/20/30 min of exercise 3-4 days a week (keeping the weekend clear which is a personal preference).

I'm no personal trainer and I believe that the modern world severely over-complicates things when it comes to maintaining a healthy lifestyle. It's just about diet and exercise after all. In this book there are no work out plans or schedules to follow and I know people will be at different levels when it comes to their current state of fitness. So if you do consider yourself to be out of shape, why not start by doing a 15/20 minute walk each day and maintain that for a set period of time and gradually build yourself up from there? This is certainly not about doing or getting to the point where you can do some action hero work out. If anything it's as simple as committing yourself to a healthy lifestyle. Is there a better purpose than your children for doing this and your role as a parent?

I would also acknowledge that it's very easy to feel pressured these days in getting back into shape. I can only imagine this is the case for women in particular after such a major life event like giving birth. You often see pictures of celebrities who lose that baby weight in no time at all and have wash board abs showing on a beach somewhere in a bikini. My view this is not the real world for the majority of people. This book is about real world parenting and so in my view, achieving something like this is not realistic, certainly not in the short-term. Of course you can get back to being in great shape, I'm not denying that either. The proof is there for all to see when you see the images online. I'm not even suggesting the photo shop tool is used but what I'm skeptical about is how such results can be achieved in a short space of time. The sceptic in me thinks that in such cases and particularly with celebrities, they have the resources, mainly financial, to have as much help as they need whether it's personal assistants, nutritionists, or nannies, so that they can work out to lose that baby weight as quickly as possible. I'm not criticizing people who have personal assistants or nannies but, to re-iterate, this is a book on real world parenting, and in the real world most parents don't have assistance like this to look after their children so that they can do something like hit the gym. I repeat, this is a personal view and I would not want to be seen as critical of anyone as each person's circumstances are unique. But again real world parents won't have the luxuries that the rich and famous enjoy so more than anything I just think it's unrealistic to compare to someone who does have significantly more resources at their disposal. This is not condemning those who can because they have earned it and of course have the right to do what they want. All I'm saying is that most don't have such options/resources to consider or call upon in the real world.

I say all of this because I think for both men and women, it's easy/natural to compare ourselves to some model/celebrity we see online. But when I talk about exercise, this chapter is really focused more on reality and just looking to stay in some form of shape, to benefit our overall lifestyle so we can remain active. When I say remain active, I really mean active with your children. I think for the majority of us we only have a certain window each day to allocate to something like exercise. So with that, I think our expectations should be realistic enough to reflect what is actually possible as to what we can achieve. It might well be that you can only do 15-20 minutes which is fine. Generally speaking, I think for the majority of parents on a regular day with everything that is going on, that is probably all most could spare. It's not about bulging muscles or killer abs, as although they may well be desirable, again I will bring it back to reality and being a real world parent. I don't think too many of us actually have the time to dedicate to achieve such results. I just want to flag this as somewhat of a balancing act because I also think it's so important not to neglect exercise and use the excuse of being too busy. But at the same time having the realization that your schedule is probably more inclined to focus more on trying to keep you healthy, rather than be the next Mr or Mrs. Universe. I have to generalize here, so I acknowledge we will all be at different levels of current health/fitness and will have goals that are unique to us. But there is no hiding from the daily challenges parents face, so I believe it's best to try and look at it in this kind of way. I think if you understand why you're exercising and understand what is realistic for you, then the more likely it is you will stick at it and keep exercise as a priority in your life. For me it's not about trying to be on the cover of a fitness magazine, I simply want to feel good about myself and I simply want to do active things with my kids both now and in the future.

For some ideas, I think a positive now-a-days is that it doesn't really need for you to be creative when it comes to your work outs. There are so many websites and videos available online for you to do a beginner/intermediate/advanced short work out (all for free). You can do this straight from own your home, on your device and on the days when you don't feel like going out or when it might be too hot or cold outside. So why not put your phone to good use? This can also add variety by mixing it up, so that it all stays fresh/exciting where it's something you might even look forward to. Not just that there are endless amounts of jogging strollers available these days where you and your child can get some good old fresh air whilst you go for a walk/run. There are also many facilities available at gyms where you can have someone care/look after your child whilst you work out. I know some options may be a little more practical/suitable than others and I'm sure you'll have your own preferences, but the point I'm trying to make is that there are many things out there these days which make it a whole lot easier to stay in shape. Failing that, I personally see nothing wrong in putting a TV show on for 15-20 minutes whilst you do a quick work out in the house. Yes this might go against some of my other advice, but if that is the only way your child will be sure to sit still then do it for that short period, so that you can ensure you can stay fit and in shape. I'm sure you'll agree in many ways as parents we need to be flexible and may have to improvise here and there on certain things like exercise to still fit it in. So whatever works for you I say go for it, because overall I think you will see so many benefits no more so than making you a better parent because you will just feel good about yourself.

Although it might not jump right out at you, the more you think about it the clearer it becomes that our personal health is such an important asset as is our time. I will repeat throughout that the purpose of this book is to provide advice on becoming a better parent and I think a healthy lifestyle contributes to this. This illustrates itself in your outlook, attitude, your ability to play outside, and to also having the energy to do "things" with and for your kids. We've all heard the saying "No Pain, No Gain" when it comes to exercise. In this sense I think it's important to recognize the pain which I think for most parents would be to not just fitting it in, but also having the energy to do something physical when you feel drained of it. I don't know sometimes in life to see or gain a benefit in something you have to sometimes do things you don't always want to do. However, I say this so that you can look to keep your children at the back of your mind as what better motivation to stay in shape then for yourself as a parent and your kids? From a personal perspective, my daughter at times seems like the energizer bunny and will go all day long. There is no doubt that being a parent is energy sapping. This makes it ever so more important to stay in shape so that, at least, you have that fighting chance of keeping up which I mentioned at the beginning of the chapter! Trust me, you will not want to turn your kid down if they want to play with you outside but you don't have enough energy to do so! I will say it again – this book is about becoming a better parent and I believe by placing high importance on exercise you will be doing just that. I think this will be something you will be able to really see and feel for yourself if you commit.

15 TAKE CARE OF YOURSELF

This is also very much a follow on from the previous chapter but this is more about taking general care of yourself on a day-to-day basis. I don't want to appear or come across as patronizing in anyway, that is certainly not my intention at all. What I'm referring to is that it's very natural for parents to put their kids first and I'm not saying that this is not what you should do. To give you an example which I hope will make my point clearer. There are many mornings when my wife is busy getting my daughter ready for school and doing chores or jobs around the house, such that she forgets to have breakfast. Or there may be days when she is so busy taking care of everyone else that she doesn't drink enough water when it's so important to keep the body hydrated. It also came across in conversation recently that it has been over a year since she has had her hair done professionally. As parents it's easy to be guilty of things like this. Her selfless response is that this is not important and that she would rather spend that money on our children. But really that's not the point at all. In my wife's case she should be making sure that she takes care of herself and not to feel selfish in any way at all. In many ways it's admirable when you see many instances of when parents make small, and sometimes major, sacrifices for their children but I do feel that it shouldn't always be at their own expense. Remember that we, as parents, set an example to our children so we should show them that we do take care of ourselves and place great importance on doing so.

I know there are some parents who are super organized when it comes to their kids. They can be described as almost methodical with everything they do when it comes to their children. But for all that care and attention they give, some may not do the same or apply the same approach to themselves. Look I'm not saying you need to overthink this but are you a parent who lives by a routine of some sorts? Do you prioritize things like your children eating breakfast in the morning, having a healthy lunch/dinner, bath/shower before bed, a set bed-time; simple things like this? You probably know what I'm getting at, in that if you believe it's so important for your children then you have to understand it's these simple everyday things are so important to you as well. Let's face it and I will say it again, being a parent can sap the energy or life out of us but don't add to this by not taking care of yourself with everyday things like nutrition and hydration. The way so many parents are selfless is admirable with the love for their children, but by neglecting everyday needs on yourself which you place great value on for your children, is not playing the hero in anyway. To put it in the most simple way I can, you need to take care of yourself and place great value on doing so if want to be a better parent. We've all the heard analogies like a car with no gas/petrol is useless so whilst this will be nothing new to you, I think such an analogy is perfect in this context. You may have told your child this before or something very similar. To break it down a little more, I'm sure many parents say to their children breakfast is the most important meal of the day. Do you say this to your child? If so, do you ensure that you also have breakfast at breakfast time? What this chapter is getting at, is that with such things where you understand the value and importance for your children, you might also need to tell yourself the same message from time to time so you act on it. Again understand this has a purpose with the purpose being becoming a better parent, so I think the more you understand that, the more likely you will do the things you need to do. Don't think you're playing the hero because you skip breakfast or lunch as a sacrifice for all the running around you have to do for your kids. I think the message here is for you to consider that by doing such a thing will actually be to your detriment? Again the focus is on becoming a better parent so think about it for yourself.

Like it not, whether it's taking general care of ourselves, working out or eating right, we, as real world parents, have an easy cop out. We can easily pick a reason why we can't do something. I'm not saying there is never a legitimate reason, and that every reason for not doing something should be labelled as an excuse. What I'm saying is that excuses are easy to come by as we're parents after all. I have said this before; I'm never going to try and pretend to be some perfect guy who has never used his kids for an excuse not to do something. Regrettably I have, and I'm sure I will again. I know when I'm kidding myself and it bothers me even more after the fact, if I have used some lame excuse for not doing something.

So my advice is not to neglect the simple things when it comes to taking care of yourself which you might not intentionally do, or even realize that you're doing. The point is that if you take time to take care of yourself when it comes to sleep, nutrition, showering, hydration, cleanliness, appearance etc., in an indirect way I believe that it will actually make you a better parent. We all live in the real world and this book is about modern day parenting. I'm not trying to contradict myself here as I know doing these things for ourselves can be a challenge in our hectic lives. Let's touch on sleep a little more as this seems like an obvious example when it comes to parenting as we all lack sleep from time to time if not all the time. The point in taking care of yourself is being consciously aware of this, rather than being unconsciously aware to the extent that you may not be getting enough rest. I made an earlier point of intent, and I'm sure that everyone's intent is to have sufficient sleep so you, in turn, have to make a conscious effort to actually try and work on this. It might almost be as basic as allocating yourself somewhat of a bedtime, like a child, or making sure you leave your cell phone out of the bedroom so you don't have this distraction when you're trying to get some rest. There is so much out there on this subject these days, telling us how we need to disconnect if we are truly going to get some valuable rest. I say this because I know so many people who do this and I too have been guilty of it before. To give an example, it might be 10pm and I'm exhausted. I get into bed ready to go to sleep, but then I pick up my phone. Unknowingly for the next hour or so I mindlessly go from site to site on things that pop into my head whether it is news, sports, weather etc. I feel I have made considerable improvements with this, but I would say that I'm by no means perfect with it either. My suggestion is if you're just focused or at least more mindful not necessarily of a set bedtime, but just getting some more valued sleep, you might be then less inclined to be tempted by such distractions so you actually get an extra hour or two of sleep! I know this is hard too as we often joke about this with friends. I hear people say that it might be 9/10pm before they finally get a minute to themselves, so that they don't want to immediately go to sleep as they want to enjoy that free time. Whist I understand that, my suggestion would remain that you should try and use that time to take care of yourself. I mean this by not necessarily allowing something to distract you, where your mind suddenly becomes active again. I think you don't want to make it hard on yourself to finally get to sleep when you're physically exhausted. I think you'll also not want that feeling the following morning wishing you would have gone to bed that little bit earlier because you just can't seem to wake up.

It's really a question of being conscious and self-aware so, to touch on more examples, it's making sure that you make time to eat breakfast in the morning, or have lunch at the right time rather than 3 o'clock in the afternoon. Or it might be making sure that you take a shower at a regular time of day rather than putting it off or just forgetting to take one. Now I can hear a lot of people turn around and say this is a lot easier said than done. I agree in some sense. There will be days, and we have all had them, when nothing goes to plan or when it's even more hectic than usual; I get it. But in the main I think they're the exception rather than the norm especially if you have structure to your day which I highlighted in the opening chapter with good planning. I do believe that it does take some self-awareness to ensure that you do take care of yourself. Call it discipline, habits, or what you want. But we all want to lead a good lifestyle and so you're ultimately responsible for taking care of yourself. Sure we rely on our spouse/partner for support, but at the end of the day I think we need to lead by example in this area. Again this requires practice but I also think the best reward is that it will make you a better parent. I genuinely believe this and it's hard to demonstrate in a tangible or direct way, as I said before it's more of an unseen benefit when taking care of yourself. But if you think about it in a logical or common sense way, if you have had some good rest and/or are well hydrated, well-nourished and feel good then, in turn, you're more than likely to be less stressed and have a positive attitude. We all understand the modern day term of being "Hangry" which tends to make us smile when we hear it as it's used in a joking or sarcastic kind of way. But you can even look at this in parenting because if you're not keeping yourself nourished at breakfast, lunch or dinner time then as the saying goes you might become "Hangry" meaning you are irritable, impatient and short-tempered around your children. Hopefully you understand my point here and I'm the first to acknowledge that something like this is hard to see, prove or measure. But I do consider that a knock on effect of taking care of yourself in many different ways is that it makes you a better parent – the purpose of this book!

It's only normal to put your child first, but deliberately taking positive actions for yourself is really nothing to feel guilty about. Some parents may feel selfish, but I'm only really referring to taking out a few minutes to eat your breakfast as an example. More than likely you will be on the go at this time or at lunchtime so if you are, make sure you eat something and something nutritious if this is the case! By the way and thinking more realistically, you will probably be doing this on the run and not necessarily sitting all calm/relaxed at your breakfast table, listening to the morning birds chirp outside. I'm not saying that's a bad thing either, I just want to make the point which is to have breakfast at the right time of day and not at 11am or not at all. Speaking more generally, I'm also not implying that you should have a daily massage or a daily spa day or anything to that extreme. I think you'll get what I mean in terms of taking care of yourself. A lot of the points I make in the book such as this, need to be put into context as there are different ends of the spectrum. So, in this case, don't be so preoccupied in taking care of yourself with two-a-day gym sessions that takes time away when you could be with your child. This is at the one extreme, and at the other, don't make it all about your children such that you neglect yourself and your general health. It's a question of balance and clearly the obvious answer is to try and fall somewhere closer to the middle, if you're closer to one end of the spectrum. You don't need to overcomplicate this either – just be honest with your own judgment as I'm sure you'll full well know where you do fall.

This may sound rather blunt but we have all heard of someone saying that he/she has let themselves go after having a child. For the PC crazed people out there please don't pretend that you haven't heard someone say something along these lines before! It might sound harsh but at the same time there is truth in the matter. What I would highlight and emphasize here is that it applies to men as much as it does to women. I think that, more often than not, when someone refers to someone as having let themselves go, as a parent it's commonly directed more towards the mother. Not for nothing, but it's all too common with dads too. It might not even be drastic in that a dad, for example, might not put on an excessive amount of weight but does having a baby mean that it's now ok not to exercise anymore? Or start to eat more junk food rather than looking to maintain a healthy lifestyle? No one is saying it's easy, but what is easy is to fall into a trap of gradually letting things slip in certain areas, and appearance and health is an obvious one. I reiterate it's not simple/easy, but you have to find a way of making it work and this means making the effort to take care of yourself. Make the effort to where you don't let things slip, because it does really then become a slippery slope which then requires so much more effort to overcome.

We see it all too often that parents use their children as an excuse or for justification as to why they can't exercise or they can't do something. I would suggest that you don't fall into this trap of using your kids as an excuse for an easy way out. I will say it over and over again, that it's hard, but find a way. This is because if you gradually let things slide, the changes are so subtle that you don't notice any difference from day-to-day, but in a year or two you might be horrified if you're out of breath just running around with your kids. This will certainly be the case if you're someone who was used to being in shape. I do genuinely believe that it requires practice to be self-aware and know what is happening around you so that you can have more control. It might seem a bit odd to say that as we use the term "practice" in the sense of developing some form of practical skill, but I think being self-aware is a skill in itself that does require practice.

I also believe that it's important to ensure that you keep up with your dental appointments, eye/vision appointments, hair appointments, check-ups, things like this so you're indeed taking care of yourself. I will reiterate an earlier point: At the end of the day, we're role models to our children and they will look up to us and follow our lead in many ways. If we can demonstrate how we take care of ourselves and its importance, then I believe that this is something they will pick up on with longer term positive effects. Of course there are no guarantees but chances are they're more than likely to do the same as they continue to grow up. Let them follow your positive lead. Take care of yourself to become a better parent!

16 VACATIONS, HOLIDAYS & TRIPS

Rather than just say that I advise you to take a vacation or trip with your family, I want to provide a practical tip which I find useful. It relates to some of my previous advice on forward planning. I don't think I really need to explain the benefits of taking quality time away with your family. I believe that it's very important to visit new places and experience new things from which you can form many lasting memories. A lot of my fondest childhood memories actually came from vacations/holidays that I took with my family. Nowadays, whilst I also like taking a week or two away, I also really like short weekend breaks to help recharge the batteries. I don't know what it is about getting away from the day-to-day grind but it's so beneficial to do so. For me it not only allows me to recharge my batteries, but it allows me to reflect, get perspective, and reinforce what is actually important in my life so that I'm ready to go again!

So clearly my suggestion is to take time away with your family; nothing really new here I know. My advice to you however relates to planning. I believe that its best if you look something like a year in advance when your calendar tends to be a lot clearer and I think you'll find this will actually be the best time to book that vacation. I'm not necessarily talking about a weekend break, although this might still prove useful, what I'm really referring to is an extended vacation for a week or two or even more. It might seem a long way away at the time but you will soon find how quickly it comes around and the beauty is that you will all have something to look forward to. It can also serve as some form of reward or something to work towards for everyone's hard work during the year. Another benefit of this is that it's also then confirmed in your calendar and in everyone's diaries. If then there are any conflicts, or something comes up closer to the time, you know you will not be able to commit to other things as you're already committed to going away – essentially you will be in a position and have a reason to say no. But if you don't do this then in the present it usually works the other way around, where you find it hard to get away because your calendar is already full of commitments.

I tend to find where people make a mistake these days (including myself) is that we tend to look at everything in the short-term. When you know you're busy with work and other commitments, it's hard to even think about, let alone book a vacation and just get away at the drop of a hat. Speaking from experience my intention was to make a trip back to the UK once our son was born. We didn't book flights for very good reason as my wife was having a high risk pregnancy and we didn't want to commit to anything until our new baby was born. After he was born in September our thoughts then were to make the trip in November to coincide with my Mothers 65th birthday (sorry Mum), but we ended up being indecisive and in the end didn't make the trip. However, if flights were booked in advance, then the indecision actually goes away and you just go on the vacation. Think about it now, in the current moment I'm sure your schedule is full and you may have so many different things going on. Whilst a week away sounds amazing it's probably hard for you because it may seem you and your family have to stop everything that's already going on which makes it almost impossible. At the same time you might think that there is no point looking at booking a vacation 1 year or 18 months from now as it's too far away, you don't have to think about it right now and you can book it another time. But my precise point is that in such a moment it's the perfect time to get everyone together, look at dates down the line (way down the line if needs be) and book your well-deserved extended vacation. Once it's booked, it's booked, so nothing will get in the way of it. And when the time draws nearer everything will work around your pre-planned vacation rather than you having to try and plan a vacation around all of your pre-planned activities/commitments.

So my suggestion to you when you're feeling a little stressed, burnt out, and when you feel that it's impossible for you to get some time off, take a step back and get some perspective. Look ahead and book a vacation, even if it's a year away. Don't just put it off for another time. This way you will know that it's confirmed and set in stone. There will be no excuses for how busy you are when the time draws nearer as this has already been pre-planned and you're committed to it. I'm sure you'll thank yourself in some way if you do this, as and when the time does come around for you to finally get away with your family. Before I move on, I also want to make a general point about booking time off, mainly in relation to your employer. Again this is a broad brush statement and won't apply to all as I know of many employers who actively encourage personal time off, where some even make it mandatory. But rather than focusing on the employer, I want to focus more on the individual. Regardless of what I just said, I still tend to find that some people are almost scared/worried about taking time off or an extended amount of time. I think there is some crazy statistic out there of unused vacation days, particularly in the US. Look the way I see it is that life is way too short to be worrying about taking some time off, certainly if you're actually entitled to it. The reality is that a week or two goes by in a flash, so before you know it you will be back into the swing of things anyway. I don't think anyone should think they're playing the hero for never taking time off with their family. I think there is also so much out there which actually supports the benefits of taking time away to actually boost efficiency/productivity of an employee over time. My view is take the plunge, go for it and get away - nothing excessive whereby you're taking advantage, but merely using/utilizing the vacation/holiday time you're given. If not, I think this will be something you will later come to regret.

So after it's all been booked, let's now look a little at the vacation itself when the time does arrive. I think some more common sense advice, and reverting back to another chapter in the book, when you're actually on vacation with your family this is the vital time to be well and truly present. I will refer to some professional development advice which I have come across several times before which I like and has always stuck with me, as I think it basically sums up what you should do. I don't know it word for word, but essentially it's along the lines of: "When you're at the office, be at the office and when you're at the beach, be at the beach." I think this advice is very self-explanatory by not mixing the two. This type of advice is already out there, but I like it as I too believe it's equally as important to be present when you're working. However, this is focusing more on your family time. So if you stick to this approach you can have that work hard, play hard or play harder attitude.

I will emphasize the importance of this as I will give you a personal experience where I was not fully present on a vacation and it spoiled the whole experience for me. It wasn't an extended break, just a short, two nights get away, but even so I think the same rules still apply. At the time I had invested some money in some stocks and it so happened that the market took a blip around the time of our getaway. So I was stressed as I was seeing my stocks lose value and I ended up constantly monitoring the prices during the day and debating whether to sell or not. Sure I was still playing with my daughter in the pool and we were doing things as a family, but my mind was elsewhere at times. I was also irritable because, although I wasn't losing huge sums of money, nonetheless the value was going down.

Being present is so much about the mind and being fully focused on your family and really not caring what else is going on around you. Think about it, and once more I will refer to the point about living in a bubble and being mindful of that, so you don't neglect other things around you. Like with one of my previous examples when I talked about watching one of your child's activities, it might sound contradictory but when you're on vacation that may well also be the perfect time for you and your family to be in your own little bubble. So for that time away it's all about you and having that quality family time. Even something like this sounds a little artificial, but I'm sure you can appreciate what true quality time means without the need for any grand statements or gestures. I don't think you need to try and manufacture things and pretend or even worry about everyone having the most perfect time. I personally think it's more about being in a position to take it all in, by once again being truly present. This way you can connect and this doesn't have to be anything deep or over-thought, just more about enjoying as well as fully appreciating the time you have together. Although it sounds a little cliché, nothing else should really matter. If you can relate to the mistake that I made you should understand that the feeling of not being present on time away with my family proved to be a lot worse that losing some money on stocks!

I know, I know, I have already gone on and on and on (it doesn't stop here) about the use of social media and cell phones, but I would like to make another point in relation to vacations. I disconnected a long time ago from social media, but I often here about people posting photo after photo and making online albums whilst on a vacation. I know so many people do this, so I may be the odd one out here, but whenever I hear things like this I just think why on earth would people want to do post after post whilst on vacation/holiday? I appreciate I'm being blunt with my points here, but isn't it all rather self-indulgent saying look at Me, Me, Me? That's why I keep saying I think it's crossed the line to where it's not really about being social anymore and it's more about Me, Me, Me and attention seeking whereby you're then fixated on what people say/think about you and your posts. As I said I know I'm being blunt here, but I don't want to try and sugar coat the point either, especially when I think there is something much more important to consider, which is trying to become a better parent. Let me make clear I'm relating this specific to parents so I'm thinking this more of people away with their families. I know so many people who do this and I just don't get it. I get why parents want photos and videos of their family, but to post it all is the point I don't get especially when you're actually there. Back to the point of being present, I think if you're more concerned with posting snaps to social media then it takes you away from your family time. I think you then become more concerned of looking for that perfect but somewhat manufactured photo of you trying to paint the perfect picture of your family get away to show off to your friends. You then get caught up on the comments you get or don't get and keep checking on your phone to look for any responses. I'm sure people might say I want to share with close family and friends, but back to an earlier point how many of your online friends do you truly connect with? If it's more for grandparents then you can easily share photos and such with your true loved ones once you get home. I also think it's got to the point now with social media when people over post on things like vacations, it actually just annoys people and not in a jealous kind of way either. I don't know maybe the way I'm talking is like a dinosaur about to go extinct, but I will be honest throughout the book and here is no exception.

A counter argument to some of my points might be that it only takes a few seconds to upload a photo or post a video: So what's the big deal? Yes that maybe true that it does take just a moment, but all I would say is that you're still in distraction mode. I see it all the time first hand where people have their phone constantly in their hand and are constantly checking it where in this case it would be to see if anyone has responded to that photo/video post. So I would argue that you're then in a permanent state of distraction mode where your mind keeps skipping from one thing, back to your phone and then to another, back to your phone and it goes on and on. So I would just ask the question back: Why would you want to be doing this on your precious vacation/holiday time? For me vacations now means certainly for the most part unplugging. Look I get we all have things going on in our lives where we may need to check in for any messages or calls once or twice a day. So again living in the real world I actually understand it's not as easy to completely unplug. But what doesn't make sense to me particularly for parents when away with their families is when they choose that time to be as active as ever on their phone posting everything for the world to see. It's not even a privacy issue for me again it comes back to being present and fully focused on your family. Look this book is about becoming a better parent so for what it's worth I think for this to happen when looking at a vacation is to have that time where you're fully focused on your family. For all the time you spend thinking about and posting updates and photos, I think for some if not many, might actually be massively underwhelmed of those who actually really care to see and read those constant updates.

To conclude this chapter, I will share something that I find beneficial when on vacation. It's obviously not for me or anyone else to tell you how to spend your time away but I would like to share something which I like to do. You will already know that I like to keep to a schedule with good planning so that I'm making the best use of my time and, as a consequence

I typically know what I will be doing most days/weeks during the year. But when it comes to a vacation, I like to then put all this to one side and really unwind and not have to think about a set routine or schedule. This is when I can completely switch off and go with the flow and not have to think about what I should be doing, where and when. Whilst I find it extremely beneficial it's nice to take a step back and refresh so that I will be ready to go again after that break. I stick to the same rule regardless of whether I'm away for a long weekend or on a one or two week, longer vacation. Like most parents/families, you're so busy day-to-day and week-to-week where your schedule/calendar is already full with activities. With that there is no much room to do anything spontaneous. So I find when on vacation that is the perfect time to be spontaneous, to do things you perhaps wouldn't normally do and see where the day takes you. A kind of go with the flow approach if you know what I mean? In summary my suggestions are to plan that extended vacation well in advance, be spontaneous when you're away if you do happen to normally have a strict routine/schedule, but above all else when you do get away BE PRESENT (BE AT THE BEACH – your mind that is!). Again bear all of what I just said in mind in relation to becoming a better parent.

17 SUMMER BREAK

I touched on this subject in the opening chapters in relation to planning; taking stock and time management, and I now want to look at this in more detail, specifically when it comes to your children's summer break. I'm mindful that this may only apply to some, purely depending on where you live, the school and how much time they actually get off in the summer. My daughter goes to school in the US (Florida) and she gets approximately 3 months' vacation during summer. Personally, I think this a long time but I'm certainly not looking to debate the length, good or bad, as I really see this as outside of my control as a parent. What I do want to focus on and advise you as a parent is to consider where you do have control, for want of a better word, in looking at what your children do with all of that free time.

First and foremost my suggestion to you is see this as an opportunity and make the most of it. As the saying goes "it is what it is" so don't waste energy moaning about whether it should be shorter because you now have the full responsibility for keeping your child occupied for a long period of time. Some may see it as a chore because your child's day is usually mapped out but now the whole day is clear and it's really on you as the parent to figure it all out. So, before I continue, embrace this and I will reiterate the point - don't see it as a burden but as an opportunity. Looking at it from a very basic level and breaking it down where 3 months is 12 weeks. This won't apply to all, but let's just give 2 weeks up for when you will actually be on true "holiday/vacation" potentially meaning away from home. In this scenario, that leaves 10 weeks of free time for your child over those summer months.

As a parent in the real world this can seem daunting, trying to figure out what your child can/will do each day. It might be after those first few weeks that you start to wish for the school year to start again so you don't have to entertain or keep trying to come up with new ideas for something to do. Not just that, if you work full-time you certainly won't have the same luxury of having 12 weeks to just take off. However, my advice to you is to really see this time as a chance/opportunity, for your children that is, to do some really positive things by fully taking advantage of all that free time they have.

Hopefully you will have gathered a general theme of my advice throughout this book looking specifically at how and what your child does with their time. I'm mindful at times that I may go on a little or seem to be repeating myself somewhat, but I don't think I can emphasize enough the importance of this. Someone once told me that repetition is the best form of communication, so although I admit I'm certainly guilty of that throughout the book, hopefully you can see it in that kind of way where I'm trying to make an impact or get the message home (loud and clear). But don't underestimate all of the good things that can be done. Remember this book is about you becoming a better parent and I think by taking charge of this you will be doing just that by doing/ensuring something positive for your child. So when I say "control", like it or not, you play a major part in deciding what your son/daughter does with their time over the summer. The way I see it you can be passive or active, active in the sense that you're not micro managing every minute/second of the day, rather you're just looking to ensure that your children use their time productively – putting it to good use.

Now with the extensive summer break, I will share with you my outlook. I see the amount of time as an opportunity/opening to do something which will benefit my child. I look to ensure the time is used wisely. Before I continue this is not necessarily advice for you to adopt but I'm sharing with you my perspective. First and foremost, I want my daughter to have fun as well as enjoy each and every day. When I talk about using time productively it might immediately sound as if what I have in mind would not be fun at all. However that is far from the truth as I think that it's important for my child to play for hours on end with friends, have beach days, pool days, play until the sun goes down etc. So fun/enjoyment is the theme to create those fond memories which I certainly have from my childhood during the summer.

So referring to the time not away from home on your main vacation, I see the opportunity lies in doing something which I see as extremely valuable for nothing more than 2 hours each day. Let me make it clear, this isn't some form of chore. I think this sort of thing should be something a child as well as a parent actually looks forward to. Speaking personally, what I think is important is that my daughter does some form of educational activity so that when she returns to school she has a natural advantage. They have a saying here of the "summer slide" highlighting the importance of reading and other such activities so that your child doesn't "slide" back down after all they have learned during the year. I think "summer slide" as a term itself strikes a chord as it certainly does with me as a parent. It obviously depends on where your child is at, but given my daughters age it's working on things like sight words, reading introductory books, writing, gaining more confidence with numbers, and counting etc. There are endless resources available to parents these days, such that you don't really need to think too much as those resources (things like worksheets) are given to you so, really, it's just a case of executing – it really doesn't require too much thinking/creativity on your part. Bringing a point back from another chapter, be proactive by reinforcing things that your child may need to work on over the summer with open discussions with his/her teacher at the end of term. Again, if you did something like this, I'm sure that they can provide additional material for you to make the task that much easier. You will have everything you need, it's then on you to make sure that you do it with your child or they do it themselves bearing in mind their age/maturity.

Sports are already a big part of my child's life so the other hour I think it's beneficial to try and ensure that she practices one of her sports which, in her case, are either golf/tennis. The way I see it this is again using time purposefully which has benefit to my child. She enjoys it too and when you have this amount of consistent practice I feel there is great opportunity for progress. For some children the rate of progress will be more than others but either way progress should be seen as a success. So this is my take on it and I think you can probably gather by now that as a family we love sports. Personally, I see many benefits of introducing children to sports. But at the same time I understand that it's not necessarily for everyone and there are so many different ways for your child to be active. Not just that there are so many different things other than sports your child can do – I just want to share the principle more than anything. Either way my advice is find some form of enjoyed activity and commit to doing it each day with your child. It might be that you can't always take them, so this is where your planning is key when you might need to call on help, or research what classes are available in the summer to join/sign up.

In my example, I see education and sports as the main areas of opportunity to use the huge amount of time available, doing something productive over those summer months. As just mentioned, the same principle can be applied to so many different things, obviously sports other than golf and tennis, but to name just a few alternatives how about learning to play a musical instrument? Begin to learn a new language? Essentially learning anything new, but at the same time, if your child already has a love and passion for something like a sport or art then take advantage of all the time available to further enhance their current skill level. Work and apply more focus to something that they're already doing. I think that by committing to, and doing such a thing over the summer break you will see that it's all worth it at the end with the progress your child will ultimately make.

What is key is that having decided on an activity before summer break then you must commit and see it through by doing it each day (say each week day – leaving weekends free). Again I know that as a real world parent you won't always be available, but this is where your planning becomes key to ensure you can somehow make it work – calling on some help, adjusting schedules, working with your spouse/partner etc. You must commit, as the parent, to ensuring you can/will do all you possibly can to make it work. Let's not forget that your child must also commit and see/understand the benefit. If they're old enough and can take on the responsibility for themselves where they're not so much reliant on the parent then all the better – all I would say is to remain that support mechanism to help them stay on track. It's key for them to want to do it, so encourage them to have a set goal. It may be to make varsity (first team) of their sport for the next school year. This will give your child something to work for, keep/remain focused and ensure their commitment. This I feel is the only real way to see benefit. I don't even think you need to track progress, just stick to the process and let the process itself be your focus. The process being ensuring that you do it each and every day. Just picking one idea, as an example, if your child is acquiring a new skill such as learning to play the guitar or drums, then by having a lesson for an hour one day but then failing to practice what they learned for a few days will reduce the impact of that formal lesson. That stop/start approach or doing a bit here and there will benefit no one and might actually lead to more frustration for your child. So scheduling and planning once again become key, as well as the communication plus teamwork as a family to making it all happen.

Clearly all this needs to be worked around your work schedule, coaches, available sessions, and also strong consideration needs to be given to cost. There are many good as well as bad things that could cost a lot of money but at the same time there are plenty of free or less expensive things you can do. That's where you come in to be creative, perhaps by doing that background research. Don't just randomly sign your kid up to something because your friend or neighbor might be doing it, because it's cheap or that it takes up all the day. It could also be that you can take them to the court, to the field, to the pool and you work your day around it so that you get to enjoy the experience with your child. Many parents take on the unofficial role as coach of some activity so if you do happen to have a skill for something, then why not help teach your child? As with the example given, it doesn't mean you have a formal lesson from an instructor every day, it could even be once a week. If, in between those lessons your child works on and practices what they were taught by the instructor, then the next time they have a lesson they're more likely to demonstrate a little progress.

Bottom line is that after that couple of hours or so, of using time productively each day over the summer means there is still all the time in the world for your child to play to their heart's content, spending hours at the playground, playing outside, playing at a friend's house, pool days, beach days, the list can go on and on. If you go with an approach similar to mine in a consistent way it becomes entirely possible that your child continues to develop that passion of theirs. Then they might naturally want to keep playing at it for much longer than say an hour each day. It will also help ensure they're ready to go back to school when the time comes. This can then help to make that transition to the next school grade, after the educational work you also did. Referring back to the opening chapters, once again your planning as a parent is key and perhaps the most important element in all this. Funnily enough, I overheard my wife's friend say to her at the end of our last summer something along the lines of how it feels like there is so much time at the beginning of summer and then suddenly it's over. So the point here is that it's perhaps easy to take all the time your child has somewhat for granted especially in the beginning. Therefore, I urge you not to be so nonchalant about what your child will be doing because they will have so much free time on their hands. On the same note, I'm in the real world, so this isn't about having a regimented summer schedule where every minute/second needs to be allocated with something deemed to be productive by you the parent. Again there is a balance from this extreme to the other where you're perhaps too calm/relaxed about it because there is so much time. I think all it needs is for the parent to take charge a little before the summer starts to plan out what their child will be doing then help them see it through day by day.

In my opinion it's about having some focus and setting goals over the summer in addition to all of the play/fun/free time. Then, when the new school year starts you can look back and feel satisfied that your child has done things which will continue to have a direct benefit for them. Without such goals there is a danger trap where summer days are consumed with movies, TV, commercials, social media, web surfing, video games etc. I've used such examples before and the same applies in this case, where I'm not necessarily saying that you need to fully prevent/stop any of these things. What I'm saying is maybe just ensure that these types of activities don't take up too many of those valuable hours during the many days over the summer – or at least pull back a little on such activities to ensure of things that are more worthwhile/productive. I firmly believe that you will have great joy and satisfaction in using that time to good effect. Don't let one day roll into the next and have a feeling of regret at the end saying something along the lines of "Where did the summer go?"

As already mentioned not all of you reading this will necessarily have kids who get 3 months of summer vacation from school. Regardless of the length, my advice would still be to follow a similar approach. Have dedicated rest and a family getaway, but then look to utilize the remaining time wisely, however long it maybe. I just don't think the whole summer should be seen as an opportunity for your child to be doing nothing even if they're always doing something during the school year. The reality is the same principle applies for time out of school whether it's school holidays or not. The reason I have just concentrated specifically on the summer break here is that typically it's an extended period of completely free time. Therefore, with so much free time it can either be taken for granted, or valued where you as parents take advantage of it and see it as an opportunity for your child to do something beneficial to them. My ultimate advice is seeing it as just that and I will say it one final time – see it as an opportunity! By doing so I believe will help you become a better parent.

18 RELATIONSHIP WITH SPOUSE/PARTNER/SIGNIFICANT OTHER

I think any general parenting advice when focusing on your relationship, in my case with my spouse, would stress the importance of finding time for each other. This is an area where my wife and I could maybe improve so I may not be best placed to give anyone advice but I want to highlight the importance of trying to find the time. As parents we have a very natural tendency, like most, to always put our kids first and before anything else. This may mean we can neglect other areas or parts of our life, none more so than with each other and our relationship.

So this is about looking for and finding time alone with each other without the kids. The obvious one these days is having some form of date night. Sure my wife and I do this from time to time, but it's not something we have on a set schedule on say a weekly or monthly basis. If you set an evening each week when you want to go out with each other, then it could work as part of your routine/schedule. It might even be something that will just be set in the calendar. I'm not criticizing date nights by any means, but the idea is, I think, a little easier said than done. Firstly you need to determine the best day to do it. Do you do it during the week on a school night and when you have work the next day? This might be a time when your child or children have sports or activities, so you don't necessarily want them to miss out on those. Then the alternative is going out on the weekend but, speaking personally, this is the time I like to spend as a family which is now the four of us. Again, and without being a complete buzz kill to the idea, but you may have to arrange a sitter, be it a friend, grandparent or other family member. It's a lot more difficult to keep doing this on, for example, a weekly basis rather than an ad hoc one. Without trying to kill off the romance of your relationship you also have to consider the cost. When you go out for dinner and a movie and have to pay a sitter as well, it's not a cheap night. Who said romance was dead hey? Now I certainly don't consider myself a cheap skate although I'm not doing myself any favors with what I'm saying here, but the reality is that, living in the real world, you have to consider such things as cost. There may be some of you thinking here; I'm glad I'm not married to this guy! Sure, if I was in a privileged position and money was no object, I could look to do the text book date night to the best restaurant in town buying my wife a dozen roses. But I think most will know it's not as simple as that. I'm not saying it's a fantasy either, but I'm just trying to be realistic and I think this is the case for a lot of people out there. Sometimes you have to acknowledge, when looking at things like a date night and going out for a meal and few drinks, a sitter, that it's not only time constraints that you have to consider in trying to schedule something. You also have to consider financial ones too, in respect of whether you can afford it. Of course there are cheaper options out there and you can be creative in some things you do, but all I'm trying to do is make the point that it's not necessarily as practical or simple/easy as it seems at face value.

If I'm being completely honest, I really do like a date night, but we tend to do it more I would say every now and then. They could even be a few weeks or a month or two apart. I think sometimes society creates an ideal, or you might see a couple out on social media or on some reality show and you then try to fit in with these perceived social norms. So I think that you need to find what works for you. Speaking personally my wife and I enjoy nothing more than being together, but also with our kids. I will give you an example. We went away a couple of years ago for two nights for our anniversary and my wife's parents looked after our daughter at the time. Now we did have fun and enjoyed quality time with each other, but we did talk about our daughter a lot. We missed her and wished she could be with us at times where we knew she would love to be seeing this or doing that. I know it was only for a couple of days but we missed her so much. I'm not going to label it as separation anxiety which you hear of these days, I don't try to overthink things, and it was just a case that we wanted to be with her. All couples are different so this certainly won't apply to everyone, but my wife and I are definitely on the same page in that we just prefer to do things as a family together, with our kids. In our way our version of a date night is a family day/night together. This is just our preference and I do understand why people place high importance on some form of a date night to ensure they do get some quality alone time together. All I would say is that if you do place great importance on something like this; make sure you do the same type of thing together as a family as well.

Before I move on I would like to make another point in relation to compromise and sacrifice. I will look at compromise and sacrifice later in the book with different areas, but I think the same very much applies here. Sure as a couple we could look to have more trips or weekend breaks away together or could go out alone on say every Saturday night. But in order to do so, that would mean we would then miss out on time with our children and time as a family together. The way I see it you can't always have it both ways or be in two places at once. I keep saying I'm talking as a real parent not as an ideal one. Yes in an ideal world my wife and I would have that bit more time together when it's just us, but in the real world sometimes you just can't have it all ways. So the reality is we do compromise or sacrifice some nights out together or a weekend away because as in our case we just prefer to do it as a family. When looked at in that way and understand that, you then may realize you're actually not really compromising or sacrificing anything? You're just doing or going with the option that you want based on the options you have. So in our case we pick the option of a family night out or a weekend getaway rather than just a couple's night or a weekend trip for two. Hopefully you get my point here as I'm not really saying this applies all of the time where you never go away or for a night out with just you and your spouse/partner. This is referring more on a regular week-to-week basis.

I said at the opening of the chapter that spending one-on-one time with each other is something we could do better and that still is the case. But I think you have to work it out as a couple and find what works for you. If you love a weekly date night, and really look forward to it, then keep doing it – who am I to tell you to stop? At the same time don't necessarily feel the need to follow social norms of what other couples do. The reality is that you don't need a fancy restaurant to spend quality time with each other and you certainly don't need to always go to any great expense, although there is also nothing wrong with treating yourselves once in a while either if you can afford it. With what I'm saying now do you at least consider that I'm somewhat of a catch? Ok don't answer that…

So as a real world parent, I will share some advice which is working for us and doesn't need a manufactured date night. I think this will relate to a lot of couple out there as I will focus on the time you do actually have alone each day, which might tend to be when you put the kids to bed. Don't worry; I'm not going to go into details on being intimate here! Look our reality was, and still is to some extent, that once the kids are in bed fast asleep that is our "me-time" (my favorite ever saying (not!)). So this is the time when you and your wife/husband/partner go in complete opposite directions meaning dad goes into his man-cave (or people cave being the

Politically Correct term) to watch sports or play video games and mum goes into another room and goes on social media whilst the latest reality show plays in the background. Sound familiar? Jokes aside, as this is speaking very stereotypically and I'm not meaning to offend. But I think the reality is that this is what a lot of parents do.

I don't actually have a man-cave, but this picture is what quickly became the norm for my wife and I: We would put the kids to bed and then we would go to separate rooms to do our own thing. Now we all need a bit of alone or escape time after a long day, but all I'm saying is to try and look at this time you have alone together and make better use of it. I'm not saying to manufacture something or force something either but, hopefully, you understand the point I'm trying to make in making use of this time to have some quality time together. It might just be 15-30 minutes you set aside for each other at the end of each day where you remove all TV and devices and just spend time with each other. Now you really don't need me to provide you with ideas or suggestions here, but even just as simple as sitting down for a coffee/drink with each other. Now this doesn't have to become a daily task or a chore where it's fake and you both are going through the motions, doing it for the sake of it. But if you think as a couple you need to find more time for each other and you can relate to some of the things I have said, then be mindful of this time when you will be alone so you can make better use of it. It's really all about prioritizing time with each other and placing great value on it. This still will mean that you continue to put your kids first, but if you think this way, then perhaps you're less likely to sit in different rooms when you do have an opportunity for some time alone. Then, many of the same rules apply insofar that you're present with each other. Put away those distractions and value the time you do have together.

Thinking about it the same thing applies for a "family night" or "family day". Clearly it's as important for you all to spend time together but again the reality of this is it's easier said than done to arrange a time/date when we factor in our jobs, school, practices, lessons etc. When we do find some time, we might feel the need to go out and do something which can be costly. Again, whilst dinner and bowling or something like that sounds great, let's be honest it's not cheap either. So again the same advice applies when there might be 30 minutes a day where you're all in the house together at the same time. Rather than be in separate rooms or on devices my advice is to make better use of this time together. Call me old fashioned, but pull out a board game, play something, eat together, have a drink or have some dessert together. Again it might seem a little fabricated at times, but this is much more manageable and reasonable without you necessarily feeling the need to do something extravagant each time you can get together. Sure still go out from time to time and do nice things, but I'm just being a realist in that it's harder for some to do this. This book is about real world parenting so I know for many of us it's not always as simple as it may seem. Again it's all about just being a little creative, using your imagination, taking advantage of the time together, when and wherever it may be.

This is something my wife and I are still working on. When I say working on we're doing just that as we certainly haven't perfected it yet, as I occasionally just crash and go straight to bed after the kids are put to sleep. But we're doing better at not just going straight off into separate rooms when the house has some peace and quiet. In our case we have a porch outside where we just go out to sit/chill together. I think if we continue to do this we need not worry or think about the need to always have some form of date night on a weekly basis, providing we continue to make better use of the time we have alone together on a daily one! A final point I would like to make in closing this chapter is that many of the points are connected to help you to become a better parent – none more so than your relationship with your spouse/partner. So a healthy relationship will no doubt help to add to as well as maintain you becoming that better parent.

19 TEAMWORK

I wasn't really sure what to give the title of this chapter, but I went with teamwork. In this instance when I say teamwork, it's focusing on you and your partner/spouse and even your wider family given your personal situation. My advice relates to my experiences with my wife. But first I will share a story. I once met a guy who was giving me a ride somewhere and we got talking and he was sharing details about his wife and family. The way he talked he was so proud of his family - his wife, children as well as grandchildren. I cannot remember the exact number of children and grandchildren he told me he had, but it was a lot. He explained how his children are all successful in their own right and I remember asking in a joking kind of way "what's your secret?" I do vividly recall him saying that he and his wife made a great team and worked so hard with each other to raise their family. In his own subtle kind of way he implied the hard work and sacrifice was so worth it for the rewards they now enjoy, seeing their children make something of themselves. I was getting my car serviced at the time and this man was happily retired enjoying the fruits of life. He worked a few hours a week to drive people around wherever they needed to go whilst their car was getting worked on. He didn't need to say he was happy or content, you could just tell.

So call it what you want whether it's teamwork or something else. You don't need to give it a slogan or anything like that, but when raising children you and your wife/husband/partner are a team both wanting what is ultimately best for your child. Therefore teamwork is key. In terms of my advice focusing on modern day parenting, I want to break it down a little further because things are not always equal, no more so than running a household and raising a family. My wife and I have what I would call petty arguments frequently over who does more around the house, who cooks more, who's more tired, or who's worked more hours in the day, things like that. It's petty because we should not be wasting our energy arguing about this as it's not a competition or contest. I know there are many couples out there who argue about similar types of things. There are times when I admit I don't fully appreciate what my wife does and I can sometimes do a better job of telling her how grateful I really am. It's easy to think sometimes that getting your kids ready for school is an easy/simple task, but as I'm sure you full well know this can be an operation in itself. When my wife was unwell recently and had to spend a few days in hospital, I had both mum and dad duties for several days during that period. Needless to say both dad and my daughter not only missed mum, but we really needed her back home as things didn't run quite as smoothly. It's at times like that when it's only just for a few days away that you realize everything the other half does.

Another point I want to briefly make as I will touch on this again a little later, is to say, try and make sure you're on the same page with things. I don't want to spell out the obvious here or give some text book advice on the importance of communicating with each other. I mean this in a sense of having no surprises. To give an example, I might sign my daughter up for something related to her golf or tennis without checking in with my wife first. I'm not saying that I need to check in with her because I need her approval or anything like that; I mean it more just to confirm we don't have anything else going on. It sounds simplistic or common sense advice but I'm often guilty of this. It might be that she will need to take her and I kind of just assume she can without seeing if she actually will be able to first. Speaking more generally, I think it's very important you're on the same page with what you sign your kids up for, what they're doing in their spare time bearing in mind the frequency with how much/how often. Again back to my daughter with sports, there are times when my wife and I might disagree with how much practice she should be doing. So this is another point where I don't mean to patronize, but the best thing to do is just talk it out to get to where you're on what I have been referring to as the same page so to speak. I think all of this even requires teamwork as you understand the role you play as parent, where it might be the case that you're the one having to take your child somewhere. So when I say you're working as a team, I mean this in a way where you're all dependent on each other. One parent may sign the child up for something, but then you as well as your child are then reliant on perhaps the other parent to physically take them, get them ready, make sure you have everything you need, feed them, bathe/shower them after etc. This is all very much every day stuff, but nonetheless I think it's extremely important and should not be undervalued. I'm sure you all play your own part so appreciate what everyone does and understand the "team" element where you all depend/rely on each other for things to run as smoothly as they possibly can. I say this as I think you'll quickly find out how it can all fall apart or the wheels can fall off, if you don't work as a team.

So the point I'm trying to make is that it doesn't really matter on your position - you could be a family where you both work full-time or one when there is a stay at home parent. Everyone's circumstances are different. All I'm saying is not to underestimate what your spouse is doing as ultimately you rely on each other. My mum has a saying and jokes that all of her work is behind the scenes. Essentially there will, no doubt, be a lot of things you do as parent that your spouse may not even realize. I think this will apply to both parents in different ways insofar that, day-to-day, you essentially get on with it and there may be many important things you do that go unnoticed. I say this in a sense that you're not being intentionally ignored or that you need some form of recognition for everything you do. I highlight this point to make clear that to keep everything flowing and running smoothly it needs that "behind the scenes" work. So don't underestimate the importance of what you and your partner do, as some of it might not be directly or glaringly obvious at face value. Again this is about working together. To reiterate the point don't try and keep track of who does what, who does more, who makes more money - things like that. We have in the past and it's silly really. It's an impossible task to even try and keep track, it wastes your precious energy and to the point, I'm sure there are many things your partner does without you even knowing.

If you think about it, it's inevitable that one will do more than the other in certain areas so as long as one is not doing completely everything, just know that you're working together as a team. Don't keep score, but as long as it's not all one sided I think you will find over the course of time things naturally even themselves out anyway if you really do work as a team. Well kind of anyway! I mean this in a generic sense rather than looking specifically at one task or house chore. Your spouse may not always be in a position to help get the kids ready in the morning, but I'm sure there are many things that they do which are just as important. Sure there might be days where you seem to be doing a lot, or most things, but there will be inevitably be others when you're not in a position to help as much as you would like. There will be times such as it is currently for me where certain days of the month I'm very busy with work and I'm more dependent on my wife who has that added responsibility of doing almost everything when it comes to the kids. I'm sure you can appreciate it's not easy to bathe, do homework, feed and get two kids ready to bed by yourself with no help. Take my advice from where I have gone wrong in the past by making sure that your partner knows how thankful you are. I think we can all perhaps be a little guilty of taking everyday things for granted from time to time, so I'm just saying try not to underestimate the team element.

You can call it what you want but it does take teamwork to pay the bills, get the kids ready, get them off to school, take them to practice, do laundry, help with homework, clean the house, get the dinner prepared and everything else, down to washing the dishes and taking the trash out – regardless of who does what, who does more and what is deemed more important. If you look at it in this kind of way it helps as you naturally want to help each other out. You may not be intentionally acting selfishly but it might be that you reconsider if you're in fact working together and helping each other out by sharing more of those everyday responsibilities. It might be that you think you're done with all you need to do so you can now crash but, if your partner is still busy folding laundry for example, go and help them put it away so you will both be done with all you need to do for the day. You might also sense that your partner is having a rough or bad day, so that will be the time for you to step up and do a little more. The team then obviously extends to your children as they get older. My daughter is still young, but it's good for everyone if they can help and learn to take on some little responsibilities; simple things like making their own bed. As our family grows and our children get older I want them to understand that we all work as a team; supporting each other and helping each other out. So I think if you have the approach of using the analogy of where you're on the same team and you're not competing against each other then you will see the benefit. Remember this is about becoming a better parent, so by working together more as a team, I think you'll be doing just that.

20 LEARN TO EMBRACE & OVERREACTING

In this chapter, I will pass on some advice that I previously came across, which I would like to share to let you know how I applied it to my benefit. It was an article or an extract from a book on parenting and one of the key points that it was making was that, as parents, we should try to embrace certain things instead of letting them stress us out or annoy us. It was getting to the point that as a parent you have to accept certain things as part and parcel of parenting. I'm paraphrasing here, but I think essentially what it was saying was to consider how you can change your attitude in situations which you may see as a negative and try to look at them in a kind of positive way. I will provide an example of how I applied this in a fairly simple manner. Now I certainly don't consider myself a neat freak, but at the same time I don't like clutter and a messy house. So after a long day at the office when I was tired, maybe a little stressed and hungry, I would come home and there would be toys all over the house – something like the saying that it looked like something exploded or a bomb just went off. But back to the article of the advice I had received, it was basically saying to embrace such moments. It can be considered normal for a toddler to be playing with toys or things around the house and making a mess unconsciously. Instead of letting this stress you out, you can look at it in a different way as such behavior/moments like this are only to be expected. Now this example was when my daughter was between 2-3 years old and I'm not advocating a child to create a mess or anything like that as, when they become older, they need to learn to clean up after themselves. The point here is that the situation depends very much on the age of your child as different norms will apply.

So whatever the age of your children, I'm suggesting that you just consider some of their actions or behaviors which may cause some minor, in the moment stress. See if you can, embrace it in a positive way or try and look for some positives, as it might only be very normal/expected behavior. Of course I'm not saying embrace everything that is negative. What I'm really referring to are those in the moment things that we can catastrophize like the world is coming to end when, in reality, it's so minor and doesn't really matter – like a messy living room of toys which can be easily cleaned up. Just take my experience as an example as we're all unique as to what may or may not bother us.

It can be anything such as taking your kids to school. That can be a little stressful at times when you're rushing in the morning, getting everyone ready and out the door, hitting every red light, or stuck behind a slow car. What this advice is saying is take a step back and actually enjoy the moment you're in, like in this instance, appreciate that you're actually taking your kids to school. The stresses are so short-term and in the moment it's not worth wasting your precious energy. So in a way try to embrace the minor stresses of parenting which come with the territory as, let's face it, we signed up for it. We're all guilty at times of making such a big deal of things that don't really matter in the grand scheme of things – so this advice is saying to try and embrace at least some of it.

There is a lot out there these days on the importance of gratitude and almost practicing being grateful. I actually believe in its importance, but I do think it can be looked at in this slightly different way when it comes to parenting, more where you're learning to embrace. With the example I just gave on taking your kids to school, I really do think with something so simple/every day such as this, is where you can show/feel gratitude where you're grateful/thankful for being able to do just that. This is what I would call more rational thinking, but being a real world parent I know and see first-hand that's it's not always easy to be so rational. We're always on the go, stressed, and tired, to where we have different levels of energy throughout the day, whereby our mood swings with it. I'm exaggerating a little, but I do think as parents it's easy to be/get flustered. So specifically applying the advice in this chapter it's more about not trying to over-react, where you're embracing certain things rather than make a huge deal of something. By embracing it doesn't mean you start to jump for joy when you're tired/stressed it just means you're not letting something overly affect you to the point where you become even more stressed/cranky. I say embrace rather than grateful because I don't think you will necessarily be so rational where you're thankful in my other example of walking into a messy house which you feel that you will have to clean up. Again talking as a real world parent I don't think you will be grateful of walking into a messy house, but I think if you embrace it to a degree there is a difference in that I think you will be less inclined to overreact to where you feel the need to shout at the top of your voice. If you embrace I think you will take more things in your stride to where it doesn't overly affect you as you understand/accept such things will just happen from time to time.

There will be many different ways that I believe that this advice can be applied and yet again it will most certainly differ depending on the age of the child. At the end of the day, accidents happen and let's face it; kids of all ages are prone to accidents! The point is to apply it to what works for you. By looking at something in a different way, I was able to prevent myself from wasting energy and stressing in certain situations that used to bother me. To summarize, you basically have a choice in how you respond to a situation or how you look at something. This means you have control. Apply it in your own way, as I did. I consider these minor day-to-day stresses as all part of being a parent. So consider what you can learn to embrace so that you almost go somewhat full circle with how you react to something by embracing the moment – like that messy living room for me! It might not always seem the natural response, that's why I say somewhat, but either way just try and look at some things a little differently.

Speaking generally about embracing, I like the sayings "embrace the madness" or "embrace the chaos" when it comes to parenting. This is not putting a negative spin on parenting at all and speaking personally I love nothing more than being a parent. All it is doing is acknowledging the fact that our lives as parents are busy and hectic - day after day. Therefore if we embrace this rather than moan about how we have no longer any time for ourselves, then I believe that this will set a parent up to be a better one. By embracing it you understand that there are just certain things that come with the territory of being a parent. By accepting and embracing I think this can make you more of a positive parent and less inclined to overreact/dramatize/exaggerate every time something goes wrong. I also think if you take this approach of embracing, this will also make you more inclined to do things like plan/schedule and purposefully manage your time which I highlighted in the opening of the book. This is because you will understand that life is chaotic at times so, as a result, you need to take control of your days, otherwise, and I will say it again, they will control you.

This leads onto the final point in this chapter and I want to focus a little more on trying not to overreact to minor things. Sounds simple enough and basic common sense, but when it comes to parenting it can be a little harder in practice. For example, things like when your child accidently spills a cup of water, or bruises their knee, breaks a toy, gets stains on their shirt I could go on and on with these type of examples and I'm sure you can certainly relate to the type I'm referring to. I'm sure you also can think of many more for yourself and those that are more personal to you. As real-world parents we often feel overwhelmed, tired and stressed. So when your child spills their juice on the floor that can somewhat be a tipping point where it's easy to blow something out of proportion and you end up taking your frustration out on your child. It's very easy for me to sit here say "don't overreact" or "don't blow everything out of proportion." However, in the heat of the moment, I'm sure as a real world parent it's perhaps easier to understand we can have moments where we can dramatize/overreact or simply make a big deal of something so little. In terms of a solution to the advice? I'm not going to try and answer this for you by saying something like "count to 10 before you say anything" and "take deep breaths" - things like that. For me I think as a parent it's important that you realize you're vulnerable to such moments, so it's really more about being self-aware and reflecting or being honest with yourself when you do overreact. This is another area where I think I need to briefly pause and clarify the point. What I'm referring to here are the times when we as parents can be prone to being a little stressed, cranky, frazzled, grouchy, irritable or snappy…you name it - so its things like this I'm getting at! When I talk about overreacting I mean it more in a way where I think it's just making a bigger deal of something that really doesn't need to be when we're feeling like this or this way. This is another reason why I think it's better to look at it more of embracing such things rather than always looking to be grateful for them as I think it's much more applicable to real world parenting.

To give an example, I have done it before when we were out as a family and my daughter accidently spilled hot chocolate on her new pair of boots. At the time, I overreacted by being a little snappy in the moment which did spoil part our evening out somewhat and I set a bad example to my child. So I was honest with myself and I admitted there was no need to act in such a way like the world was coming to an end – if you know what I mean? So the way I try to prevent such behavior from happening again is immediately refer back to the time when I did overreact the next time an accident occurs. This enables me to remember how disappointed I was in myself and how I got worked up over something so minor or something like an accident which are bound to happen. When I do this I find it helps me to remain calm and immediately apply some perspective to what has just happened. Let's face it, we're all human including our children and kids will be kids. That's why I think it's also important for the parents to stand up and apologize when they're in the wrong. As your children grow up there are inevitably going to be moments when mishaps occur and they will be common to some extent, again depending on your child's current age. So try to look to apply my advice in that firstly, learn to embrace such incidents as it's all part of being a child and a parent. Secondly, by having such an outlook this might enable you not to over-exaggerate the significance of something, but this does take practice. I personally do find that it helps to refer to a time when you were mad at yourself for doing so! A lot of this advice is already out there, I'm just trying to apply it a bit more specifically to parenting and everyday life. Essentially, as parents we have the choice of how we respond to something. When you look at it that way, I think you really begin to understand the importance of all your choices where you do have that element of control as a parent. So if you're prone to any of this my advice is to try this sort of mindset shift. Embrace rather than freak out and even if you make some form of positive adjustments, then I believe this will be another way/area where you can improve to become that better parent.

21 DIET

There is a general theme with some of the chapters in this book, in that most tie back to the opening one on the importance of scheduling. I believe this is no more evident than in the diet of your child/children. I'm no dietician so there are no meal plans or anything like that from me, but I'm sure you have all heard of sayings like "You are what you eat" showing how important our diet really is. I don't want to give you any obvious advice such as that it's so important for your child to have plenty of protein, fruit, vegetables and for them to say stay well clear of sugary foods/drinks, fried food and junk food in general. I'm certainly no expert, especially when it comes to feeding time. An ongoing challenge we're facing with our daughter at the moment is that she is a painfully slow eater and we still sometimes have to help her eat. However, what I would say is that she does eat healthily and tries new things with no issues, so she will eat almost anything but it just takes a while! Another benefit of this is that she eats what we eat and so we don't have to prepare separate meals or even plan for different meal times.

Going back to some of the opening advice in the book, I think it does relate to scheduling. This is because if you do take a little time to organize, do a weekly food plan, which takes care of your meals/lunches for the week ahead, you can ensure you have control of your child's diet. Elsewhere, I also mentioned where you can become so strict with a diet that it begins to take over. So to clarify I'm not downplaying the importance of your child's diet. I just think living in the real world it's perhaps making life a little hard on yourself if you don't have any leeway to where it becomes almost an obsession of yours. This chapter is going into more detail about being proactive so that in the main you're eating healthy meals. This chapter is not about being so stringent/rigorous to say your child can never ever have a bowl of ice cream, a slice of pizza, a soda, a burger & fries or some chocolate. Like with many other points in this book some common sense comes into play which is why I just don't think diet needs to be overcomplicated. I don't think I need to spell it out in such a way by saying something like you need to give you child such things in moderation.

So let's focus on what I think is really important which is being proactive. If you don't do a little forward planning an easy trap to fall into is when you are home after a busy day, there is nothing in the fridge, you're tired/cranky, your kids are whining so what is the easiest thing to do? Get fast-food, and sure there are kids out there who love healthy foods but given the choice I think most kids would go for an unhealthy option such as something fried over a plate of vegetables. I think this is where it can become a vicious circle if you fall into this trap as I hear parents say things all the time like "my child hates fruit" or "I wish they would eat some more vegetables". But if they're used to fast foods that provide a short-term instant satisfaction then that's what they will like and usually choose when given a choice. Another beauty of planning all your meals in advance is that it removes the hassle/chore of having to think about what you will be eating for dinner that day. Again I'm talking as a real parent where sure, in an ideal world; you will have all the time in the world to pick something out for whatever you're in the mood for that day. But let's be real about it – when you have kids I think most would prefer to make life easier on themselves which is why that forward planning once again becomes key.

I'm not saying your child should never have a choice. But as a parent particularly from an early age, you need to realize that it's you who has full control/authority or whatever other word you want to use, when it comes to your child's diet. Or to put in another way, what you decide to put on the table. Don't get frustrated if you constantly give your child sugary sweets/snacks and then they flat our refuse an apple if you randomly try and give them one. In that sense, I think kids or people in general become somewhat accustomed to eating certain things. I know of some families where the children eat so healthily so without overthinking it – is that just what they're used to? On the other hand if a child is accustomed to junk food won't that be what they're used to? Look at something as simple as what your child drinks. Does your child drink enough water or do they always go for the sugary drinks? What are they used to having? What do you give them? Do you see what I'm getting at here? Maybe sometimes if you only give your child water then that's what they'll drink, if you don't give them that option. I don't think this needs to be done in some super enforcer way where it feels like your ordering your child to eat this or drink that. If anything I think you just down play it or not make a big deal of something and go with that assertive approach of this is what we're eating tonight.

This isn't rocket science advice, but do plan the day and time that you can do that weekly shop. Before you go, decide on what you will be eating for the week and plan lunches at the same time. Again this is where you need to be proactive – look at your schedule as a whole for the week. If you realize that one night is really busy when you will be on the go and you will not have time to cook, then make an extra portion of something the night before so you have some good left overs for the next day. Or, if time is tight, arrange a simple meal or can you make a batch of something and freeze it? Let's be honest as a real world parent some nights it might even be eating in the car with everything going on, but if you know this will be the case, then you can pre-make something rather than go to the nearest drive thru. To echo the point, if you do all of this ahead of time you have control and after a stressful day when you may get home a little flustered, you will already know what you're having for dinner. You will have everything you need so, although you may not feel like cooking at times, you will at least have everything prepared in advance. I'm certainly no Michelin Star chef and cooking more is something I definitely need to work on. But at the same time I would say I'm all for making life easier, so even as a novice cook, I can easily get a stew full of meat and vegetables ready with a slow cooker in no time. I can then leave it for the day until we're ready to eat. I don't want any of my advice here to undermine in anyway and I'm not trying to call anyone out if they're not making fresh home cooked meals every day – as a real world parent I know that's unrealistic. I'm simply highlighting an easy trap which I think anyone can fall into. So for those parents who have children who do have a healthy diet maybe you can understand or relate to some of these points, which may work for you? Another point I want to make is that I'm not generically labeling, that all parents do this; I just want to continue to highlight the importance of preparation/scheduling and apply it in this context.

Other examples may be that you're going out for the day or the afternoon/evening and you're not sure what your child will eat. In that case can your child eat ahead of time or can you bring something with you that you can easily prepare in advance? Again not rocket science, but it just needs that little thought for you to think forward. An additional benefit of such an approach is that, no doubt, it will save you some money as well as knowing that your child will be eating something nutritious. You know because as a parent you have taken the time to plan it out. I don't think this requires a lot of effort and if anything, it's making life easier for yourself – it just requires a little discipline and being that bit more mindful.

I would like to reiterate that I know many parents do this but, on the other hand, there are many that don't. For those who do, I do hope you can relate to the fact that forward planning plays a key role in maintaining a healthy diet for your family. Connected to this I would like to make a general point on the book as a whole at the close of this chapter. I do want to acknowledge that some of my advice will not apply in certain instances as you may already be doing things your own way and maybe with better results! I fully appreciate that some of the advice, particularly in this chapter, is pointing out the glaringly obvious. I don't think I will be amazing anyone with advice on preparing for meals ahead of time and making enough so you have left overs for the next day, things like that. Yes, there are so many parents that do this, but at the same time there will also be many who don't. Either way the main point I want to highlight is that, as a parent, you control your child's diet particularly from an early age. With the groceries you choose to buy, like it or not, you're deciding what you're feeding your child and family. This may also be obvious to some but nonetheless I want to make it abundantly clear. At one point or another I think that most parents will have challenges when it comes to the diet of their child but I think the key takeaway (excuse the pun/dad joke) is that you understand your responsibility as a parent. You also have the choice to be hands-on/active when it comes to what your child eats as well as drinks.

To round up, although this chapter is titled Diet, I didn't really touch on anything too specific with foods/drinks, as deep down I think most will know what's good or bad. I'm also going with the assumption that most if not all parents understand the importance of diet, but perhaps fall into some of the danger taps which I highlighted which can be easy to do. This is why I wanted to focus more on looking ahead and planning/organizing, because I full well know how we're more likely to be on the go, rather than necessarily having the time to eat as a family at the dinner table every single day. So I think you will become a better parent if you take more control in this area, take the responsibility and take it on yourself to make it work based on your no doubt busy schedule.

22 DOING THINGS FOR YOUR CHILDREN

I would like to share some advice that I have read or have been told several times before so you may have also received it. Either way, I think it's worth sharing or repeating as I think its great advice. Now I can't remember the exact words or how the saying goes but essentially the advice is not to do anything for your kids which they can do for themselves. I think the principle of this advice can apply throughout childhood. It will just obviously be dependent on, and will change given the age of your child as they will be only be able to do certain things subject to how old they are. This advice relates to very simple things and the examples of how I applied it relate to my 6 year old daughter, but hopefully you will get the point and apply it accordingly. Now I must start by saying I'm guilty as I still do things for my daughter when I know full well she could do it herself. I do it instead because it might save some time but, with anything, its practice so I try to constantly remind myself of this advice and apply it. So it could be something as simple as cleaning up toys. She is now old enough to do this herself. I personally don't see anything wrong in sometimes helping out but the key point of the advice I think is to ensure your kids don't become lazy, entitled or expect everything to be done for them. Parents need help and it's great when your child can start to assist with such things but, in addition to them doing you a favor, it also starts to instill some simple yet important principles. Another point of clarification here: this is not about getting to a point where your child can do an endless amount of chores or where you don't or no longer help or do anything for your child. For me this is about preventing it to where the parent does everything for their child and that it becomes some form of expectation from the child that this will just happen – time after time.

I will explain when I say I'm guilty and I know, and have seen, other parents do the same. Back to the toy example, it might be that I'm a little tired or stressed and I could ask my child to clean the toys but she still needs a bath and to get ready for bed, so my thought is well it will be a lot quicker if I just went ahead and did it. Or it might be that I ask my daughter to make her bed, but then she might not do it as neatly if my wife or I did it and again it will take her a little longer. Other simple examples include my child wanting a snack or needing to get dressed and it will be a lot easier/quicker if we just got it or did it for her.

I think as parents we also have a tendency or it's only natural to want to do things for our children to help out. But this advice is basically saying that you're not actually helping if you do everything for them. In the long-run it might actually do more harm than good. In addition to wanting to help them out, I'm sure you can all relate to my point of thinking that it saves time and it's a lot quicker/easier if we just did it for them. This may well be the case, but again I think this advice is saying to consider the long-term over that short-term/instant first thought of what is best for you in the moment. My advice is to start early with this as I think we'll all know of a kid who moans/whines just because someone asked them to do something. I think this sort of advice is generally saying take that step back and consider what is best in the moment. Back to my toy example for my daughter to clean up herself it might take 2 or 3 minutes against my 30 seconds of quickly putting everything up and away in the drawer. So I'm only saving myself a minute or so to do this when I could be teaching my daughter that she needs to learn to clean up after herself. So my advice to you, and I'm sure you have been there in such moments - when you just want get something done or out the way, this is the time to take that step back. If your child can do it, let them do it, even though it will mean prolonging something, no matter how painful that is.

Another example is my daughter learning to feed herself. I have touched on this several times in the book where the ongoing challenge for us is that she is a slow eater. So with that there are times where we might put her food on her fork/spoon and then in her mouth, essentially feeding her just to try and speed things up a little. The advice is relevant for us in this instance, in that when we do this for her, we're not really helping as she should be doing it herself. This is an example of some advice I'm sharing where I would be the first to admit we haven't got it right or all figured out. But we're continuing to work on this. I think this helps by sometimes acknowledging that you shouldn't really be doing this/that – like in our case of spoon feeding our child. With that, I think you do have to give yourself those mental reminders or ask yourself whether this is something your child can or simply should be doing. So maybe be mindful more than anything particularly with things which happen as a result of impatience or laziness. Both come into play in this simple example where as parents if we do sometimes feed our child, this is lazy on our part as well as our daughter's. Not only that we're impatient in the moment trying to hurry something along, but other than saving ourselves a few seconds, there is no real benefit of that either.

There is an endless list of examples and I think its age specific. Something I want my daughter to start doing is that when she has tennis or golf, to be responsible for her equipment – Does she have everything she needs? Does she have enough water? - Things like that! We haven't fully got there yet, but again the same principle will eventually apply. It will be easier as the parent to get everything ready and do everything for her, but I think by always doing this/that I will be missing a trick. It's important for her to become responsible for her own things and not be completely reliant on my wife and I as parents. So when I talk about expectation, if my wife and I continue to always get stuff ready for her then in a way my daughter won't even think about it or that she needs to do it. So just as the other points, clearly getting her to start doing this herself is a logical move.

Somewhat related is actually giving them the time to learn, to be patient as they will make mistakes and not get it right first time. Another simple illustration and something which again I'm a little guilty of so maybe you can learn from my mistake. My daughter was recently learning to tie her shoe laces. It was not easy for her and took a little time. But what is great, and I know most kids do the same at her age, is that she wanted to try and be that big kid and do it herself. However, there were times when she was learning where we were in a bit of a rush and my daughter still wanted to try and do it herself. But I may have been quick to tell her she couldn't as we need to go, so I took over in the moment and tied them for her. I get frustrated with myself when I do things like this because what actually was more important? I should have just taken a bit more time, that minute or two, to let her try rather than just be in a rush somewhere. In such moments, I think, as parents, we need to show that patience, as it's essentially a teaching opportunity for us to help our children learn something new. In moments like this it might well be just taking that extra minute or two. At the same time I think if there is somewhere you really need to be, like in my case, it would not have been appropriate to sit for an hour, or leave only after she learned how to do it. Some things take longer than others. All I'm saying is that in such situations we should, as parents, just slow down a little, let them try, and encourage as well as praise our child for wanting to learn and do something by themselves.

So the next time you're doing something for your children ask yourself "is this something they could actually do for themselves"? If they can let them. I think the more and more you choose/decide to do this; you will be making more of those step by step improvements in another area, thereby helping you overall to continue to become a better parent.

23 TV OR NOT TV

TV or not TV? That is the question. This is not the longest chapter in the world but I do think that it's worthy of close consideration. It may not be an issue for some, but I have to say that it does bother me when I think that my daughter has been watching a little too much TV. I just think there are so many better ways of spending that time. I'm sure there are many different thoughts on this from limiting the amount of time per day to not having a TV at all in the house. I can actually understand this approach to a certain extent, as I'm sure most would agree that reading a good book or just playing outside is far better than watching any old cartoon. So I think the jury is very much still out on this topic, but either way I will address it in this chapter.

We do have TV's in our house so I can't say we have done it yet but the thought has crossed my mind to cancel our cable subscription. However, I currently think a more logical/sensible approach is maybe more beneficial. There might be the odd day here and there where your child might watch a little too much TV but, with anything, there is balance. As a parent you need to know and recognize what is too much which makes me believe that a timer or an app which monitors how much they watch isn't really needed. Some kids would watch their favorite movie all day long if you let them so I believe some parental control is definitely required. Also a child may have watched their favorite movie three or four times, but if they have watched the same movie say over ten times, then I think as a parent you really need to consider if you're ok with that? I'm not referring to old time classics here, more the default movie you may just stick on as a go-to thing so your child zones out. Only you can answer that question and this can easily just happen if you don't have some form of control. I think a good way to look at it is that if your child is watching TV for an extended amount of time each day, and then ask yourself whether they could be doing something different and more beneficial during this time or at least a portion of that time? This is in line with comments I made earlier in the book about taking stock of how your child uses their so called free time.

Speaking personally, I have and I know a lot of others out there have too, binge watched a series on TV. I don't know about you but in the moment it's great if you're hooked to a gripping show, but at the end of it I almost feel as if I have wasted the day or time by doing this. This is the same line of thinking I have with my daughter. We have had so called lazy afternoons where she would watch a couple of movies. Whilst in the moment it feels great to sometimes just kick-back, switch off and relax, I cannot help but reflect that this was to some extent a waste of valuable time. This is not to say that as a parent you can never relax, hit pause and that you always have to be doing something or be on the go. But this is more about looking at your child or what as a family you're doing with your time when you might be all together.

I know for us there are times when you're flat out exhausted or just need a little break, so I personally don't think there is anything to feel guilty about if you put the TV on for half an hour or so. I think all parents can relate to times when you all just need to chill out and take a little time for yourself. Or there might be times when you want to clean the house or some chores and if your kids are not quite old enough to help out too much, again I see no harm in putting the TV on. However, there are still better options to consider, so what I'm saying is not to always have it as your go to thing to settle down your child, essentially having it always as your first resort. Again why not have them color or play with some of their toys as alternative options when you need a little break or "time-out" yourself? I say this because as parents we do have to be mindful of the norms we establish. So if we always put the TV on as a "norm" in this example; why would a child suddenly say one day I want to read instead? I'm not saying that could never happen, but chances are this is going to be unlikely.

It's like when you see a kid with a phone or tablet playing a game or watching a cartoon in a restaurant. I used to say before I became a parent that I would never in a million years allow my kid to do that. I do have to say I slightly eased up on that thought after having children. I still don't really agree with it to a certain extent, but sometimes needs must. My view is that if your toddler is having a monumental tantrum or breakdown in a restaurant and you know that if you let them watch a show on one of your devices it will settle them down, then it's a no brainer - do it. I don't think this is the time to try and set an example and make a scene - it will obviously cause you stress as well as the others trying to eat their meals who also need consideration. Of course another option is to take your child outside, but if you know that they will settle down if you put a show on and you, and everyone else for that matter, can enjoy a meal in peace I don't think many would hold it against you. However, my advice here is not for it to become the norm – we have all seen a family of four at a restaurant, all on their mobile devices/tablets, not saying a word to each other and I think we would all agree that the other extreme is certainly not the way to go. Back to the example of settling down your child, this also goes against the advice of thinking long-term over short-term. In this scenario you would be going with the short-term option but, hey, at the end of the day we're real world parents so occasionally needs must. That is the point my advice is do it sparingly and as and when it's really appropriate for you. To put it another way, I'm not saying that the TV should necessarily be seen as a last resort, but my advice is not to have it as your default response/first resort or go to thing, just to get some peace and quiet. That's when I think the norm for what I have been referring to can easily become established.

I suppose we could debate this subject all day long and I still don't think there will be a definitive answer other than some form of moderation. I think you can actually make a good case for both in a debate – to have and to not. Of course, I suppose what your child is watching is important too so I'm not saying you can't be mindful of that either. However, I do believe there are some great benefits of watching certain things on TV. There are, of course, things like nature shows or educational programs. My daughter is developing a liking to golf and tennis and I think it's great to see her watching the pros on TV and then getting a club in the house imitating a putting stroke or swing for example. You can't measure the benefit but surely it's great for your kids to witness someone winning a gold medal at the Olympics, learning about the hard work, sacrifice and dedication that it takes to get there? Similarly if your kid loves sports, I would encourage them to watch games, matches, events and have role models that they draw inspiration from and can aspire to. We all see kids wearing the jerseys of their favorite player with pride. They may say something like "I want that to me someday playing in front of a big crowd" and the reality of this is that this comes from them watching their role model on TV. I'm sure many kids out there have got or wanted to get started in something after seeing an athlete or a singer on stage on TV as just two examples – so my view is that it's certainly not all bad.

Aside from this, I occasionally love for our daughter to get into bed with us, snuggle up and watch a movie, particularly at Christmas time. Yeah there are a lot of cheesy holiday movies that may not provide any educational value or anything like that, but I would still consider this as quality time together when it's done once in a while. Using an example like this I think relates to some of points elsewhere in other chapters, when I advise to not worry about always doing everything by the book or step by step.

So to conclude here I don't think TV should be ruled out of the household completely - just my view of course. The pros and cons of having a TV in the home can be debated/looked at all day long, so I think this is very much a personal call. However, my advice to you is to give this area at least some more consideration, and have a good idea of how often your child watches TV. As a parent, my view is that you should know if your child watches too much TV and think of other positive ways they can spend their time; thereby reducing the amount that they're sitting in front of a box. Sure there might be a day or two over the summer, for example if the weather is bad on a rainy day, where they might watch a little too much or have an afternoon of watching a couple of movies. I personally don't see any major harm in letting that slide. But as in other chapters, I have highlighted the importance of how your child spends their time, so just make sure when this happens it's on more of an occasional rather than a frequent basis. Perhaps like with certain things when it comes to parenting, with TV being no exception, there is no need to overcomplicate it or overthink it, that is if common sense is applied. I don't really see the need for a strict set of household rules or guidelines. I will talk later in the book on the importance of being honest as a parent and here is no exception. As a parent, only you'll know if your child watches way too much TV. So whether you have one or not, or are in favor or against, to become that better parent I think at least consider all this and keep going back to ask yourself: Is there something else/better they could be doing? – Certainly if indeed they do watch a little too much. It all comes back to your child's time. Truly value it and if you always place high importance on how they use it, then this all should really take care of itself. So if anything this may be an area just to be a little more mindful, attentive and considerate again to help make you become a better parent.

24 COMMITMENTS

If you come across any personal/professional development tips/advice or study traits of successful people in general, a common one is that they learn and know how to say no. Now I think this is good advice for anyone, but specifically and significantly for any parent. This relates back to the importance of the opening chapters of scheduling/planning/time management, as it lays out your priorities. Therefore, when you know that you have your own commitments and are disciplined in sticking to them, then you're in a better position to say "no" to something as you know you already have other plans/priorities. As parents we have so many different responsibilities/obligations from personal/family related matters to work/professional as well as other external commitments. When our plates are already full it's easy to feel some outside pressure, especially when you're asked to add to your full list because even though you may do so much, with the world we live in there is an element of the; What have you done for me lately?

Before I go on, I must clarify that this doesn't mean you now say "no" to everything that comes your way and refuse to do anything that impacts your schedule. I did also highlight the fact that you need to be flexible and adaptable. So if your parent needs a ride to the doctors, or something else of importance comes up, you obviously need to adjust. What I'm referring to here are the types of things that you don't really want to do, have little importance and are insignificant. Listen, some people are better at saying no than others. Sometimes it's hard when you're put on the spot and you don't want to offend/upset anyone or anything like that. Even your response to these types of situations takes practice and time to be confident to do so. For me, I don't really like being put on the spot for anything so I always tend to respond with a genuine response that "I need to check first and I will let you know". When I say "genuine" I mean it. We all know, as parents, how busy things get, so you do need to check in with schedules and maybe other family members to even see if it's a possibility. This time then allows you to actually assess if you do want to do something if your schedule permits. This little bit of advice is more of an aside of letting you know what works for me.

As a parent there are times when I think you just need to put yourself and your family first and I definitely don't think there is anything selfish in doing that. To illustrate my point, I will try to give some hypothetical examples, but hopefully you will get what I'm saying and can think of your own by drawing on past experiences. You might be asked to sign up for a weekly class, go to an event, help plan an event, volunteer, join a club, go on a weekend trip, sign up for a course outside of work and the list can go on and on. If something sounds appealing and you want to and can do it, then go for it. What I'm saying here is that if you're asked to do something that you really don't want to do then my advice to you is not to sign up. The bottom line is that if I'm going to commit to something that is going to take me away from my time with my family, it had better be worth it. I will quickly refer back to an earlier chapter which might seem a little contradictory when looking at living in your bubble so to speak and not shutting out the rest of the world. But this is really about not stretching yourself way too far with additional commitments (unexpected or unsolicited) when we all know how stretched we already are as parents.

This might not apply to you, but I think we all know of someone who doesn't like to say no, or offend, or feel like they're letting someone down, or create any tension, things like that. As a result, it's hard for them to say no. Or, on the other hand, it might be something which you have been asked to do which everyone else is doing so you go along with it. So it might seem much easier in the moment to say "yes" and sometimes you might even feel pressurized into doing so. Again, my advice here is that, if you already have too much on your plate and say yes to something you don't want to do, then this is really when your family suffers. I think we have all had times when we take things out on the ones we love because we may feel overwhelmed with other things/commitments. It could be something so minor that tips us over the edge and this can, more often than not, happen with a loved one who is actually the last person you want to take any frustration out on. If any of this resonates with you my advice is for you to become a little more selfish. Put yourself and your family first if you're doing too many other things for the benefit of others and not for yourself or your family. Does this now make you a selfish person by being a little selfish in this instance or from time to time? In my view it certainly doesn't. I think there is a huge distinction between a selfish person and someone who merely prioritizes time with their family. Again when I say putting them first, I mean it bearing in mind any additional commitments to your already existing ones. Quite frankly it might not be fair for you to commitment yourself to something else, certainly if it takes more time away from your family and certainly if that time is already extremely limited as it is.

It's worth repeating that learning to say "no" doesn't mean you now don't do anything for anyone else. I'm sure as a parent you may need to call on a friend or a family member sometimes for a favor and likewise they made do the same with you from time to time. So if a friend needs help and you can help, then do so. The only thing I would say be mindful of is to make sure that a one off, or a once in a while favor, doesn't become an everyday one. For example, it might be that you're asked to pick up another child one day after school along with yours and look after that child for a couple of hours in the afternoon. But then that one off favor might turn into a weekly request or even possibly a daily one. This is where you need to recognize what's going on and step in before it goes any further and no longer do it – only if you don't want to of course. The reason I say this is that I know that my wife and I, using this example, couldn't look after another child after school as we already have commitments which would get compromised if we let something like this happen. So we're just not in a position to where we can/could even consider it. Sure we can do something like this every now and then for a friend or neighbor but all I'm reinforcing is to learn to say "no" when someone else is maybe asking too much. This is just one example, so it may well be something else. As parents, I think we can all relate to a past situation when someone else is perhaps taking advantage, when you, yourself, have enough on your plate!

To touch on one more example in more detail which might be more personal to you, let's look at a course offering that might be available. It might be one offered by/through your employer or one that you're considering to voluntarily sign up to. Now there are so many different courses out there these days, so with something like this I think you need to take some time, do some research, and then determine if it's all worthwhile. The point is that, whilst there are some good if not great courses available, on the same note there are some bad ones too – or it may be just a case of something's not relevant to you. A course might a good one but it might just be that it's not relevant to you based on things like your current level, current qualifications or years of experience. My advice is don't just say "yes" immediately because you think it will be another thing to add to your resume/CV. Ask questions, speak to people who may have previously done the course, ask yourself: What's really in it for me? Will it be worth my while in helping me on the job, or to learn a new skill? Will I learn anything or something new? Is it linked or related to what I'm currently doing or looking to do? A motivation might be that it might help get you recognized, help with a promotion or pay rise but you really need to analyze the reality of any of this happening.

The reason I say this is that I have done a course or two before that took me away from my family on weekends and in the evenings, plus it required additional study in my own time. Now I can safely say that after completing the course there was no real benefit gained from doing it. I didn't really learn anything new and it has made no difference at all to my current position or career. I was the person who was quick to say "yes" without doing that bit of groundwork/research beforehand. I didn't fully consider the commitment required and how much time it would actually take to complete. I appreciate you need to look at both sides, so I will also say you don't necessarily need to check/tick every box to justify why you should sign up for something like a course – sometimes it might well be you don't know until you try. If something sounds really interesting and you want to learn more then go for it. I suppose I'm just trying to make more of a general point here. I would guess at one time or another, something has come your way which you weren't really sure about - where it's a case of should I, shouldn't I? You may want to be seen as doing the right thing or appear to set some form of impression. If anything, I think all of this goes back to establishing all of your priorities where you're only doing things that are important to you, when you do have a choice. To cover my own back, I want to make it very clear this is not about refusing or turning down things which are directly linked to your priorities – like something for your job/employer. I want to make the distinction between the necessary or the things that you're perhaps required to do vs. shall we say the optional. It's for those optional choices where there is no obligation, when I think you really do need to consider the commitment when it will be taking time away from your family. After consideration you may determine you need/want to do it and there is nothing wrong with that, the main thing I suppose is that you carefully thought it all out before it's too late to change your mind.

To further clarify, sometimes it's sort of natural to jump at something which is offered to you, such as a course offering or some form of invite to an event. It also might not be straight forward as you may not have a choice if you're effectively told by your employer that you need to do a certain course or travel to some form of event/function. My personal example relates to something which I essentially volunteered myself to do – to the point I just made, it was optional. So when you do have a choice and there is no, shall we say, pressure on you to do anything outside of your regular work commitments, then I reiterate, my advice is to make sure it will be worth your while before you say "yes" or sign up. So let me make one final point on this before I move on so there is no misunderstanding. I do think courses, learning, education which all fall under, whether you want to call it personal/self or professional development, are extremely important. As they're extremely important my advice is to take that time to carefully select any additional optional/elective offerings which are available to you so that you make best use of your valuable time. Because if you don't do this I think you end up missing out in two ways – one, you don't learn/develop (you miss that opportunity) and two, it means you lose out on time with your family. It's the second point I would really like to emphasize, as there is nothing more frustrating than missing out on things with your family for something which has no value – and certainly if you signed up for it!

Let's look at some other examples. It might be that you volunteer and you enjoy it, doing what you can, when you can, but are then asked to do more of the same. My view here is that, even if it's for a worthy cause, don't feel pressurized or feel bad if you're already doing all you can and simply can't do or take on anymore. Sometimes it might be the case you actually would love to do more but it's just not physically possible with all of your other commitments. As the saying goes, I find honesty is the best policy here. I think if you're open, honest and transparent I think you will find it becomes a lot easier to deal with the many different things that come our way as parents. Even now with our daughter's school there are weekly events that we can sign up for as parent volunteers, but the reality is that it's impossible to do, and sign up for everything. Even something like this requires us looking ahead and being selective as to what we can, can't and actually want to do. So if there is a field trip we know about in a few months' time where volunteers are needed, we can be more selective with our commitments and make sure we do all we can if we do want to go.

We all know the saying that time is precious. I think we all come to realize this or understand more of its importance at different stages in our lives. For me, becoming a parent made me realize this more than ever. So I will keep saying it, the point is if I'm now going to do something that is going to take me away from family time, it better be worth it. We all have commitments in life and some things we can't escape from or sometimes we can't just simply say I'm not doing that. Well not as a real world parent anyway. This is definitely not about saying no to the things you really need to do or are actually "committed" to. So what I'm really referring to here are the other commitments we have outside of work, voluntarily sign up for, or where we do have choice or more of a say in the matter. My advice to you is to seriously consider those and anything extra you commit to as, essentially, this will take you away from your family time and moments shared with your children. I always remember a term from an economics class I took in College, which is the "opportunity cost" of something. In the economics class it looked more at money or cash where essentially or the way I understood it, is that opportunity cost is looking at what else you could spend or use that money on. I think the same very much applies in relation to time and not just money. So in reference to time the opportunity cost is looking at what else you could you could be doing with your time – when I say what else I'm really meaning could that be with your children/family? So I bring that up as I think you really do have to consider the alternatives - especially with your own time and especially when it comes to your kids.

I will try to highlight the point even more providing other personal experiences and giving different types of examples. The first one is that I used to play for a soccer club purely on a recreational level. The standard was ok, we had a good team, there was a good group of guys and I enjoyed playing. In terms of a commitment we used to train twice a week after work and then play every Saturday. This was more than manageable before I had my first child and for me, even in that first year of my daughter's life when children do sleep a lot. But it changed for me when my daughter became a lot more interactive and suddenly I was faced with, essentially, a dilemma. The dilemma was that I was committed to a soccer team three days a week and that was taking valuable time away from me and my child/family. So I made the call at the end of a season to stop playing as I was gaining some more responsibility at work and for me, it was too hard to do it all.

We're all different so I'm not trying to offend anyone here who plays for a team or a club and has children, as I fully understand the need to have a life outside of your own kids. My advice is not to quit a team or anything like that, I'm just trying to get across my point of view and that I came to the conclusion in this case that I couldn't have, or do it all. Saturday was a day off for me and if we had an away game with travel I would be gone for most of the day. So I did what I wanted to do and decided to give up my commitment to the recreational team because I now wanted to spend that time with my daughter. The way I saw it something had to give. Sure in an ideal world I could still do both but in danger of stating the obvious as a parent you can't be in two places at once! Sometimes you might feel some external pressure from, maybe, teammates in my example to not give it up. But this goes back to the opening statement in this chapter by learning to say "no" when you no longer want to do something. You ultimately make the call what's right for you and what you want to do.

Another example is that a friend of mine is nearing retirement and she belongs to a group outside of her work where she is a board member. To clarify in this instance this group was not related to my work or employer so this would very much have been me voluntarily signing up. She approached me to see if I would be interested in replacing her as she was looking to step down. In this case I asked for all of the information she could provide, learned about the group and what it did and what my commitment would entail. Here I didn't just say "no", I did give it full consideration, but I decided to decline as it wasn't for me and I anticipated I would have some schedule conflicts. I looked at this in a couple of different ways. I didn't want to miss out on anything with my family but I also didn't want to be in a position where I would be seen as unreliable. I would hate to sign up for something but have to regularly turn people down or have to turn around at the last minute to say I can't attend something.

Speaking more generally, you might work for a company that offers many resources to its employees. These might include events outside of working hours and access to different social groups/activities. Let me also make it clear here, if this is the case, I think that is great and I would recommend being active with such groups/offerings. I actually think it's very important to do so. All I would suggest and on the same line, is that you ensure that you do a bit of research before signing up or learn the specifics of an event before you go. I just think that you need to find out more about things first before you say yes to something, particularly if there are many different options available to you. Occasionally I find people try to please everyone or are quick to jump on something and I just don't think you can do that with your time as a parent. I repeat this doesn't mean you're selfish or have anything to feel guilty about if you feel the need, at times, to put you and your family first by saying no to something.

I have come across advice before saying that you can have it all. But when it comes to time and commitments, I would argue against that ideology. Take my soccer example, don't get me wrong I did enjoy playing and it's not like I just suddenly wanted to stop playing. I genuinely just wanted to spend as much time with my daughter as possible outside of work so the way I saw it, something had to give. Similarly, it could be that you're a season ticket holder of your favorite sports team or that you play a round of golf every weekend. Again I'm not saying you have to stop doing your favorite things, but ultimately some sacrifice may need to come into play at some point. Or it may be that you compromise a little, so that you can still do the same activity, but not as much. That weekly round of golf with the guys now might become every other week or once a month. Or, as in my case with soccer, I signed up for a work team with my previous employer which played games more on an ad hoc basis. It was still fun but the benefit for me was that there was no formal commitment, no weekly training sessions and therefore was a lot more manageable. All I'm saying is to consider your existing commitments if you're frustrated with the lack of family time that you have. The same also applies to new commitments. This is ever evolving as there will always be new things you're asked to do and consider, so my advice to you is know what you're signing up for and getting yourself into. Not only that, know what's really feasible based on those existing commitments.

The difficulty in all of this is that I know the importance of having a life outside of your children. Some of this advice at first-hand might give the impression that now you have kids you have to shut yourself off to the outside world and your whole life now completely revolves around them. So, in relation to this point, if you really do love doing something and you don't want to give it up, then don't. Don't stop doing something that might in a way lead to resentment. The reality is that there is no simple answer and you have to determine what is really appropriate in your situation. If anything, this chapter is really highlighting the importance of considering those potential new commitments which are presented to us all the time. For a real world parent our days and schedules are already at capacity, or so it seems, so if anything just be mindful of the new things/requests which come your way. I don't know about you but there always seems to be something going on with my daughter be it sports, or school, where new things come up all the time. So we do really have to consider what we can feasibly do and sign up for given the fact that we now also have a new born son. Some may not agree with my decision to stop playing for my soccer team but I'm sure you would agree that this takes time away from my family – its fact. So it's a big predicament really. Sometimes it might be a case of having to give up something that you like/enjoy, and still want to, but it's just that now you are choosing something else which is actually more important to you. That maybe the main and only reason. This may well help you by looking at something in more of a logical/objective way like this, that is if you're currently experiencing a similar type of predicament.

I wanted to share this with you and explain how my stance and position has changed over something which I used to really care about and has been affected, since I became a parent. We all know priorities change and this is one that certainly changed for me. So it might not even be a sports team, but look at where some of your priorities lie and assess if they're actually in line. I reiterate that I'm sharing my personal experience here and this chapter is meant to be more thought provoking. Thought provoking mainly in how we direct our energy to certain commitments because for me, I adjusted some of my commitments/priorities after becoming a parent. An important point to make here is that I chose to make the adjustment as this was something where I did have a choice and could make such a decision.

I hope my examples have presented you with a good picture of how to look at and how to deal with new and existing commitments. It could be that your season ticket for your favorite sports team no longer gets renewed but a compromise is that maybe you still go to some of the games, just not all of them. Or that weekly night out with your buddies turns into a monthly one. You don't need me to tell you that there are other options, so you can make it work if something is still really important to you to not give up entirely. Also another quick point to consider is a commitment such as new pets. I don't want to be a buzz kill here because I love animals. I say this because we do have a dog so I know first-hand what's involved on top of having kids. If you do decide to get a pet, this is a huge commitment. You should know ahead of time what will be involved bearing in mind your existing commitments, as you will have to consider the animal to ensure that they will get enough love and attention. Maybe looking at something like new pets requires a bit more focus, but I at least wanted to bring it up because it certainly relates too many of the points already made in relation to commitments. We're fully committed to our dog and I don't want to discourage in anyway as he is very much part of the family. We wouldn't change him for the world and it's great to have a dog as part of our family, so if anything I would encourage it, I just want to keep highlighting the level of commitment that's involved. I'm actually thinking more about the pet here as like I said you really need to understand what's involved in having as in our case being, a dog. I think it's best summed up by the saying "A Dog Is For Life, Not Just for Christmas."

As parents our commitments ever evolve with our children as they get older. It's difficult to manage at times but the key is that you don't want to be in a position where you have to say "no" to things you want to do because you're already committed to things you don't actually want to do. Maybe a rule of thumb is to be as prudent with your time outside of your work life which includes your family time, as you probably are with your money, when consider your existing as well as those potential new commitments. I think if you do this, then this will be another way in where you can become a better parent.

25 JOB/CAREER

I did reference your job in the previous chapter in relation to potential course offerings and other commitments outside of your regular working hours. The main focus in that area is to ensure that if you're going to sign up or say yes to anything which maybe optional, then it best be worth your while/valuable time. Essentially do some background research to know what you're signing up for and getting yourself into. Now I do want to shift focus to look in more detail at your current job/profession, career and future career aspirations/next steps. As I have said in numerous chapters, clearly we're all from different walks of life, have different jobs, all live in different places and pursue different professional careers. However, I do think that most would agree that it's hard to manage both professional and family life when it may seem at times, that they're pulling you in opposite directions. I think it's so important to have a chapter on this topic as a parent. I can imagine for the vast majority that time at work takes/makes up the vast majority of their day, week, month and year. Essentially our life, so needless to say that as parents we do need to consider this so closely given the fact it enables us to provide for our family but it also takes time away from it. Clearly you can't have one without the other so this is not about choosing between providing for or spending time with your family, so with that let's start to look at this a little deeper.

You hear all the time these days the term work/life balance. Again this will have some differences in meaning to some, but what is clear is that it's as important as it's ever been. Work/life balance obviously doesn't only apply to parents, but when I come to think of it, when we refer to balance with our profession, I'm sure more often than not that people would refer to their family time away from work – especially if you're a parent! Speaking personally, work/life balance is so important to me. I want to spend time and be with my family/children as much as possible and I don't want to miss out on the oh so many firsts, events, and the many experiences with my kids. Some things you just can't get back and are priceless, like being there for their first day of school as just one example. This is where the term "balance" is key. Don't get me wrong, I know of the importance of my professional career and being in a position to provide for my family so I'm not underestimating or downplaying the importance of this either. Again to emphasize it's about balance; quite simply you can't neglect either side as you will potentially suffer the significant consequences.

Before I go any further when I refer to balance in this instance, I think I've been around the block enough to understand this is not about some perfect 50/50 balance where your time is equally divided. Again this is about being a real world parent, so I full-well know it's unrealistic that each day has a seamless balance between your work and family time. I get that there are times for all of us where some days, weeks, months or a certain time of the month is going to be more hectic or busier than others. So this is really taking a step back and looking at your life and career in an overall sense, to make the determination if you do get to enjoy enough regular quality time with your family?

I won't go into great depth about my current role and who I work for but I will touch on some key aspects. I'm fortunate in that I currently do have a good work/life balance – I'm extremely grateful for this and certainly don't take it for granted. Benefits related to this are having every other Friday off and having flexible working arrangements. This means I can enjoy quality time with my family particularly after work and at weekends. As I have said on many occasions, my daughter has developed a love for sports, most notably golf and tennis. She has progressed so well for a girl of her age. Some might say it's a natural talent, which may well be true, but I'm also a firm believer in practice and hard work. Now I don't want to take any credit away from my daughter because she is the one putting in the practice and hard work. But she has the opportunity to do so because I have the time to take her as a result of my schedule. This is mainly after school and at weekends too – we also benefit from the climate in Florida where we can do things outside all year round. These are precious moments I get to share with my daughter on an almost daily basis and I have the joy to see first-hand my child's development.

I think a professional career balanced with the role of a parent is so difficult to master when, at times and as already mentioned, it's as if your career and family life are pulling you in different directions. On top of that, although you may have choices which I will touch more upon later, the choices themselves are not simple or straight forward. Let me explain. So to continue with my current job, I do enjoy a good work/life balance but I would be the first to admit that whilst I certainly don't consider myself underpaid, at the same time I think like most families money can be tight at times. I also think that, like most modern day parents, what comes in each month goes out in paying bills. So essentially we live pay check to pay check so to speak. Now I will give you another example of someone we know who made this point to my wife when she met her in the grocery store just the other day. She too has a daughter who plays golf and she saw us practicing one night and she made a comment to my wife along the lines of: "I wish my husband could do that more often with my daughter." I'm going to generalize a little here as I admit my next comments will have some presumptions but I do know that the lady I'm referring to lives in a multi-million dollar home. I also know that her husband travels a lot so I'm again guessing he is very well paid for what he does - although I don't even know his profession! Now this is not a criticism, but a simple example like this shows how your career and family life pull you in opposite directions. You may be able to provide everything your family needs, live in a wonderful home with nice cars etc. But sometimes you have to ask yourself is that all worth it if you hardly ever see your kids? Money may never be an issue and paying the bills may never be a worry, but sometimes you may need to consider what's more valuable. As the saying goes, money isn't everything, but I'm not going to try to be all ideological/philosophical with no sense of reality and try to pretend it's not important either. In my view earning a living is vital when trying to raise a family, I don't think there is any hiding from that. So I think this provides another example of how two very important things can be going against each other.

Without being all philosophical you do need to consider what a successful career looks like to you. It's simplistic, but perhaps natural, to look at someone who earns a lot of money with a big house and a fancy car and think he/she must be successful. There is no getting away from it, how much you earn does link to how much you can provide for your family so again the individual who can give a child everything they need may again be seen as a success. You have probably figured that I'm leading you down a path here to come to the point that may all well be true, but if that person hardly ever sees their family because they're working all the time then is that person really a success? Only you can respond to such a question but I do acknowledge that it's not always a straight forward answer as individual circumstances vary so much. For me, a successful career is one where I can provide for my family, but can also enjoy a healthy work/life balance. I just think you can't put a value on being such a big part of your child's life as they grow up – it's priceless.

It's not easy to make simple comparisons as it's never really comparing apples to apples but, speaking personally, I would not want a job even if it paid a huge salary, if it meant I would hardly ever see my kids. If it resulted in me having to travel and work all the time with no sense of balance in my life, again for me it would just not be worth it. Looking way down the line when you approach the end of your life, I can only presume, but at that point the house, the fancy cars and the material objects are now worthless. Sure you may want to leave your kids with a healthy inheritance, I get it, but I think you can still do that with good financial choices – but that is a whole other discussion.

There is no doubt about it there is pressure on parents to raise a family. It's natural to want to provide and give your children the best possible life or give them things or opportunities that you never had as a child. But I think the reality is that you have to weigh everything up and trade-offs may be required. It might be that you don't live in the biggest house, don't have a brand new car, but you do have that regular/frequent precious time with your children. It might not seem a big deal in the moment but being able to play with your child each day after work and at weekends is certainly something not to take for granted. Again I reiterate we're not presented with a simple choice of "pick one or the other" as our career can naturally evolve and gravitate you in a direction or to a position which is then hard just to walk away from. For example, I can only presume that it's not straight forward for the CEO of a company to say "I now just want to become one of the workers." Or it may be that you own your own business and with that great responsibility it would be hard for you just to turn around and say one day "I don't want to do this anymore". As we all know life is not that simple.

However, I do want to touch on your job or your potential next steps in your career as a parent and for those of you who might be reading this as an expecting parent. This is where you may have some control/choice and bearing in mind what I have just shared, it will at least enable you to consider what is actually more important to you. Throughout this book I'm always trying to be "real" and in the "real-world" so to speak. So I don't want to give some ideological career advice to you and say that you should pick a job which you will most enjoy, provide endless fulfilment whilst also being able to enjoy quality family time, earning a big salary. That is the ideal/perfect world, but most parents live in the real world. Therefore, I think it's important to consider the realities rather than fantasies, although this is still not to say you're not ambitious with your career.

When I hear career advice which encourages you to do what you love, follow your passion, I just think its ideological advice coming from someone in a privileged position. I'm sure there are plenty of stories out there of people who are great parents who do what they love and enjoy a great quality of life, I'm not denying that. At the same time, I know there are many parents, whose main concern is providing for their family first, paying the bills and putting food on the table. So whilst it would be great if they could do this doing something they love, I know for many this is very much not the case. Doing what they love is not the main concern as the primary focus is to earn a living. Generally speaking, I personally think that a lot of people don't love their job, but they do it as it's necessary to provide for their family. Now I can almost hear someone respond to this with something along the lines of "if you're not doing something you love, quit or do something else." But I think such advice is almost useless if you're a real world parent with a family to support. Sure this advice needs to be applied individually but at face value its saying quit something, but quit at the expense of no longer being able to pay the bills, rent or mortgage? It's a lot easier said than done. We can talk about all that philosophical stuff but, at the end of the day, let's face it, would the vast majority of people do what they're doing if they weren't getting paid for it? You may also hear things like money doesn't matter, but I think that's nonsense especially when trying to raise a family. I get it that money is not the be-all and end-all and there is a lot more to life, but there is no doubt that you have to factor it in – again when trying to bring up a family. That is my view anyway, where perhaps there is even a balance or trade-offs required with something like your salary. All I'm trying to say is that you can't just ignore its importance. If you have all the money in the world then yes you can perhaps be a bit more philosophical, but in the real world we have to face reality.

In essence what I'm trying to say is that I think that, for most people, their work is considered a job and as a necessity more than anything else. However, it doesn't mean they hate it. I'm certainly not saying for all, but I think for some if not many a job is just that, a job. I admit and I repeat, I'm generalizing here as there are people out there who get paid a fortune doing what they love - sports stars being an obvious example. But again this is a book on real world parenting, so I think that for most in the real world this doesn't apply to them. It's more about doing your job and getting paid – that is perhaps the main priority. As this doesn't apply to all, my statement is a sweeping/broad brush one I know that. But to give an example, I know of so many parents, after they have had a baby, who would love nothing more than to become a stay-at-home parent. That's what they want to do and they even hate the thought of having to go back to work because they don't want to leave their baby with someone else. I think for those in a position where one of the parents can stay home, I tend to find that most do just that. Obviously some can't because they need to work financially, but I think given the choice many would prefer to be home with their child. So the financial element is more of a necessity than a love for a career. Or it may be for some when child care is that expensive that it actually pays for one of the parents to stay home because the net effect is that you would essentially be saving money. So again in such a case it's not the love of the job or career where returning to work is the parent's main concern or priority.

Again I know that some people love what they do, are great at it and are great parents too – they make it work. So these points I repeat certainly don't relate to everyone and some parents may want to go back to work and I'm certainly not saying that there is anything wrong with that either. The main point that I'm trying to make is that I think you sometimes hear of advice which tries to romance a career, things like "do what you love and you'll never work a day in your life". You know I have been honest throughout and as a real parent and with the parents that I interact with all the time, in the real world I think this is all somewhat make-believe. I think that for some, certain things need to be thrown out the window after having a kid in that they simply have bills to pay and a family to support. So the notion of following your passion or doing something you love may be great but if that doesn't put food on the table how can that work or be sustainable? Or what about the parent working multiple jobs to make ends meet – are they doing this because they love it? Can you just quit your job to follow your passion? I dare say that it's not as simple as that. Can you risk everything to start a new business? Sure you can, but the risk may be far too great for some especially for parents who are financially responsible for raising their family. I personally think a lot of career advice you hear is from people who are in a privileged position and they have earned that right, so this is certainly not a criticism. There are also many rags to riches stories out there, or examples of parents or families who had nothing but then went on to enjoy great success. There are no doubt stories out there to inspire us all to prove that it can be done but, again, I think that for a real parent with the day-to-day challenges we face, it's certainly a lot easier said than done.

So I say all of this to help you gain some perspective. I have only worked for two companies and my previous employer was great to me but on reflection and comparing it to the company I currently work for, I did not enjoy as much of a work/life balance. Like many, I worked long hours but one of the main downsides was that I always felt that I was "on call" outside of regular office hours. It wasn't quite a 24/7-365 job but nonetheless it was demanding. In my current role, I'm no longer on call all of the time outside of working hours and feel I do have separation in that, when I do log off, I'm off. I think this is important as it works both ways insofar that when I'm at work I can fully focus because I have that better balance. My job is still demanding and can get hectic at times, but I feel that I can still enjoy that separation, particularly in the evening, weekends and on vacation. Now I just don't think I could go back given the choice, having experienced a different side where I didn't have such a balance. Back to my previous point, I do think work/life balance is somewhat of a luxury to have and in that sense I'm lucky - I certainly don't take it for granted! Not everyone can enjoy that work/life balance in their job/industry/profession. Now if I was to move up levels within the company and into different positions with additional responsibility, then this may all change so again it's about whether I want to actively pursue that. When I say it would be hard to go back given the choice I emphasize the word "choice" as, don't get me wrong, if I had no choice such that I was going to lose my job for example, then obviously I would do it. It does all depend on individual circumstances.

So let's stay on the element of choice and when we're faced or presented with one such as a new opportunity. I haven't really mentioned the death of my daughter Emily in this book and that has been intentional as it's far too personal for me to share. What I would say is that my outlook on life has drastically changed after her death. My whole perspective on life has changed to where my career ambitions have altered. That is not to say that I'm not ambitious, but I just want to take a different route as I value my family time too much. Consequently, I want to take a different career path and that is my choice. Sometimes I wonder whether you can have it all? Can you have the top job with the highest salary and be the best parent you can be? I believe there are exceptions to every rule so I'm sure there are people out there who can/do. But I think for the vast majority that it's somewhat of a fantasy to have it all in that sense. The main thing I consider or factor with all of this is time, actually having the valuable time available to spend with family – nothing else really. You can never be in two places at once so when I refer to having it all, sometimes I just wonder how that's even possible. Related to this, technically you can try and do two things at the same time, constantly check in on messages, taking calls trying to switch your mind from one thing to the other. However, whilst some are better than others at multi-tasking and whilst it's practical or somewhat of a necessity in some cases, I just don't think it works as far as family/work time is concerned. I have previously highlighted the significance of being present when with your family which I believe is so important. So again this is another thing to consider, whether you do have enough opportunities to be truly present with your children on a regular basis?

Looking at it from a very simplistic point of view, if you're stressed all of the time, your schedule is always full of meetings, your head is constantly spinning, then how can you balance this with being the best possible parent that you can be? This is where it comes back to the question of what you value more? Perhaps, and arguably the biggest gift you can give your child throughout their childhood is your time. Your time then translates into love and attention. The aim being undivided attention but as we all well know, for the modern day parent, this is becoming increasing challenging. I think that if you work all hours of the day, travel, are on call, stressed etc. then it is hard to have it all when it comes to work and your family. I reiterate my point for some out there you don't have too much of a choice. As I have already said I would do the same thing if I had to, and if it was the only way to provide for my family. Some might turn around and say "you can quit your job if you don't like what you're doing" but we all know that it's not as easy as that when you have a family to provide for. Personally I think that this too is ideological thinking which isn't really applicable to so many people in the real world.

Let me explain a little more with choice, providing a real life example. The point is that not everyone has a choice with multiple options. It was not that long ago that we went on a short family vacation – we went on a mini-cruise for 3 nights from Port Canaveral which is close to where we live. Many of the people working on the ship were from countries all over the world. You could almost sense it with some that, without them directly saying anything as I saw it in their face, how much they missed home and their family. When they looked at our family together with our daughter at the time you could not help but think that some were trying to see their own little boy or girl through ours. Some people working on the ship would go months on end without seeing their family. We did not go into too much detail but essentially you got the impression that they had no real alternatives or choices and they needed the job to provide for their family as there were few opportunities in their homeland. So I suppose, in a way, that it's almost survival mode as providing the essentials for your family is the first priority. So what I'm saying is that if I had no choice and it meant I had to do a certain job to provide my family because I had little or no other option, then of course I would do it. Not everyone has a choice - I get that!

Related to this I also acknowledge that there are people who serve their country, for example in the military, sacrificing so much for their family and for the benefit of many other families across the world. So it's hard to generalize in this sense and put everyone in the same basket, as certain careers are so unique where the purpose and sacrifice is actually sometimes for the greater good. So like with many of the other chapter in the book, consider the points made, apply what's relevant to your own circumstances and make your own conclusions. I appreciate some things won't be relevant and there are many more things to consider when it comes to a career and raising a family. So perhaps the main thing is just to give all of this the full consideration it deserves.

However, for some, you may have a choice or at least more options, particularly if you work for a big company/organization which provides so many different opportunities. You may be presented with new opportunities from time to time. It might be a promotion, a new challenge, a new job. If this is the case, my suggestion is not to feel pressured or obliged to accept. It's easy to say "yes". Previously I know I would have more readily jumped at the next opportunity that came my way, without much hesitation, but my circumstances and my whole outlook on life have changed. My priorities have changed in that my fundamental priority is now to have that work/life balance. This doesn't mean that I place any less importance on my job/career or that I'm not ambitious with my career. If anything it's the opposite in that I have that separation that allows me to be fully focused on my work when I'm working, and fully focused on my family when I'm not. I'm grateful for my circumstances which, if anything, make me work even harder on my role. It also doesn't mean that I'm not motivated about my professional career because I am, all I would say is that I have adjusted or realigned objectives so I'm now focused on a different career path.

This is also not to say that, because you're a parent and that like me you do value work/life balance that you now reject or turn down every new opportunity that comes your way because it will result in change. What I'm saying is for those of you considering a career move or applying for a new position, make sure that you do your research and know what you're getting yourself into. Again, in this instance, you have more of a choice as you're deciding/initiating upon the action. An obvious thing to find out if you're a parent is the potential amount of travel required. I don't know about you, but I try and avoid business travel as I personally think it's massively overrated. It might sound good when you're talking about your job saying that you get to go here and there, but spending a lot of time at airports, on planes, and in hotels is not appealing to me. Not just that, and more importantly, this would take valuable time away from my family. So if you're on the same page as me, I would advise you not to look to apply for something if, after some research, you find out you will be travelling 50% of the time. Again, I'm just sharing my views. Our careers are so personal and I'm certainly not saying that I'm right or wrong. But what I'm saying to you is to give it the consideration that it really deserves based upon what you truly value and place great importance on.

Another point which I think is relevant to make is that you may already be in a good position, earning decent money and actually enjoy a good work life balance, but are looking to make the next move up the traditional career ladder. All I would say is that sometimes it's as if there is an internal or external pressure to continue to get to the next level, get more money, essentially keep wanting more and more. With that you may need to reflect and come to the conclusion that you actually have the right job for how you want to live your life. I won't say the perfect job because again let's face it you're never going to tick/check every box of your desires. Sure, living in the real world we could all do with a bit extra in our pay check each month, but you have to weigh up that next move to determine if it will actually all be worth it. An obvious point to make, but if your personal situation drastically changes because of a new role having a negative impact on your personal life, then it might not be worth it for that extra bit of money/cash in your bank account each month. Again what is more valuable? What is more valuable to you and your family? Speaking personally, and to reiterate the point, just because you don't apply for that promotion or want to become a manager or director doesn't mean that you're not ambitious with your career and that you don't place great importance on it. Someone who is incredibly committed to their family will also be incredibly committed to their career in order to provide for their family. That's how I consider my current situation in that I place great importance on both and I feel I have the appropriate balance to be fully committed in both my professional and personal life. As a parent I feel that it's vital that you're mindful more than anything of every decision you make when it comes to your career. Sometimes it's hard to go back on a decision once you have decided to go down a certain path, so make sure before you make such a decision that it's the right one for you and your family. I would also say don't try to play the hero, where you feel the need to be seen as always working late or that you never use your vacation/holiday time. I think we all know there is a difference of being busy and being productive. It's how you use your time that counts to benefit both your employer and your family so that there is an all-round benefit.

I previously mentioned that I had been in a somewhat 24/7 job and I would only go back to that if I had no choice now. In my current role there are times when I'm very busy but I feel that, once I log off for the day, for the weekend or for a vacation, for the most part I'm officially off work.

This allows me to have the so called balance in my life. I actually think the benefits given by my employer are returned in such a way that I'm happy at work, remain motivated and committed to what I do. In my case it certainly helps in retention as I don't feel the need/want to look for something elsewhere at another company. Back to my earlier comment, it gives me the gift of time with my children and it in turn gives my children the gift of my time too, because as I already said the time/attention a child receives from their parents in my view, is perhaps one of the most important factors in their childhood. When you're with your children do you feel you're in a position to be fully present/attentive or are you elsewhere because of the stresses and demands of your job/career? Do you need to dial into meetings, take calls, and check/respond to emails outside of regular working hours? Or more simply do you have enough energy to get out and do things and be active? Or are you burnt out where by the time you get home all want and can do is just crash out? Sometimes I'm sure it's a case that it's dependent on the profession/industry you work in. So if anything consider more of where you do have a choice or option as to what you actively pursue, as I think you do have to factor these types of things in. Of course what you do with your time is what really counts but this is about actually being in the position to give your time. Work/life balance in my view, is similar to time management in a way in that it is very difficult to master, so all we can do is continue to work at it and as I keep saying give it the full consideration it deserves.

I will summarize with one word the challenge of balancing your career and parenthood: Complicated. Sometimes external factors dictate and ultimately the first priority is to provide for your family. So in order to do so, for some, this may well mean having to sacrifice time with their family. I get it and as loving parents if there is no choice then there is no hesitation of what you need to do. However, although it's complicated look at areas where you do have a choice. It might be a current area of study, a new career that you're considering, and a change in profession or even a promotion. It might even be looking down the line in looking at where you want to go in your career and which path you want to pursue. This is where you need to give close consideration to the effect that this will have on your family life. You also need to factor in things like having/planning for more children and considering that impact. By reflecting on what's really more important to you this may affect your decision one way or the other. It might be as simple as answering the question: Will I have a work/life balance? Again balance in the sense of being in a position to spend regular quality time with your children. Or will my life now be fully consumed by work? I also want to re-emphasize the importance of placing equal importance on both as we can't neglect either - especially if you want to be a better parent, which is the reason why you're reading this book!

As I begin to wrap up this chapter, I think for the modern day parent in the real-world, that work/life balance is so important these days. Therefore it's needless to say that you need to choose carefully if you have the luxury of choices/options or are considering a career change. It's a lot easier said than done when we have bills to pay and need to put food on the table. But you do have to consider how it will impact your personal life, because this will directly affect your role as a parent. Again and I stress this is perhaps looking at it more where you do have an element of choice/control and maybe initiating a move in one direction or another. I mentioned in the opening of the chapter how providing for and spending time with your family are so important but can sometimes have you going in opposite directions. How drastic that difference is can obviously differ significantly so when we look at balance it might just be a case of placing as much importance on both. It's not trying to overly complicate it and it's not about ensuring there is always a 50/50 split. If anything I think it's having the understanding you can't have or should I say really enjoy one without the other, so with such a realization I think be constantly mindful of this with your career choices.

In closing for me it comes down to this: I don't want to be the guy with a glittering career, plenty of money in the bank, but to achieve it meant that I had to sacrifice a very significant amount of time with my family. It meant I missed out on so many little and big things. It meant I was not present in mind even when in their presence. It meant my kids saying something like "daddy always worked" or "we didn't get to see him too much growing up." Looking ahead I already know if my kids would say something like this when they're adults it would break my heart. I think by doing this you risk your relationships with the ones you love most. That's when material things really don't matter. I wonder what use is a fancy car or a big house and the like if it means work, work, work all your life? For me it's just not worth it. This is merely my personal view and take on things so it's not really any advice that I'm offering here just my thoughts for what it's worth. You may agree/disagree with some of the points I have made in this chapter and that's fine. I go back to the most important point which is I think the key is that as a parent you need to give this area the full consideration it deserves, because of the fact it's so personal, as ultimately it will directly impact your role as a parent one way or another. By constantly looking at the potential impact on any career move/decision you make on your family, by always keeping them front and center, I believe will make you become a better parent.

26 COMPROMISE AND SACRIFICE

Now I will try and explain my thoughts as best as I possibly can here based on personal experience. Bear in mind the essence of this chapter is really to assess or analyze your priorities and also consider that you may need to sacrifice or give certain things up. I think as parents we can all understand that we have to make personal compromises/sacrifices for our children. In doing so understand that, essentially, this means that you're doing something, or giving something up to enable you to become a better parent for your child. The crux of my advice in this chapter is that something may have to give when you have kids. Sacrifices are needed and priorities need to be realigned – in my view anyway. I'm going to use sports teams as my main example. This relates first hand to my experience, where I initially sacrificed something that once took up a lot of my time before I became a parent. I say initially sacrificed as I now see that I'm not actually sacrificing anything as I would now choose time with my kids over my favorite team any day. Also think about time as you read through this chapter as that is what I tend to believe is the root cause of compromise and sacrifice. As the responsibilities and demands of a parent rise, the available time for the parent does the opposite, going the other way and falls.

So I will explain more shortly focusing on my experience, but I hope you can relate to this, to something which you spent a lot more time doing before you came a parent. If you're still doing it now as a parent maybe some of my advice will make you reconsider what is more important. As I said I will use my following of a sports team as this is a real life example of mine but it could be one of many other things. It could be someone who was used to going to the gym every day or even twice a day. It could be your subscription where you used to binge watch a marathon series or it could be that you used to play video games for hours at a time. Just a few alternate examples, but essentially the advice is to consider partially sacrificing such things/habits now that you're a parent. Now there is potentially nothing stopping you from continuing to do this, but you do at least have to look where your priorities lie – again bringing it back to your personal use of time.

For example, a parent could still go to the gym every day or twice a day but that would surely mean sacrificing time they could be with their child? In this instance, I'm thinking more of a parent working full-time. This is not about completely revolving every second of your life around your children but at the very least placing the utmost priority on the time that you do have together during a typical day. If you work full-time, chances are you probably only have a short window each day that you can spend with your child also factoring in their education/schooling. So it might only be 2-3 hours when you will have the opportunity to be together. Yes, you still need to have a life outside your kids, I get it, so I know that might be an immediate push back on this advice. I also previously highlighted the importance of something like exercise so I'm not going back on myself here either. I'm just saying that your previous regimented schedule where you were in the peak shape of your life may no longer be a viable option. Staying with this example, should it be the case that you try to cram a little time in with your child after the gym or vice-versa?

As I said earlier, I place a high priority on my health and exercising which is why I had a chapter focused specifically on it. I think it's so important, but I can honestly say I worked out way more than I currently do before I had kids. I just had more time. So when I said realign my priorities at the beginning of this chapter, I did realign in such a way that I adjusted my typical work out purely based on the available time in my schedule. I personally don't want to go out for a run when I get home from work as that is my family time. I need to be creative in where I can fit it in. I know others do the same and if your schedule permits where you can stick to a regimented schedule that doesn't interfere with time with your children, then great, go for it. All I'm saying is that I don't think this will apply to many real world parents. We all have different schedules, so perhaps the main point of advice is that you should consider not focusing on such personal things during the time which is open to you when you're together with your children – as like I said you may only have a short window of time together each day as it is!

But let me break this down a bit more with a specific day-to-day example, demonstrating the regular issue of conflicting priorities with our time. As already stated, I place great importance on health/exercise, but there are days when the only real chance I have to do something would be at the same time I would take my daughter to her golf or tennis lesson. Although exercising is one of my priorities, whenever I'm faced with something like this I would go with my daughter's lesson every time – it's even more important to me and therefore an even higher priority. So that day I would sacrifice my workout or I might compromise to where I do a much scaled down version of a workout towards the end of the day, whenever I get the chance. So I think this simple example shows compromise and sacrifice in its simplest form. I'm not saying it's necessarily a dilemma/predicament but as parents there are times where we just have to pick one or the other. Both maybe important so you end up compromising or sacrificing a little on the option which might only be a slightly lower priority. So although I'm stating the obvious here, before I had children, I had so much more time to focus on working out. I never had an issue of having to compromise/sacrifice this time for something else. Now I do have children, sure I could still work out as much as I did in college, but that would then mean that I would be compromising/sacrificing so much day-to-day, with my children.

With these initial examples and the many others as well as the ones that will apply directly to you, let me make something crystal clear. I'm not criticizing or suggesting you need to suddenly quit everything and stop doing something you love or are deeply passionate about. If anything as you read this just continue to consider the amount of time something takes up or that you dedicate yourself to. It's the time element which I think is most relevant when I talk about compromise and sacrifice. But be aware that both terms being compromise and sacrifice, to me imply that you do stop doing something you want to do or that you're having to give something up you actually don't particularly want to. The reason sometimes is because there is no other choice and we go with the option that is most important or has that higher priority. I will briefly refer back to the commitment chapter as I think an example I made ties in with this. The example being that I stopped playing for my soccer team/club. I said I didn't really want to stop or quit but as I just mentioned, in my case I personally didn't think I had any other choice. I previously also put that I couldn't be in two places at once and with my spare time being so limited outside of work it basically came down to what I valued more. Spending time playing soccer for an amateur team or spending time with my daughter/family? When I just said I had no other choice I didn't mean it in such a way that I was forced to quit to spend more time with my daughter. What I really meant by saying that was that it was a no-brainer decision for me. I would pick my daughter every time without hesitation. I repeat yet again, this book is about becoming a better parent so in order to do so I believe needs you to look at how much time, energy and passion you give to things other than your child.

So let's now look more at my main personal/additional example with sports teams, professional sports teams that is. It amazes me really how fanatical we can get over a team that we support/root for. I'm originally from England, and in Europe the main sport is football/soccer where the love and passion for a club can be described as almost tribal like. I now live in the US and I see the same love and passion for teams here. Whilst soccer is growing in popularity I see similar traits in people when it comes to American Football, Baseball, Ice Hockey and Basketball amongst other sports. With American Football, I also see that same level of passion for College teams, not just NFL where people's affiliation with a college is so strong, that same passion runs deep.

I want to continue as I can speak first-hand about this as I'm one of those fans who have that strong connection with a team and always have. I have always loved to watch soccer, not just following my team but the game as whole, and I consider I have had deep knowledge of other teams/players. Like most, my team is my hometown team, Birmingham City, which is currently a second division team in England. I wouldn't necessarily say I was ever a die-hard fan but I was a season ticket holder for many years, wouldn't miss a game if on TV and my weekend mood would be affected one way or the other depending on the result. Ok so maybe I was. On game-day, if I was not watching a game I would be constantly checking the score for updates on my phone throughout the 90 minutes. Even before the game I would read up on pre-match news, interviews, the team line-up and the current form of the opposition amongst other things.

As an aside, I would like to make an analogy where I think we should all apply that same love and passion we do to our family/children as we do to our sports teams. You will be aware that there are people out there who know every stat of a team, player, league, so surely that same knowledge should also apply to our children's activities? This point certainly won't apply to all and some might think it's even crazy to suggest. What I'm not saying here is that I think people love their team more than they do their own kid. But what I'm saying is that they should look to apply that same passion to everything that their child does like their favorite team. I'm referring to things such as how, for some, they won't miss their team's game and will move everything to make sure they get to watch it. That's how I think you should approach all your child's activities with that mentality so you don't miss anything. Or in another example it might be that a fan may know every stat on their team for the season or on a key player, but doesn't know how their child is performing at school –

essentially their school stats for the school year (season)! Do you really want to know more about your team than what is going on in key parts of your child's life? The reason I say to ask yourself this question is that such behavior is fairly unintentional. You don't purposely act this way by deciding between your favorite team and your child but it can easily happen in a sort of unconscious way where it's not so glaringly obvious.

Before I go on and to provide another more generic example to reiterate the point, what about all of the reality shows that people watch these days? I'm not even going to get into looking at or criticizing the show content. But what I would like to make comment on is the fact that some people are more concerned with how others live their lives, rather than focusing on, or paying more attention to, what is going on in theirs. Some are quick to mock, gossip and judge others on these shows by taking a hard look at others without taking a hard look at themselves. They may know more of what is currently happening in a reality star's life than they do their own. It might sound crazy, but for some it's not too far off/from the truth. It might be that someone can't miss a show and revolves their day around it, placing the utmost importance on it. It can become almost obsessive, rather like the sports team, in that you read up on, follow online, watching or looking out for everything that is going on in someone else's day-to-day life. However what people need to consider is that person/celebrity/reality star doesn't even know who you are, your name and to be frank doesn't care one bit about your day-to-day life.

Related to this and back to my example with some similar comparisons, I would also share that, whilst my team will always be my team in that I will always root for them, I have to say over recent years that my level of interest has waned. In fact it continues to do so to the point where my level of interest is nowhere near where it once was. One of the main reasons for this is being a parent which is why I think it's relevant to raise the point. I think so many can at least relate to the passion they have for a team and I know because I was that guy. So why has my level of interest dropped? It may sound a bit cliché/corny, but I just think I should be using that passionate energy elsewhere. I have been that guy on game day who switches off, constantly checking my phone and then I have been in the worst mood if my team loses. It kind of got to the point when I told myself this is ridiculous. Firstly during valuable time with my family, I would switch off completely like I wasn't there and it would then affect how I interacted with them for the rest of the weekend depending on the result of a game. Personally I have come to realize that the outcome of a soccer/football game, good or bad, ultimately has no consequence in my life. So why should I let it affect me? The type of questions I ask myself is do the club and players care as much about me as I do them? Will this game matter in 1 year, 5 years or 10 years' time? We all know the answer to this question is no. In addition to this, when it wasn't game day I would constantly be checking in on updates from the team, the league and the game in general. In essence, so much of my time and focus was being applied to soccer/football throughout the week – especially on my team!

Now don't go all politically correct on me here with what I'm going to say. I can imagine that I would lose some man-points or that I will be going against the guy-code by saying that I'm no longer as much into my favorite team or sport. But I would respond and say what other option do I have? What's the alternative? I have to speak a little hypothetically here as I no longer live in the UK. Sure someone can have a season ticket, be on the road to go to every game home and away – no one's stopping you or anyone from doing that. But going back to a term that has always stuck with me from an old economics class is that you still have to consider the opportunity cost. The opportunity cost both in terms of time and money. For all the money you spend on your team, could that be put towards something else like a family vacation? Or just good-old family days out? If you're on the road on a weekend watching your team what else could you be doing with that time? Are you missing your own child's game or practice? Could you use that time to play your favorite sport with them instead?

I know my passion for a team and sport is replicated across the world in different teams and many different sports. My advice to you isn't to ditch your team, as I said; I still root for my hometown club, but let's just say my love/passion is much less intense or nowhere near where it once was these days. I get that it's not as easy as a switch which you can just turn off. Come game day, sure I want my team to win, and I get a little disappointed if they don't, but win or lose my mood doesn't drastically change. Of course I still like to watch some of their games or highlights, but I now spend less time following them and give more focus/attention elsewhere, that being with my children/family. I redirected that extra love and passion to my family. Like I just said, this sounds a bit naff/corny, I know, so to perhaps cut to the chase, I just think it's more important to place a higher priority on time with your family/children than something like a sports team.

Again it all comes back to how we use our time and we all have a choice. As you know I now live in the US and many soccer games being played in the UK are shown live on a Saturday morning one after the other. Saturday morning used to be kick back time for me where I watched these games. But again it go to the point when I started to ask myself or tell myself for that matter, that this was the time that I should have been playing with my child. I work full-time like so many parents so Saturday provides a perfect opportunity for me to still switch off, but do that with my child and family instead. Although I do enjoy a good work/life balance this means that I utilize the time I have away from the office the best that I can as this time is still limited. Again, most of my days off are at the weekend and if I spend most of my Saturday watching soccer, then I feel that this is actually time wasted because I should be doing other things with my children.

I see it here particularly with American Football and come Sunday afternoon many people are tuned into their game and fantasy team knowing every in and out of it. They know all the stats of the players and teams. My points in this chapter are to provoke thought more than anything else. So I'm not suggesting that you never watch your team again. But in this instance, I would at least ask yourself such a question – what is more beneficial, being glued to the TV and phone all day Sunday with your team and fantasy team or actually playing out with my child? I say this because this may only be your true day off! Not just that if you're physically going to the game there is the added time as well as expense to do so. Sure, you can have a great family experience if you all go together to a live game, I get that too, but I think this is better to do more on an ad hoc basis. In the real world I also don't think many can actually afford for all their family to go to a ball game especially all the time and so perhaps the reality is it might not be family time for all, after all. For me, I would never even consider buying a season ticket now as I feel that I would be investing a considerable amount of time, energy and money into something which actually has no real benefit to me or my family – especially if they're not going with me.

Personally if my team are now on TV and my daughter asked me to take her to the pool instead or practice one of her sports as an example, I would not even hesitate and I would pick my daughter every time. Again ask yourself is the result of this game actually going to matter this time next year? I just want to reiterate, I'm not suggesting that you suddenly ditch your team or stop watching sports or anything extreme like that. I know first-hand how you can have a love and passion for a game, sport, team and it doesn't really go away – certainly not in an instant! What I'm saying is that if you put things into perspective you may no longer be that intense or take the result of your team to the extreme where it impacts your life as parent which was the case for me.

We all need some form of escape from time to time – I get that too. But my advice here is not actually saying to completely stop doing something. It's saying look at your current or past priorities and determine if some compromises or sacrifices are needed. Essentially something may have to give for you to become a better parent. One way to look at it is that you might be choosing something else over your children such as a sports team, the gym, that series or reality show. So when it's presented that way or that bluntly then it might become a no-brainer for you, like it was for me, to reassess how you focus your precious time, energy, passions to then make those comprises/sacrifices. So on the other hand maybe it's not all sacrifices. I say that in a way where I think sometimes compromise or sacrifice means that you're giving something up and not getting anything back in return. In some cases you might learn to find that having made such a decision you don't compromise or sacrifice really anything, as what can be more important than your children? You never know after giving something up, you may well eventually find that you do indeed get so, so much more back in return. In doing so I think you will see first-hand of how you become a better parent.

27 SPORTS/HOBBIES/PASSIONS

For this chapter my advice will focus on sports, as this is an area in which I have experience as my daughter plays both golf and tennis. However, I believe the principles of my advice apply to other types of activities that your child may be learning or is actively playing/participating. So for this chapter what I'm saying is focus more on the message because I don't think it really matters whether your child is into dance, gymnastics, is learning to play a musical instrument or participates in any other sport, as I think so many of the same things come into play. For those of you thinking about getting your child started in something, hopefully this will provide you with some good things to consider before you do.

Before I go on in this chapter, I will repeat a point that I have reiterated throughout in that it's vital that you, as a parent, commit to something. When I say something, I mean anything. Whatever activity you get your child involved in or signed up for, my fundamental advice would be to commit to it. I cannot emphasize the point enough, which is why I have repeated it throughout the book in other examples, and I will do more of the same, particularly in this chapter. I'm sure that most parents would describe themselves as committed. But I have already seen many examples of where this is not the case when exposing their child to a sport/activity. Same goes for dedication where most if not all parents would say they're dedicated to their children. So my advice would be to commit or dedicate yourself to something not in some obsessive or over the top way, but essentially just following through. I'm sure you have said something to your child like "if you're going to do something, then do it right" well if you have, I think the same very much applies to you as a parent in this instance. So that's what I mean by dedicating and committing, where if you're going to sign your child up for something, then you might as well do it right. If you believe that you're a committed and dedicated parent, I think you have to show it through your actions with these types of things. To give a rather blunt example, I know of parents who have got their child a set of golf clubs, but then done almost nothing after that – they end up sitting in the garage somewhere. In a way I see this as sort of signing your child up to something, but if you don't follow through with arranging/organizing/scheduling practice, lessons, going to the range or kids clinics etc. then it's probably not worth buying them in the first place. As I said that might come across a bit blunt or even a little harsh, but I say it because I think if you're going to do something like this, then beforehand you need to determine if you really will be committed for your child. Again I will refer back to the saying you might preach to your kid something along the lines of if you're going to do it, do it right/properly. I also say all this because I know how valuable your time is as a parent, so you do need to ensure you know what is and isn't feasible or what realistically you can/cannot do.

For me commitment means going all in, going to every class and it means sticking at it for the long haul. My blunt and honest view is that if you don't commit or do something half-heartedly, then you're kind of wasting both your own and your child's time. Parents should be setting their children up for success and you do that by committing. It doesn't necessarily guarantee anything, but by setting them up for success, you're doing your part. If you don't commit then I think the opposite is true in that, in essence, you're setting your child up for failure, although I admit it's not so glaringly obvious and certainly not intentional.

I also want to recap on some of the points made in the chapter, Choices, as I think they're very applicable here. So when I hear parents say things like "we're going to let our child decide what they want to do" or "let them find their passion", I just think by saying that it's rather wishy washy. What does that really mean? Given the choice not all, but a lot children would choose to watch TV or play video games. My view is that if you're going to let your child decide you still have to take control by essentially giving them an opportunity/chance with something and exposing them to new things. Once more, if you're going to sign up for something you must know what you're getting into, what's involved and then commit to it for a prolonged period of time. Prolonged is vague but it certainly doesn't mean after one or two attempts - it could be over several months or even years. Don't do one off things and expect your child to instantly take to something. It does require some experimentation, or trial and error, but at the same time you can only stretch yourself so far. You have certain resources available to you and there are only so many hours in the day, so my view is to pick something that you know you will be able to commit to. It could be anything like a sport, music or art class, something like that. Go all in for a period of time and just see how it goes – essentially don't give up which is something I'm sure you tell your kid all the time. Back to our earlier swimming example, which I have referred to many times in the book, it might even be a year before your child starts to really enjoy something once they get used to it or the hang of it. This simple illustration shows how something can develop over time. Our commitment as parents was key as there was no instant love/passion for swimming from my daughter. In those early days we had to drag her to the pool and now we have to drag her away from it when it's time to go home. I said this ties in with the chapter looking at choices where in this example, my wife and I very much called the shots and not our daughter. I say this because I think this simple example shows how choices/decisions as a parent can play such a vital role in letting something develop. Our daughter now has a passion for something and as parents we were the ones responsible for having that long-term outlook of the importance of her learning to swim if anything just for safety reasons alone. In this case there was no way we could really let our daughter have a choice as she would have initially decided not to ever go to a lesson. Rightly or wrongly we made her go. A general example might be that a kid in the moment may not really see the benefit of or even care to learn something new as the video game or TV show they're currently watching is more than good and that's all they want to do right now. But surely the parents need to take charge sometimes and understand what's really best for their child and the right thing for them? You never know they may well figure this out for themselves sooner rather than later and may even thank you for it! So again your commitment as well as choices/decisions as a parent to whatever it may be will be vital, if you're going to overcome those inevitable initial obstacles/challenges as well as the many more along the way. In our case, as parents, we were a lot more assertive and essentially got on with it. Now we see the benefit of such an approach.

You also need to give very close consideration to services you might pay for whether it be classes, lessons, clinics etc. with a coach or instructor. This is obviously something separate to something you might do with your child alone in terms of an activity. My advice is to ensure that you do some simple background research. Ask around about what people think about a class, a coach or a club and ask to go and watch the next time there is a session on to see what you think so you can decide for yourself. You can also ask if your child can come along to try something out so that you can observe what is going on, as well as their initial reaction. The main thing I think you should pay attention to here is whether you're getting value.

Value not just in how much it will cost but perhaps more importantly your time and your child's time. Trust me, I have already seen a lot of classes which I personally think are a waste of time and aren't cheap either! For example, I have seen kids in classes where there are so many children that they may just wait in line, standing around for an hour and have one or two attempts at something without any coaching or much playing at all. This is primarily your responsibility to find out about a certain offering and then ultimately you form your own judgment, to decide what you think will be best for your child. Also, bear in mind that, although a lot of kids might be involved in a class, that doesn't mean that it's actually any good. So my advice is to do your homework to see what's out there. Find good classes, coaches and programs given your resources. On your part, plan and schedule accordingly to ensure that what you sign up for is realistic with your timetable. There may be a great class offering, but it might be a two hour drive to get there, so be realistic in that it probably won't be viable or sustainable for you to commit/consider it.

When kids are very young and starting out in something I agree more than anyone that a key element/emphasis should be on fun/enjoyment, I get that. I'm also not saying that a coach needs to have an instant impact on your child where they are suddenly shooting three pointers, hitting home runs or driving the ball 100 yards. It's not that, what I'm getting at as progress is ever so gradual when starting something new and that is not just for kids, but adults too. As parents you have to be, and remain, realistic throughout. But as I just said, I have taken my daughter to a class or two and observed other sessions where kids are standing around, waiting in line and not really doing anything for the 30 minutes or an hour – essentially it's just a waste of time and money. Trust me, young kids waiting in line and standing around in the heat or cold isn't really a good combination. You have to consider whether there is something better or something else your child could be doing that might be more beneficial? I don't really want to come across cynical in anyway as there are so many good coaches and instructors out there offering great things for kids – my point is that, in my opinion, there are some bad ones too so make sure you take the time to find a good one. This requires some effort on your part beforehand and paying close attention to a potential offering. Trust me, this will definitely be worth your time if it stops you signing up for something which you regret and will end up causing frustration all round.

I do recommend a small group setting as being beneficial as it allows for some personal focus from a coach, but at the same time the group allows your child to begin to make friends with other kids. If you have experienced something like this you will see the fun and enjoyment escalate when you child is playing something with his/her friends. So this can happen and evolve naturally whilst at the same time they're doing some form of activity which is beneficial. Kids natural push each other without you necessarily noticing or having to force it in anyway. So I would strongly encourage you to place high importance on your child making friends related to the same sport/activity that they're involved with. I think every parent wants their kid to ask them to practice rather than the other way around, where it feels more like a nagging parent asking their kid to practice. I repeat that a child needs to take responsibility and be accountable – the notion of practicing and working hard when no one when else is watching or asking. There is no simple formula to get to this point but I think that, having friends who are developing a passion for the same thing as your child, can only help.

This is why the parents' involvement and their choices become crucial, particularly in the early years and when starting something new. If you think about it, the parent is the decision maker here and the child is totally reliant on the parent firstly for any opportunity that they're given. Your child is not necessarily going to know what's out there. Looking at it just from a simple logistical perspective, it's not just the opportunity, it is also providing things like transportation and then scheduling. Scheduling is something I continue to emphasize, and was one of my most important points at the start of the book. I will elaborate even more in this chapter on this specific topic as well, as I believe scheduling goes hand in hand with your level of commitment/dedication.

But before we go further you might even wonder what to introduce your child to? I live in Florida and where we live there are so many programs to choose from and we obviously benefit from the climate which is good for year round sporting activities. If you're looking at sports, providing you have done some good background research on finding a good program and coach, I personally don't think it matters too much what you introduce your child to, it could be any sport really. Also, I personally don't think that it's selfish at all to get your child involved in something for which you have a passion – why not? It's kind of an obvious choice really. You will have passion and excitement and will get so much joy in watching your child try it. If you think about it, it seems logical in a way that if a parent has experience in dance, an instrument, soccer, tennis, basketball, or whatever; that they will introduce their son or daughter to that same thing. The parent has the advantage of knowledge and experience to know what to look for and if it will be beneficial. You can also help to teach them. If your child begins to enjoy and advance you may start to get sarcastic comments that you're living vicariously through your child, which is nonsense really in my opinion. As long as you don't take it to the extreme it seems almost common-sense to introduce your child to something that you're passionate about. If your child then starts to develop that same passion which you then share, you will no doubt begin to form a very special bond in a certain activity which you can begin to form so many long and lasting memories/experiences.

It's strange that it didn't work out this way for us as my wife and I both played soccer in college and have a passion for the game but our daughter ended up getting into golf and tennis. In terms of how she started out in golf she had a plastic playset at home which she seemed to like to play with. We then heard about a class in our local area which was recommended to us, we tried it out plus we kept going and it all naturally developed from there. We kept going because she liked it and as parents we thought it was good for her, so once we got going we essentially committed ourselves to it. In terms of what you introduce your child to when I say it doesn't matter you will of course need to factor in things like climate depending on where you live and what activities are more readily available. Although we didn't think this way at the time, if you did want to think about it a little more why not consider introducing your child to something which could last a lifetime? Like golf or tennis? If my daughter continues to develop her passion there is no reason why she can't continue to play throughout her life. Or what about an instrument like a piano? Again the same applies where your child could play for years on end. So maybe that's another way to approach it rather than playing the odds of which sports provide the most amount of college scholarships.

The only thing I would flag here, which goes back to the opening advice in the chapter relating to commitment, is that in my opinion, you do have to give consideration to the difficulty or complexity of something. This is because something which is very technical in nature, again in my opinion, will need much more commitment/dedication from the parent and child. This is only a presumption so I'm sure someone out there will correct me if I'm wrong when looking at something like the piano. I have no experience in learning a musical instrument like the piano but my simple, uneducated guess is that it requires an enormous amount of discipline, dedication and commitment to not necessarily master but maybe to even become remotely proficient.

Something I do have more experience with now is in golf. The pros on TV sure make it look easy, but I have to tell you that it's such a difficult sport to learn. I'm not saying that's bad either, it's such a great sport but it's technical in nature and its complex. Don't believe me? If you've never played, go to the nearest range and just try to hit the ball. I say this because when we're getting our child involved in something we will all have different motives and differ in how far we want to go. All I'm saying is to consider a child doing something like golf or the piano, doing say a 30 minute class a week and that's it, nothing else outside of that in terms of practice. Now I'm not saying that's a complete waste of your and your child's time, but surely you want to give them every chance of being able to progress with something? I don't think there is any point in trying to sugar coat this. So with something very difficult in nature, if that is all you're committed to, then I think the reality is that you will see very little progress.

I'm sure that you want to set them up for success so when considering what your child should do, take the advice of doing some background research to determine the true level of commitment required. Speak to a parent whose child plays the piano to a high level and get an insight into how they got there. What does their weekly schedule look like? How many lessons do they have each week? How much extra practice do they do? As for something like golf, in addition to lessons, it's practicing on the range, practicing on the putting green, chip shots, bunker shots, different lies, different distances; I could go on and on. So you have to actually consider, firstly, in terms of schedule: Can we physically do and commit to something like that? Then secondly: Do I actually even want to do all of this in my spare time? Speaking personally I love nothing more than being out with my daughter. But the reality for me in terms of what I'm doing at times is nothing glamorous at all. For example, I'm essentially nothing more than her glorified ball boy at tennis when she's with her coach and when I'm at golf with her, I'm collecting up her balls on the chipping green. But I wouldn't have it any other way! So again consider things like: Do I want to be a ball-boy/ball-girl going around collecting all my kids balls so they can do another round at practice? As a parent am I willing to fully commit to this? To answer whether you're willing, maybe find out what it takes ahead of time. For the parent to commit, your passion is equally as vital, meaning that although it will be a challenge you will want to do what it takes with your child.

So you also have to know what you're signing your child up for. Educate yourself - observe other children who might be more advanced and speak to their parents to get some insight into the process. If you see a kid smashing golf balls with pin point precision on a driving range or see a girl hitting tennis balls like a champion, my guess is that is a result of a lot of hard work, patience, persistence, grinding, commitment, dedication (call it what you want!) over a considerable amount of time - rather than just turning up and taking to it like a pro. If you sign your child up for piano lessons then understand something like this will require a long-term commitment. Once more that commitment is vital from you, the parent and then of course the commitment of the child. I emphasize the commitment of the parent though, factoring in the reliance children have on parents. A child may be willing and fully committed, but if they can't get to something or have the opportunity to practice, or where it's not scheduled into part of their day/week as a priority then their willingness or commitment becomes somewhat irrelevant as they might not even be able to act on it. Is a kid talented or do they have to work really hard at something? I think the more you learn and gain insight the more likely you'll understand the hard work plus level of commitment actually required – that's my view anyway.

The next chapter will be very much linked to this one in that it looks in more detail of how progress for your child will at times be so very gradual and, as a result, your patience is vital. This is having patience in the moment, but perhaps more importantly having that long-term patience which comes with your commitment/dedication. That is perhaps the key point of this chapter in that, no matter what your child is doing or signs up for, be sure to commit to it for the long-run. This is because it's won't necessarily all be plain sailing particularly in the beginning and the stop/start approach will, more than likely, cause frustration in lack of progress. But how can your child progress if your approach is stop/start? Like the piano lessons, say a kid does a lesson here and there. I think this stop/start approach will result in frustration more than anything else, particularly with something difficult, as it might be hard for the kid just to get past square one. Teamwork as a family is also key for success as touched on more in the Teamwork chapter. Teamwork, particularly with the parents, is crucial in that you're both on the same page when you commit to something and know what you're signing your child up for – there are no surprises. This is to ensure that you then remain committed because if you're not on the same page early on with what, how much, the cost, who's taking who or how often your child is doing something, the wheels can quickly fall off.

So whatever activity it is, perhaps the key ingredients for your children developing a passion are commitment and opportunity. Give and expose your children to something which will then give them an opportunity to develop a passion for something. But I think one of the most important things to be mindful of is that I truly believe that a passion for something is developed over time. It could be a considerable amount of time but either way, I think it would be rare for a child to have an instant passion for something. They first need the opportunity, and then your commitment/dedication in order for the passion or the potential of that passion, to have the opportunity to continue to grow. To become a better parent in this area for me to say your commitment is important is rather pointing out the obvious. But for this to become true, for you to become a better parent that is, it has a lot more to do with your actions – particularly with something like helping your child to develop a passion for something. Prove that you're committed with what do rather than what you say to become a better parent.

28 LESS IS MORE

My comments in this book are purely my own personal opinion so I must reiterate that what I'm saying are my views based on my personal experiences. It doesn't mean that I'm right or wrong so my advice is just that, advice, so you can ultimately begin to form your own opinions based on your own experiences. So my personal opinion on sports/hobbies/activities is that less is actually more. At the time of writing this my daughter plays golf and tennis. Scheduling two sports with time/resource is a challenge in itself, where we could not simply do no more. I can only imagine how this challenge is multiplied for parents with two, three, four or even more kids, all doing different activities. We're not at that stage yet given the age of our son, but no doubt you have to bear this in mind when you have more than one child, which is why I think that will also support the view of less actually being more.

The counter argument to this trail of thought maybe that exposing children to multiple sports/hobbies/activities at a young age helps them become well rounded and multi-skilled in different areas to become somewhat of an all-rounder. I can personally see where people are coming from here. But, again, when looking at time, schedule and your personal resources you have to ask yourself whether what you're trying to do is sustainable and realistic? Can you really commit? You also have to work to find a balance because I also think that you should not throw all your eggs in one basket either and concentrate on just one thing from such an early age. Two works for us right now and another thing to consider is maybe focusing on one or two activities at a time for a certain season/part/period of the year (like summer). Then you could do something different in the winter, as an example, so that your child does have that variety if that is a route you prefer. But my advice would remain the same being, over a given period;

just concentrate on one or two things. I want to clarify when I say my daughter just currently concentrates on two things in golf and tennis. What I mean here is structured activity which is more focused with practice, lessons, clinics etc. Of course we do other things like swimming, riding bikes, playing catch, kicking a ball, going to the playground, things like that, but these activities are not structured or as regularly scheduled. I say this because you also have to have time to do things like this so it quickly shows how hard it is to even try to fit it all in. I completely understand how sports can complement one another and you can continue to develop things like hand-eye co-ordination. My point is that we still do this with our daughter but just focus more concentrated time and effort, currently into two sports.

It's a balancing act and there is no simple formula for success. I know parents who have their child in piano practice one day, tennis the next day, then golf, then math class, dance or gymnastics. The week quickly becomes consumed with activities and I'm not criticizing a parent for doing this. Rather the opposite as the intentions are clearly positive with love for their child and wanting them to succeed in something, providing so many opportunities. But is this a schedule you can commit to long-term and, back to my earlier point, is it sustainable? Can your child make real progress if they're involved in so many things rather than just concentrating on one or two? Again, and back to what I just said with the piano or with golf, it might be that some kids are doing so many different things, but not really making progress in anything. It might be nice to say that your child is learning to play the piano, but saying and doing are two different things. Are you really committed such that your child is really learning and progressing? We're already finding it to be challenging to do two sports as my daughter is progressing well at both, and is now playing golf tournaments but is still a little too young to play tennis tournaments. I'm sure there will come a point, sooner rather than later, when we might have to prioritize one over the other purely for scheduling purposes as to what is realistic. Again I'm talking as a real world parent here facing the inevitable realities – there is no hiding from it. In an ideal world we would keep doing both as much as each other, but in the end that's just not realistic for us to commit to. Another thing we will have to consider is our son when he gets a little older as we will want to give him the same opportunities, so that is where we will have to give it even more thought. Sure you can stretch yourself, but only so far! Let's not forget, you also have to factor in work and school which is a challenge in itself! For some it may seem natural to want to expose your child to as many things as possible and do everything so to speak. However, in the end you may be setting yourself up to fail. I say this in a way, given your time and resources available and being able to really commit to such a challenging schedule in the long-run. Not just that, rather than trying to do it all consider that, after all, less might actually be more beneficial for your child to have the opportunity to really develop in something. By not doing many things doesn't mean that you're not committed as a parent, this is actually more about being a real world parent and looking at what is realistic for your family.

To go slightly off topic for a second not only do you need to factor in the importance of resource and scheduling with activities, I also think you need to place great importance on your kid being a kid as well. What I mean by that is that your life, or their life, gets so consumed by something which prevents your child from doing the so called ordinary or typical things a child would be doing given their age. Again this is age specific so as a parent I will share my take on my daughter who is 6. As a parent I place high importance on her continued practices so that she continues to develop. I want to give her every opportunity to do so. I will be the first to admit that she does practice a lot for a 6 year old and I believe that this is perhaps the key reason why she is so advanced for her age in both sports. Whilst I place high importance on this, I'm fully aware of the importance of it not taking over, whereby she doesn't do things a normal 6 year old would do. So when I refer to importance I understand how important it is that she plays at the playground, rides her bike or scooter, plays with other kids in the neighborhood, goes to the pool/beach, has play-dates, colors, birthday parties, plays games and the list goes on.

So this is another thing to factor in and by doing so you soon realize actually how difficult it is to even try to manage. Which is why I think that, by taking all of this into account, a less is more approach is just more realistic in relation to sports, hobbies and activities. When I say I place importance on my daughter doing things a 6 year old should do, I mean it and the only way I think I can do this is with my actions. So whilst I take her to her practices as much as I can, I also do everything else too like riding my bike, coloring with her, playing chalk, playing school, playing outside, playing shops, tea parties, you name it. Doing things like this with my daughter are equally as important to me and as enjoyable. So I'm not going to deny that my daughter does a lot for her age in terms of practice in relation to her sports. But, as her parent, I can honestly say that whilst this is true, I don't believe that it's at the cost of anything else or that she misses out on anything right now. I'm mindful as a parent that it may not always be equal, but I certainly don't want to neglect a vital part of my child's life, given her age. I understand that as kids get older they may progress in something whereby it does take up a big part of their life, but I still don't think you can just completely abandon or neglect everything else. Even when considering this it shows the real challenges that we face as parents.

My advice is to not downplay this in anyway as our children are the most important part of our lives, which is why I think we need to think carefully and take everything into account.

Staying with sports, there are obviously many kids out there who are great athletes and have a love for different sports. This process evolves over time and I'm not discouraging this, particularly if the love and passion for multiple sports is there. I actually think that you can make a very strong argument for this approach so let me make that clear. But I think that is in an ideal world, and the theme of this book is being in the real world as a real world parent. Speaking personally, I would actually love for my daughter to do some additional things, but when you factor in our time and resources it's just not that easy or even possible for us to consider. Again speaking as a real parent, sure it would be great if my daughter could do many more things like learning a new language or an instrument, but I have to be realistic as to what is possible. When I say less is more, I think it's really relevant here more in terms of quality over quantity. Take my daughter for example. She is very good at golf and tennis because of the amount of practice. But if she did so many different/additional things then she wouldn't have had the opportunity to develop anywhere near as much as she has in those two sports – hopefully that makes sense?

As I already stated, clearly there are relationships/similarities between sports which complement each other and can actually help you get better in one thing by doing something else - might be something like footwork. Staying with tennis, I'm often told how soccer and basketball can complement tennis, specifically with footwork. I'm going slightly off track and it's really for another debate, one which you could probably write a whole book on, but to reach a high level in anything, particularly in one sport, I believe that you do need to give more focus to that one sport – even from an early age. This is not saying that you focus all efforts so that your child can look to become some form of professional athlete. This chapter is a follow on from the previous chapter, looking at developing a love and passion for something like a particular sport/art/activity. I think the main challenge is actually your child developing the passion itself where they develop that love for something where they would want to continue it for the rest of their life – because they want to and not necessarily just because you want them to. Essentially to the point where they want to keep playing, where the enjoyment is pure and for all to see. The notion of practice when no one else is watching is important too and that only really happens if the individual has that passion. Otherwise it's on you and you can end up becoming that nagging parent.

I really like the term and I have used it throughout the booking being, "Set yourself up for success". That applies to you as the parent as well as your child. So my view is set yourself and your child up for success so that they can develop a passion in something, and this in my view does require a "less is more" approach. Make it realistic and sustainable given your time and resources so that you can commit long-term. People caution against burn out with children and I'm not denying that this also needs to be a factor. Something which may also deserve more attention is the actual burn out of parents. If you have a full time job and want to do so many things for your children, you may suffer burn out by trying to do too much. I don't know about you but for all the fun and joy I have running around and doing things with my kids, particularly with my daughter right now, taking her here and there, it's flat out exhausting. Safe to say most days when my head hits the pillow I crash, and I'm out like a light. So this is about your child developing a passion, but your role is vital in the process in terms of support be it logistics, resources and the time you physically have available. A child is somewhat reliant or totally reliant on what opportunities they're given by their parents. When I say opportunity it can be as simple as whether the parent can actually take their child to a class or practice? Are/will they be available to do this bearing in mind their schedule? Some might think I'm overthinking it a little here but I'm just sharing my experience and what I also see/think. If you stretch yourself too far as a parent, again you might be setting yourself up to fail sooner rather than later. The reality is that it's not as simple as it might appear at face value. This is why I think you need to give all of this the consideration it deserves and then go with your own view of what's right for your child.

I may be laboring a little on this point but don't underestimate the importance you play as a parent ensuring that your child develops a passion for something. My view is that if your child jumps around with too many things, they don't actually have the opportunity to really learn and progress with any one thing. Not just that, it makes it tough on you so alternatively, if you do have one or two things to focus on, it actually simplifies the process for you as a parent and makes it more manageable/realistic all round. With more concentrated effort and learning, I believe that this does set your child up for success by increasing their opportunity for progress/improvement. Note I stress progress and improvement and not becoming the best at something as I fully appreciate levels can vary. But if a child sees that they're progressing, learning and improving in something specific, whilst there are no guarantees, at the same time, I feel this has to increase the likelihood of them developing a passion for it. We're all human, both kids and adults, in a sense that once we start getting good at something it's just natural to want to keep doing it. So once that passion starts to develop, they will want to keep coming back for more and the fun/enjoyment that they will be having will be very natural. This is what this is all about, helping your child develop a passion for something, so again you as the parent are such a key player. Ultimately you will have to find a schedule that works for you, but what is important is that you know you can commit to it long-term, not just for a one-off or for a week or two. So if you're flat out, running here there and everywhere, wishing for a few more hours in the day and if this resonates with you in some way then maybe you'll find the less is more method is the way to go. But remember the reason for doing this is so your child will get MORE. In this case I believe more opportunity to progress, more opportunity to grow/develop, more opportunity to develop that passion and more of an opportunity to succeed. I think you'll see and understand this term firsthand, but you can perhaps only know through experience. So to become a better parent learn for yourself and then decide for yourself on the approach which works best for your family.

29 LONG-TERM PATIENCE

Patience, Patience, Patience. The word has, and will be forever be used and associated with parenting. It's true that you need patience in abundance, and patience is a trait which isn't only vital with a parent, but also with children too. As the saying goes, patience really is a virtue, and I don't know about you but it seems to be getting harder and harder to develop the trait. I refer to a similar point elsewhere in the book, and this is purely a personal opinion, but I just feel that in general, society is becoming more and more impatient. What is odd about this is that we get so many things now at the touch of a button. But what's almost strange is that it doesn't have the effect of making us more patient, if anything it just adds to the desire to continue to have more and more things in an instant. As a little aside, and this might purely be a geographic thing about where I live, but this is demonstrated in how people drive these days. People can't wait that extra few seconds as they need to pull out in front of you, ride the backend of your car, run that stop sign, run that red light or just drive like a maniac just to get wherever it is they're going that little bit quicker/faster. Not just that but I think some people would almost run you over to get a closer parking spot at the local grocery store! Like I said, this is a bit of an aside, but nonetheless, I think my personal opinion is relevant, particularly with the thought that society/people in general are becoming more and not less impatient. I therefore consider this has relevance for parenting, because I think patience isn't a switch which you can easily turn on or off, to where it only applies in certain circumstances/situations. What I'm saying is that I don't think it's simple for an impatient person to pick and choose their moments. Essentially they will generally be impatient most, if not all of the time and as a result will also have an impact on their behavior as a parent.

In many ways, the world we currently live in we have come to expect things immediately, sometimes as easy as at the push of a button. However, the only thing with parenting is that nothing is instant in our fast-paced world. Nothing. It even starts at the conception process, then the pregnancy itself if you're fortunate enough to be able to have children. From there, the progress of us as parents, and the progress of our children, is gradual and can be so subtle at times that we don't even notice. Patience, or lack of it for that matter is definitely one of my flaws but the truth is that patience is vital in so many ways as a parent. Patience from waiting for your child's first word, first crawl, first walk and the many other firsts we want to see. There are times when we need patience in the moment when we've had enough or we're stressed out/overwhelmed. You will particularly need patience in the moment if your child isn't listening, they're uncontrollable or in flat-out meltdown mode. We also need that prolonged patience when supporting our children when they're learning a new skill like learning to ride a bike or catching a ball. These are perhaps simple examples, but my view is that if you want your child to excel at anything be it from something simple to something else like school, a sport, an art, you're going to need patience in abundance to ensure that you and your child stay the course of your chosen path.

I tend to find that, with parents and kids, we associate patience very much in the short-term and in the moment. For example, a real life one currently with our daughter is that my wife and I might be in the middle of a conversation and we kindly ask for her to wait until we have finished talking without always interrupting. But she is going through a phase right now where she keeps calling our names until we respond. This is a simple example of where our child shows impatience. On the other hand, I'm sure you can relate to many a time when you've asked your child to do something and they don't respond first time. So at the fifth or sixth time of asking it's very easy for you to lose patience. Another real life example for us at the moment is that we can easily lose patience with our daughter when she is eating. I have said it elsewhere in the book that generally she is a very good eater, will eat most foods and is also open to try new things. The only issue is that she is very slow at eating. So it can be a little frustrating at the dinner table sometimes when my wife and I can easily lose patience when she is still chewing the same mouthful of food for several minutes. In a sense we then become part of the problem.

So these types of examples are very much day-to-day, in the moment and are really short-term/momentary things. I don't want to give too much focus to the short-term examples/incidents when looking at patience, although I don't want to downplay the importance in anyway. I actually want to focus more on long-term patience and shift gear a little. I want to continue with the theme of relating it to a sport/hobby or activity your child is taking part in. My advice also focuses more on you as a parent. I feel that if you begin to demonstrate patient behavior, as well as understanding the importance of being so over the long-term, then I think this can only have a positive effect on your child. In the process, I believe you will become a better parent where you will see/feel it for yourself. I don't really want to focus on what I would call the little things with patience that may lead to a minor meltdown or temper tantrum if your child doesn't get their way. I want to look at what I consider long-term things like education, sports and activities for your child. In time I think that, by developing your child in such a way where you have a long-term focus, it will actually help to reduce those poor behaviors which leads to the moaning and nagging from you as a parent in the short-term/day-to-day present moments. I say this as I think you will be less inclined to get so worked up in the moment.

I will continue to use sports as my example and I have referenced a similar theme throughout. I really want to bring it home when it comes to patience as a follow on from previous chapters with some of the points I have already made. I will give a very simple example. What I really recommend is, from an early age, doing very simple things like throwing a ball and playing catch. I always played throw and catch with my daughter which I think is great for hand/eye coordination and hand/eye coordination is beneficial for so many things. It's so simple and it's fun too! So this is where you can do something so easy with your time and I think it's very beneficial. I don't think I need to provide a coaching guide here but even progress in throwing and catching a ball is so gradual and you have to start with low expectations. But if you keep doing it, over time you will soon be amazed at the progress made. Patience really is a virtue here in that you have to keep at it on a consistent basis over time which does require discipline. The same applies to so many other things. I just want to use throw and catch as I think it provides a very simple example for you to consider as well as put it into context with many other activities.

I often wonder whether parents do have the patience to play catch for 30 minutes when the child might initially never catch the ball? Are you prepared to do the very slow and tedious things which produce such minimal results in the short-term? It's so important for you as the parent not to underestimate your child in anyway. Realistically only you as the parent will take the time to do the slow and tedious things that require a lot of patience and for you to essentially grind it out, little by little, day by day. Your child needs you to believe in them so, if your child is struggling to throw or catch a ball, don't assume and definitely don't use throw away comments like "my kid is just not a natural athlete." Sure your child may need more time to take to something than another kid, but again this is where the parent is key. Invest your time with your child and keep going at something even if the process can be painful at times. Try to embrace the journey, so to speak, without being all philosophical. Again, I repeat, throw and catch is a simple exercise, but core principles like patience, persistence, dedication, practice, discipline, repetition etc. apply to so many things your child is trying to learn from the so called small things to big things. However one of the most important factors I believe comes down to the parent and the parent having patience so that they invest their time, when again they're committing to the process.

Another example where I think we enjoyed success in having patience is with our daughter learning to ride a bike on two wheels. This is a good example as we know of some kids of her age who took to it almost right away. Our daughter needed more time to learn. I think even something like this requires patience on the parents part by not becoming frustrated and putting pressure on your child because other kids can already do it. Something like this needed our patience because we took her out many times to learn and the process was slow, progress was gradual and at the few times of asking I will admit we didn't really get too far. At such times you need to ask yourself whether you willing to stick at it and have the patience to take your child out after a long day at work or get up early on a Saturday morning to try again? I will say it again, even with such a simple example, patience and commitment are key. To put it bluntly - your kid needs you! They need you to simply take them and work at it with them, giving nothing more than your help/support.

I often get comments on how well my daughter can focus compared to other children for a class which may last for an hour. I can't pinpoint the reason for this but I certainly think that exposing her to classes from an early age, and attending consistently certainly played a factor. We also practice and work on many things with each other. It's sort of a combination of many different variables coming together. A point I made earlier which I think is such an important one for you to consider – progress is ever so gradual. So gradual at times that you may not even notice it until you refer to an old video from months ago. The level of progress can obviously differ from child to child but in the main, using my experience seeing kids playing golf at an early age, no one just picks up a club and can drive it far, putt well or chip expertly. In fact I think golf and tennis are two good sports to provide this illustration as they're very individual and technical. So I now want to look at making progress in more detail.

When progress is so, so gradual this is where the parents patience becomes so important. One of the previous chapters focused more on your commitment, but the focus is now on your patience. Yes, the kids need to stick at it but so do you. Back to an earlier point on scheduling and picking which activity, this is where you need to use some common sense. Sign your kid up for something you know you can commit to and you know you can make each week – then remain patient in the process mainly in relation to progress/improvement. If there is a class that runs once a week but you can only make it once a month or every now and then, then my advice is not to sign up. My view is that there is no benefit to the child and it will actually begin to cause some frustration, even with you as a parent if you don't see progress at all. If you think about it, how can a kid make progress in something if there is no consistency? I see it all the time particularly with the golf clinic my daughter attends every Saturday morning which I have previously mentioned, and she loves. We have just made it a habit of going every single week – we don't miss a class unless there is something really important, so you will be sure to find us there - every week! I admit, to a certain degree, it depends on the activity itself. If it's something very individual then I just don't see how a stop/start approach can really work.

To put a different spin on it and something I think we can all relate to. I'm mindful that I use sports a lot for my illustrations but, as I keep saying, I believe that many of the same rules apply to so many different things. So let's say if you (you in this instance, not your child) decided that you wanted to learn a new language, and we can use French as an example. Individual motivations will vary as to the reason why you're starting out, just like when you're introducing your child to something new. Personally, when you begin learning, you will want to see progress little by little and therefore it's logical to want the same for your child. Again this does not mean that you're getting carried away. The key is to have realistic expectations, not expecting instant/dramatic success, understanding that it's a more gradual process over time. I'm sure you would agree that to learn a new language requires discipline, hard work, effort and consistency over a long period to achieve some positive results. Essentially you need to form some form of schedule to set yourself up for success, and stick to it. Now on the other hand, say you start and do an hour one week, a few hours the next and then have two weeks off. You then pick it back up by doing an hour a day only then, through ill-discipline you don't work on anything now for a month. Essentially you're constantly stopping and starting and it will almost feel like you're at square one when you get back to it. Doing this sort of ad hoc practice will only have the potential to increase frustration, reduce enjoyment/motivation and will mean that there is a greater chance of you giving up at some point. I think this analogy perfectly illustrates the importance of why it's important to stick at something with your child, to give them every chance of success. No doubt as a parent you will get frustrated too if you see your child frustrated. But if you have a schedule which is non-committal, I stress that you will end up with this stop/start process which quite frankly doesn't work for anyone. I can speak firsthand of this as I tried to learn Spanish a few years ago, but I didn't get too far as my approach was rather sporadic and so in the end I didn't really get anywhere!

I'm a great believer in hard work and practice if you want to get better at anything. Nothing more so than in sports and that is what I put my daughter's progress to date down to. Again, I continue to reiterate that the progress is so gradual; it's at a snail's pace at times. Before you say anything, I'm not suggesting that just because you're getting your kid involved in something that they need to work to become some form of trophy kid or mini superstar – that is not the point. Every parent will have a different approach/motivation, but I think most will be on the same page in that first instance, in that introductory phase, the emphasis should be on fun and enjoyment. Related to this though is that parents will want to see their child make progress which then starts the process of beginning to develop that love, passion and enjoyment. Again I emphasize the word "progress" as this is not about your child scoring the game winning goal all the time. As long as the parent is realistic and realizes that progress is gradual, I promise you that you will see your child progress. Again, I reiterate that it doesn't mean for them to be the star of the team, but you will be amazed at what gradual/tiny improvements can do over time. So, back to my earlier point to give your child the best opportunity to succeed, commit to something you know you can do and stick at it. Sticking at something, anything for that matter is the key driver in all this.

I will provide a tennis example now to show the importance of "sticking" with something and having that patience. My daughter was in a group class when starting out; with this boy who must have only been five/six years old and he quickly made very good progress and was very impressive. He stood out in the group. This was a weekly class and then weeks went by when the boy no longer attended. It must have been months later when his mother randomly brought him back to the class. By this time my daughter and others had made gradual progress and were becoming better and better. But as the boy had not played for some time he had forgotten the key fundamental skills and was starting out again. He then was quickly becoming frustrated in the lesson, seeing others execute some of the simple drills when he was having difficulty and previously could do with ease. You could sense the mother was frustrated too and after that they didn't come again. I don't know the full story here and I might be a bit presumptuous but my guess is that there is a good chance they gave up. Of course there can be personal reasons so I don't want to be judgmental, immediately jumping to conclusions; it just goes back to the key point of signing your kid up for something that works with your schedule. The boy was previously excelling for someone so young and was clearly enjoying it but all he needed really was consistency so he could keep playing. I'm not going to say anything like that is a huge waste, or that he could have been a future world number one or anything silly like that. But the kid had potential so he just needed the opportunity to be able to keep going/playing. I also see similar things with the group golf class which I have mentioned many times which I take my daughter too. There are many kids you see kind of just randomly show up. Might even be once every couple of months. Sometimes I can get a comment of some sort like "wow how did she get so good" when referring to my daughter after seeing her hit. I don't like to overthink things really and I essentially think she is good because she plays on a consistent/regular basis. I mean, let's make it so common sense using another analogy. Who do you think will be in better shape? Someone who works out all the time or someone who hardly ever works out/exercises?

The point I want to continue to make, linked to patience, is that I think if you sign up for something, then commit to it. How long you commit to something again is something which is open to debate and really needs to be your personal judgment. At the same time, I don't think it's wise after one or two tries if your child says they don't like something, to give it up. If however, your child obviously hates or dreads going to something and he/she really did give it their best shot over a sustained period of time, it then might be worth calling it a day – again use your common sense. I think your responsibility as a parent is giving your child the opportunity to succeed and that is where I think consistency and patience become key.

So patience as a parent is also vital and this is where realistic expectations come in. I hear frequent stories from coaches on how parents are so impatient with their child's progress that it almost adds a form of pressure, not only to the coach but to the child too. I will use tennis as another example to make a point which I hope you can apply to your situation. The serve in tennis – watching a pro they certainly do make it look easy. My daughter has only over the past few months been introduced to the very basic mechanics of the serve. I soon realized how technical it is and when you break it down, it's something which I think is actually quite complex. Not only when you advance you have to consider the accuracy and power but from the beginner's stage where my child is at, you realize how important the body position is, the grip of the racquet, and not only that the toss of the ball. The toss has so many factors, even where and how you hold the ball before you even throw it up. Then the height to which you throw it is very important, the speed/pace and then the position of the ball in the air is another variable as to what makes a toss good or bad. I could go on explaining the complexity of the serve, but the point that I'm trying to make is that everyone needs to be patient when learning something which, at first glance, might not seem so difficult. But when you break it down, like I have done in this example, you realize the multiple steps involved. So obviously the coach and player, in this case my daughter, need patience, and so do I as a parent. Realistically, something like a serve takes many years to even develop, let alone master, so by just applying some basic common sense you then have realistic expectations for your child. As a result, no one becomes frustrated as there will be times it might appear that, for all the hard work, no significant progress is really being made. In this example, it's having the understanding that it's going to take a lot of time and practice. Therefore, patience is fundamental going hand in hand with commitment.

Yes there are children out there that may be more naturally suited to certain things and will make progress quicker than others, but remember the classic tale of The Tortoise and The Hare? The Tortoise wins in the long-run, but you and your child have to persist and remain patient as well as committed in the process. If anything improvement or progress can move at snail's pace at times. If you picture improvement as a spectrum, I think you will find in most things that improvement does go at a snail's pace. You might well say that's ok and only to be expected. But like with so many things these days, I tend to find people what to see improvement or progress at a much faster rate than say a snail. So actually that spectrum of improvement becomes more of a spectrum of patience to determine your level of tolerance. But I would strongly encourage you to remain patient and committed. If you stay with my analogy for a second referring to improvement moving at the pace of a snail, think about it; it's so, so slow/gradual. But think of it this way if that snail keeps moving at the same pace wouldn't it get a long way in say 6 months' time or even a year from where it started out? Of course it would. So I strongly recommend you to look at improvement/progress in the same way. Yes it might be tedious at times to watch something move at a snail's pace, but I think the ones who do and remain patient see the benefit down the road. Hopefully you see where I'm coming from with the point I'm trying to make here, because sometimes I think all it requires is a little patience to see something out to really start to see the benefit. I may come across a little cynical, but I tend to find people in general (not just parents) want to see something (results) much more quickly these days. So bringing this specifically to parenting, a parent may sign their child up for something and find that their child isn't really getting anywhere early on and their child might be getting frustrated too. So at that time it might only be natural to think: What's the point? Should we try something else? A blunt way of posing the question is to ask: Can you really be bothered with it? It's hard not to generalize with these types of hypothetical examples and I know every case is unique, but all I'm saying is consider being more patient at times when these types of things are going through your head. My advice is remain committed as it may just be your child is moving at the pace of my snail friend.

I really like the saying progress not perfection. If you approach things with this mind-set then you're a creating a pressure free environment for your child which allows for them to make mistakes. Mistakes are a fundamental part of making progress and learning so remember this key point too. I speak to many coaches and to give you examples in golf and tennis many say how parents become frustrated and expect their child to be smashing balls within weeks of lessons. This not only creates unrealistic expectations for the coach but also the child. In this scenario typically frustration wins and therefore quitting is the easy way out. Back to my daughter's example with tennis I have to say I was amazed with how technical the serve actually is. As I just said, everything from the position of the body, the grip of the racquet and tossing the ball up is an art in itself. My daughter has made very good progress on her tennis serve, but I would be the first to admit that the progress to date has been very slow and tedious. Now I'm not patting myself of the back here, but as a parent I expected this and was realistic about any progress to be made as the skill itself is technical in nature. Therefore, frustration doesn't come into play, as I felt I understood the process and still do, in that there is much more improvement to be made and that all just takes time. I'm going to generalize now, but a tendency might be to get frustrated if you don't see that improvement right away. Or it might be you see another kid of a similar age performing much better. At such a time, I think this is when the parent needs to step up as they may actually need to reassure their child to keep working at it. There is no doubt kids can get frustrated too if improvement is so gradual that it's hard to even notice it. Using the theme of choices in such cases looking at the potential of frustration/quitting, I personally think it's best for the parent to initially take control and then they can gradually involve their child in decisions when the time is right based on maturity. When this will be is purely a judgment call on your part as there will be no cookie cutter recipe/formula.

Staying with having realistic expectations this is where you as the parent again play such a key role. My advice to you is be part of the process. Looking for those gradual/incremental improvements which work wonders over time, but, at the same time, keeping expectations realistic. Do whatever works for you and your child. You could have a chart with goals which you can track/monitor over a set period. Whilst there are a lot of things which are subjective and hard to measure, at the same time I'm sure you can find some more objective things which you can. In my view it doesn't have to be over complicated, the beauty is in the simplicity. So look for things you can do where you're involved, part of the process and where your encouragement is key. If you child plays basketball you could track how many free throws they make in a row and then you can use that as a baseline to try and improve on that number. You then re-baseline after the next target is reached and you can see how it can evolve very naturally. The same can apply in soccer, with something like juggling, or golf with putts, or tennis with serves. In can be applied in many other settings too like in education - how about in spelling or with sight words like in my daughter's case? This is where you now have a purpose and focus to practice with the main focus being on patience, improving, but in a very gradual way. Using this example you may need to stay on a certain number for an extended period and that's ok too. It's all about application and sticking/committing to the process over time so that you can overcome the inevitable challenges along the way when progress might seem slow. If you understand this, then pressure is removed by staying patient throughout as you understand that you need to be and how important it is.

I keep making the point that progress is very slow and there might be times where you think your child is taking a step back, but that is ok and to be expected. I say this because the easiest thing to do when frustration kicks in is quit, no longer sign up and be done with it. But I think kids go through so many different phases, certainly over the long-term, both good and bad, so with the bad it may be as simple as just riding it out. A good analogy showing the slow process is like with the growth (height) of your child. If you're with your child every day you won't necessarily notice any growth (in height) because it's so gradual. But parents get comments all the time and I make it to other parents on how their child has grown – we notice as we only see them every now and then, or on an infrequent basis. I think this principle can be applied when your child is learning something new. Providing they continue to work on a sport or instrument for example, progress for the first few months or even years will be so gradual that it will be almost unnoticeable if monitored so closely. However the gradual improvements over time do become significant, and although they might not be striking to you as it has been so gradual – trust me, the results will be worth all of the effort. Some might say that it's worth the sacrifice, but I don't see how I can be sacrificing anything if I'm doing something that will benefit my child.

This is why I recommend taking videos every so often, and there are plenty of good apps these days which make it so easy for you and it automatically logs everything by day and time. I have done this with my daughter with golf and tennis and this point rings true. I don't really notice significant progress in her golf swing, or accuracy, or how she rallies in tennis. However, if I refer to a video from, say, six/eight months ago my wife and I can quickly see the almost dramatic progress she has made. The videos are not only great for that purpose but I now have these forever and I'm sure I will cherish looking back at them in say ten years' time. I think this is something all parents can easily do these days as, let's face it, we all love taking videos and photos of our children. So whilst all along I have been saying to put the phone away, bring it back out of the closet (or back pocket) as there is a purpose to this to help show that improvement over time. You can build up a great memory bank of videos and photos – for you and your child. You will probably say something like here we go again, but my advice would be not to have such a memory bank on social media. Take the external out of it as this is internal to you and your child/family. This isn't about getting all caught up with constant posts, comments and praise, so you can hear your social network say things like great job or get so many likes. I think it's best to remove such noise and distraction as it's getting away for the main reason/purpose of what you're looking to achieve.

I'm not going to deny this is easy and by bringing it back to the opening of the chapter, the difficulty is that we are, as a society in general, becoming more impatient. It's very easy for me to sit here and say to have a long-term focus for everything you do, as having such an outlook in the present/moment can be challenging at times. But when I say have patience I mean it in a way so that you don't get carried away at times when you might not think your child is getting anywhere. I say to be committed so that, at times, you just get on with it as you just know that's what you need to do. Many of these chapters are linked and I would be the first to admit that some, if not many of the points made are quite repetitive. I know I go on and on a little at times, but I repeat some of the points for a reason. I really believe in their importance, so I think it's relevant to perhaps make the same or a similar point in a different way/setting or with different/additional examples. So this chapter really focuses on patience with the understanding or how progress is so gradual. Once you have that patience and understanding, I think this will help keep you committed. Looking at it the other way, impatience can cause frustration which can then ultimately question your commitment to something when quitting or giving up could ultimately win. Long-term patience is just that long-term and for a long time. My advice is stay the course. Every road is unique/different so if anything have faith in the principle/concept. I don't want to close out this chapter to say something like become more patient to become a better parent as this would be another way in just pointing out the obvious. In this chapter, I looked to provide that context where I have applied the concept in the real world. Hopefully you understand what I've been trying to say in different areas, so you can apply it for yourself to help you become a better parent.

30 BE PROACTIVE

I do believe that you have to be proactive as a parent as well. So let's now look at this concept and once again apply it to some of my previous examples. Back to my daughter's golf. She goes to a weekly clinic and we get there early every week, hit some extra balls after, and make best use of the time we have there. From an early age my daughter was making gradual progress. I don't want to come across boastful/big-headed here or anything like that; I just want to make a clear and honest point. The point being that my daughter is better than most kids and is very advanced for her age - it's evident by just observing as well as considering her successes from many different tournaments. You can argue the reasons, but looking at it from a logical, objective, not subjective or biased point of view; I believe one is that we make best use of time. We always arrive early practicing before the clinic and hit extra balls after. So from just one clinic I would say my daughter would probably make double the amount of shots in that class than any other child – when you multiply that over a year or two you then see the positive results. You then understand the outcome as it's almost common sense. Someone may see her first hand and think "wow she is talented" as she does stand out when comparing with other kids. But when you consider that she is hitting way more golf balls than anyone else then it's a lot easier to understand. I'm not saying the "wow" element necessarily goes away, but when at first-hand someone might be a little surprised to see her hit, but when you understand how we got to that point it kind of just starts to makes sense. To use an analogy like a magic trick. We can be amazed at seeing a magic trick, but when we learn how it's done – you then understand and you're like ok, so that's how you do it! As a result, that somewhat element of mystery or that wow factor actually kind of goes away.

As her father you may think that I might be slightly biased, but that is why I emphasize it's from an objective not subjective point of view. A key point I have made throughout is that I'm just being honest. With that, I think that, whilst it's important to share with you experiences where we have made mistakes, I think it's also as important to share with you examples where we have enjoyed some success. More simply, my reasoning for why I think she is better is because she does more than others. Sure there are other variables too, not least what we and others do outside a weekly clinic which I provided in my example. In her case she does do a lot of additional practice outside the weekly clinic, but even so I think this approach of utilizing practice time has significantly benefitted her. Can you at least relate to some of my points? Your kid might not play golf but like much of my advice throughout the book, the same principles apply. Think to yourself whatever your child is doing can you do a little more? I have no doubt that it will benefit them. Can you arrive a little earlier or stay 10 minutes after and do that little extra of whatever it is that he/she is doing? Can you child use/utilize 15-20 minutes of spare time in the day to work on something? Again, this all goes back to making the best use of your child's time for their ultimate benefit. This also doesn't have to overly impact you or your time as a parent – you're already going or will already be there so take advantage of that.

I want to stay on this point a little more just to further illustrate the point from an objective point of view to actually remove my or any opinion. Let's just look at numbers. I will keep it simple, continuing with this golf example and this one clinic alone. Again, to get to a certain level you need to look at more than just one class or clinic but I want to illustrate how to make best use of your time. So say she hits 50 balls (ranging from putts, chips, driver etc.) before and 50 balls after, that's 100 extra balls from one clinic alone. There are 52 clinic in a year and let's say she goes to 50 of them. Clearly there will be some give and take here with the numbers but, like I said, I want to keep it simple. So basic math's (math – for my American friends) will tell you she will hit 5000 more balls over the course of the year than other kids in that same class alone. Now I won't pretend this is new advice as it's out there where you play the numbers game so to speak. Clearly there is also more to it than just numbers as it has to be beneficial. With this golf example, if my daughter had a really bad grip or was doing something fundamentally wrong 5000 times, then it might have an adverse rather than a positive effect. However, in her case it really has made a positive impact and the key thing I want to open your eyes to be that when applied correctly, "playing the numbers game" correctly no doubt works. But even saying that, I would still go back to the main point that this is more about using time wisely and being proactive rather than necessarily focusing on numbers.

Another key point is that it's important for your child to want to do this extra practice and that only really comes if they're developing that passion. But you have to help them develop that passion so in our case, by doing more, she naturally becomes better, starts to enjoy it more and then naturally wants to do more herself. When I say be proactive in this sense it's not that we even have to really go out of our way as parents in terms of scheduling. It's just really about being organized so we can get there ahead of time and then we just stay a little after, something like 15 or 20 minutes. Why should I be in a rush to leave if she wants to stay to do more and we can do this? So for me being proactive does not necessarily have to really think outside the box or be over imaginative. Sure some days you may have something else on or need to get to somewhere, but on others consider if you're rushing to get away to then get home and do nothing. The way I see it, we're just making better use of time, all for the benefit of our child. It actually doesn't really put us out at all and I'm more than happy to do something like this as I know it benefits my child.

Continuing with my daughter, I'm not getting carried away, but she has made some great progress. It's kind of logical in a sense in that she practices more, hits more balls, and spends more time playing than other kids, so in turn she is better. When you look at something in a logical way then there is no real surprise/shock for why she is better as the reason is rather obvious. The talent label is a completely different debate – I value hard work, effort, attitude and practice. Sure, there will be some exceptions to the rule and examples out there which might argue against this but I think you have to play the percentages so to speak. This means giving your child every opportunity for success. The results still may differ from child to child if everyone did that in terms of the rate of progression, but let's be honest; everyone would at least be better at whatever it is they're doing.

This is where you can play a vital role as a parent, giving these extra little, seemingly insignificant in the moment, advantages to your child. That's what being proactive means to me as a parent. Again, in terms of scheduling, it requires you to plan and forward think a little, maybe get up a little earlier, things like that. But trust me; anything like this where you can be proactive is so worth it. I get it as parents that we need to be flexible; there are simply times where all the good planning in the world goes out of the window as life can throw so many unexpected things at us. So don't be too rigid, be flexible when you need to, but trust the schedule in terms of planning as your time management can either give, or not give your child additional beneficial opportunities. Back to my earlier example of arriving early to my daughter's golf clinic is something I have committed to and it has essentially become a habit. Again, by doing something like this you don't notice the benefit instantly; it is only over a period of time. So if you're going to start doing something proactive like this, to see results you even need to commit to that. Develop good routines rather than showing up early only for a week or two and then doing it again only a few months later, as it won't work that way as intended. It requires discipline and not much on the child but more on the parent to actually do something like this. I'm sure if a kid is really into something they would jump at the chance of doing more. I'm sure some parents might not want to associate words like discipline, habit, consistency when introducing their child to a hobby where you just want them to have fun. I'm not saying it needs to be super serious where something starts to take over. I think these words need to be looked at in context with the points I'm trying to make and hopefully you can apply such perspective to your personal situation. But when I say it's on you as a parent, it really is. A young child won't necessarily think about getting to a class early or think about doing a little extra when he/she sees all the other kids going home. You're the one to get ready ahead of time and determine when you leave and go home so again, like it or not, you really do call the shots, even on things like this.

So my advice is to ensure you're more than doing your part in helping your child by getting there a little early or staying and hitting those few extra balls once everyone else has already left. Apply this analogy to your child's current activities. Not just that, do additional practice time with them and essentially bond over a sport or activity. If you commit to something your child will have the opportunity to have great experiences, as well as the opportunity to potentially develop a love and passion for something which may last a lifetime. I really believe that you increase the likelihood of this happening by setting them up for success so that they can make that progress and improvement. Again being proactive as a parent can only help. Let's face it, this is not just kids, but if we're getting better at something we naturally enjoy it more and then, in turn, want to do more. As the parent you will get to enjoy the experience too and see first-hand your child develop. But you have to play your part, do all you can and be hands on to help your child get to that point where they're starting to get really good at something. If done right there are so many knock on benefits such as your child developing belief, confidence and a level of maturity. My advice is for you to really understand how you play a critical part in the process, where the sooner you realize this, the better it will be for you and your child. To use an analogy you may be like the conductor of an orchestra where you may not be the one out there with the instrument in your hand, but you're perhaps just as important when it comes to bringing everything together. So when I say be proactive to become a better parent, I don't mean it in such a way where you need to think of something new or innovative. I mean it more by perhaps just being a little creative or mindful in things like making the best use of your time. I think the more and more you think like this where you look to and can be proactive, then becoming a better parent will go hand-in-hand with such an approach.

31 FUN

I do want to touch a little more on the notion of having fun. This is something that I'm going to throw out there for your consideration more than anything, as I don't think there is a perfect answer. In an ideal world your child will always be having fun doing whatever it is they're doing, but let's just stay with sports. My take is that is actually more of a fantasy than a reality. I think the simply reality is that it won't always be fun. As part of the process in developing and getting out of your comfort zone things like failure, rejection, setbacks, bad days, losses will inevitably happen and will continue to happen along the way – if indeed you do stay the course. I'm not saying that this will be the norm as on the flip side of that will be the opposite with many great days. The ups and downs will be part of the territory of developing which again is why it's key to get used to being out of your comfort zone (both parent and child). I will look a lot more on getting you as the parent as well as your child out of your comfort zones in a forthcoming chapter. So when looking at the realities of occasions when there will be failure, rejection, defeats, setbacks, bad days, losses, then the reality is that those days won't be fun at all. But I think that's ok too because, as I touch on throughout, it's all part of the process. If anything it is to be embraced as it's only to be expected, although in the moment I appreciate that you won't be thinking so rationally. I think that, for this reason, it's more important that the love and passion for something is developed, which does start with it being about fun, so that your child would want to bounce back from any set backs down the line.

To stay on this topic, what about things such as your child working really hard, pushing themselves, grinding it out – in those moments will a child always be having fun? Can every practice be fun? Sure, in time they might learn to love going that extra mile, but the point that I'm trying to make or get you to think about, particularly when children are younger, is that it might not be as easy for them (or you for that matter) to have such a mindset. Things are not always constant in that your child won't always have the same level of excitement. In reality they're not going to have the same level of excitement as when they're trying something for the first time. Love and hate are opposites but I think if your child has a true passion for something you will see both of these feelings over time. If anything, the hate your child may feel in the moment when it's not all fun may actually prove the passion that they have. Obviously this hate would need to be a short-term feeling rather than a long-term one. Their love/passion will want them coming back for more in those challenging times. Challenges and responding to challenges in such a way can help build things like resiliency, another great trait. I'm not trying to overthink it here but I'm just trying to point out some knock on effects/benefits which might not be considered in shall we say tough moments/times. So what I'm saying is that if you focus on everything being fun that might neglect such moments which ultimately can build character in your children, as well as other traits like resilience, positively responding to setbacks which are so beneficial. Overall isn't life or something actually fun when we overcome obstacles/challenges all for the better? Wouldn't it be fun to see your own child do just that? Is it actually fun if everything is easy or manufactured/artificial/fake with no challenge? Do you want your child to be in a manufactured environment? Is it fun to stay in the comfort zone? Sure it might be easier and seem more appealing in the moment but consider such questions.

So my advice is really just give this some closer consideration for yourself. I don't think there is an easy, right/wrong answer. If you read any advice on sports or activities, or ask a parent or coach what is the most important thing for the child, I bet the most common answer would be to have fun. Let me make clear, I'm not denying the importance of fun or downplaying it in anyway, but I can't help but think that sometimes, as parents, we're made to fixate on something always being fun. I say this because when there are times when it does get tough/hard for your child, the parent can easily feel some guilt and assume responsibility. Then you can easily think things like: Is this all worth it? Am I pushing my child too hard? Should we stop doing this as it's stopped all being about fun? I say these things because these are all common emotions and reactions which we will face or continue to face when out of your comfort zone. But I just want you to consider it from the other point of view for a second because should you actually feel any guilt? Perhaps not, if you come to the conclusion that in fact it can't always be fun all of the time. The reality is for some kids doing that extra work, practice and hard work means that they won't have a beaming smile on their face while doing it. You may inevitably get some push back where they don't want to do the extra practice or work that little harder. Or it might when they're done they won't necessarily ask to do some more.

So I want you to consider that maybe it can't always be about fun and maybe that's ok? That's something you really need to decide for yourself. I say to consider this because if you have the mind-set that it can, and should only or always be about being fun, that's fine or all well and good, but does that translate in the real world? Does that mean that you stop or quit the moment it's not all fun and games? Again speaking as a real world parent there will be days when your child might be playing for a soccer team as an example and using a slang term the team might get "tanked" say 6-0 or 7-0 or 8-0? That can happen in any team sport or individual sport for that matter. So will that be fun when you get thrashed by another team or opponent? Despite how much perspective you have as a parent and how much you look at the bigger picture, in the moment it won't be fun for you or your child. I'm sure if you've played sports yourself you can relate to a time when you got well beaten in something. Come to think of it I bet most if not all professional athletes can recall a time when they got "tanked" in a game/match. The reason I say all this because that it's ok. It comes with the territory, is to be expected and is perhaps fundamental to actual development to have the different range of experiences and emotions. I personally think it's also important for you to experience and go through these range of emotions as a parent in relation to your child. Sure it's easy when things are going good but my view is that you have to deal with the other side of it. That's when I think you'll learn a lot about yourself as a parent. So I highlight this to not let it be a reason why you stop your child doing something because you will have days that aren't "Fun". Again you will know a result of a match in the grand scheme of things is rather irrelevant. Despite that I think you'll find you will be human in that it will still not change your feeling in the here and now where you're not going to be bouncing up and down with joy. However, my view is to not to suddenly overreact or blow something out of proportion because you only signed your child up for Fun.

I just think advice on it being fun is rather generic and it's a kind of stock answer that everything has to be fun. I would put such a response in the bracket of that ideological/make believe advice or approach because I just don't think its real world advice. Personally I don't think it's so clear cut and actually needs to be given more context/consideration. This is why I'm highlighting it here. Again I stress that having fun is vital but maybe we should be less obsessed with everything having to be fun all the time, because is that realistic? There is almost a degree of hysteria around things always having to be fun all of the time with children. I reiterate this because of that external pressure we may sometimes feel that everything has to be fun. As a result, perhaps you shouldn't have any guilt at all. I think that, as parents, we can then put internal pressure on ourselves around something like this, which is compounded in part by external pressures. The external pressure in this case being focused on everything having to be fun and this could come from friends, neighbors, family members, teachers, coaches and others. I know that, as parents, we can put pressure on ourselves for many different things so in this instance I would just question whether we should allow for this to happen? I think it needs close consideration and it's certainly not a simple yes/no answer where it's so clear cut. I'm certainly not getting to anything extreme where your child is doing grueling things and of course the age of the child is a major factor here. To break it down a little or to look at it a bit more simply, all I'm saying is to perhaps look at it in a different way when you're faced with these different types of challenges. Maybe be a bit more logical during times when it just might be that things don't go your child's way – again I say this as I think it will inevitably happen. I don't even want to say at one point or another as I think children go through so many different phases which you as a parent have to deal with and work through. So I think this is very much a continual thing you will have to deal with and face head on rather than look to avoid in any way.

We get a lot of cues as parents in relation to fun, particularly with the level of excitement. I did just mention it and I want to talk a little more about your child doing something for the first time with my own example. I was thinking the other day about my daughter and her first golf tournament. When we pulled up she was screaming in the car (good screaming with excitement) like it was Christmas day. She no longer does this when we pull up for tournaments although she has a lot of fun and is excited in different ways, such as seeing and playing with friends she has made. It did make me think though and question whether she should still have that same level of excitement. She has played in over 25 tournaments now so I suppose the novelty factor has worn off. I say this and want to make this point because that first time excitement is just that, the first time. As a result of your child developing in something, I think you will go through different stages/phases where fun actually starts to have a different meaning as a result of the continued experiences your child has along the way. So I wanted to share this to demonstrate in another way that things being fun when looking at something at face value, might not be as simple as some might think.

I also think the idea of fun is subjective and is actually very personal. Put simply, what's fun to someone might be like watching paint dry to someone else. So it's more of a perception really the more you think about it. I think this is another reason to not get all caught up about things being fun because it essentially has a different meaning to each and every one of us. Is easy and simple really fun? Or how about working so hard at something to master so that it's now fun? Can someone learn to have fun by learning something? Can something become fun once it has been learned? It might require a high level of discipline, commitment and determination which might not be fun during the process, but it may all be worth it in the end. That is why fun is such a perception or so personal to an individual and not some broad notion that applies to everyone and everything. I appreciate that some of these questions to consider maybe over-thinking it a little, particularly if you're only just introducing your child to something new. But I think the deeper you all get and when you run into your first few hurdles or obstacles then at least some of this might start to become more relevant. I actually think this will happen a lot sooner than you may think.

Another way to look at it is not putting fun where it is solely considered in isolation. What I mean by that is that I believe a parent, coach or teacher can be fun whilst at the same time appropriately pushing your child at the right time to improve. Or that parent, coach or teacher can still be fun whilst also being disciplined too. So maybe fun can't always be considered as the most important thing or in isolation? Also that parent, coach or teacher might be considered fun, but that also doesn't mean that they need to be fun all of the time. It therefore should possibly be considered in more of an overall sense. An exaggerated example might be a teacher or a coach that goofs off with your child all the time which might be fun in the moment, but sometimes you might have to ask yourself whether fun is the only real benefit and at the expense of your child's development?

I want to make a distinction here. This is not referring to a situation where your child might genuinely hate something but you don't want them to give up so you don't let them quit. This is not about being forceful on your child, them crying at just having to go where they flat out don't want to be there. Although I must admit we did go through this when our daughter was learning to swim as her safety was our main concern, so I will touch on this again in a moment. But this is really about when your child does have a love and passion for something, but faces challenges on the way. With those challenges, I think again the reality is that your child won't be having fun for every second of it. Hopefully you understand the point I want you to consider and determine whether it's actually ok that, at times, it won't always be fun. Or alternatively you could only sign up for things for your child which don't have challenges, where it's always "fun". But is that fair on the child? At one point or another they will be exposed to the realities of life in the real world, so is it best to try and hide or always try to protect them from that? How about something as simple as losing? Do you want to get to a point where you're child can't experience losing at anything because losing is not fun? Or it might be your child looks to avoid certain situations because of the potential of losing and that is certainly not a good thing for their overall development. So the reason I want to make these points is that in those challenging times that might be the time for a parent or child to say that they no longer want to do something because it's no longer fun. So I just want you to ponder whilst we would love everything to be fun, in reality if your child is really going to progress in something can it always be fun? Or in other words what's good, or what's best for a child might not always be fun. I keep going back to my child learning to swim as an example but it's such a simple illustration and proves how something can develop over time. The point being there was no instant passion or love of her wanting actually go. She would never have, in a million years, asked me to go to the pool. It was a case in those early days of us essentially making her to go a lesson, call it what you want but that's what we essentially did. Our child's safety was paramount so at that point we were less focused on it being fun and, trust me, it wasn't fun. Fun was secondary to our child's safety. With us all having worked through that difficult period she now has all the fun in the world swimming. So again all I'm saying when thinking everything has to be fun, perhaps it's not so black and white and more thought is actually required.

Let's think or look at it another way. I'm sure you can draw on your own past experiences with a coach or teacher who may have been a little strict at times but, on reflection, it was the best thing for you. Or, let's look at ourselves for a minute. Are you, as a parent, always about having fun with your child? Whilst I love the idea of me, as the parent having fun every second that I'm with my child, being that fun dad all of the time, again that's living in an imaginary world. In a basic example if your child is acting up are you going to respond to that thinking about being or acting all fun? In another context is something like studying or homework always going to be fun? I think we all know that the answer is no but we understand the fundamental importance of something such as homework or study. In this instance we're not concerned or worried about our child having fun and certainly wouldn't encourage them to stop, quit or for them to not do their homework because they won't necessarily be having fun doing it. Also, when looking at your comfort zone, this is not to say that you can't have fun when you're out of it either. I just want to make these points as I think that, at times as parents, we perhaps can be a little fixated on things being fun when maybe that's an unrealistic expectation.

So I encourage you to think more than anything about the notion of things being fun. I want to make it very clear that I'm on the same page as people with the importance of fun. But I think it needs more thought, where it's not looked at in isolation as I also think that the meaning of fun can actually evolve over time. Whilst I'm certainly not denying the importance, I would not essentially obsess over it, as by thinking something always has to be fun maybe a false hope. Regardless of what level your child is currently at, I think you will actually come across this somewhat of a dilemma a lot sooner rather than later than you might think. I have said it throughout, this book is about real world parenting, so whilst in a perfect world it might be nice for our children to be having fun all of the time whether it's at home, school or playing a sport, ultimately is that realistic? Perhaps the key takeaway in this chapter is for you to give this topic the consideration that I think it deserves. After that make up your own mind to decide how you will deal with or approach the notion of fun, as this will certainly be ongoing for you and your child. To become a better parent have the understanding of fun and its importance, but you may well come to the conclusion it can't be fun all of the time. Will that actually be the best thing for your child? Only you can answer that.

32 READ/EDUCATE

When I say it's important to read/educate so you can learn, I'll admit this isn't earth shattering advice - I know. But I do want to put my own take on it from an everyday parent's perspective. Firstly, I consider myself fairly well educated but I would be the first to admit that I haven't really read many books outside of formal education. It has only been over the last 3-4 years where I have really started to do so. I suppose I used to have a fairly ignorant view of reading and I never really saw a great benefit of doing so. I only really ever read the books assigned to us in school and that was essentially it.

I have now been converted on this and see so many benefits from reading. If you come across any personal development advice a common and recurring theme is reading, to support the notion of continual learning. I can't say that I know about how, and the reasons why in terms of the science, but I genuinely do believe that when you do read, it ignites a certain part of your brain. I think it also helps you to be more creative whereby thoughts almost start unexpectedly coming into your head, which perhaps wouldn't happen if you weren't actively reading. I will let you into a little secret though. When I say read, I'm lying a little, as a lot of the books I now "read" are on my way to work, in audio form. So I tend to listen to them on my commute to and from work and any other time where I'm alone in my car. Another benefit of this is that I have control of what I'm feeding my mind rather than what is given on the radio in the morning. From a personal point of view, I get aggravated by the commercials and mindless gossip on some of the radio stations. I consider myself fairly active or as my wife would say I have ants in my pants, so I don't really like sitting and reading a book. I find audio books as the perfect solution and I think you will be amazed at how quickly you get through a book this way. I also feel that there is something unique if the narrator is a good story teller as they make the content that more interesting. The audio option I think will also appeal to most parents as I keep referring to the fact that free time is very limited, so this is about being inventive and using opportunities like commute time wisely for your benefit.

There are endless lists of top books to read, whether it's in personal development, finance, autobiographies, to name but a few. I think you will find many of the key benefits are consistent that you receive from reading a good book. Hey, why not read another one on parenting? I will touch on this a lot more on what I suggest you read up on. It might not also need to be a book as there are many good articles out there but the difficulty I suppose is that there are so many; it's about subscribing/finding something which relates to what you're looking for. This is another area where I'm not trying to call anyone out, but this maybe some more advice where a parent might say I just don't have time to read a book. I know, I know I have gone on enough already, but if that is you, but you do find time to read up on celebrity gossip, look online at random photos/videos, watch reality shows, check social media, read up on the latest timeline etc. then perhaps you do have time?

So this is fairly general advice which is already out there and essentially applies to everyone. So I will try and be more specific when it comes to parenting using my own example. I also use the word "educate" as part of the title for this chapter, as I think reading and education go hand in hand with something that helped me. I have mentioned throughout that my daughter has developed a love for golf and, as a consequence, so have I. Growing up I would say I was a golf fan in that I played recreationally on a very occasional basis and watched the major championships on TV. So I certainly wouldn't say that I had deep knowledge of the sport. So as my daughter quickly developed, she started to play tournaments and I became what is known as the caddy daddy. The focus is very much on enjoyment and development, but nonetheless all the rules of golf essentially apply when she is playing. In addition, I quickly learned there is a lot more to being a caddy than just carrying the bag of clubs. So I took it on myself to get a book with tips for parent caddies and US Kids Golf, who run the tournaments my daughter plays in, also had a recommendation for an online course for parents with kids involved in competitive sports (Positive Coaching Alliance) which I completed. I'm also reading up on some of the golf rules and etiquette which will become more relevant as my daughter matures. But that way I see it, is that it's my responsibility to help and teach her some of the rules as she grows. Not just that, but I also want to learn more about something for which my daughter has developed a passion for so I can gain more of an understanding myself. I now have much more of a personal interest, so essentially I want to educate myself more and more. I do want to highlight here that I'm not taking it to the extreme to become an expert and know every rule or all the ins and outs, but ultimately, I don't want to be ignorant either. I personally feel that it's on me to take the time to do this and at the end of the day it's something I really want to do anyway.

Hopefully you understand what I'm getting at here and it doesn't necessarily have to be a sport, but if your child is developing a love and passion for something which you don't know much about, why don't you also learn more about it? Learn the rules, get some coaching advice as well as some tips you can reinforce at home. Why not read an autobiography about someone with great success in the industry/field/sport that you're looking at to learn about their journey in how they rose to the top? I'm sure you can pick up on many good fundamentals that were important to them along the way. Why not register/sign up for newsletters, articles or magazine subscriptions? At this point I want to clarify, along with my earlier point, that this advice is not saying you're doing this to become a fully qualified coach in a given field. I also think it really doesn't matter what level your child is currently at, it could be advanced or beginner. All I'm saying is to take a deeper interest and there are endless resources (like books, where many are now in audio form) out there these days to take advantage on any given subject.

So, read a book, take a course or even watch one of the many different videos online now with practical advice with visual demonstrations. There is so much available now (a lot of it free), that there is definitely no excuse in this area. In doing something like this you will become a lot more engaged with the hobby that your child enjoys which ultimately can bring you closer together. I think there is always the opportunity for parents to help reinforce that enjoyment and I feel that it's your responsibility to do this also. My golf example is very specific to me but the same principles apply, certainly across sports. So don't sit on the side-lines and think to yourself what is going on, or what happened there, or why did the linesman flag that offside, I don't understand the rule!? Well, my belief is that you should. Maybe not right away but if your child has been playing soccer for a year and you still don't know the offside rule then maybe that's a sign to take some action. Take it on yourself to learn and educate yourself here and whilst it might take time for it to click, and that is ok, that's not really the ultimate test. No matter how long it takes - learn the offside rule! Jokes aside, it's all about trying to help your child and I think you can do that if you learn more about what interests them. It might sound a little blunt but don't be ignorant or oblivious to what is going on around you. This is not about learning all there is to know but at least playing more of an active role. Again, all of this is with the purpose of becoming a better parent. At the same time you may not have given something like learning the rules of a sport (if this is relevant to you) some thought, so in that sense I hope this suggestion has given you some ideas for consideration.

By being proactive in this sense, I think this will also enable you to reinforce some things a coach might be working on with your child. Speak to your child's coach to see if there are some things you can do with your child together to given them an added advantage. If your son or daughter plays soccer and you never played it before and have little knowledge of the game, it's perhaps an easy excuse to say that and you leave everything up to coaches. Point is that your child will only have so much time with coaches and I think you will find that, in the main, kids who are showing greater progress put in that added work/practice over and above those regular practices/sessions with coaches. So sure, the kids can take it on themselves, but for particularly the younger ones, they do need some assistance. When I say excuse using the soccer example, I mean just that and I think the same is true for any other sport/activity. So staying with soccer, speak to the coach and have him/her show you some simple things you can do. By having this conversation hopefully this can help highlight some areas that need to be worked on anyway. Again you're educating yourself in the process! It also doesn't necessarily have to all be with the ball either and be overly technical. There are all type of different footwork or conditioning drills you can do. But this is also the time to take advantage of all those different videos and online resources that are available which, in some cases, literally take you step by step through drills which anyone could implement. I can't tell you how many times I have looked up videos for my daughter's tennis and they're all mainly simple drills that relate to footwork as that is an area for her to work on. So use soccer as my example and apply it to whatever your child does so that you become a part of the process too. This doesn't mean that you need to become a coach-like figure where you try and do everything your child's coach is currently doing or that somehow you're trying to takeover. I know there is a lot of advice out there which goes against just that. If anything, you're just assisting/facilitating in reinforcing the skills that your child may be currently working on. I think you will be surprised how quickly you can actually pick things up because, if your child is developing a passion for something, it's only very natural for you to want to mirror that passion as the parent. You may even surprise yourself with how quickly you pick things up if you're actively looking to learn.

A little aside but, I make such a point because again as a real world parent whilst it might be great for your child to have a full-time coach in something, this may be completely unrealistic for a number of reasons not least financial ones. I'm really not trying to look at or debate whether a parent should also try and coach their own child. What I'm saying is that I think a parent will have to be very active/involved if they want to see their child progress in something – make of that what you will. To give you a specific example using tennis with my daughter. She currently has two 45 minute private lessons a week. That's certainly enough for her right now as I look to reinforce what she works on outside of her lessons. But if I'm being honest we can't currently stretch ourselves (financially) to anything more than that. I do think additional practice time is very important to help her develop but it's more of a necessity that I do this, purely as there is no other option in that we can't afford more lessons even if we wanted to.

Or take my daughter's golf where I'm the caddy at her tournaments. I know a caddy is different to a coach but I do think there is some cross over. So I think it's on me to at the very least know what I'm doing. This is another little aside, but I raise it because I think this even needs to be put into context – like Fun or Control or Pushy Parent. It's all well and good for someone to advise you that your child should have their own coach and you leave them to it where you never coach/teach your child - just focus on being the parent. I get it, but all I would say is that I think this is a bit of ideal world advice. Where yes in an ideal world your child will have access to the best coaches and you get to just sit back and go with the flow. But for many I just don't think this is feasible, realistic or remotely possible. I think it does depend a lot on the sport/activity and I think this applies more to individual/technical sports or activities. I may be wrong, but I don't think many real world parents can afford endless private lessons for their son/daughter. In the real world parents can't afford full time coaches. I tend to find many examples where parents have to essentially volunteer to be a coach particularly with team sports for many reasons, one of which may just be out of necessity – who else is going to do it? Back to my caddy example, looking at this ideal world advice, am I supposed to get my daughter her own experienced caddy in each tournament? We all know that would just not be practical or even appropriate on so many levels. So it's on me to do it.

Looking at it another way; is there a difference when helping your child out with their homework? Or teaching your kid how to ride a bike? I think a simple point I'm trying to make is that we can't always reach out to a tutor or a coach for everything where someone else is on call or by our-side 24/7. That's simply not living in the real world. Yes in an ideal world we would have a math or science genius helping our child understand something with their homework if we're having difficulty trying to figure it out ourselves.

I'm exaggerating to make the point here, but I hope you get what I mean? There might be many everyday things you can think of where someone else would be better at helping out your child with a specific task or skill, something as simple as homework. But at the end of the day we're the parent, so I don't think we can just sit back and say that's not our job because it is. Again I just think there will be so many times where if you don't take the lead and help your child to work on something and improve then who else will take that role? So bringing it back to the theme of the chapter in educating yourself, if you do take the lead, I think you will actively seek out ways to improve yourself to ultimately help your child with one of their passions. This will no doubt make you become a better parent and as I said if anything see it as your responsibility.

I get every case is unique and if a child really progresses to a certain level they may have access to somewhat of a full time coach where the parent can then start to focus on just being a parent. But I think as children are learning particularly in the formative years, I think in some cases they're almost reliant on their parent to help coach them in some way. So bearing that in mind if a child is to do any additional practice time it's somewhat inevitable for the parent to have an important role to play. Who else other than you, the parent, will really reinforce this additional practice? Essentially if you don't, then who will? I raise this as another thing for you to at least think about. As I said I think this is another area that needs to be put into context and applied specifically to you. Sure there are horror stories out there of parents taking it to the extreme as a coach like figure. But I would not be put off by such stories because there is always a flip side with examples to inspire us all. I also know of many who assisted or were volunteer coaches on their kids team and have so many great memories from doing so. So this is something where some common sense might just need to be applied in that you're not looking to become a professional coach or coach of the year. You're really just trying to assist in any way you can to supplement/reinforce/complement things your child might already be doing. So again when I say read/educate it's so you can do these types of things rather than just sit back. It's certainly not about taking over and becoming all over-bearing. As a result you may have the understanding and learn that if you don't get involved then your child might be missing out on additional opportunities/practice time to help them make those incremental improvements.

Going specifically back to educating yourself, be fully engaged when your child is being coached or playing a game. Try to continue to gain more and more understanding on what the coach is working on with your kid. I know I sound like a broken record with this but if they're having a lesson with something, "be present" and without wanting to sound patronizing, watch, listen, and learn. Don't switch off to be on your phone accessing social media, or gossiping with other parents, because this is when you will miss things. Again, use common sense, this is not saying that you should turn up with a note pad and pen, are lazer focused every time your kid has a practice, and that you can't talk to other parents whilst it's going on. At the end of the day you're the parent, not the "coach", but at the same time I think you should look to be active/involved rather than completely ignorant to everything that it going on around you.

My examples are specific to sport but I think the same principles apply if your child is learning to play an instrument, learning a new language or developing a passion for a certain subject at school. My advice is to take that extra step by getting involved in something that they enjoy by learning more about it. If they have a favorite book then you read it too – I think things like this are so simple, no-brainer actions but really show how much you care. I think that, as parents, we have the responsibility to continuously learn and improve. Just like you're doing reading this book! So why not apply this scenario to where you learn more about an area of interest to your child? If you agree it's on you to learn/improve you have to apply/action this and I think this is a good area to do just that.

Before I close out the chapter, and connected to reading or educating yourself in relation to your children, there is another area I want to touch on. It's rather loose advice, but it's essentially to take the time to read anything that you're given related to your child. This could mean one of many things which I will touch on shortly but when I say take the time; I really mean digest anything that you're given. I don't really want to get into it about how we live in an age where its information overload and it's all about trying to determine what you should filter out as being the biggest challenge. I think most have already figured that out, but this is about reading things which are specifically related to your child. I will give you some examples of what I'm referring to, specific to my children. I'll start with my daughter. Every week she comes home from school with a folder full of papers. The typical things included are pictures, general school papers of her work and then information for parents on things like forthcoming field trips, school events, school news etc. Now I will just share my view of what's important, and consider it for yourself. For me it's important that I take the time to read this information, see how my daughter is getting on in school, see what's coming up, essentially, digest it all. It could be a day or two later when I find some quiet time, grab a coffee and read it through when I have no distractions. I won't deny that sometimes when picking up my daughter from school, when the day is already hectic and you see a load of papers in your child's folder it can feel a little overwhelming. You're probably not in a position to look at it in the moment so it might be that everything goes back in the folder and put away, almost forgotten about. So what I'm saying is that, whilst I can't just stop and read it right there and then, I ensure I take the time to do so, at the right time. I also think that it's important that my daughter sees that I take the time to look at her school papers. I'm sure to let her know when I do so, as well as tell her of things I liked, that she did or worked on.

I will give you another example, this time with my new-born son. We recently went for a check-up and it was very routine. At the end the doctor gave us several handouts of general information relating to children aged 0-6 months. For me it was important that I took the time to go through it in detail and digest it, not just put them in some drawer. I get it that, in both of my examples, not everything is going to be relevant, but some things most certainly are. So this is another aside for the chapter as it's intended to focus mainly on educating yourself in an area of interest to your child. This advice is to take the time to read up on anything that you're given related to your kids. But in saying that, you're arguably educating yourself whether it's reading up about an upcoming event at school or some medical advice. I reiterate the point to take the time to digest rather than skim read or glance over something to then just put it away. Most, if not all of the time, when you're given something you won't be in a position in the moment to look at it, so I will say it one more time, find that time to do so. This is to help preventing things like… "I wasn't aware that"….or "I didn't know about this"…. "Nobody told me that…." Hopefully you get what I'm getting at here, to make sure that you don't miss any important information about your child because you didn't take the time to read up on something that you were given.

So to round up this chapter my suggestion to you is to read to support that continual learning and to keep your mind active/creative. But I want my advice to be specific to parenting so look at some of my suggestions on learning more about something in which your child has an interest. In essence, I'm saying yes, read, but maybe don't necessarily just pick any book. With limited time you will be only able to get through so much so be sure that you take the time to select one which will benefit you. In addition to this, take advantage of things like audio books to use up some of your time more wisely. As this book is focused on parenting and becoming a better one, my advice to you is to do this in an area which has relevance to your children and your role as a parent. If you take the time to read up/educate on an area of interest for your child this is certainly taking steps in becoming a better parent which is what this book is all about!

33 BE HONEST

Be honest. In this chapter, I will refer to several different things in relation to honesty, and I will start with being honest with how your child is behaving. Sometimes it's a lot easier to provide an excuse for your child, or justify it in some way, if they're playing up. In some cases there may be a legitimate reason, but this is where you come in as a parent and back to the opening statement of being honest. If your child is acting spoiled, being selfish, not sharing, not listening to name few common behaviors, let's face it; most, if not all children, will act this way at some point. However, what I think is important is that you, as a parent, recognize these behaviors so that you can act accordingly and your child can learn from it. It doesn't mean coming down really hard on them or anything like that, but take it as an opportunity to correct an unwanted behavior. But, and I repeat the point, you need to be honest with your child and essentially call them out when you see something wrong. I see this a lot with parents and I have previously been guilty of it myself – my wife too. I think as parents we can sometimes try to overthink something as to the reasons why, but in this chapter when I refer to being honest, I'm just getting to the point where you simply try to say it how it is.

To explain more, I think it's natural, or to put it another way it's an automatic response, to defend/stick up for your child, even when they're in the wrong. It's as though you're in denial to some extent as you don't believe that it's possible for your child to do anything wrong/bad. A kind of response like "Not my boy"…or… "Not my girl…" Speaking generally these days, not just on parenting, it's easy to pick flaws in others, but when the role is reversed and the finger points at you or your child then it's a different story. A kind of "you can dish it out but can't take it" analogy. So the point of advice I'm trying to get to is to be mindful of such tendencies and be more honest if and when your child is acting up. I say this because our parenting style and anything related to our children is so personal. So with the saying "truth hurts", it can hurt even more when it comes to our role as a parent or anything negative related to our kids. I think it's important to acknowledge this because at times it will be hard to be completely honest with yourself, but nonetheless the importance still remains. Or it might be that you need to reflect on something related to your child – good or bad. Again, my simple advice is to be honest in your reflection. If possible try to look at something from an objective point of view rather than a subjective one, so that it helps to eliminate any bias which we might be more inclined to have when it comes to our own children. Don't bury your head in the sand pretending something didn't happen or there isn't an issue when there is – that's what I mean by being honest. Before I go on, I do want to highlight the importance of being honest with good behavior too as it works both ways. Again, the same still applies in being honest with what you see so that you can look to reinforce something that is working or, on the other hand, you might need to change something which is not.

Slightly related to this is not to be ignorant or oblivious to what is going on around you either. This probably won't apply to someone like you who is reading a book on how to become a better parent! Either way I will get something off my chest which I frequently come across with other kids/ parents when my child is playing at a playground, birthday party or even in the neighborhood as just a few examples. There might be a group of kids playing nicely and, not saying that there is always one, but there are times when a child is acting up for whatever reason and the parent is doing nothing about it. It maybe that they're on their phone, or talking to someone else, but essentially they're oblivious to what is going on with their child. It then creates a rather awkward feeling as it's hard for you as another parent to intervene or take charge, especially as the child's parent is actually there. So this is basic advice in not being oblivious or ignorant but I want to highlight the point, particularly in a group setting. I say this because, if a child is acting up in the group, I would like to see their parent deal with it, just as I would do the same if my child was playing up. The point is that you need to be present to see what's going on. This doesn't mean you have your child by a tight leash either. Its common sense really in that it's obvious when a child is misbehaving so again, the advice is not to be unaware to what might be going on right in front of you. This does require honesty on your part to recognize if you child is acting up, but it doesn't mean that you need to make a scene. I think if you're honest with yourself and the situation then you will deal with it appropriately without any need for an overreaction.

We all know that there is no such thing as the perfect parent, and the same is true in that there is no such thing as a perfect child. When looked at it in this way it's easier to understand why children make mistakes or misbehave at times, as it's only really to be expected. Although in our eyes our child may seem a "golden child", the reality is that our kids will misbehave as well. It may well be the case that it takes time to correct an unwanted behavior which may be fine too. But don't fall into a trap of continually allowing things to slide by, essentially, turning a blind eye or being in denial. I have been guilty of it and you see it all the time with other children and their parents where it might be something simple such as they're not listening, sharing or waiting their turn. A parent might say something like "well he/she is tired today" – we've used that one before. This is where you can fall into a trap of excuses. I have to say I'm not one for making a scene; there is a time and a place for certain things. So if my child is in a public setting, I would not choose that time necessarily to set or make an example of her by coming down hard in front of a crowd. Again this is where your own intuition would need to come in.

I think that, as parents, we continually want to defend our children, it's only natural. However, if we do genuinely want what is best for our children then there will be times when we do need to be true/honest, which will, I believe, serve everyone for the best in the long-run. Like other things in this book you will need to tailor this advice to your child, based mainly on their age/maturity. However, I do think that the message of being honest in relation to your child's behavior is applicable throughout their childhood. I can only presume that it's equally as important in the teenage years. There is no simple solution for this as parents occasionally may need to let a thing or two slide so that you don't become that nagging parent, so how and when you pick and choose to act is also an important consideration. Even then there is a fine line of letting the odd thing slide to continually turning a blind eye to anything bad. I don't think it does anyone any good to brush things aside or look the other way. But the crux of the advice remains that you should not be in denial about your child if you're going through a testing time/period. Depending on the age of your child, the range and size of current challenges will vary. Sometimes you may have to ride something out because there won't always be a quick fix. Regardless, the same advice rings true, you need to be honest as a parent in a given situation. This doesn't mean that you're against your child. If anything you're approaching it in a way whereby you're on their side in that you may be working to help correct a negative behavior which may just take time. I'm sure it won't feel that way for your child in the moment, but by following such advice, it will ultimately be of benefit to you and your child over time.

Another thing to consider as a parent where again your complete honesty is required, is to determine if your child is ready for something. Let me explain using real examples which I hope you can relate to and apply in your own life. My daughter is really good at tennis for her age and we're at the stage where we have considered entering her into some very basic entry level tournaments. But, at this stage, I still think that she is not ready and I need to be honest about that. I need to be honest in the sense that it would be me who would sign her up for such a tournament. If I asked her if she wanted to play in a tournament, she would jump at the chance but she doesn't quite fully understand the concept. I don't need to tell her that she's not ready. I'm just not signing her up right now or in the short-term. I'm mindful that she is on the borderline of being ready, and my reservation is that, if we rush and jump in the deep end too quickly, then the experience might be negative, or even traumatic. So my view at this stage is "why even risk that"? Why take a short-term risk which could have such negative long-term consequences? I later talk about the importance of getting out of your comfort zone and I think this is as important for the parent as it is the child. But I want to make clear I think it's important this happens when the child is ready. You could easily pick my words apart here as I know to get out of the comfort zone requires your child to perhaps try to push themselves in unfamiliar territory, but all I would say is that this can still be done in a progressive/gradual kind of way using common sense – like the next level skill or trying something new within a particular discipline. As for my daughter, I do fully intend to introduce her to tournaments and it will be sooner rather than later. But I think as parents we sometimes have to use our own intuition or just apply a little common sense to something, particularly given their age. Again there will always be a borderline of rushing into something and then taking something too slow which is why I say parents do need to use their own intuition based on their own unique set of circumstances. To give another example my daughter is ready and does regularly play in golf tournaments. I have seen a couple of examples where there are certain girls who have entered, but are clearly not ready for competition. Let me make it clear, I'm all for inclusivity/participation. But I say this because I remember the one girl who was crying most of the round, even though she had plenty of encouragement from other players and parents.

I think the main issue for kids is for them to recognize for themselves that they're not ready, as it can make for an all-round bad experience, not just for the parents, but most importantly the child. Tears can flow, meltdowns can happen, and, although this is the worst case scenario, be mindful that it could happen. The point that I'm trying to make here is really about trying to protect your children a little as they won't necessarily know if they're ready or not for something. So your honesty plays a key role and, like in my case with tennis, you don't even have to say anything to the child which would be perceived as negative, you just delay signing them up to something until they're actually ready. Again there is a borderline of jumping in the deep end and then being so far off being ready. Some kids may respond well to jumping in at the deep end so to speak, but again your judgment and honesty is key. Sometimes as parents we might get excited and want to sign our kid up for something, which is all well and good, but at least know what you're getting yourself in for or into. It might need you to do some digging and research first, go to a tournament, go and watch a game/show, seek advice or whatever, and then honestly judge for yourself if your child is ready. Remember, this is all in the best interests of your child.

Alternatively seek those entry level options or introduce/expose your child to a non-competitive setting so they can have that experience before diving right in. Something like this also works both ways because if your child is advanced for their age, but you're entering them into things for beginners, then you need to be honest and determine if that is good for your child? Bottom line is that there is nothing wrong in taking a little more time if needed to do extra preparation or practice so that your child can be ready for something where you can help to set them up for success. So you have to weigh things up sometimes. Sure you could be surprised and everything can go great. On the other hand it could be a disaster with tears and statements like "I don't want to do that ever again." So again at least bear all of this in mind. We all know in the grand scheme of things that the outcome of a golf tournament, or something like that, is really irrelevant. However, the reality is that it will be important to your child and a very negative experience can be damaging. So my advice is, when you're considering entering your child into something like a competition, to be honest and determine if they're really ready. I say this not to discourage anyone, hold anyone back or to strike any fear of having to think of the worst case scenario. At the core of all this remains your honesty, it's not about being negative, it's more about facing realities and being true to yourself. I just say it because I have seen first-hand when a child is not ready for something and the negative effect is has on the child. My view is that if you don't sign up because you're being honest and determine they need more time, then you must commit to practicing until they're ready. By doing this with your honesty, I believe will be making you a better parent. When the time is right the experience will be worth the short wait. This doesn't mean that you're less committed than before; if anything you might even be more committed to help get your child to the stage of where they need to be.

Before I move on, I want to make something very clear as I refer in one the next chapters to the importance of getting yourself as a parent and your child out of your comfort zone. I will explain more shortly, but what I think remains key in both cases, is to continually look for more of a natural/gradual progression which all still requires your honesty. Your honesty like in whether or not your child is ready with this past example. So whilst I would encourage seeking ways to get out of your comfort zones, again your honesty is key to ensure you're doing it at the right time. What I just mentioned was more about not being ready for something in the first instance to prevent, using an analogy of having a potential mountain to climb after a bad experience. To give you a simpler example, I have mentioned many times that my daughter attends a golf clinic and it's very entry level. But even with something like this where children need to wait their turn, I do see from time to time parents bringing children who are too young. Too young to follow any direction and as a result it's disruptive where they're running all over the place to where it does affect the other kids. Like with many things there is a caveat here, because I actually don't think that age is the main issue, more maturity. Two kids can be exactly the same age, but can handle/respond to things very differently – I think we all know that! So although age is a factor, like I said I believe it has more to do with the maturity of the child. Maybe it's just me, but in basic situations like this I think a parent needs to be honest and take into consideration others, particularly in a group setting.

I also had a personal experience with this with my daughter. I can't remember her exact age; she must have been almost 3 or just over 3 years old at the time. We signed her up for a mini soccer class where she just hysterically cried the whole time and was unable to follow any form of direction. I can look back now with a wry smile, but it certainly wasn't funny at the time. I can try and over analyze it, but bottom line was she wasn't ready for that type of activity. She just needed a little more time to mature I suppose to follow some basic directions and that became evident when she was just a little older when she was then fine with a sports class in a group environment. We did try the soccer class, but I had to be honest at the time, acknowledging she wasn't quite ready and also being considerate of other kids/parents, as it impacted everyone to have a hysterical/uncontrollable kid in a group class. I'm not trying to get a pat on the back here and I know kids can have meltdowns and tantrums one day and be fine the next. I just want to say this because I also think there are times when you do need to be considerate of others if you're perhaps trying something a little too soon. Again all of this needs your honesty. I will also say that this advice should not be confused with some of the points I made in relation to commitment. It may seem that some of what I just said contradicts some of the earlier advice, but I can honestly say in my personal example at the time it was just simply down to maturity. As parents we were fully committed to signing our daughter up when she was ready to participate particularly in a group setting and from there we have maintained our commitment to her, to help with her development with her sports. I admit certain things are just not clear cut, so all I would say to further emphasize the point is that your honesty is vital because you will have to ultimately make the call in these types of situations. The way I see it is there is nothing wrong in delaying something to allow for a bit more time as that may just be all that is needed. But what is key is that when the time does arrive your commitment as a parent must then kick in to really give every chance to your child being able to flourish.

Let's move on and now look a little more at setting your child up for success. It's somewhat of an aside, but I will bring it back to being honest. I just really like the concept of setting yourself and your child up for success. I have used it throughout the book and I think it's so relevant for parenting. Let me make clear this is not my advice as this concept/notion is certainly already out there. I think in many ways our role as parents is to set up our children for so many things in life. This does not mean that you're doing things for them, it means doing everything you can with the resources at your disposal, so that your child is then in a better position to succeed on their own. The term "baby steps" is relevant here. A very simple example I feel is when learning how to ride a bike, but I think the same principles apply to many other things. Typically you start your child on training wheels and then gradually build up to where they can ride without them. Or, when your child is learning to swim, you typically start with some form of float or arm bands. Or, like with our daughter who is learning to read, we started with sight words and are gradually working our way up. Very simple and common sense advice here, but I really do think that the same principles apply to so many different things. We have enjoyed some recent success with our daughter eating by herself with no help from us. Here we ensured that the meal was a reasonable portion and pasta, something we know that our daughter loves is relatively easy to eat, so these are the ingredients (excuse the pun) in how we set her up for success to build confidence.

I love this term and I really believe it works when applied gradually. It's not an instant process as it takes time, but in time I'm sure that you will see success. The reason I want to highlight this is because sometimes I see the contrary where it might well be unintentional/inadvertent, but parents actually set their child up for failure – like the previous golf example I just gave. Unfortunately the girl had a bad experience and clearly wasn't ready to play in a competitive setting. She was crying throughout and I want to make clear that my daughter, myself and the other parent/daughter who were also part of the group were very supportive, trying to encourage where we could throughout the round. But ultimately she wasn't ready and the tears on the day show that, in one way or another, she was set up to fail. Now of course this was unintentional and would not have been done on purpose by the parent. I'm just using the term here. But this girl clearly had a bad experience and there was certainly more harm done than good. At the same time I think that, as parents, we do have to take responsibility and look to set up our children for success by making sure that they're ready for something if you sign them up for it. I bring all of this back to honesty so that you, as the parent, are honest and you can look to prevent something like this happening with your child. In this girl's case it would mean doing more practice, perhaps going out on a course with her parent by herself so she can get to the point when she is ready. This is just one example when jumping in at the deep end was the wrong option. I just think it simply needs honesty. There is nothing wrong if your child isn't ready for something. The only thing I think would be wrong is if you then did nothing about it in terms of helping your child prepare/practice to get to the point to where they're ready.

You may have a child, or know of one, where it helps and you see benefit in "throwing them in the deep-end" so to speak. So whether it's swimming or something else, again we come back to that grey area, or fine line of jumping in the deep-end or not being ready at all. So I revert back to the term "baby steps" and by taking those small gradual steps, I believe that you're then setting your child up for success. But you have to take responsibility to set them up for that success. In the simple examples I provided, you need to practice with your child those sight words, go to the pool with the float, on the bike, on the driving range etc. You are key in the whole process as it requires you to take the time to do this, take those gradual steps, stick to the process and then with your honesty, determine when they're ready to progress perhaps to the next level like a tournament/competition. All of this requires your honesty as a parent to make the right call and at the right time. Again, linked to your honesty is your commitment to ensure you're committed to the required steps that need to be taken after your honest assessment.

Staying with the theme of being honest, I believe it's vital that you're honest as a parent – with yourself! I keep saying it that there is no such thing as a perfect parent, so we can't beat ourselves up when we make mistakes. However, what I do think is important is to acknowledge it ourselves when we do. There have been many situations where I have tried to excuse myself for behaving the way I did, but I don't think that helps. I think it's best to hold your hands up when you overreact, lose patience and are short tempered. These are the type of things I'm referring to which I think are common for all of us in the real world when we're tired and stressed. There are times when it's easy to lose your cool and patience over little things. My advice though is not to give yourself the excuse and think its ok when certain situations like this happen just because you're tired and stressed. Being honest with yourself in this sense is not looking for excuses or reasons which might justify your actions. Admit it and, if an apology is needed, then apologize whether that is to your child, spouse or anyone else for that matter. This is about holding your hands up to yourself, as you're not being judged by anyone else in this case either. This is also why your complete honesty is crucial, otherwise anything less than that makes it rather pointless. So perhaps the main thing is that you take responsibility.

I often smile when I hear sayings these days like "Own-it" which can be applied in many different ways but the same applies here. "Own-it" being the good and bad when it comes to your parenting, without any finger pointing. But let's face facts for a second as parents we're going to make a ton of mistakes and I think it's important to not hide from the fact. There is absolutely nothing to be ashamed of when making a mistake as a parent as we're exposed to so many new things all the time with our children, to which we have no prior experience. So the advice is saying "Own-it" and hold your hands up when you do as I think that will be making you a better parent. I'm not meaning that you become better because you act so humble/noble, I mean it more so you can perhaps learn from it which then helps your future response. You have to know when you're in the wrong so when a similar situation happens again you deal with it better next time out. It might not be that you drastically go from someone who is impatient to becoming patient, but hopefully you know what I'm getting at. It comes back to being self-aware so that essentially you get better in certain situations by recognizing your own tendencies which, in turn, helps you to become a better parent – certainly if you react more positively next time around. I have generally focused on negative behaviors which we need to be honest with ourselves about. But as I mentioned earlier, I think that as parents we also need to be honest with ourselves when we're not positive enough. So with even something like this I think it works both ways where you're also looking at positive behaviors as well as things that do work well for you. It might be that, at times, we don't give our child enough praise or encouragement when it's really deserved. For whatever reason, I think it's a lot easier to be hard on your child when they're doing something wrong, so be honest with yourself if you need to do a better job of recognizing/praising what your child does right. Therefore, be honest with yourself in such times on a positive note when you act in such a way which positively influences your child, so that it continues to reinforce such behavior. This is something I needed to be honest with myself when I wasn't giving enough praise or encouragement in certain situations. So, by being honest, I became a lot more mindful of my actions recognizing that there were times when I was perhaps quick to jump on a negative, but then not doing the same when something positive happened. As a result, I think I have improved at giving more encouragement/praise to my child as I really understand the importance that I play as a parent in helping to instill belief and confidence. Have I perfected this? No. But after being honest with myself I think I'm improving.

The reality is there will be times when you might come down a little too hard on your child for something. On the same note and on the flip side of that, there will be times when you might have been a little too soft on your child. Either way, in both instances your honesty will be key so you learn from it. There is something I have come to realize and that's as a parent you're constantly learning on the job so to speak. As children grow and develop there are constantly new things and experiences to deal with, ones which we have not come across before. I think the more and more you understand this learning concept, the more inclined you'll be to be completely honest with yourself, helping you to become a better parent along the way. Speaking generally I'm sure most parents would admit they have dealt with or responded to certain things better than others. So that's why I think it's important to look at the good and the bad and to be honest with both to help us understand even more what works better. Hopefully you can start to see that without your complete honesty, the opportunity to grow diminishes.

I will give you a couple of other examples when I needed to be honest with myself as a parent. The first one was in relation to my daughter learning to eat by herself. I have mentioned this several times throughout the book and on reflection, at times, I have been part of the problem. As I have already said, my daughter is a slow eater and we often needed to help her eat. This frustration added a level of stress and anxiety to our family meal times. In a way I was putting pressure on my daughter, but we also needed to have done a better job of setting her up for success at mealtime. But, perhaps the main issue was me and I needed to be honest with myself to admit, I was part of the problem. I just found that, by really just chilling out a little, providing more reassurance/ encouragement and not getting overly worked up, helped all round. This didn't mean there was radical progress but there was progress nonetheless. Ultimately I found out how to deal with the main issue where, in this case, it was me and my behavior/reaction.

I want to make more of a general point here as there are many more examples. I will be honest based on experience from mistakes I have made, but I also see it in others where the main issue at times is actually the parent or parents. I say this because it's easy to fall into the trap of being the main part of the problem as the parent by maybe adding pressure, anxiety, worry, concern, nervousness, stress etc. to a given situation. We don't intentionally do it, but it can easily happen. To give another sporting example, there is a term often given to parents with a warning not to over coach your child. I have seen it where parents try and give too much instruction to where it gets to the point of confusion for the child and sometimes it might just be best for the child to figure it out for themselves, learning from their own mistakes. So back to the main advice it's saying that if something isn't currently working with your child, then you may need to be honest with yourself as you may be part of the problem. Honesty is key. Again there is no point in trying to justify how you acted in a given moment if it contributed to something negative. This doesn't make you a bad parent realizing and admitting that you're part of the problem with something. I believe it's actually making you a better parent (the main reason for reading this book) as, by admitting and acknowledging your mistakes, you're more likely to understand what you now need to do to help improve things. I think that, as parents, our overprotective/worrying nature can lead up to catastrophizing things, assuming a worst case scenario, and thereby being part of the problem.

Another one if I'm being honest with myself is that I could do a little more around the house and with our new born. I could change more diapers, I could cook more and essentially help out a little more at home. Again this needs honesty and my advice is be honest with yourself if you may be part of a problem or could do more of something. If you're honest with yourself I think you will find that you're more likely to take steps to improve in a certain area where you might be currently lacking. Let's quickly look at me actually saying I could do more. In this case I'm being completely honest with myself; I'm not looking for excuses as there is no point. I could say I'm just so busy or I have too much on at work, but I think that is taking the easy way out and again it defeats the purpose of being honest. To look at a general example we previously looked at in other chapter, (yes phones again), if you spend too much time on your phone when with your child, my advice is to be honest with yourself about it. Be honest so that the next time round you will put the phone or other distraction away so that you can give your full attention to your child.

Linked to being honest, I also want to look at "failure" with you. Firstly I want to take it away from the context of parenting before I bring it back. Speaking very generally there are so many successful people in the world who have "got to the top" by failing many times along the way. There are countless stories of movie stars, business moguls, professional athletes who failed and were rejected, not just once but many times on their journey to success or you could say to the top. If you read any professional/personal development advice I'm sure you have come across sayings like "don't fear failure" and "fail frequently and often." Interpret this how you like but essentially my take from it, is that failure along the way, is fundamental to getting better at something/anything. So now I will bring it back to parenting. It may have been but I'm not really sure if parenting is looked at or considered in a similar means where failure is considered part and parcel of getting better or improving. The difficulty I think with parenting and our children is that it's so personal. I'm not pretending to be an exception here. I'm sure most will agree that if anyone offended you as a parent or your kids, in any way, then you would not take kindly to it at all. I repeat, it's so personal. Therefore, I think it's hard for us individually as parents to also be really critical of our children or ourselves because, let's face it, sometimes the truth hurts. As a result, it's tough to be honest sometimes and admit any failure.

Taking it one step further, when bringing the actual word failure into the mix, that makes it even more complicated. Now I'm not suggesting for one minute that you start calling yourself or your children a failure, but let's bring it back for a second. If a sports star got to number one in the world by failing many times on the way would it not make sense that, in order for you as a parent and your child to be a success, you will also need to fail many times? Now I know there is a distinction and I'm not suggesting that down the line there is some type of reward for the world number one parent or child, that's not what I'm getting at and that's not what it's about. I actually want to go full circle on this and back to the title of this chapter of being honest. My advice is to try and be honest with yourself and with your children when you have failed at something as a parent, or they have failed at something. I think if you understand and accept that failures are part of the process then, if anything, they're to be encouraged/embraced - certainly if you want to improve as a parent, or your child wants to improve at something they care about. It's so difficult to be completely honest with yourself and your children when it's so personal, but my advice to you is to try and do just that. I repeat this is all personal to you based on your own true/honest personal reflection; it's not about calling you or anyone else for that matter out. Again this doesn't mean that you're now going to be calling your child a failure for everything they might do wrong. It's going back to the root of being honest so that you can improve as a parent to help them also develop at a time when they may have "failed".

When I talk about honesty with failures in this context, I'm referring to everyday things rather than anything extreme. It could be that you didn't attend an event that your child took part in, and you come to the conclusion that you should have been there for them. Therefore, in this context you might deem it to be a failure on your part. By being honest with yourself in such an instance, I believe that this will make you a better parent. Although you can't turn back time, I'm sure that, with such honesty, the next time something similar is scheduled you will move everything to be there. Or it may be that your child was rude, somewhat disrespectful, lacked manners or had a bad attitude in a certain instance. Again by being honest with such a "failure" you can look to ensure that this won't happen again. So in this case you're not really focused on an activity, but actually looking to make your child a better person. I think the big and small cases like this require your honesty as a parent, firstly by looking at yourself and then your child if you have failed in anyway. Again I want to highlight that "failure" is the word just being used in the context so you understand the point. I think that some of you reading this might not like to associate with this word but I just want to continue to make the point crystal clear that it all requires your honesty!

This is all internal to us. This is not about someone judging you or your children, or you doing the same of others. This is about you being honest with yourself and your children. It's personal and as I said, I'm sure you won't like to associate the word "failure" with yourself as a parent or with your children. So as you're reading this, I don't want you to get the wrong idea or the wrong end of this stick on this in anyway, it's just been considered in this context. I'm not talking about any drastic "failures" on the parent or child's part, rather more of the day-to-day things where you could say we might let ourselves down a little. Or perhaps a better word to use is setbacks, which can be frequent at times in the real world. However, if you understand that failure is about being successful in anything, then I believe parenting is no exception. I think the more you understand this as a parent the more inclined you will be to be honest in difficult or challenging times/circumstances. This is because if you have such an understanding then I think that, in a way, you would embrace "failures", take them in your stride and you certainly won't overreact or be in denial. I purposely associated the word "failure" with the small day-to-day issues as I think they're as important to being honest with as the so called bigger ones, if again you're to become a better parent.

With so many things with parenting like this, there is no "one size fits all" answer. That is what makes parenting so challenging, but at the same time, so rewarding when things do work out. Continuing with the theme of being honest, I want to focus a little on expectations. I don't know about you but what crosses my mind in relation to this are the expectations that we set on ourselves and children. Again, this is a challenge and somewhat of a juggling act. Common sense would say to have high expectations on yourself and for your kid. But is the bar set too high? Are your expectations as a parent realistic? This brings it back to the theme of the chapter in that you simply need to be honest. Because there is no one size fits all solution to the many challenges we face as parents, the responsibility lies on us to do just that by taking responsibility. There are so many variables and factors that come into play when looking at a situation for any child as each child's circumstances are so unique. Sometimes to do this requires taking a step back, looking at things a bit more objectively and taking some of the raw emotion out of decision making. Another thing to consider is maybe asking for some constructive criticism in a situation if you can call on additional opinions for whatever it maybe. This may be a challenge in itself to ask, and then listen to some constructive criticism especially if it's directed at your parenting and/or your child. It might be that you're talking to your child's teacher or coach but if the trust is there and you trust their opinion, then my advice would be to ask them to be honest in their assessment. Appreciate that honesty. Turn a potential negative into something positive such as an area that they need to focus on to improve. Speak to your own parents or other parents about challenges you're facing, or issues you're dealing with. I think you will be surprised in that many will be going through or have experienced similar issues/challenges before. So again, be open and honest in your discussions if there is trust because, again, that all comes back to being a better parent. All I would say with anything like this the objective is honesty which I'm sure you've already been told is the best policy; so why not apply it to parenting and more specifically to your own parenting? If sometimes the truth hurts, respond by taking responsibility and make those necessary adjustments/improvements, because that is exactly when being honest will serve its purpose.

Hopefully I have got across the main point of advice which I want you to understand in that, for you to improve as a parent or your child to improve at something or to correct some unwanted behavior, then your ultimate honesty plays a key role in the process. To become a better parent, I believe your honesty will be and remain vital from the small to the big things in our everyday life. Remember that this is with a purpose so, if you need to face some cold and hard truths about yourself or your child, face them. Face them in a positive way because through your honesty you will be making steps to improve on something, thereby making you a better parent. I also looked at linking honesty and failure together for you to consider as in other fields/industries/professions, setbacks/failures are what help shape people to become better and improve to then go onto experience success. Expectations were also considered but it's not really just these things. As I think about it many if not all of the chapters in this book and the areas considered need you as the parent to be honest in your reflection. So if you're using your valuable time to read this book an obvious piece of advice from me would be to totally honest in those reflections because it's all for a purpose which is to make you a better parent. To look at it logically anything less than your complete honesty would reduce the chance of that happening, so then there is then no point in the process. Hopefully you'll see/understand this more than ever with something as important as your parenting/children, so that anything less than your completely honesty is actually doing a disservice to you and them. BE HONEST to Become a Better Parent.

34 COMFORT ZONE

I will try and give advice as best as I can here by sharing a personal experience and I hope you can relate to this in a current or future scenario. A lot of personal development advice these days in a professional/career setting talks about the importance of getting out of your comfort zone to develop. It might be that someone is anxious/nervous about public speaking so to get out of their comfort zone that individual will actually seek opportunities to do public speaking and there are many forums available these days to do just that. I won't provide any more examples as I think this is a good one, so to bring this back to parenting my advice to you is to seek opportunities to get out of your comfort zone as a parent with your children. Resilience is another personal trait I hear more and more about these days which is common in successful people. There are different interpretations, but the way I interpret being resilient, is being able to come/bounce back from something. That something typically being a challenge, something hard/difficult/testing or even a negative experience. I say this because I think that, being out of your comfort zone and being resilient very much go hand in hand. I believe that you, as a parent as well as your child, will become more resilient the more you look to step out of your comfort zone and embrace the challenge of doing so.

I actually think that this relates to you as the parent more than the child in some ways and seeking opportunities to get out of your comfort zone. I say this because I think that kids are generally much better than adults in taking new things in their stride. So my personal example relates to my daughter and being introduced to golf tournaments. Now to my point, I would not say by doing this has really put my daughter out of her comfort zone at all as she saw this as something new and exciting when finding out that we first signed her up for a tournament. This continues to be the case and she has been playing in tournaments for over a year now. I think in this sense getting out of the comfort zone is much more applicable to me, the parent, as speaking from my own experience, I know I was certainly out of my comfort zone for those first few tournaments. I still am today, even though perhaps on a different scale, as I start to come across new/different challenges as she develops. As I already mentioned, I highlighted the importance of being honest to ensure your child is ready for something. But bear in mind that when they're ready it does require you as the parent to act to ensure that you then sign up for things, so that they can continue to advance/grow. My advice is to actively seek those opportunities. When I say getting out of your comfort zone with a child, I mean it in ways where new challenges or next steps can bring a level of anxiety on your part. So, although it may bring some level of nervousness, my advice is to not hold back, again providing that your child is ready of course. Again, there is even a fine line here because you may want to hold off on something because your child may not be ready. But on the flip side, when they're ready it's equally as important that you don't hold them back. So to use an analogy in this sense; if your child is now the big fish in a little pond don't stay there as they need to progress to the next level/challenge.

Speaking openly and honestly as a parent, I feel slightly vulnerable, particularly as I also act as the caddy daddy for each event. Now I can hear people saying "for crying out loud your daughter is only 6 years old and you should just be out there having fun". That is true and without doubt it is key for it to be fun and we do have fun. But even so as a parent when I say I feel vulnerable, I mean those normal feelings of wanting your child to do well, enjoy it, build confidence, not have traumatic experience in anyway, make friends and develop a love and passion for the sport. So if you actually don't get what I mean by this, then this might be a good message for you as it might well be that you and/or your child aren't getting out of your/their comfort zone. I don't think I'm alone in this one as I hear it from many parents. Whatever your child is doing, be it soccer, tennis golf, dance, gymnastics, whatever; the moment that they cross that line so to speak, you have a sense of vulnerability as they're out there on their own. You have a range of emotions from joy, pride and excitement to being anxious, nervous, worried, scared you name it. Or, to put it another way, you're out of your comfort zone! I think these opposite and wide ranging emotions add to that sense of vulnerability as there is a fine line at times or a tipping point to where you child can go from experiencing delight to despair. I'm not trying to imply you're on a knife edge or anything like that, but our children do become our world so to speak, so there will be no one else who will care as much as we do. I don't know yet but from speaking to some I don't think these feelings drastically change either when your child gets older.

Now if you have played golf before I'm sure you can appreciate that some things are a lot easier said than done. Whilst it's without doubt a great sport, it also brings many frustrations. It's a very difficult sport and my child is out there on her own. There are no team mates to cover if she is having an off day – it's all on her. So my main point is to actually try to value this and seek such opportunities when you will, no doubt, feel uneasy at times. Using my daughter as an example, she has developed so much over such a short space of time. She is improving as a golfer, growing a love for the game, making friends and building confidence as she is doing well on the course. She is seeing a direct link - the more she works hard and practices the more she sees improvement in her game. That is not to say it has all been plain sailing since we started out. It hasn't been turbulent by any means but we have had some ups and downs along the way – dare I say it comes with the territory and will only continue. So, as frustrating a sport as golf can be when you can play great one day and off your game the next, with that brings a range of emotions/feelings, none more so than with the parent. As a result you're, most of the time, out of your comfort zone. This is because you're dealing with many new things you haven't experienced before and, particularly in my case, where I'm not experienced at all within the sport. As mentioned, typically your child is out there on their own and whist you can encourage and support you have no real sense of control.

As there are times when I will be out of my comfort zone, the easiest option for me as a parent would actually be to not sign my daughter up for that forthcoming tournament. It's easy to avoid that stress, having to experience those conflicting emotions or that new challenge as I don't have to enter her into anything. As a parent I have that control and I can make it a whole lot easier by avoidance. Or it could be that you decide to take a break for a little while in doing something. The break may well be justified and no doubt you would have to look at it more case by case but, speaking more generally, how long is that break? Is it a set amount of time or does that intended short break gradually become an extended one? It might well be that after that break, or taking some time out, that the challenge for your child to start back up again is now greater than if you just kept going at it. That greater challenge could easily then become a greater turn off. In life and generally speaking, I'm sure you can relate to a time when you may have taken that easy option by taking no action or avoiding something. In my case hopefully you have figured out there is no good for me or my child if I avoid something in the short-term, just so that it will mean that I will not be out of my comfort zone having to deal with those stresses/tensions/worries it may bring.

Thinking of another example, this time was actually with my parents and going back to my childhood. I was 16 at the time so you could say I was a young adult but I went on a school trip to Costa Rica from the UK, where I went with a group of students for a month and travelled the country. It was something organized with my school and it was extremely well prepared with teachers and also experienced tour groups/agencies. I loved every minute of it and the whole trip was a new adventure, so at no point did I really feel out of my comfort zone even though I was in a new country, speaking a different language. However, when speaking to my parents today, this was a big deal for them. Although they really wanted me to have the experience, they were out of their comfort zone knowing that I would be in a foreign country for a month. So all of that came with that general parental worry until I arrived home safe and sound.

Like some of the other examples throughout this book there is even perhaps a scale of low to high with this looking at getting out of your comfort zone with your child. And there will be different thresholds for different parents as this is a personal thing and that's ok too. We all know by now that all things are not equal. So, whatever your threshold may be as a parent, I encourage you to step out of your comfort zone rather than to avoid something - especially if it means that your child will have the opportunity to develop themselves by doing whatever it may be. In my case it was the new challenge of being a caddy and my child playing in tournaments. For my parents, it was me taking a trip half way across the world and trust me in both cases it was worth it. Hopefully you understand the opening points I've made here particularly with the golf example. This is not about taking something super seriously and creating pressure on yourself or your child. All I'm trying to say is that I think there are many times as parents when we will face new experiences/challenges, when we're in unfamiliar territory having experienced nothing like it before. We all respond to or deal with new things or change in different ways, but looking at it specifically as a parent with your child, value it's importance. Value the benefits it can bring to you and your child. I will admit there might be an element of risk vs. reward at times but I guess the key is not to stand still especially when there is a long, long way to go in something. Although it may mean that you're out of your personal comfort zone, you will have the understanding that it's all in the best interests of your child.

An idea, and I suppose an obvious one at that, in looking to get you and your child out of their comfort zone is exposing them to new experiences. Forgive me for providing yet another sporting example but, again, I think the concept applies for many different things. The advice I often hear from coaches is to look to ensure that your child combines playing time with practice time. Let me explain with golf and tennis and I will start with tennis. My daughter is a good example in that in practice she looks really good and can rally no problem. One of the things to bear in mind is that whilst she is practicing a lot of balls are hit to her in her so-called "strike zone" to develop her technique, as well as build confidence. I have recently started to take her to some play/match days which introduce kids to scoring and playing actual games. When she was exposed to this I could see that she was out of her comfort zone as she was not used to trying to score and the ball was now coming in more unfamiliar directions. She is learning very quickly and some advice stuck with me from one of the coaches saying that it's important for kids not to be good practice players who are then unable to execute when playing. I think the same is true in golf where you might see someone look good on the range, but then they find it hard to translate that onto the course when playing. So essentially the advice is that kids need experience of playing, not just practicing along the way.

Looking at it in a very common sense way this is to be done progressively and not looking to throw your child in the deep end all the time to see if they sink or swim. Trying to use other examples with this concept, say if your child is learning to play an instrument or is singing/dancing. I have no experience in this area so I can only presume that something similar applies in that a child should be introduced to performing when they're ready, where they continue to combine this with practice time. Being progressive with experiences is, I think, a good way to approach anything. I have never learned another language proficiently but I was told that the best thing for someone at the right time or when they're ready is to go to the country that speaks that particular language, exposing themselves to the real life experience. I think this is a simple example of where someone putting themselves out of their comfort zone is actually the best thing for them to develop/grow/learn. I could use more words here and whilst they might sound like fuzzy buzz words, either way, I think they're valid/applicable. So I just wanted to throw this out there and, again, apply this to your circumstances. Think of ways where you can potentially introduce a new experience to your child for whatever it is they're doing. It could just be as simple as playing somewhere new or with some different kids; again this is not about doing anything drastic. I will make the point again that this is not about just throwing your kid out there to see how they get on and hoping for the best. This is about making gradual progressions. I will refer back to an earlier chapter where I referenced the importance of commitment. If you're committed and in it for the long haul then I think you will realize more than anyone, there is no need to try and rush things for the sake of it. If applied correctly I think that such an approach can really benefit your child as well as you as a parent with your range of experiences. The experiences help as the more and more you're exposed to new experiences, the more you'll learn and I think the better you'll all become at dealing with new things or even change.

Related to getting out of your comfort zone as a parent is also not giving up when you or your child face adversity. This ties into developing resiliency which I mentioned at the opening of the chapter. I say that it's related as; in such challenging times; you and your child will no doubt be out of your comfort zone. I stress this because sometimes it might not seem that you're giving up or have given up. It might be that you decide to take a break from a certain activity that your child has been involved in because of a bad day, bad game, bad experience. At the time you may have the intention to start up again but that is when the notion of the comfort zone comes into play. This is because it's a lot easier to stay in the comfort zone rather than look to go back out of it. You choose to avoid something because it has the potential to cause you more stress or anxiety as a parent and why do that when you can enjoy an easy day at home? As parents it's certainly easier when things are going well. I think any parent can look and act like a great parent when everything seems to be going their child's way. But how about when it gets a little tough? How about when your child has bad game? How about when they show bad attitude or bad sportsmanship? How about when they lose or suffer a big defeat? I say this, and of course you need to ask the same questions to the child, but as this is a book on parenting such questions are just as vital to the parent. This is because the emotion isn't only shared with your child, but arguably it's multiplied for the parent when it comes to your child. Not just that, as I already said you lose a sense of control as your child is out there on their own. It's easy for me to sit here and say something like try and take the good and the bad in your stride. I can also say how it comes with the territory, but as I've said before in the moment I think you're probably not always going to be thinking so rationally. It's perhaps more on reflection when you come to such realizations. But I think being resilient is about responding to something bad in a positive way with the attitude that you will keep going at it. A bad experience is not about blame, excuses or finger pointing. So when the going gets tough how do you act as a parent? How do you act or treat your child? It's a lot easier to act dignified when all is well but the true mark may be how you react on a bad day. This is where the notion of not getting too high or low, which I will discuss further in the chapter, Complacency, may become crucial. Not just that, again your honesty is crucial when you do face certain challenges.

I talk about not giving up and this very much relates to the parent, not just the child. I'm sure parents out there often have times when they might feel like throwing in the towel; don't feel like doing it anymore and asking themselves whether it's all really worth it? Again, this is about being a real parent where everything will not always go to plan. We can talk a good game and say this doesn't apply to me, but I think if you go through these first hand experiences you will no doubt have these type of things cross your mind. Especially if you're regularly out of your comfort zone! To touch on a point earlier in the chapter, at times like this your level of resilience will be tested. There will be different levels of challenges you might face, but this is when you may need the resolve to dig in and bounce back as a parent and show resilience. As parents we certainly won't like or cherish challenging times in the moment, particularly when it comes to our children, but the reality is that challenges, or some hard times, are only to be expected at one point or another. Essentially it will be normal so don't treat tough times as something abnormal where you then decide to flat out quit. This doesn't mean you need to like or enjoy it, it just means you don't think about it in a way where this should never happen to you or your child. The severity will vary but even when facing some minor hurdles we might feel as if we have been knocked down so to speak, so being resilient is all about being prepared to dust yourself off and go again.

I believe that if you can look to instill the value/principle of resilience in your child it will have so many long-term benefits, no more so than overcoming something or not doing something because of fear. I think there is a pressure on people today to come across, or look perfect, so to step out of your comfort zone actually then becomes a risk. This is because you increase the likelihood of "failing" at something, particularly if you're trying something or experiencing something new for that first time. But I think that being resilient is actually about seeking ways to step out of your comfort zone and facing any fears head on. I appreciate some of this narrative on resilience does sound like it comes straight out of a text book and not necessarily applicable to a child or real world parenting, so let me try and continue with an earlier example to paint a picture. I'm not referring to things which from the outside looking in would appear to be a big deal. Again I can only make some assumptions going back to where a child might be singing or performing in front of a crowd/audience. You might think no big deal, but the point is for the parent/child it is a big deal and a really big one at that. I firmly believe as parents we need to develop resilience when it comes to our children because if you think about it there are so many things we're exposed to that we haven't experienced before. Your child may have no experience in something new that they're doing and you may also have no experience in how to deal with it.

Some of this sounds as if it has come straight out of a manual, but I think as parents we're always learning and ever evolving. Therefore, if we embrace this, embrace stepping out of our comfort zone, embrace any failure/rejection/setback as a way of growing, then the resilience will naturally build in yourself and your child. I think it can only be a good thing if this trait is developed by you as the parent as well as your child. I also think this is more likely to occur at times when you're out of your comfort zone. I think that this point is a really important one for you to consider, not necessarily agree with. I think a lot of the points in the book are linked in some way, so I will go back to look at fun and apply it here. As parents, we can expose our children to somewhat manufactured environments to ensure they will have fun where everyone will have big smiles on their faces. So just consider if you or your child might be missing out on some more important things if you don't ever look to step out of the comfort zone.

I believe that, when you expose your child to sports or competitive events or a show, you learn so much about yourself as a parent. Think about it in job/career setting where it's fairly obvious that learning on the job or gaining experience is crucial to development. So I think the same very much applies in when looking at experiences, but just in a different setting, being parenting. So when talking about learning about yourself, I don't think there are many better ways to do this. Not just that I think you can learn so much about your child and they can learn so much about themselves. Look we're all human and it's easy to sit and read this and talk in an ideological/fairy tale way and say that it should all be about fun and enjoyment. Whilst this may be true, as I said, we're human and, trust me; it's a lot easier said than done to act as an ideological parent in the real world when it comes to your kid. As a real world parent, I believe it's more realistic to say that there will be days when you will be frustrated as a parent even though you're really trying not to be, or even when you perhaps know you should be acting in a different way. There might be a time when you're sitting on the side lines knowing you should just sit back but then you just can't help yourself to get involved or say something. There may be times when you will feel upset, discouraged or irritated. Of course, overall you will always be proud of your children in that overall sense. All I'm saying and the point I'm trying to make is that not every game, performance, experience will go according to plan, be all rosy and that you as the parent will always act as that model/perfect parent. The ups and downs your child will experience will also be experienced by you as the parent. How you act/behave/deal with such moments I think will help you to learn so much about yourself, where the same very much goes/applies to your child! Sure, you want to act in a perfect way, but in the moment as in many other cases, to act with model behavior at all times is a lot easier said than done.

So this is the second bit of advice in this chapter being not to give up when you are faced with these tough moments, challenges, some difficulties or experience those range of emotions. In these tough moments you will be out of your comfort zone but what I'm also trying to say is that the same tough moments will help build that resiliency. It might only be short-term but even so, it's not only important for your child to persevere, but you need to give them that opportunity to persevere by actually persevering yourself as the parent, setting that example. I think this advice can ring true no matter at what level of activity your child is current participating in their area of interest. The same principle of advice applies in that for you as a parent, it may need you to get out of your comfort zone to get your child into something new or expose them to something they have never experienced before. Or it may be they are now ready to go to the next level and be further challenged which may cause some unease to you as a parent. My advice to you is get out of your comfort zone. Again what I would say here is that it's easy for someone to criticize and ask why would a parent be anxious as it should be just about having fun. That is true to an extent but, again, until you're in that moment, experiencing it first-hand, I think that it's only normal for a parent to be apprehensive, nervy or even scared at times. When it comes to your own child the range of emotions will come into play in all walks of life. The point being it's not just the big things, but very much the small everyday ones too.

Hopefully by sharing a current real life example of mine will help demonstrate the range of emotions in one situation. I will refer to an even simpler one. Currently we're trying to teach our daughter to ride a bike on two wheels instead of four. With that comes pride, joy, love (yes even with something as simple as this) as some positives but at the same time as a parent I feel nervous, worried and a little anxious (yes even with something as simple as this) that my child will fall off, hurt herself and then won't want to try again. Not just that it can be frustrating too as it might take a little longer than first thought and you see plenty of other younger kids riding around on two wheels already. I can try and come across all ideological, but I prefer to share real life emotions as it's these real life emotions that do put us out of our comfort zone. I think simple things like this are a big deal for parents with their own children even though it won't be for anyone else. Take this example, it's very common for a kid to learn to ride on two wheels as you hear and see it all the time. Nonetheless, this doesn't down play it in any way for you or your child when they finally do it! So let's apply some of the things I just said in this very basic example. To stay in my comfort zone as a parent would mean I don't look to take her to learn as I just put it off. The next stage would be to go, but she falls off, grazes her knee, so that means we won't try again as it caused too much stress. Hopefully you can see there is no benefit with either approach, by not trying or then giving up.

To round up, I will repeat what I believe is key and important advice to a parent. Step out of your comfort zone with your child as this applies as much to you as it does to them. I think that if you really want to learn about yourself as a parent then I encourage you to look for opportunities where you're out of your comfort zone with your child. Not just that I believe that you will learn so much about your child in the process too. Additionally, don't give up when it gets tough and remember that giving up doesn't need to be glaringly obvious. If you're avoiding experiences for your child in the short-term but then that leads to the long-term, you need to ask yourself whether you really did give up? As I have said throughout, we're talking here as real parents in the real world. With that in mind, I think it's better to deal with the realities we face rather than something make-believe. If we understand the realities then I think we will then be in a better position to accept those ongoing challenges to help build resiliency. Therefore we may learn to accept that being out of your comfort zone at times is all part of the territory if you, as a parent, and your child are really going to develop/learn/grow. So get used to being uncomfortable. By doing so, I think you will learn so much more about yourself to help then make you become a better parent. The added benefit of this is that I think such an approach will be so beneficial to your child in the long-run, providing you deal with those ongoing short-term challenges. Again remember this is all about becoming a better parent, so all I would say is reflect and decide for yourself on these points to determine what would actually be best for you and your child.

35 COMPLACENCY

Hopefully, by now, you have gathered that I have tried to apply all of my advice or topics in the chapters specifically to being a real parent, so I will now do the same focusing on complacency. There are different ways to look at the subject of complacency and I'm sure that there are books out there which concentrate on this subject alone. The way I look at complacency is that it actually follows something which has been a success. The term being complacent implies that you take your foot off the gas, stop doing what has worked or on the other hand stood still and not looked to further develop. We can look in much more detail of the definition on complacency in different circumstances, but I want to look specifically at how it applies to us as real world parents. I'm not sure how much this topic has been considered when it comes to parenting, as well as children, in becoming complacent with something. I have a tendency to believe that it's associated less with children and parents, and more with reference to something like a sports team or organization. I also tend to think that it's more considered or obvious if you like, when there has been a very notable drop in performance, but performance at the very highest level. Or alternatively, it might have been a drop in the level of success, but that success was a major achievement. What I want to do here is strip that down and look at complacency when it comes to parenting and your children, very much looking at the day-to-day experiences we regularly deal with. I think it's all relative to a degree where a major success or achievement for our children may appear to be no big deal, but in our own world of being a parent some things are just that - a really big deal to us. I say this because I think some of the underlying principles apply or are at least relevant.

I also believe in the importance of considering or looking at complacency for your major successes/achievements as a parent, as well as the same for your children. I think the big and the small should be considered and I repeat it's all relative, but nonetheless, the significance shouldn't be ignored. A major achievement for a child will be completely different to a major success for a global brand or a superstar athlete. But what I think would be good for you to think about is that, although that is very true, do some of these underlying factors/causes/principles of complacency still actually apply?

Before I do, let's just look at some general illustrations of complacency which are easy to relate to and I think this will help when looking at some parenting examples. Speaking broadly the sporting world or business industry provides many examples of where teams, individuals or organizations that were once successful, at the top of their game, or even the best in the world/industry, no longer enjoy such success. I highlight that I'm speaking broadly here as there are obviously many factors that can contribute, and every circumstance is different, but being complacent has certainly played a key part for many in the past. It might be that the world number one athlete who got to the top by outworking everyone else suddenly no longer applied that same work ethic after reaching a certain goal. It might be an organization which achieved huge profits by focusing on customer satisfaction, only for their focus on customers to drop after achieving that success. These are rather broad brush examples, but in everyday life, something we can all relate to is that we all must know of someone who has been on a diet. Someone can suddenly lose weight, get into shape, eat healthily etc. But once they reach their pre-determined goal the intensity fades and the success becomes short lived by resorting back to old/bad habits. It might not be the only factor but I think that when this happens, complacency certain comes into play.

So let's now apply this to modern day parenting. I want to look at real life examples, not looking at someone who may be parent of the year but then misses out on the award the following year. I want to concentrate on day-to-day issues. For us right now with our daughter we're going through a period where her listening is ok, but there are many occasions when she doesn't respond at the first time of asking. So this is something my wife and I have paid close attention to of late. When we do and essentially stay on top of it, her listening does improve, and she does things like cleaning up at the first time of asking. What I mean by "we're on top of it" is by enforcing it and this may mean that we are a little stricter/firmer than usual. However, what I do find is that when we see improvement we might ease off a little and then the unwanted behavior slowly returns or creeps back in. So in this case she resorts to doing something after the third or fourth time of asking. You might think there are additional things to look at, but the way I see it is that my wife and I need to take some responsibility as a key one is that we became a little complacent after some initial success. Or to look at it another way, it requires constant work. Whilst improvement is great and desired, it doesn't mean that the job is now finished/complete and that you don't have to think/worry about it, or do anything anymore. It might even be as subtle as not giving something as much attention, where you kind of assume it's all taken care of.

I like to focus on the simple day-to-day challenges that we all face as parents and consider something like complacency. Again, the goal here is for us to become better and improve at parenting, so I think the principle of complacency can apply to how our child acts/behaves. Sure kids can get complacent but I want to concentrate on the parents here as we can easily get complacent without it being glaringly obvious. I don't like to over complicate things, I like to keep it simple, so let's look at some other examples. The reason for this is, hopefully, for you to look at and analyze what your children are currently doing and determine if you have become a little complacent in a certain area. Say, for example, that your child was struggling a little with Science or Math. For several months your child does some extra study and works hard to improve their understanding. Months go by and the improvement is there for all to see. It might not be even related to a grade at school; it might just be that your child understands the subject matter in a better way. So your child gets to that point. Does he or she stop the same work ethic? Do they take the foot off the gas? Do you, as a parent, stop checking in to see how they're doing because they are now doing much better? Do you now assume that everything is ok and that you or your child no longer needs to pay as much attention to it? This is a very simple hypothetical example but the premise can be applied to so many things. In this case, it could be that your child achieves excellent grades in one term/semester by studying and working really hard but then the next semester/term grades fall after a reduction in the level of effort. Or it might be your child does extra practices to make the team, but then that extra practice stops once they get playing time or win a trophy, league or tournament.

I just want to highlight this as a key topic for you to consider as a parent with your child. Let me make it clear, I totally get that success is relative to the child. It's not always about being number one in something. Like the example I just gave, a major success for a child might be making the team, so that is relative to that child. All I'm saying is that, regardless of whether the success is making the team or actually being number one at something, the same principles apply when looking at complacency. In terms of responsibility, I think it does lie with the child but perhaps more so as they get older. As a parent, I believe that you share the responsibility of preventing complacency after your child achieves some success, be it in something big or relatively small.

I do want to keep stressing that success can be on many different levels; again it's not all about winning the league or some tournament. Another success for a child might be getting more playing time in a season. There is nothing wrong with that. The key is to look at the way your child achieved that success and look to ensure that their level of effort/attitude/focus is maintained through your support. Don't let it just be from time to time or only when grades fall or when your child doesn't make the team. Try and be consistent regardless of the so called wins and losses because if not, in my opinion, you're more likely to see frustration as a result of cyclical or up and down outcomes. Sure, it has to be something that is achievable and sustainable; but if your child improves, generally speaking, at anything by working a little harder should that suddenly stop once you see improvement? If a child improves their shooting accuracy at basketball by doing 30 minutes extra after practice, should that individual stop doing this if they're now making more shots?

I won't go any further with this but hopefully you get the point. I provided a very simple example with my daughter listening, to then looking at a child's grades or performance in their sport. What I'm saying is that I do think it's easy to fall into a trap of becoming a little complacent after we start to see improvement – we're all human after all. Speaking personally with my daughter's golf there have been a few times where she may have struggled with something during her round - like her putting. So I then look to ensure I help my daughter by staying on top of things helping her by scheduling additional practice time. But I know I have not responded in such a way after a good round, where I don't think as much about her next practices or make it more of a priority. But using myself as an example this shows somewhat of an inconsistent approach as why should I look to only prioritize some added practice after a bad day? If she's doing well because of that extra practice should I now ease off after a good day? I think these are some good points for you to consider for yourself in your own similar type of circumstances, where it may be much better to follow more of a long-term consistent approach regardless of any short-term outcome.

I highlight this as I just think this is something to be aware of and take note. For things big and small, when you see your child improving at something which is as a result of an increase in level of effort, practice, hard work and attitude, make note. With your child, you can then look to ensure that such behavior continues, where it's not a one-off type behavior/response. I think that, by at least being aware of the risk/threat of complacency, you will be in a much better position to prevent it from happening. As the saying goes "prevention is better than cure". What I mean by that in this case is that it's perhaps more common for parents to act by reacting to something negative/undesirable. Like that drop in grades I've used in this chapter. On the other hand, if you take a consistent approach whereby you're not being complacent then this helps to prevent unwanted surprises which you, as the parent, feel the need to suddenly act upon. Hopefully your child will also begin to understand and recognize this. Eventually the ideal scenario is that, as they mature, they will take it on themselves to maintain more of a consistent approach to something and thereby helping to stop any complacency from happening. But I do want to bring this back for a second, speaking as a real world parent as I did say we're human after all. I think a steady/constant approach is realistic and where you will get that consistency, but I fully appreciate it won't always be such a smooth process. I highlight it more to help try and avoid having to use those types of knee jerk responses, where you're in that constant state of reacting or even overreacting to things. On a similar note, the same applies when only looking at or giving attention to something when you see some form of swing.

I do also think that you have to consider the other side of complacency and remain realistic by keeping perspective. Let me explain a little. What I'm about to say may even slightly contradict my own advice, so as with anything in parenting I'm sure that you will agree that there is no simple formula. When I say the other side of complacency, I mean always looking to do more, or extra of something. Going back to the math example, it might be that your child has improved at school by essentially working harder. Now they have got to a good place the advice of preventing complacency implies for the hard work and application to continue and not to just suddenly stop. All I'm saying here on the other side is that, as parents, sometimes we can also see that improvement and there is an obvious correlation for hard work/effort essentially doing more of that activity. So it might be that we now want to see our child not only sustain their effort, but increase it. Then further improvement might be made so we want them to keep working and working at it, increasing the intensity and time. I'm not saying that there is anything wrong with the concept of continuous improvement as that is clearly how so many different people have become successful in many different things. They don't stand still. Point I'm trying to the highlight is there still has to be a balance, especially with children. Finding that balance is such a difficult thing to do.

Let's look at one of the other examples. I mentioned the sporting one being where your child makes the team. It might be that they have worked really hard to improve and they have enjoyed the process, but the key is then not to take it too far and push them too hard. I think we all know the dangers of burn out or taking enjoyment out of something. So is there an answer? With many things in parenting there is not a simple one. I think with the many questions we have as parents there is no simple yes/no answer or where something is clearly black or white. Essentially there are so many variables when it comes to parenting that have a grey area where it's on the parent to figure it out for themselves. So I think it's no different here. This advice is more about taking the time to consider and apply the principle to your own life.

Overall, in terms of advice to prevent complacency from happening, I think a good one is to find balance so that you or your children don't get complacent. When I refer to balance in this context, I'm looking at your emotions. Like in other areas of the book I will call on advice from the sporting world and apply it to parenting. I think many core principles apply in both where there are many parallels. In many cases, be it with coaches or athletes, when I have read about them or read quotes about what works for them in relation to complacency, I have come across similar types of responses. Responses being that they don't get too high when they win and they don't get too low when they lose. Now you might think that it is a little ridiculous at first to draw parallels with this when it comes to parenting and those everyday kinds of examples, but I really do believe that the same principles apply. Of course their gains or losses are different, where yours might not be exactly the same as the result of a game where there is a clear result/outcome. But let's look at one of the examples I just mentioned, being a grade at school or result in a test. Using both extremes this advice takes the emotion out, or at least reduces any extreme reaction one way or another. What I mean by that is that if your child aces a test, it doesn't mean you give a huge reward, jump for joy and now think that your kid will be the next valedictorian. On the other hand if your child doesn't do so well, that doesn't mean that they won't graduate, need to be grounded/punished and that suddenly they're no good at school. I say this because I think it's so easy for emotions to control or take over and be at one end or another of the spectrum. It's easy when something goes wrong to think that the world is coming to an end where everything is a catastrophe and it's also easy to think your kid is sure to become a pro after hitting that home run. Like with most of the advice in this book, I say this because there have been many occasions when I may have needed more balance or have that level head – not getting too high or low. I also see this all the time with other parents.

What I must make clear, particularly with the high moments, is that by taking some of this advice on board it doesn't mean that it reduces the pride that you have in your children in anyway. It also doesn't mean that you no longer get excited, or you don't celebrate or reward a big achievement in some way at the end of long season. As I said, what happens in our own parenting world with our own kids is a really big deal to us individually. What this advice is saying is that really; just don't go overboard with every single positive moment. This is because living in the real world as a parent; we all know that it's not all smooth and plain sailing. For every positive there are setbacks along the way, or rejection or some if not many losses. These are moments when your children may get low, but this is where they need you not to overreact. I have touched on it throughout, but so called setbacks or failures are all part of actually progressing and succeeding so, if anything, they're to be embraced. It might seem hard in the moment, but if you reflect on periods of difficulty this might make sense for you as the parent and the child as well.

Let's go back to our education example and not getting too high or low, regardless of a grade. If your main focus is for your child to work hard/study hard and continually practice whether it is at Math, Science or any other subject, then would it not make sense to not make a big deal with one grade from one test? Just because they got an "A" doesn't mean that they can now stop that same work ethic, and on the other hand if a child "flunks" that doesn't mean they stop that same work ethic either. In that second case, it might be easy to have the attitude of "what's the point? I worked really hard last time and failed so what's the point of me doing that again"? I admit that its easy reading this to agree that this attitude or logic is not the answer, but the reality is that in the real world it will be hard in the moment to perhaps convince your child otherwise. So this is where not getting too high or too low becomes crucial. If you keep the focus on the work ethic and gradual improvement as the most important thing, whilst there are never any guarantees, I find that, in time, grades and such will take care of themselves. Again drawing very common advice which is already out there in the sporting world as well as in education, you're more focused on performance or the process than the result/outcome itself. This is certainly not my advice as so much is already out there on the importance on focusing on the process rather than the outcome, but I do want to reference it as I do believe in such an approach. I do think such a method also helps instill positive lifelong principles which are applicable in the real world. I will also acknowledge that kids will progress at different rates and with this logic some will progress quicker than others. As the title of the chapter is "complacency" this really looks at the period after a success so the advice to the parent or child would be not to actually get too high. I think you can get too high by focusing more on the result/outcome rather than the process. So by focusing on this kind of practice I think will help to reduce complacency as the theory suggests you maintain the same consistent approach regardless, so that you're not always looking at something in isolation – whether it's good or bad. I said that is the theory so with real world talk, it may be better to just say something along the lines of don't get carried away or ahead of yourself - in order for you to maintain/keep doing what's working.

I want to give a final point on the concept of not getting too high and low and applying it as a parent with our child. This advice is something else I have previously came across which I would like to share with you, as I think it also has relevance. Again it's related in a sporting context and what you do after a match of a certain sport, something simple as getting ice cream. The advice was basically saying don't only do things like this after a win or a positive outcome. If you were planning on getting ice cream before its saying don't suddenly change your mind because the team lost or that your child had a bad day/game. Hopefully you get the point as it looks for a more consistent approach with more of a long-term outlook so that you don't get overly caught up either way in the present looking at one isolated event.

Wrapping this chapter up my advice is give this concept some consideration. Is your child a top student or athlete, but of late performance has dropped a little? Have they dropped their standards and essentially become a little complacent? Have you as the parent stopped checking in, assuming that everything is still going well? Are you still on top of things? Are you keeping track of progress? Similarly are you a parent that sometimes lets emotion take over? Do you get very high or very low one way or the other? My advice in both cases is try not to let complacency set in and try to keep more of a level head. This is a lot easier said than done at times I know. This also doesn't mean that you and your child now need to take a relentless approach to everything you do to prevent any complacency from ever setting in or ever happening. I did suggest to consider your emotions which I think will help with this by not getting carried away whether or not something is good or bad. This is because complacency can easily set in after something positive and an overreaction can easily happen over something negative. I think you'll agree both ways are not the way to go, so my advice is to look to maintain some form of consistent approach regardless of short-term outcomes – again no matter if they're good or bad. This will help so you're not always reacting and feel like a drastic form of response is required. At the same time you do have to consider the other side of complacency where it can go too far and to the extreme. This may not only result in some form of burn-out, but if your child ends up spending way too much time in one area as a result of some form of overreaction to try and fix something, then no doubt other important areas will start to suffer or be neglected. Therefore, balance is key so, again, this is where you come in and play a vital role as the parent, by helping to ensure that there is an appropriate level of balance. This is where we then fall back into a grey area as people will interpret this and apply it in many different ways. This is what makes you, as a parent, and your child so unique, so try and cherish that fact to make it work for you. All I would say to close is whatever your approach may be, consider the underlying principles of complacency, not letting something slip or go backwards after progress, no matter how big or small that progress or improvement actually is. Remember, at the heart of all of this is to become a better parent.

36 BELIEVE IN YOUR CHILDREN

Believe in your children and let them know that you really do believe in them. Mean it. Give your child confidence by believing in them. I don't want to come across patronizing or undermining in anyway, but I think that sometimes as parents we're quick to jump on our kids when they have stepped out of line or made a mistake. It's easy to fall into a trap of becoming somewhat of a nagging parent, getting on your child's back, criticizing them every time they do something wrong. I don't know about you, but as a real-world parent I know it myself when I'm nagging my child and I even start to annoy myself at times as I'm doing it. My advice to you is, when the opportunity is right; let your child know how much you believe in them and how proud of them you are. However, I think even this isn't as simple as it seems – when I say you have to mean it, you really do and I will touch on this point a little more. Another reason why it's not as easy as it seems is because you need to strike a balance where you believe in them, but you don't want to give false hopes or unrealistic expectations. At the same time you want to set high expectations for your child, so this rather confusing/conflicting opening is another example of how complicated and complex it really is to raise a child!

As a parent, I think you play a vital part in instilling belief in your child so that they have the confidence to believe in themselves. I think confidence is such an important thing for children and anyone really for that matter. In some cases it's providing them with the resources to set them up to succeed which then breeds/builds confidence. In other cases it might be repeating the importance of core values/principles like practice and hard work, which can help them, improve at anything. It's not rocket science, but I think it's just human nature in that the better we get at something, the more confident we become. I highlight and emphasize the word improve as I

263

think that should always be the focus rather than necessarily being the best or number one. Again, where it gets even more complex looking at expectations, you don't want to have a situation where your child doesn't aim high or doesn't set high enough expectations for themselves, as this will help drive them. But on the same note, it does all need to be realistic/achievable. It sounds rather common sense, but if your child needs some help with a forthcoming science test where they got a grade C last time out, then to immediately focus on the end result of an A might be completely unrealistic in the short-term. It might be much better for your child's focus to be on improving in the short-term by studying harder, asking for help or where you might be able to give some added resources. If this helps them improve their grade then that should be seen as a success. Even if they improve their score and remain at a C grade improvement has still be made. If this constantly remains the focus over time, then I think results and grades don't really need to be worried about as much. This is where I think the concept of looking at process, not outcome, can be really applied. By working this way in a consistent manner as already considered looking at complacency, I think that you will find in time that things like grades/scores tend to naturally take care of themselves. Providing you stick with such an approach of course!

So breaking it down further in this example, you're instilling belief focusing on the behavior or actions rather than the actual result, where you believe your child will do what it takes to get better. When I say "mean it" when you're telling your child that you believe in them you really do have to mean it. Otherwise your words may become somewhat insignificant, will have little impact on your child, so they, in turn, might not believe you when you say it. Continuing with the same example, if you know your child hasn't studied or worked hard at a subject they have been struggling with, should you say that you believe they will do great on the next test? Should you tell your child you believe they will do well knowing they haven't studied? Should you say how proud you are of your child in this instance? If you say things like this when it's not really warranted, I tend to believe it dilutes the impact for when it actually is. In essence, say such a thing when you do truly mean it. That is my view on it anyway.

This example relates to something I will look at even more shortly, in focusing on your child doing their best. So more on that to come! In this case, I think you need to look at the situation in isolation focusing/concentrating on behavior or actions rather than any result/outcome. With complacency, I did just talk about how your consistent approach can help where you're not having to overreact every time something goes wrong. On the other hand you also don't just suddenly stop what's working well after something positive. However, I do think even with such an approach you need to break it down sometimes, but only to where you're looking at the behavior rather than any result. I think complacency looks more on following a consistent way of how you react to things. But to allow you to do this, I think you do need to have the knowledge or reassurance that the approach/preparation/behavior has remained consistent. Hopefully that makes sense. With this hypothetical example which I will continue with, the advice is don't get worked up or make a big deal say with a result of a school test/exam, but I think there is a "but" to this. The "but" is providing your child has done the somewhat obvious in preparing and studying for it – which is what I mean by a consistent approach where in this case your child always looks to study/prepare appropriately. So this is where sometimes I think it's warranted to look at something more in isolation like the behavior/approach. This is what can enable you to not have to then make a huge deal about an outcome one way or the other – again providing the consistent approach has been followed. By looking more at the behavior is where I think you can genuinely believe in your child. To stay with this example, knowing they have studied and prepared for the school test, you believe in them knowing they're doing their best which we will look at in more detail in the next chapter. To recap, if your child has worked hard, done some extra practice, you can now say with confidence that you believe in them and they'll be rewarded for their hard work sooner rather than later - if they continue with this attitude. You're still not focusing on a grade in this instance. Therefore, regardless of the outcome you can say that you're proud of your child. Again, I'm not talking about being proud of your children in an overall sense, as that will be a given, this is looking at it a little more step by step/case by case.

Let me say this again before moving on. Of course you're going to be proud of your children in an overall way, but in such a particular or individual circumstance, in my opinion, it doesn't make sense to say it if/when it's not warranted. It also doesn't make sense to say that you believe they will do great if they haven't worked at it/something. It also doesn't mean that you no longer believe in your child, again you're just looking at something on its own. Because you're looking at something in isolation, I think it also doesn't mean that you now come down really hard on your child either. All I'm saying is that you can't always just say things when it has no real meaning/impact and isn't justified. So sometimes I do think you do need to detach and look at something by itself to determine if your child has really done their best which I think is very much linked to believing in your child. When you hear things like "can do no more" or "giving it their all" perhaps this is taking it to the extreme, especially with children and something like a school test. Again this is real world parenting, so I don't think you need to overthink it to assess whether your child has given every ounce of their energy to something to where that's the only time you say you believe in your child. So when I speak to you as a real parent it may be just as simple to look at effort and consider whether your child has at the very least, tried or tried hard enough.

When you sincerely mean it when you tell your child that you believe in them, then I think that will reinforce their positive behavior and attitude. This will no doubt give them confidence and they will start to believe in themselves once they see the positive results. I repeat, don't just focus on the result of a test as the marker. Focus more on the attitude, behavior and work ethic. Down the line these values are much more important than a one-off test in class or the result of a game. If you believe in your child I think this will, in turn, instill belief in them. I think this chapter is so significant as forget the example for a moment, the main purpose of this is to look at ways to instill that belief/confidence in your child, as I repeat I believe it's so, so important! I think this creates a win-win in that, and back to our school test example, you now know that your child understands the importance of studying/working hard. The more they learn/understand, the more confident they become and they know they can do it (belief). As a result, you believe that they will do just that for the next one, developing that consistent approach to help prevent any complacency from kicking in. Essentially you help to build up a trust so they can learn to take it on themselves. It does sound like another generic affirmation/slogan to say something like believe in your child. To become a better parent, saying you believe in your child/children may be a given. But at the end of the day these are just words/statements. So I think even something like this needs to be put into context, looking more at actions. My advice to you as a parent is do your part by giving your child opportunities and all the resources you can, to help set them up for success to build their confidence/belief. From there my advice is to focus more on your child's behavior in relation to effort/work-ethic/attitude, because if that is all positive, you can then truly say you believe in your child regardless of any outcome. I say this also from experience, as with my daughter the more she practices or works at something, the better she becomes and as a result her confidence/belief rather naturally or gradually builds. Think about this more for yourself, because I think any belief/confidence you can help instill in your child, will no doubt be making you become a better parent.

37 AS LONG AS YOU DO YOUR BEST

In many ways this chapter continues with a very similar theme as there is some cross-over to what was just discussed but, I do want to drill some of the previous point's home. I want to focus a little more specifically on the saying "As long as you do your best…" or in the past tense "As long as you did your best". It has to be up there with one of the most used phrases as a parent. We hear it all the time in the context of school or sports or any other activity for that matter where the key message is that the main thing, above all, is that the child does their best. I have to say I like this advice. I'm not criticizing it at all and I often say this to my child. But back to some of my previous points. You have to be honest sometimes and reflect, to actually understand the message itself. I think the phrase is used rather loosely and bandied about these days without full consideration from the parent or child. So to reinforce the example I have been using, if your child has a test at school and you say that you don't mind on the result as long as your child did their best (the process), that is all well and good as long as it's true. Let's recap on some of the questions you may need to consider. Did the child prepare for the test? Did they study well in advance? Did they ask for help if they needed it? Rather simple questions and there are others you could also ask, but nonetheless they're important to answer/consider. If the answer is "yes" to all of these and other similar questions, then you can reflect on the result/process regardless of what it is and say with confidence that they did their best.

On the other hand if the answer is "no" to these questions, but you ask your child whether they did their best and they say "yes", and you don't dispute this in anyway, then this is the type of example where the phrase is essentially meaningless. In such cases, as the parent, you also need to ask whether you did do your best? Continuing with our school test as our simple hypothetical example, consider in the first instance whether you knew that they had a test a school? Did you help your child prepare? Did you check in on progress and how they were getting on with their studying? Did you ask if there was anything you could do to help? This doesn't mean that you become a controlling parent as you will no doubt want your child to take ownership, particularly as they get older. But by doing such things, I believe that it's not being controlling, you're merely showing interest in your child and you're offering to help them if they need it because at the end of the day they might well need some help or form of assistance.

In this chapter, I will continue to use a school test as an example, but you can use the underlying principles in sports and other activities. When we say "do your best" it's very much in that specific moment in time such as doing a test or playing a match. However, I think the phrase tends to lose focus on everything else around it like practice, effort and preparation. These are the enablers to your child actually being able to do their best and then say that they did their best after the event. I think as a parent that you have succeeded if your child actually understands what it means to do their best. When this is the case then the saying does have significance to both the parent and the child when it's used. Another thing to consider is to sometimes ask the question directly to your child: "Did you really do your best on this occasion?" I think this encourages your child to reflect and be honest with themselves where, down the line, they assume full responsibility, so your role as a "nagging parent" becomes somewhat redundant. So what I really want you to consider is that sometimes it's not appropriate and you can't always just throw out a phrase like "I really believe in you" if you don't see your child doing their part (doing their best) and you don't truly believe it yourself. Again this is when looking at something more in isolation I think becomes relevant where in this instance the focus is more on looking at whether your child is doing their best in something? I will once again refer back to the complacency chapter to point out that this is perhaps why that consistent approach is crucial. Some of you reading this may think I'm over-thinking all of this a little, that maybe true, but I just think you at least need to give this area some additional thought so it can have more of a positive impact on your child. Again with all of this I'm just thinking more of the child's ultimate benefit. I say this because I believe a child will no doubt benefit from having confidence/belief in themselves and understanding what doing their best actually means.

Before I go on, I do think it's worth considering the point just made of what your child giving or doing their best really means or looks like. I'm not trying to trick you here. I say this as I want to bring it back to real world parenting. A child giving their all for their forthcoming school exam might mean they do nothing but study between now and then. I think we all know that's not realistic or practical. So I think it just needs to be looked at as I think it might be easy to look at your child doing their best where they have something as their sole or primary focus. We all have so many different things going on so to expect that, again I say would be unrealistic. So maybe you can kind of look at it in a way where they're doing their best, within reason. What I mean by that is your child not having just one primary focus which results in other important areas of their life being neglected. This is another instance where we can discuss balance, but again this is not about looking to perfectly allocate time into slices/chunks where it all seamlessly comes together. Sometimes common sense comes into play which perhaps doesn't help with any specifics. But I think the parent and child will know for themselves if more could have been done within reason, if they're truly honest with their assessment. I touched on it in the previous chapter and maybe sometimes all you need to really look at is the level of effort. Did your child put enough effort into something? This is rather vague, but I think as parents we all know deep down when our child hasn't really shown the right attitude or tried hard enough. So I say this because your child doing their best may even need to be put into context sometimes. But as I said, I think you will know for yourself when looking at effort/practice/hard work/attitude whether they've actually done enough. Sports are another great way to illustrate the point. Another hypothetical example might be that your child might have a bad game. I think we all know by now that's ok. But say you ask did you do your best and they say yes. They say yes when they didn't prepare as well for the game or they might have been slacking/goofing off a little in practice. So I say this because I think such a saying can sometimes be a bit of a cop out and the parent may need to take a step back and also answer the question from their point of view. It might be a really good lesson for your child to learn, that the reason they perhaps didn't do so well at school or in a game is because they actually didn't do their best on the occasion or the build up to it. The reason I say this is because hopefully that can help them understand so that next time out they can focus more on really doing their best!

As a follow on from the previous chapter, looking at belief, but now specifically in relation to doing your best, as parents I think you can relate to the desire of wanting your child to believe in themselves so they can actually do their best! It's so important and I believe the key is confidence and, as parents, we can play such a key role here. But again, all I would say is to be realistic with your child knowing their current capabilities. To provide a real life example with my daughter, I mentioned previously I'm the caddy for her when she plays in tournaments. There are times when she might be a little tentative with her shot and not really going for it, or she is holding back a little not really believing in herself. She might hold back on one of her putts or chips and it will fall way short of the hole. This is where I try and instill belief in my child as I know she can do it or go for it by being more positive as I have seen her hit hundreds of similar shots before and with success. Point is that I know she can do it, so I can really mean it when I say that I really believe in her with this specific/particular skill. This is so that, on the next shot or next time around, I hope she can have the confidence to be more positive and really do her best - where in this case it's going straight for the hole rather than being a little timid with her approach. In this case I think encouragement is different to belief in that you can and should encourage your child when you believe in them. But I think encouragement is key before your child can do something and whilst they're learning plus working hard at it. As they're learning, the encouragement is key and once they can do something, then you can encourage, but that's when the belief and confidence in the child themselves may actually be more important so again they can truly do their best.

So when we talk about doing your best, I think it not only applies to the child, but the parent too! So let's focus on our role right now as parents. Play your part in the process. Give the resources they need to help set them up to succeed. I find that there may be many people that love and care for your child - from family and friends to coaches and teachers. They all play a role and are an important factor in your child's life, but I think the responsibility lies solely on the parent to go that extra mile. It's doing everything you can so you can set your child up for success and give them the confidence that they need to succeed. It's your responsibility to do that. Other people may love and care for your child, but the reality is that they won't go to the same level, degree or depths which may be required to help them truly succeed. I mean that in a sense that you're the one responsible in relation to helping them go that extra mile, going to those depths and levels which are sometimes required. Hopefully you understand my point here. This is not about a contest of who cares the most about your child. This is about doing your best as a parent for your child which no doubt you preach the very same message to them in relation to doing their best. Let me put in another way looking at something else. I once was talking to someone about finances and he said something along the lines of "no one will care about your money as much as you do". Yes, you might have a financial advisor that cares, but not to the same degree. So bringing it back to parenting in this context to give your child belief and confidence in something may be about doing all those little extra things. Doing more practice, taking them where they need to go, signing them up for something, doing research, help with coaching, planning/scheduling, getting a private instructor again going to the depths which no one else will, because it's not their responsibility – it's yours! Or to perhaps put it more simply, if you're not going to do, or be prepared to do this for your child then who else will? This is what I mean when I talk about doing your best as I think it applies to us more than anyone and for us as parents to lead by example.

By doing all of this I think addresses the somewhat two parts, starting with the previous chapter which looked more at belief/confidence and combining it with this focusing more on doing your best. Firstly by giving your child the resources or added opportunities to develop, this in turn can help develop the confidence so that your child can really believe in themselves. Secondly if you, as the parent, and your child do go that extra mile then, regardless of any outcome, you can both be sure to say that you really did do your very best. I obviously feel confidence and belief are vital in children and as parents we play a vital role in instilling it in them. Linked to this, is to consider when you tell your child that you believe in them to make sure that you truly mean it. Really understand if your child is doing their best (within reason) and encourage them to be honest in their own assessment. Reflect on your role as the parent and determine if you're doing your best or doing all you can to help your child develop/build that confidence which then helps to instill that belief.

Linked to this is also having expectations that are realistic for your child. This may require you to look at things more in isolation or case by case, particularly when considering if they could realistically do no more. As I said, we will always be proud of our children, but sometimes for you to help them it might need you to be more honest in an isolated incident. This is because there will, no doubt, be times when your child will not do their best for whatever reason – could just be as something simple like a reduction in effort. If that is the case, I don't think it requires a song and dance about it or some form of overreaction, more simply at times maybe just acknowledge it and say it how it is. But, coming back to the theme about this book, becoming a better parent, if you're honest in those isolated incidents and your child also gains an understanding so that next time out there is improvement, then it all serves a purpose. Then you can say how proud you are of how they responded, again looking at it in isolation. Of course you don't need to look at everything in isolation and you don't always need a reason to tell your child how proud of them you are or how much you believe in them or constantly assess if they're doing their best in everything they do. All I'm trying to say is to sometimes give it more consideration so that your words when you use such a saying do have a real impact/meaning of giving your child that belief and confidence to succeed. This in turn may increase the likelihood of your child really doing their best, be it at school or sports and taking it upon themselves to do so. But I think we really do need to be more honest at times when making that determination of whether you or your child did their best (again within reason). Otherwise it just becomes more of an assumption or general thing you or your child just say without it really meaning anything. So to become that better parent understand what doing your best truly means to you and your child/children. You make the call on that.

38 SHORT-TERM VS. LONG-TERM

I have purposely put this chapter towards the end of the book as I intend to reference previous chapters, highlighting the daily choices that we all have. I say this because I firmly believe how so many things are connected/linked/related to help make you become a better parent. I will just quickly pick two of the earlier chapters out, being taking care of yourself and exercise to illustrate the point. I believe both work together in a way, going hand in hand or side by side, helping you to become that better parent. I say this because if you take care of your health by exercising frequently, then I think the more likely you will also place importance of some of the general examples I gave in taking care of yourself; by eating healthy and at the right times, getting your checkups, keeping up with personal appointments etc. I just picked these two out, but as I said I think there so many things that we do or don't do that are connected/associated and have a knock on/domino effect which can be good or bad. Continuing with this example the knock on effect of taking care of yourself in an overall sense by eating right, keeping up with your appointments etc. is that you also exercise to help maintain a healthy lifestyle. I want to emphasize this as I believe in its importance as that same knock on/domino effect can work in reverse or the opposite way. So again sticking with the same example if you don't or are less inclined to take general care of yourself than I think the less likely it will be that you will regularly exercise.

As a parent my advice is to give some of your everyday choices some consideration to allow you to further consider whether any short-term choice/decision that you make will have any long-term impact. I say this, but this doesn't mean you need to over-think or analyze every single choice that you make. I'm not suggesting that at all. All I'm saying is to look at a few of those choices and take a step back, as it may open your eyes to something you can improve on. I keep saying that this book is about becoming a better parent so, whilst I'm not saying you need to be overly critical of yourself, you do need to realize that there is always potential room for improvement. This applies to all of us, so no one is singling anyone out here. I believe that, if you embrace this notion rather than reject it, then there is no doubt you will improve as a parent, which in turn will have many positive benefits for your children. In addition, also bear in mind with what I just said about the potential domino/knock of effect of your everyday choices/decisions, as I think you will find that so many things, if not everything is related/connected. I will give you a personal example as this has happened to me before and very much links to the example I keep referring to. Maybe you can also relate to this, but I think it very much shows the knock on effect that one choice can have. It's sort of mysterious of how the mind works really and I will show you both sides, like I said from personal experience. It might be that I have an unhealthy lunch or dinner and now that I have done that I think to myself; well I may as well have a cheat day now, so I keep going where I continue to eat bad foods for the rest of the day. Because I'm doing that the thought of exercise is a now a complete turn-off or no-go where I don't even think/contemplate going. Now looking at it the other way and if on the other hand I do go to the gym or exercise having a really good work out, my mind-set is different with what I eat/drink. This is mainly because I don't want to feel like I have wasted all the time/effort I just put into my work out. So hopefully you can see where I'm coming from? This is just one example, but I think the concept of this knock on/domino effect works in so many other ways. So bear this in mind with the specific goal of becoming a better parent as I think so many things have to work together to actually make that happen!

Before I go into some more examples, when I talk about the long-term in this context, I'm not really focused on things like saving for college or your daughter's wedding. I'm not downplaying the importance of such things, but I want to focus more on the everyday choices that we make which do actually have a long-term impact one way or another. So let's look at these everyday choices which obviously relate to the short-term. What I want you to think about or bear in mind here is that, in the short-term, it's so much easier as well as more tempting to go with the easy option. Some rather generic obvious reasons for this are because we're tired, stressed and the day has got the best of us. I want to speak and relate as a real parent and I think we have all had days where we've had enough and we can't wait for the kids to go to bed so that we can have five minutes to ourselves. This is just being honest and maybe taking it to the extreme a little, but what I'm trying to do is acknowledge why the easy option is so tempting. Therefore, my advice to you is to try to identify when you do go with the easy option, and then work on avoiding that route on some occasions. I want to highlight that, by avoiding some of the short-term easy preferences; you will enjoy long-term benefits, making you a better parent. Again which is what this book is all about!

A real simple example is that, towards the end of the day when you long for that 5 minutes to yourself and you're putting your child to bed it might cross your mind – should I read them or have your child read (depending on age) a bed-time story? A voice in your head might say "it's ok, you don't need to tonight" and you quickly put your child to bed. I hope you have come to the conclusion that I don't pretend to be the perfect parent and here there is no exception. There have been times when I'm exhausted and have decided against reading a bed-time story. I would say that I've rarely done this but it's important to hold my hand up and admit that I've done this before. In this case, I chose the short-term easy option/preference. Where the long-term impact might come into play is if I repeated this course of action on a few consecutive days. That regular routine of reading a story before bed can quickly turn into reading a story every once in a while, before the norm actually becomes just putting your kids to bed without a story. There is then a long-term impact because by going with the short-term easy option, your child no longer reads with you. You then have to determine the effect over a year, which I would say is long-term in this instance. The effect between a child who reads with their parents or a parent before bed being one scenario, against the other scenario of where they do so infrequently. I appreciate that I may have exaggerated the point here looking at the extremes, but I want to also highlight that this can easily or unconsciously happen, with no real intent. I think a parent won't purposely go out to avoid reading to their child but it can just not happen. I have spent a bit of time on this example, but I want to demonstrate that sometimes the easy option isn't worth it in the long-run. Don't rush to get those 5 minutes to yourself when there are more important things for you to do.

There are many more examples I could provide. My daughter is also learning sight words and has a set to work through but I could easily say to myself "let's just skip tonight" or "let's do just one page". So it might be that you're desperate to get to bed because you're exhausted but do you get into bed to go to sleep or do you get in and just go on your cell phone? You might be desperate for some rest but are you really resting when doing something like this? All I'm saying is not to justify doing something or not doing something with your child because you're exhausted, but then spend the next hour or so on your phone after they've gone to bed. You might feel good about the easy option in the short run but I assure you that won't in the long-run. Before moving on, I also want to make the point that I know there is a lot more to it than just looking at reading a bedtime story, but I'm just using it as an example when looking at short-term vs. long-term. This is looking more in a general sense as I know there are other equally as important things to do with your child like helping with their homework etc. I get it and again like with anything else apply such an example to your own circumstances.

Again back to my own examples, I want to be honest with what I just said as I have been guilty of such behavior in the past. I won't lie; there has been the odd day or two where I couldn't wait for my daughter to get to bed so I could just have some downtime. It might have been that I rushed bed-time and skipped that bed-time story. But I think when doing so, it's important for me to consider: What for? I'm sure if other parents are honest they would have done something similar one time or another. Now, on reflection and just looking at it in a logical way, when you rush something like this, something so important consider: What do you end up normally doing? In my case, it might have been that I rushed bedtime, only to zone out watching some TV show or for others it's rushing the process only to jump on social media or some reality show. I'm sure that some may work or study and essentially do something productive. But I have a feeling that those cases are few and far between, and in most cases it's really just to zone out. So when I say to look at it in a logical way, then I think it's a lot easier to come to the conclusion of what's actually more important so that you keep going a little longer. This is because, when given the choice, it's a no brainer decision of what to do in the present moment (short-term) – even when you're really tired! Now, as with most things in this book, apply this type of advice to the age of your children. I labored a little on the example of reading a bed-time story which I would imagine is more common with parents with young ones rather than those with teenage kids – well maybe? Just look at the core of the advice and principles. This is really looking at whether there are times when you rush something, or don't do something with your child, just to get a few extra minutes to yourself. If you do that, then consider whether it's more valuable than what you could have done with your child. A little wordy here, but hopefully you get the point.

I will now give some more examples but I won't go into the same level of detail. But consider the same principle that I have just shared and how the short-term easy option could have negative consequences in the long-term. I will bring in areas discussed in previous chapters, but I also encourage you to consider some of your day-to-day choices in this context and apply it specifically to your lifestyle. Before I do go on, I would suggest that you apply some common sense. I'm not saying every day is the same and that we live like robots. But remember that we're creatures of habit to a degree. So whilst we will all have differences, I'm sure that, if you look at your day-to-day life, there will be a lot of similar/regular occurrences which can, in the short-term, form habits which then do have that long-term impact – good or bad.

So let's recall some previous examples and apply it looking at short-term vs long-term. It might be that you go with that take out or fast food option against that home cooked meal or healthier option. When I say "you" in this instance I really mean your family, including parents and children, so in this case you all have it together. It might be that you put on a TV show rather than playing a game together as a family. It might be that you go on social media, check emails, respond to texts whilst at the playground with your child rather than just being fully present. It may be easier to stay inside if it's a little cold or the opposite a little humid, rather than going out to play a sport. It might be easier in the present to let your child play a video game rather than having to go out somewhere and do something. It might be a whole lot easier to not go swimming and stay in when your child doesn't want to go even though they need to learn. It might be more tempting in the short-term on that Saturday morning to have a "duvet day" and stay in bed rather than go out and teach your child how to ride a bike or something else. In the short-term it's easier to put something off and say that you will do it tomorrow or next week. I'm not going to lie; there are days when I feel like doing nothing! But doing nothing doesn't help anyone and the doing nothing is where the short-term does eventually have a knock on effect in the long-term. Sometimes as a parent, even when you don't feel like it, it's a case of just getting on with it for the benefit of your child. I'm not talking about being heroic here and doing things even when you might be sick, things like that. This is about the times when we feel lazy, want to be lazy, but do the right thing and choose not to be. It's your choice!

Now a counter argument to this would be that we don't eat fast food every day or it's only on occasions, when we have a movie/duvet-day. I get that and I acknowledge that I'm exaggerating to make a point. I just want to highlight that it's easy to fall into a trap of going with the easy option in the present moment. I don't think that you need to start and look at everything you do and analyze short-term/long-term implications. If anything, my advice is that if you want to improve as a parent you will have to fight against those short-term temptations at times and just not give in. I have just provided a few very simple examples, there are many more and I'm sure many that are unique to you. To improve as a parent with those day-to-day choices, my advice is to not give in and grind it out. This is kind of a buzz word/term these days, but I think we can all relate to this as parents.

So when you're tired don't just put a movie on so that you can sit down and zone out on your phone whilst your kids watch TV. My suggestion is to play that board game together, take your kid out to play something, cook that homely meal, put that phone away when you go to the playground, go and practice a bit more with your child and go play even though it's cozy inside but a little chilly out. I could go on, but I'm sure by now you get the point.

Hopefully you can see by actually going against short-term temptations to not do anything you will actually benefit, and not just in the long-term. I actually think you will end up finding you benefit in the short-term too. You know the feeling when you really don't feel like working out but when you do, you feel so much better for it? I think the same kind of thing applies here. You may not want to get up and go outside, but after you do and you get home, and see your child has enjoyed themselves and that you have had fun as a family, then it's all worth it. On the other hand, have you ever had that feeling of eating a lot of candy or that big bag of chips and then regretting it immediately after? Again the same kinds of feelings apply the other way. It might be tempting to eat that candy, that bag of chips, zone out on your phone, put that same movie on again, allow your child to play another video game and so on. But after you do you might have that kind of feeling of regret immediately after, thinking that you wished that you didn't just do that or allow for that to happen.

I hope I have demonstrated that it's our day-to-day choices that do have long-term implications. I acknowledge that, as a parent in the short-term, it's really tempting to go with the easier option at times. My suggestion is to avoid the easy option on occasions. What I'm not saying is that you should never have some rest time, downtime or any time to yourself. This is also not about beating yourself up at times when you do take the easy option. The reality is there will be times you take that short-term easy option even though you don't want to or when you may even know you shouldn't. Speaking as a real world parent sometimes we need to take the easy route – it could be as simple as we're flat out, drained and the gas tank is empty. As real parents we won't always make the right or perfect choice. But this is more about what you do most of the time, formulating your norms/habits. Maybe it's just looking at it where it's the exception rather than the norm where you have a so called cheat day/moment. This is about looking to ensure that you use the time wisely, especially when with your child, to do productive and worthwhile things. I'm sure that you value the time that you have with your children, so this is about ensuring that the time is valued and not wasted. I repeat, this is about becoming a better parent, so I really believe that you will improve if you take this advice on board. I also think that by not picking the easy option it's not like you're now having to do something hard/difficult instead. It's really more about not going with the easiest option. I'm sure that you would agree that it's easy to play a board game or take your child out to play. But it might be that little bit easier in the moment to stay in and do nothing other than watch TV. In the short-term my advice is for you to not go with the easiest option and by doing this time after time, you will no doubt see the benefits in the short and long-term. It might end up being a complete no brainer to go and play out rather than stay in and watch TV, or play video games, or see what others are up to on social media, as you know that it's much more fun to do. If you go with such an approach, I'm sure you'll find in the process that you will have improved by making better choices, thereby becoming a better parent.

39 REFLECT

I think that it's so important to take time to reflect as a parent as it brings so many benefits. We all live such fast paced lives and, although we can't change the past we can certainly reflect on it. You can reflect on any amount of time. You can reflect on the day and ask yourself: Was I a good parent today? Was I a good husband/wife? More often than not we tend to reflect over longer periods of time such as the past year, which we tend to do at a time like New Year's Eve. I think that, as parents, you can reflect on the good and bad. Starting with the bad, we all know that there is no such thing as a perfect parent. As a result, I think we should take the opportunity to be honest with ourselves in times where we may have let ourselves down. On the other hand, reflection can be used to positively reinforce something that you're doing well. It can also be a bonding experience as my daughter loves nothing more than looking back at old videos which we have recorded over the past 6 years of her life. Before we get into the chapter, I want to make it clear when I talk about reflecting as it's nothing too deep. I'm not suggesting anything like going on some form of retreat or finding some kind of perfect spot/setting to reflect – I want my advice to be practical!

Again I will look to apply this specifically to parenting in the real world. I also think that there is great value in your child reflecting – even though they might not understand that they're actually reflecting! You may have conflicting views or have come across different advice, but I want to make clear that this is not about dwelling on the past or longing for the good old days. It might be looking at or digging out some form of memory box which will enable you to reflect on your child's experiences and achievements to date. I say that your child might not get that they're reflecting but if they're looking back at something and can understand how far they have come through hard work and dedication, then I believe that they're doing just that. There doesn't have to be an agenda for everything you do but there is a purpose for this. By reflecting it might help reinforce what you're doing, provide added motivation, instill pride, inspire a sibling, re-energize you, it can have so many different positive effects.

Without trying to overcomplicate this you may also want to consider breaking it down a little. As a parent you can reflect on yourself, your child and your family as a whole. You can then look at things in a way as to what's working, what isn't so you can then address it. I think this is something we should all purposely do more of as parents as a way of becoming better parents for our children. There is no hard and fast rule here and we sometimes naturally reflect on something typically when something has come to an end. It might be that your child has finished a school year, a season with his/her team, or they might be finishing middle school and moving to high school. At times like this it's only normal to reflect on your child as to have far they have come, what they have achieved and the progress that they've made.

So what I'm actually saying, or my advice to you, is to try and reflect more often, at times when it might not be/seem as natural for you to do so. Back to an earlier point, it requires self-awareness to purposely reflect on something. But again I'm talking here in a real way, so this isn't about having to do anything out of the ordinary or about finding some special location to ponder/reflect the meaning of life. This is more simply reflecting on the day-to-day, taking a step back once in a while out of your own bubble. When I said no hard and fast rule, I'm referring to time more than anything, as it might be that you reflect on the day, week or month. I think by trying to reflect more it will naturally make you a better parent as you can more easily identify things that have worked well and other things that may not have. The key therefore in this instance is being honest with yourself which is something I have continued to highlight the importance of. Also by doing this it's kind of preventing life passing you by, understating what's really happening in your lives, allowing you to intervene, change or reinforce behaviors which can be with you as the parent or with your child. It might be something simple that you reflect on yourself and you might come to the conclusion that you did not acknowledge or praise your child enough for something that they excelled in. It might be that you could have provided more encouragement at a given moment. By reflecting, you may determine that your child may have taken a backward step in a certain subject at school. So in this case, it might be that you can help or find someone who can bring them back on track. However, it's not just focusing on the negatives, it's important to reflect on successes too. Back to the example I just gave, if you need to encourage your child more, the next time out when you do provide that encouragement reflect on the positive effect it had. When I say reflect I mean reflect on your own actions as well as your child's.

Let's look a little more and apply this advice as I don't think you need to over-think it. I now want to focus a little more on some short-term ideas. I will continue to use my daughter as an example with her education and sports. As with most things, consider the principles which can be applied to your own children. When I say education or sports I really mean some form of activity. I will start with tennis. I have built up different little videos and photos of my daughter playing over the past few years. This is easy to do and we all love to take videos/photos of our kids! What I like to do once in a while is sit down with my daughter and watch some old ones. This alone is great to do just for the fun and enjoyment of viewing. At the same time we're reflecting but doing so in a positive way to help positively affect the future. I will touch on a specific skill being the serve which I have referred to in other chapters. Now she has made extremely good progress with her serve and some of the reasons for this are her positive attitude, hard work and dedication. It hasn't all been plain sailing and we only have to go back six months or so when she was struggling a little and was getting frustrated at times. Six months ago she could hardly toss the ball and now she is successfully serving over the net. She is even becoming fairly consistent with success. I want my daughter to take pride in her progress as I certainly do. I want her to understand that her hard work and dedication has rewards/paid off. The reward in this case being progress/improvement. I really think doing something as simple as this every once in a while has a purpose and does have the positive effects. I don't know about your child but my daughter loves to watch videos of herself. I previously mentioned about reinforcing positive behavior and maintaining motivation, to keep working hard, to keep on improving. It is basically providing proof to my child so that she can see it all for herself. Sure we can also reflect by letting her know, but there is no better way than showing proof with something like a video. I think there is great benefit for children to realize things like this for themselves. I also said re-energize, but I meant this more for the parents. What I'm getting at here is that there are times when we're running around so much that we're flat out exhausted. But speaking personally, when I look back at simple things like this, it helps re-energize me to stick at it and keep going because it's so worth it. That's how I feel anyway.

I used tennis as a specific example in this instance, but I will also do the same with her golf as well as with her swimming. As I already mentioned she has come full-circle with swimming and we pull a wry smile when we look back at the rough times that we had when starting out. We even have videos of those times to prove it! In an educational setting my daughter is still learning to read. At her school she has a page of sight words and when she successfully completes a page by herself, we can sign it off so she can get another. Over the course of the school year she has built up quite a collection of pages, again all through her hard work as she practices them almost every day. Sometimes I just pull the stack of pages out and show her the ones she started out with and how many she has now completed. Again I want her to be proud of what she has achieved. I also think this helps give her confidence.

You may not be thinking this, but I do want to make clear that this is something we do to positively reinforce what our child is already doing. It's very simple things like the examples I just gave. I believe we're reflecting although what we're doing is nothing out of the ordinary. It might even be something you're already doing, but don't necessarily or automatically associate reflecting with it. This is also not an exercise of gloating. We don't put out videos online or on social media of our daughter playing tennis or showing off the stack of papers we got through. We're extremely proud of our daughter, but I don't feel the need to really share this on some form of social platform. My recommendation is to keep this "in-house" so to speak, by not seeking or getting distracted by outside/external noise. But by going back on things and reflecting, your child can see first-hand how far they have come. There is proof, so it helps to positively reinforce their behavior, instill confidence, and increase motivation to keep at it. Not just that, I think that it's so important for the parents to sometimes be reminded of how far their children have come over a period of time and for even themselves as parents. I'm sure you won't feel the need, but sometimes give yourself a pat on the back for all of your hard work too. Again back to comments I have already made in this book that sometimes as a child's progress can be so gradual. Therefore, we don't really notice it day by day – it's only when we look back when we can perhaps notice the huge improvement/growth. On the other hand you can get a pleasant surprise from time to time. Take my daughter for example, my wife made a comment the other day, something along the lines of how she is suddenly starting to read quite well. But the reality is there has nothing sudden about it as it has involved a lot of work from everyone helping her and not least my daughter for working at it. I don't know what it is but sometimes things can start to sort of just come together where in the moment it might look a little effortless, even though it took so much effort to get to that point. Either way and in both cases by taking some time to reflect and to look back once in a while, you can understand how far you've all come.

Speaking a little more generally now I also recommend and advise you to sit down as a family from time to time and pull out the old videos from past Christmases, birthdays, school events and many more of your precious memories. You can do the same by pulling out old photos or photo albums. Again I think you will subconsciously reflect and put things into perspective of what's really important. Sometimes I feel we're so involved or consumed in the day-to-day that we need something like this once in a while to gain that perspective. I think you'll find it's also a great bonding experience as well to watch those videos and have a good laugh/joke. This, I repeat, is not dwelling on the past so just try it, as it's a great thing to do. If anything it continues to put things into perspective of what's really important for the future and helps you to cherish those next experiences even more. I have said it a couple of times, but for me, when I gain such perspective, it does help to re-energize me to go again or keep going.

Another thing I recommend for you to do as a parent is to step away when you can, as I find I unconsciously reflect on something important to me. When I say step away, I mean doing something like exercise which I highlighted in another chapter. It might be that you go for a run or walk and it could be only for 20 minutes or so, but this is some time alone for yourself. Or it might be something simpler than that such as taking the dog for a walk (if you have one of course). This may be something which is more personal to me. I don't know about you, but when I step away and do something like this, I naturally reflect on certain things. For a real parent in the real world, I think most will agree that life is chaotic at times. So I really do advise you to step away from the chaos/madness. This is not being selfish as I think by even doing this; it will help you become a better parent. When I'm stressed and if I do find time to step away and go for a run or something like that, something that may have been troubling me may now make sense. I may realize that there is something I need to do. Or it might even just help me regain a little perspective as to what is really important when I'm bogged down in the moment. Or it might be that I realize that something which has been draining me or that I have given a lot of my time/energy stressing over is not really worth it. I don't know how to explain it other than its like mini reflection and I kind of don't intend to do it as my purpose is really to get some exercise. But I find that it's natural for things to flow through my mind or have an idea jump into my head. Sometimes I think of things like: Was I too hard on my daughter for something? Do I need to say sorry? Am I part of the problem for something? Should I have done something different? What can I do next time? Either way, I really do recommend that you do take some time out for yourself whenever you can. It doesn't have to be each day, but try to find some time away from your busy life. Again, I strongly recommend exercise as I already have a chapter with advice specifically on this subject. All I'm saying is that for me a by-product of doing so is that I reflect on important things in my life without always intending to do so.

Linked to this is getting away as a family. An extended vacation is ideal but perhaps more realistic or frequent for a family would be a day trip, a night or weekend get-away or even just a change of scenery. I think it helps to sometimes look to step away from the day-to-day not by means of escape or anything like that. I can use many different words of how I think it helps you to refresh, regenerate, rejuvenate, reenergize or breathe new life into you. I may be going a little overboard but I think all such things apply in some way. Although this is a chapter on reflection, I don't think the purpose of something like a day trip is to give you time to reflect. I don't think you necessarily need to go out of your way to do this and find a remote or tranquil location on some mountain where you're doing something deep like considering life's purpose. I don't know what it is or how else to explain it, but I just find when I step out of my day-to-day, I kind of unconsciously reflect without even really trying to. Sometimes it's a simple case of things can be put into perspective a little better or you may see something a little differently. I may be on my own with this one, but maybe find out for yourself? Next time you get away, see if you end up reflecting on something in some way without actually actively trying to. Either way, I'm sure from time to time something happens which gives you a little more perspective, which can most certainly be a result of some form of reflection. As I said earlier, reflecting can be as simple as asking yourself at the end of the day: Was I a good parent today? Your honesty is key in so many ways because only you can truly answer that question come the end of each and every day. Only you can decide what constitutes you saying, Yes, to that question. You have to set your own standards and expectations on yourself as there are no standard checklists or templates to fill in. This is not about being your hardest critique either, more of just holding yourself to account and taking responsibility if you decide to reflect in such a way.

To round this chapter up, I have provided some ideas, all with the purpose of reflecting. I want to make clear that it's reflecting positively and with purpose, but at the same time not overcomplicating it. I shared with you the benefit we have of things such as looking back at old photos and videos from time to time. There are so many options out there and, again, you don't need someone like me to tell you that. You could also keep some form of a journal or log and your child could do the same, so you can then refer to it or look back at it every once in a while. I know there are also many apps out there these days that can help track things or monitor progress of a given activity over the short/medium and long-term.

Alternatively you can keep it real simple and reflect on the day, week or month in your head and I'm sure that your mind will immediately jump to the most important moments, specifically with what matters the most to you. As I said in the chapter about being honest, when you reflect, it's vital that you maintain honesty with the good and the bad. No matter what medium you use the same principle of advice remains. Occasionally, reflect on what you and your child are doing with purpose, so that you can positively impact and further cherish the future. If you really do want to become a better parent then I believe your honest reflections are key to making it happen.

40 NO REGRETS

It might sound a little morbid and I don't know why, but I often think of myself, way down the line, nearing the end of my life. Or it might be that I try and picture my kids in the future when they're all grown up. When I do I say to myself that I want to make sure I that don't have any regrets when it comes to my kids. I don't want to have the regret of things such as missing out on something that they did or not giving them every opportunity to do something better with their lives. For me it's also not about the big things, it's very much the little everyday things that make our childrens' lives so unique and special.

How often do you hear another parent say something like "turn around and they will be in high school or going to college"? Therefore, I feel you have to try and make every moment count despite the daily challenges that we face as real world parents. This is rather obvious, simple, and somewhat textbook/ideological advice. But nonetheless, I think that it's worth parents reminding themselves of this on a regular basis to prevent any feeling of regret someday hitting us out of nowhere. Sometimes it might be easy to forgive yourself if you miss out on something, but will you later come to regret it? As parents we all know that we can't be in two places at once and I fully appreciate the challenges that parents must face in this area when they have multiple children. The regret element is really more looking at a situation and asking whether you could have actually been there or done something but you chose not to or did something else.

I don't know about you but I'm sure that all parents don't want to have any regrets when it comes to their kids. I constantly remind myself of this. My daughter is now six and, as I said before, we now have a new-born son, so I'm still relatively new to parenting. However, I do look to take advice on board, certainly from parents who have older kids or even kids who are now full grown adults. I often hear them say that it only seems like yesterday when they started pre-school or it goes in a flash or turn around and they will be a teenager. I have to admit this is a little scary but I don't take this advice for granted or dismiss it in anyway. Essentially the theme or at the core of such a message we often hear are to cherish every moment and don't take anything for granted. This is because time sure does fly and time as we all know, waits for no one. Sounds very cliché I know, but I don't really know how else to explain it.

So when I'm talking about no regrets, I mean big and small. Big in that I don't want to regret not giving my child an opportunity to do something or develop in an area that she is passionate about which currently is with sports. But here I think the small things are more applicable. When I say small things I don't mean it in that they're of less importance, but what I mean is that it's about the moments that come around once in their lifetime. Like being there and taking your child to and from the first day of school. I never forget the words the school principal shared when he said that his best advice was for us to be active with our child in school, attend the events, volunteer, go on the field trips. This is certainly advice I have taken on board.

I know it's hard these days and I have a full-time job like most parents, but this is where time management and planning become so important as explained in previous chapters. This is to give you every opportunity of being there with your child on such special occasions. You might not always be able to attend; you might be on travel or on a business trip. But if there are times when it means moving a few things around, or offsetting some time by working late one day or getting up earlier on another or just using some vacation time, then my advice is do it. The principal also said something to the effect that any time with your kids is never wasted and I certainly agree with that too.

When people are asked what is important to them in life, in general, I'm sure most would say family. I'm sure this is most certainly the case for parents. But what you say and then follow up with actions are two different things. If family is most important to you, make sure your actions reflect that. For me it means that I do everything within my power and what is reasonable so that I can be present for all of life's important events – whether it's something like a dance show, school show, sport event and so on.

As an aside, but related to this in some way, there was a case I recall where

Phil Mickleson, a famous golfer, chose to withdraw from a major golf tournament so that he could attend his child's high school graduation. I don't think he necessarily divided opinion on this, but I do remember it causing some debate at the time. I recall listening to sports analysts talk about it and say what they would do in the same situation. I have to say I completely understand why he made the decision he made and if I was in his shoes, I would have certainly done the same thing. I obviously can't give you his thought process or reasoning, but I think it comes down to perspective and asking what is more important? Again, looking down the line in years to come everyone will have forgotten about the golf tournament, but he will never have the regret of not being there for something that was really important in his family's life. In his case I'm sure that, when he is 90 years old, he will remember the fine details about that special day with his child that only comes around once in a lifetime. When he's 90 years old, I'm sure he would not have remembered half as much of the golf tournament if any of it at all, if he had chosen that instead. Some things you just can't put a price on, as essentially there are priceless things in life - certainly when it comes to experiences and most certainly when it comes to our children! Certain things/experiences/events in our child's life are one time deals, they come and go and don't come round again. To look at this a little more, sometimes it's not just about the main experience of seeing your child on stage for that brief moment. It's about everything else in between in terms of the experience that special day brings from the buildup, the drive, breakfast, a private conversation, the weather, the atmosphere in your home, the family meal, I could go on.

I don't want any of my advice to come across as ideological in anyway as this book is for real world parents. In Mickleson's case some might say this guy is a multi-millionaire and has the luxury of being able to miss a golf tournament to attend such an event for his child. I appreciate others, including myself, don't have the luxury of significant resources, especially financial ones. Ultimately putting food on the table and providing for your child does come first. For many parents, I appreciate that they do have to sacrifice on missing out on special things in order to provide for their family and they certainly don't intentionally choose to miss out on anything. I get it – it's easier said than done. Sometimes you won't be able to attend something and although you will try and get to everything sometimes it's not practically or realistically possible. But having no regrets is about being there at the times when you do have the opportunity to do so, when you do have a choice of doing one thing or the other. Yes, it won't be between a golf tournament and a high school graduation, but it might be something much simpler than that. It's when you can move things around with some forward planning or organization. It's the time when you work late a few nights so you can attend something on a given date. This is where your actions of when you say "family first" essentially come into play and are put to the test.

I will give you our own little Phil Mickleson example in that my daughter, as you know by reading this, plays in competitive kid's golf tournaments. She was recently invited to her close friend's birthday party which was on the same day as one of her tournaments. It was not feasible to do both as the times clashed, so it was a case of picking one or the other. In this instance we decided it was much better for our child to go to the birthday party with her friends. Again like the Mickleson example, ultimately it's a personal decision and for us as parents it was a simple choice. Our daughter is six years old and for us what's vital is that she has balance in her life right now. I think even an example like this comes back to having no regrets later in life. I would also hate to think when my daughter is older, when looking back at her childhood she thought as parents we only focused on just one thing, something like a sport. I don't want my daughter's life to be consumed, particularly when she is so young, in one particular thing be it her sports, education or play or anything else for that matter. I believe there are no things equal in life so just looking at sports, education and play alone there will never be an even split in terms of time. But I do see our role as parents to ensure there is at least some balance and. In this case, had we chosen the tournament, I believe that we would have been neglecting an important area, which is play time with her friends, certainly given her age.

When you can't be there for something important, do take advantage of what technology has to offer these days, asking others to take plenty of pictures and videos. I often FaceTime my parents who live in the UK and when there is something special, they can sometimes watch live when they can't be there in person. What I would say is that, although such things are all well and good, don't substitute it for a time when you can be there in person. To give you an analogy, I think any die hard sports fan of a team would agree that being live at a match is so much different to watching it on TV. Ultimately you're watching the same thing whether at home or at the event itself, but the experience is that much different. So always choose to be at the live event in person, with your child that is, rather than by dialing in or watching videos afterwards, only when given the choice that is.

It's a simple and obvious statement to make but I intend to have no regrets with my kids and my advice to any parent is to do the same. I'm sure you're on the same page here. But it might require us to remind ourselves of this every once in a while when we are pushed for time or have conflicting things on our schedules. If your family really is the most important thing to you, make sure that your actions prove or reflect this. Because if family is most important to you (family first), but you don't follow it up with action, then there might be a time, sooner or later, when you have that unwanted feeling of regret. If you continue to try and become a better parent than I believe this will no doubt have a positive knock on effect, by reducing the possibility of any later feeling of regret.

41 ARE YOU WILLING?

Are you willing to become a better parent? This is not meant to be a trick question. Some of you may find it patronizing or insulting to even be asked such a question. I get that because it's a question with such an obvious answer. Even so, I want to stay with this because particularly as "Yes" is the glaringly obvious or no-brainer response. The reason I want to stay with this is because, as although this is no doubt the case, it actually needs more consideration because the initial question is so basic that it doesn't look at HOW.

Staying with the theme of questioning, I will pose some additional, very leading questions with obvious answers. The reason I want to do this is for you to consider on your own that, despite how clear/obvious the answers are, as a parent it still might be the case that in some areas you're not doing the glaringly obvious or the no-brainer action, that you need to do in order for you to become a better parent.

You hear parents say all the time things like "I would do anything for my kids…" I referenced this earlier and like with other examples, I have referred to in this book, I think such sayings are more commonly used with reference to big things something like a huge sacrifice. As I said I will use some very leading questions as examples but the intention with this is really just to get you thinking and is certainly not about calling anyone out. The questions I think refer to somewhat smaller things rather than anything big like a major sacrifice. Again the purpose here and going back to the saying "I would do anything for my kids" is to look at whether it should be applied for most, if not everything, rather than a major life event. The answer is of course that we should as parents, but again, in the real world the somewhat smaller, more simple/everyday things can easily pass us by without any real intent of neglect.

I could provide an endless list of questions here and you can think of your own. Hopefully you understand what I'm getting at here but let me provide an example to further demonstrate.

For this exercise always starting with the opening question:

Are you willing to become a better parent?

If Yes...ok then answer the next question:

If so, are you willing to put away your phone and all distractions when with your children to give them your undivided attention?

I know I have gone on and on about phones, distractions and being present in this book as this is something that I believe a parent should place high importance upon. I'm sure some won't have the same opinion as me in this respect and that's ok. But I want you to put any opinion to one side for a minute and just consider the questioning, as I will provide some different examples as well. But let's just say for now you're of a similar opinion that you feel that as a parent you should remove all distractions and be present when with your children. Say you agree but then you don't actually put away your device and you let a call, text post, email, photo, video, social media feed, you name it distract you when you're out with your child. If you let that happen go back to the opening question: Are you willing to become a better parent? If you let this happen would the answer then be NO?

I did say that this was not meant to be a trick question. But I want to demonstrate how easy it is at times despite all the best will in the world not to be able to back up our wills/intentions with the right action. Saying and doing are clearly different things. The answer to the first question like I keep saying is glaringly obvious with a no-brainer decision. Despite this and despite knowing the best thing to do at times we don't always do the no-brainer act. It's the act that is really the only thing that is important; as I'm sure you've heard many times before that actions are much louder than words!

Here are some addition questions that come to mind but before you answer each one ask the opening question first being: Are you willing to become a better parent?

- Are you willing to plan your week ahead to ensure that your priorities are worked into your schedule?
- Are you willing to plan your meals to ensure that, as a family, you

are eating healthily?

- Are you willing to persevere with your child learning something new like learning to ride a bike or swim, even when your child resists on going?
- Are you willing to get up early on a weekend to teach your child something or take them to practice when you're tired and sleeping in is so tempting?
- Are you willing to go out and practice something with your child when it's cold out, humid out, a little rainy out, windy outside?
- Are you willing to commit to something for the long-haul?
- Are you willing to remain patient when your child is learning something new where progress is so gradual it can be unnoticeable at times?
- Are you willing to ride-out and face/deal with inevitable ongoing challenges/phases your child experiences head on?
- Are you willing to find time and make effort to stay in touch with close friends or family members outside of your immediate family?
- Are you willing to say "no" to something which you don't want to do which takes time away from your family?
- Are you willing to regularly exercise and place importance on taking care of yourself?
- Are you willing to miss "your team" play to play with your child instead?
- Are you willing to get up early or work late one day so you can get to your child's next school event?
- Are you willing to give every opportunity you can for your child?
- Are you willing to be out of your comfort zone when it comes to your kid?
- Are you willing…..(think of your own)

As I said these questions are ones that immediately came to mind and I could think of many more, but I think there is enough there to prove the point. I fully appreciate that we all have different opinions and place higher value on certain things so, more than anything, just consider the concept. I have purposely put this chapter towards the end of the book as it looks at some of the areas I have addressed in earlier chapters. These leading questions are not meant to insult you in anyway but please give them some thought. Go back to the chapter of being honest as no one is judging here, this is about honest reflection so that you can become a better parent.

This also comes back to being a parent in the real world because at times it's even hard to do the things we know we should actually be doing. Like in all other areas of the book, I won't even pretend to be some form of exception here and I will recall one of my simple examples I provided earlier to demonstrate. There have been times at the end of the day when I'm flat out exhausted and I know I should read to my daughter or let her practice her reading with me. But despite knowing this and knowing this is the right and best thing to do, there has been a time when I just put the TV on instead so I could completely switch off. So back to the line of the leading questions in this context I would answer the first question: Are you willing to be a better parent? And I would say YES, of course. Ok. Are you willing to read to your child even when you're tired and don't feel like it? The glaringly obvious answer and the no-brainer response to this is also YES but there has been a time when I went against this trail of thought by going with the wrong action.

I don't want to over complicate this and I'm not saying that when you go with the wrong option that automatically means you're not willing to become a better parent. Again as a real world parent in the real world we will not always be perfect and make the perfect, or should I say right choices. The intention of this was really just to show that, despite knowing what we should do, we don't always do it. The final point I want to get to with this theme is that if you ask any parent are they willing to become a better one, all would no doubt say YES to that question. The most important thing to consider however or perhaps the more important question to answer is: Are you willing to do the things it takes to become a better parent? Your actions will ultimately show if you really are prepared to do anything for your kids.

42 MISCELLANEOUS

A strange name for a chapter I know. To be honest, there are some thoughts/advice that I want to share which perhaps didn't warrant a chapter on their own, in terms of length, so I will do my best and group it all together at the end of this book. The first part is not so much advice, but I do want to share a realization which I thought you may also relate to. I will take you back to my childhood when my parents, and really it was my Mom, who was very overprotective. Overprotective in ways such as not allowing me stay out too late or not really letting me go too far outside of my neighborhood. I remember that I always used to say and think that when I become a parent, I wouldn't be like that at all and I would be that cool dad who lets their kids do whatever they want. Well, I soon realized that when you have a kid of your own that thought process kind of goes out the window, as it's all too easy to develop those overprotective tendencies.

I'm going to move around a little here, so bear with me. The next bit of advice is to ask your child questions. I would love to know the actual number of questions that my six year old asks during a day. If we watch a movie together my wife basically won't be able to watch it properly as she is being bombarded with all different type of questions. I think this is generally seen as a very good thing for a child to ask questions as it shows they want to learn – except when you're trying to watch a movie and trying to enjoy some peace and quiet! Jokes aside, I will share something I came across when I was briefly doing a short spell of soccer coaching in my local community. One of the experienced coaches used a phrase of encouragement which I want to share, something called "Guided Discovery". There is a more formal definition out there, but basically it's a method of learning where you, in your case as the parent, ask questions to your child. It might even be as simple as asking the question: What did you learn? Essentially how this was applied using the soccer example was that he would put on a drill and then would ask the kids questions on why it is important to move this way, or why should the player be in this position or what should the player do if this happens? Essentially the coach didn't want to always have to give them the answers and wanted the kids to try and figure it out for themselves. By doing this I saw, at first-hand, the positive impact on the children which enabled them to better understand what they were doing and then execute it more successfully. Or it could be that when your child asks you a question you in turn respond with a question yourself, encouraging them to think of the answer.

I do refer to a lot of sport related things throughout the book but this principle of "Guided Discovery" can really be applied to anything. I haven't done a lot of research, but I do believe that it actually stems from education so it can obviously be used in the classroom. I believe this is well known advice which is certainly out there so if you initially like the sound of it, I'm sure you can find out much more with additional research. But like I said, I think you can apply it to even the simplest of things such as asking your child why is it important to clean up after you play? Why is it important to brush your teeth before bed? Why is it important to have breakfast? Children are obviously looking for answers when they ask many questions, but my take on guided discovery is that it allows for children to become less reliant on others for answers as they can begin to figure it out for themselves. With something like this I think a little common sense even needs to be applied here and once more the age of your child is a big factor. I don't think it's for me to respond every time my daughter asks me a question with an immediate question back to her. I think it's natural for parents to want to teach and respond to the varied and oh so peculiar questions that we may get asked on a regular basis. I also don't think you want to discourage your child from asking questions as I think that it's generally seen as a very good thing. My advice is to pick and choose a good moment to respond with a question back to your child from which you want them to learn an important message. As a parent you need to look to identify those learning opportunities. Clearly this is something which will need to be tailored to your child's age and understanding of certain things. But I think one of the keys to all this is by asking questions you're allowing children to think for themselves. It's easy to give children the answer, finish their sentence, tell them what to do or do it for them. By asking more questions I think encourages kids to figure things out on their own where common sense would say such a process would help them learn faster. Either way, I think you will find benefit in adopting such an approach from time to time. Hopefully it will have the desired effect for you.

Balance. I do want address the term balance more than anything and I want to address it now towards the end of the book, as I'm mindful I have used it several times throughout. I want to provide some clarification on what it means to me and for you to consider it for yourself. My perception is that it's becoming more and more of a buzz word/term these days. I think it needs more thought on how it's applied to each and every one of us as it's very personal. Work life balance is an obvious one to think about, but speaking in general terms balance can apply to so many different things that make up our lives and how we spend our time. So in addition to work and children you can factor in things like time with spouse/partner, friends, exercise, entertainment, rest, vacations etc. There are many more and I'm sure others which are more personal to you. So the way I see it when I refer to balance this is not about thinking that it's a pie where everything is divided up equally and you live some perfectly balanced life. Yet again this is more of a fantasy when looking at real world parenting, because with our fast paced lives nothing is constant. I also think this is not something that requires some type of sophisticated tracking system which calculates how you spend your time to ensure everything is allocated, so that you have this so called perfect balance which we hear so much about these days. I actually think all this can be looked at in a much simpler way starting with your own intuition. What I mean by that is that you don't need some fancy app. Just ask yourself questions like: Am I spending enough time with my family (children & partner/spouse)? Am I spending too much time at work? Am I getting/doing regular exercise? Very simple questions where if you're honest then you will immediately know the answers.

In a world where we always seem to be on the go, I think it's becoming somewhat harder and harder to achieve a balanced life. So to combat this when I look at balance I think it actually goes back to ensuring you have your priorities established. Once you do, it then goes back to planning and scheduling to ensure your priorities are worked into your day-to-day lives. That does sound a little idealistic or text book like, but in practical terms it just means that once you understand what's really important to you, you then plan your time around what's important. Again it goes back to taking control and not letting the day's just roll by. To give a hypothetical example, it might be that someone ensures they meet up with a close friend once a month – it's a priority. Now meeting up once a month is actually not taking up any significant time at all, which is why I don't think we need to look at balance as where everything is equally divided up. In this example, the individual might feel a sense of balance by being able to stay in touch and meet with their friend on a fairly regular basis even though it doesn't overly impact them – it could be something like once a month. The feeling of balance in that person's life comes from knowing they're doing this amongst all of their other priorities, whereby they're not losing touch with people who are important to them.

So when it comes to balance, I think it's being mindful more than anything. When you think about our priorities, say when it comes to a major live event and it could be the birth of your child or the passing of a loved one. At these times it's very natural to prioritize your time with family and the ones closest to you. But this is somewhat reacting to that life event. Let's look at it another way. You may have spent way too much time at work over the past 12 months, so you suddenly book a family vacation – again reacting. Or it might be that after months on end where you did not exercise or eat right you suddenly have the need or prioritize time to exercise and diet – again reacting. The point I'm trying to get to is rather than being in a state where you're reacting to things all the time, have your priorities established so that you ensure that you regularly find time for them. I think it's only natural at any given point where you'll find you may be having to focus more time on a specific area of your life whether it's your work, family or health. What I'm saying is that is ok and to be expected. But by having priorities established you're a lot more mindful and I think less likely to completely neglect other areas of your life which you also place great importance on.

Let's play devil's advocate a little on some of the points I just made and I will ask you these questions: Should you only prioritize time with family after a major life event like a birth or death? I want to touch on this a little more before I move on for another thing for you to think about. No matter how busy we are, no matter what is going on in our life, something like a death or a sick relative, results in us putting everything else to one side. Nothing else matters in the moment, so we find the time and rightly so. I know this is an extreme way of looking at it, but does this not just show we can always make the time? Of course not everything should be looked at as life and death, but perhaps this is why even more of the day-to-day things we get so worked up on need some perspective. I think the point I'm trying to make is that sometimes we think we can't do this; we can't do that because we're so busy with so many important things going on. But when something major happens (something truly important) that important thing is no longer important. I'm perhaps confusing myself a little here – but do you know what I mean?

To continue on this theme, should you only book a family vacation because your have spent so much time at work? Should you only exercise when you're completely out of shape? I said finding balance is very personal because of this reason in that we all have different priorities. I understand how crazy life can get at times. Speaking personally, as I place great value on time with my family and my health, I look to ensure my life works around such priorities rather than the other way around. I try and book things like vacations in advance regardless of what is happening right now as time away with my family is so important to me. By being more mindful or having such a mindset, I think it helps me to not neglect priorities in my life which includes my job/work, family, health and friends.

It works both ways in that I place great importance on my job, but to me this doesn't mean I don't prioritize time with my family. By the same token just because I place importance on time with my family that doesn't mean I don't prioritize my work. They go hand in hand so for me it's not about trying to get some form of 50-50 balance/split all of the time, as I know that's not realistic. It sounds simplistic I know but I think it doesn't need to be over complicated. All I'm saying is if you really are aware of what's important to you then I think you will be more likely not to be so caught up in one area of your life that you forget about everything else. I think this is an easy trap to fall into as a real world parent where we get so consumed by something it can take over. So if you understand your priorities, I think balance is not so much about parity in times when you need to focus attention in one particular area. For me, balance is more about not forgetting or neglecting even at your challenging/demanding times.

Let's move onto something else. I'm certainly no marriage counselor, so I don't want to give out too much advice here with the relationship with your spouse/partner if this applies to you when raising your children. However, one point I would like to make is I think that there is no doubt that you will disagree over many things. Specifically with my circumstances, my wife and I aren't always on the same page regarding the length of time that our daughter should practice her sports, what she eats, drinks, what time she goes to bed, how much TV she watches etc. Essentially a lot of everyday things which I'm sure are common for many real life parents. The main point I want make is that if you accept this and understand that you will not always agree on everything then I find, as in our case, that it's a lot easier to quickly find some form of common ground. If you talk it out and see something from each other's point of view, then it helps prevent one of you always calling the shots. Basic communication is the answer but, like I said, I don't want to put much relationship advice out there because I'm hardly giving earth shattering advice when I refer to communication. But without trying to sound way over patronizing, in this modern world of technology, I actually think we do less of the basics in talking something out and listening. Speaking personally, I know I could do a better job of keeping my wife informed of things at times and I will admit I'm guilty of not always fully listening to what my wife is telling me – you know when you're watching TV and they're talking to you? I'm sure you've all had moments when your partner/spouse said they told you this/that the other day, but you don't recall in the slightest – well chances are you weren't really listening! Bottom line is that if you also understand that you both want what is best for your child then you can quickly work it out. It can be hard if you're a little stubborn, as we both are at times. You do have to really try to put that to one side and at times you will have to compromise a little or agree to disagree. I would also say to really pick your battles carefully if you do want to put your foot down on something – make sure it's of real importance to you.

Talking of picking your battles as a general saying, I would also do this with your children. What I mean by this is that, as parents, it's sometimes easy to make a really big deal over a little thing or something so minor that our child does. So your child may do something that they shouldn't or step out of line a little, but let's remember that, like you, they're not perfect. So what I think I'm trying to say is that sometimes you may have to let something go, or let a thing or two slide which probably goes against conventional parenting advice. Otherwise, I think it's really easy to fall into the role of that nagging parent picking up on every little thing. It's hard to explain in a way as I'm also not saying that you should allow your child to get away with everything either. I think that what I mean is that if you're going to make a big deal of something with your spouse or child, then make sure it's really a big deal and not a little one.

To stay on the topic of your spouse/partner, I want to share some advice with regard to arguing in front of your child. It's not rocket science advice to say to try not to do it, as it really does set a bad example. I share this because I have to acknowledge my wife and I have little arguments or disagreements all the time. I would call them petty arguments really and we have always seemed to have done this, even in our early days of dating. It's kind of how we are and, whilst I admit we should try to stop getting worked up over little things, I think I wouldn't be alone here speaking as a real world parent. I'm not saying that all couples argue but, in our case, we disagree on things or we're stubborn in certain situations. If I could sum it up, I would say that we clash, can get down each other's throat a little or butt heads from time to time, if that makes sense? I think that it's unrealistic to think you're never going to fall out, have disagreements or argue with your spouse. So my advice, which is something that we have worked on and seems to work quite well, is to wait and discuss something. It might be that we wait until our daughter has gone to bed or if it's in the moment we should step into another room and not shout, just talk it out. We have by no means perfected this and I want to be honest in that I would admit that we're not some super perfect couple who never argue. We have argued before in front of our child, but afterwards we were both in agreement and on the same page, that we should not do it again. It upsets our daughter and it really does set a bad example. If you can relate to any of this, the crux of the advice is to try and not to do it in front of your child. I could say try not to argue at all. But again this is about being a real parent and not in some fantasy land or fairy tale where you and your spouse are lovey dovey all of the time. I think that the reality is that you're not always going to see eye-to-eye. So when you do disagree over things, or if you're the type to get a little animated/heated, then I repeat, try and not to do this when your child is watching or around.

Exceptions to the rule. I want to make a general point here and I think it's an important one when it comes to parenting and your children. I find that with a lot of things in life there always seems to be an exception to the rule or anomalies/outliers - no more so when it comes to advice on parenting! To use an analogy it's kind of like winning the lotto/lottery. The reality is that you will never win the jackpot but, guess what; someone wins each and every week. So the point is that you have to bear in mind that for all of the best advice in the world you may well find that there are exceptions to the norm which kind of go against your principles/values/beliefs. In real life circumstances, you may value hard work/practice with your child with their sports and studies. You want your child to understand that this is how you succeed in life. But you may find there is a straight A student who never studies or a stud athlete at school who only needs to show up to win or be the star of the show. These are just a couple of broad brush examples which I'm sure we can relate to one way or another. The point is not to let exceptions throw you off. In a way, I believe you need to play the percentages. I firmly believe in these examples alone that the core principle of practice/work is much more valuable in the long-run. My bet is that, again using these generic examples, a child may "get away" with it in high school. But in the real world if you don't back up something with hard work and a willingness to improve then it's more than likely the saying "a waste of talent" or "peaked in high school" will ring true. When I say play the percentages I'm not trying or even suggesting that this is some equation to solve or that your child is just a number in a numbers game. I'm merely saying that you shouldn't be deterred by the result/outcome of something which may throw you off, goes against the norm or goes against your principles. It will no doubt happen, so my advice is really just to be mindful that there are exceptions to every rule it seems, even when it comes to parenting and kids. Hopefully you get my point here when you hear someone say 99 times out of a hundred this/that would/won't happen. My take from that is this/that will still occur one time. So again I repeat don't be strayed when something goes against one of your key parental values. My advice is to remain focused on what works for you and what you believe in, so that you're not strayed by such one-offs.

No straightforward answers when it comes to parenting! I don't know about you but I don't think there are many simple answers to the constant day-to-day challenges we face. There are not many simple Yes/No options/answers when raising a child. There are so many variables and I will just pick out a few examples in this book from earlier chapters. Like your job/career or whether you let your child watch TV. With things like this I just don't think there is a straightforward or clear cut answer. The reality also is you can make good arguments for and against certain decisions/choices if you look at something in a rational way. Hopefully you have come to the conclusion that the purpose of many of the areas I have raised, is not about me trying to convert any opinion to make you agree with everything I have to say. There are so many factors to consider in our own unique lives. I say there are not many straightforward answers to important things related to parenting, so that you can perhaps look at both sides of the argument for certain things or just maybe see/look at something in a different way. This is so you can try to take everything into consideration before then deciding on what you think is right for you as a parent or for your child. Again speaking generally these days, I think there are some examples where some people are starting to lose credibility in that they're so single minded. I'm speaking in a broad sense. But I think there is a tendency for people to pick and choose things that might support something they believe in, but then completely shut out or ignore something which might go against it. I think this relates to parenting when I say there are no simple answers, because I do think at times you will need to look at all angles and/or consider things which perhaps go against your current view/opinion or approach to something. Again stick to the theme/purpose of becoming a better parent and I think you will be more open to take into account and consider new/different things. This doesn't mean to say you go with everything, but you at least give something the full consideration it may well deserve. Why wouldn't a parent swallow their pride or change their opinion on something if it actually meant they would be doing something to become a better one?

To stay on this for a moment and more of a general point of view now I'm coming to a close with this book. For anything in this book that relates to you I've said to not take something personal, so my advice is to not be stubborn and if needs be - eat that humble pie if you need to! That comes with you being honest which I highlighted the importance of earlier. You might need to be honest and say to yourself you know what, I do spend way too way much time on my phone when I'm with my children. I'm not always present; I don't prioritize enough and so on and so on. These few examples might not even relate to you but that is thing, in that not everything will apply to you in this book. Many of the points need you to consider things for yourself to make your own mind up. But it all comes back to your honesty. This is not a test where I or anyone else will be checking in or following up with you. No one will call you out whatsoever or will be judging you in anyway. It's not about that in the slightest. No one else will be monitoring your progress or see what if any steps you've taken to make improvements to become a better parent. You have to realize the intention throughout has just been for you to consider all the parts that do apply to you, so you then take the appropriate actions. You decide on what is best for you and your family having given thought to the areas which connect with you in some way. We all know the saying actions speak louder than words and they really do. This book contains a lot of advice and suggestions. But you now need to act on those which you believe will help make you become a better parent. It's essentially all now on you and no one else.

Bribes. I'm not saying that all parents bribe their children in some general statement. But I bet a very high percentage do, or have done so in the past. I have and I still do it sometimes, somewhat unknowingly. What I'm referring to is those moments when your child might be playing up or you want them to do something. You might have plans to go to the playground or something like that. I would often say "stop doing that or I'm not taking you to the playground". So when I use the term bribe I mean it in a sense that I might try and use such a tactic when trying to get my child to do what I want. The reason that I'm flagging this up and saying not to do it is because, as in my case, I don't really follow through if my child still does that unwanted behavior. In essence it backfires if I don't act on it. Or it might be that I say something which I will never intend to act on. Kind of like when it's Christmas time and I might say something like "you won't get anything for Christmas if you do that…" I think we've all used that one! When I do such a thing I am, in a way, trying to bribe my child. But it's flawed in that, regardless of whether my daughter responds, I don't follow through – like getting no presents, no ice cream, no trip to the playground etc. Hopefully you understand my point here and my advice is not to deal with any issue in this manner. Essentially threatening something you never actually intend on enforcing. It's really being lazy and I've done it before and I try not to do it when a situation arises which needs a short-term fix. So my advice here is not to consider the bribe option. On the other hand if you do follow through with something then this type of approach can work in isolated incidents if it does prevent your child from doing something again next time out. All I'm saying is not to try and reason with your child if you're not really going to enforce something if your child does disobey.

Recognize when you're about to "lose it". Let me explain what I mean by this. I'm sure that you have had a day when nothing seems to go your way, you're tired, hungry, stressed and the tiniest thing can tip you over the edge. Typically, you take your frustration out on your spouse or child. So when I say "lose it", I mean it in a sense when the day has got the better of you nothing more than that. The reality is that it will get even worse or it will deeply upset you if you do end up taking it out on them, by letting out your frustrations on your child with the smallest possible thing - especially when the reason why you're feeling like this has nothing to do with them. How you deal with this is very individual to you. So the main part of the advice is really to recognize it when you're on edge after a bad day and then you will know how to respond. The solution would be very specific to you but it might be that you call on your spouse to take over for the night so that you can step away for a short while. It might be that you don't stick to your regular nightly routine for that day. Sometimes it might be that you need to take a little pressure off, by not trying to get it all done at once and not letting things get the best of you. The reality is that we will have bad days from time to time, so don't beat yourself up if you don't feel like the best parent in the world on such days. It might be that you ask your children to help out a little more than normal. But my advice is really more focused on prevention in this case, knowing when you've essentially had enough and might need some extra help, so that you don't "lose it" at home.

Memory box. As you will have picked up on, my daughter plays golf and has been playing tournaments for the past year. The sport is irrelevant however, as the advice I want to provide is for you to have some type of memory box. Cherish those precious little things which, when saved together over time, become your own little treasure box. You can apply it to almost anything, certainly with any sport or activity your child is involved with. I will use golf as my example, but you can do so many different unique and wonderful things. I don't see anything wrong in getting ideas from elsewhere either, but there is also nothing better than creating your own authentic ideas to create those lasting memories. Not that this is the purpose for doing such a thing, but I also think that an added benefit is that it shows how much you really care about what your child is involved in. It can most certainly be a bonding experience! A further bonus may be that it helps to further develop the passion for something your child is developing in. I'm sure you have heard of sayings like "going the extra mile" or "going above and beyond". Not all, but I think most of the time, that this advice is referred to in a professional setting, to essentially getting ahead in your career. But why not apply this to parenting? Many parents do and I think it is little things like this, something fairly simple such as a memory box, where you're really going the extra mile or above and beyond as a parent. Your devotion as a parent may not be fully appreciated in the moment and the reason I say this is because I'm sure that one day it will be. It's only really now, after becoming a parent myself, that I can really fully appreciate everything my parents did for me when I was growing up.

A simple example of what I like to do from golf is actually an idea I have picked up from someone else. I was once watching a feature of pro golfer, Justin Thomas, which also included his father. His father showed all the different golf balls from the courses that his son played when growing up. After each round, they saved the ball and marked it with the date, score and he signed it. I'm not sure exactly how many he had, but over the years he built up quite a collection. I just thought, watching it, how amazing it would be just for them to pick up a random ball and go back to the time that they shared together. So although I may be accused of not being authentic, I too have started this and we have a long way to go to get anywhere near the amount they have. I do feel that we're off to a good start as we have over a dozen different balls displayed in my daughter's room, all from different events. Something like this also helps show how far my daughter has come in such a short space of time as she continues to improve so this, I find, is a further added use. A simple idea which is easy to do and the cost is the price of a golf ball. Imagine if we keep doing this and in say 20-30 years down the line we look back on our collection – it will be priceless.

Another form of collection I have are the different drawings my daughter does for me. She loves to draw and color so I already have quite a set. Pictures range from animals, to pictures of our family, or a range of home-made cards from Birthday's, Christmas, Father's Day and Valentine's Day. I have some in my office, but I keep most in a group. Occasionally I pull out the stack to take a look, and it's a very simple way of brightening up my day. Now you don't need me to come up with ideas for you, so maybe try and become a trend setter with a brand new concept. My advice to you is to save those paper cuttings, the jerseys, the photos, the banners, you name it. Keep them all somewhere safe. Make a photo album that you can pull out at any time. I'm sure that they're great to pull out and reflect on at the end of the season/year, and also no doubt, way down the line when your son/daughter has grown up. Use it as proof to show how far they have come with all their hard work. This will be a gift which will last a lifetime. My advice to you is to take the time to do something special like this and the simple idea I chose takes no time at all. All I would say is that even this requires discipline on your part as well as your child. Whether you call it a memory box or not, save those special little things that relate to your child's interest/passion. That one golf ball or newspaper cutting on any given day may not be worth saving, but when that one thing adds to and helps build a collection, then I'm sure that it will all be worth your while. I will sign off on this point, but let me just finish on emphasizing the discipline element. This requires action and mindfulness (to keep doing it) – essentially don't forget to do it. So if you think this is good advice then make sure you act, and continue to act on it, as it doesn't quite have the same effect if it's done as a one-off.

Be prepared to have difficult conversations. I added this bit of advice which essentially is about not being passive as a parent and taking issues/challenges/problems (whatever you want to call them), head on. My view is that if something doesn't sit right with you, there is no point in venting or ranting and raving unless you go directly to the source and deal with it yourself. I could provide an endless list of examples and it could be with anyone really, a teacher, a coach, doctor, friend, family member, neighbor, other parent and so on. You may have questions and my advice is don't second guess and find out what you need to. This is obviously all very specific to your child so I will give you a real life example which I think worked well. My daughter has a tennis coach and there was a period where she wasn't really that excited to go to her lesson. There was an element of where we felt there was a little too much emphasis on technique given her age and there were times when we felt that the coach needed to ease up a little. So rather than let these thoughts and feelings linger, I had an open and honest discussion with him and it all got resolved for the better. This wasn't an overly difficult conversation to have, but my main point of advice is to deal with any issues head on. Similarly, if you don't think something is right at school, then talk to the teacher. Or it might be that you need to raise an issue with another parent. All I would say is that this is not about calling people out or throwing anyone under the bus, or trying to be all confrontational. I would also recommend having such conversations in a private setting, not drawing any attention. As a parent you will have your child's best interests at heart, but this sometimes means stepping out of your comfort zone to deal with it. Like other things there will be a spectrum ranging from major issues to minor ones. But the way I see it, even when a minor issue comes up, I do what I can as a parent. I also don't suggest tip toeing or treading on egg shells around something which is important to you as a parent related to your child. At the end of the day it's your responsibility. If you're not going to deal with the issue then who will? I think this actually links to a previous chapter in relation to stepping out of your comfort zone and resiliency. This is not about being argumentative or aggressive in anyway, but at the same time don't worry about what you have to say or avoid something just because it's a whole lot easier. My advice is to be honest with any issues or concerns that you have and talk them through with the right person. Again, if it's important to you as a parent and it involves your child, then it's your responsibility to deal with it. Don't whine and moan about something that is bothering you to your spouse/partner or say with your own parents, deal with it directly with the right person to look to take care of any of your frustrations – confront them head on!

I want to touch on the importance of not being passive a little more. What I mean by this is that if I'm with a teacher or doctor and I have questions about my child, I don't leave until I have them answered and I understand. I may even seek additional clarification on something. Or it might be that there is an event at my daughter's school coming up so I ensure I have all the details in advance. This is not about being "that-parent" and being a nuisance or overly high maintenance. It's about being hands-on and I certainly won't lose any sleep over asking what might be deemed a silly question from time to time or about following up again on something. So to close this one out this advice is in two parts really. The first is that if anything is bothering you about your child, deal with it. Have those difficult conversations if you need to, if someone else is involved. Trust me; there will come a time, so take responsibility. Don't take your frustration out on your spouse or family member who has nothing to do with the issue and can't help solve it, talk it through with the right person. This is not about looking for trouble but at the same time, if something doesn't sit right with you as a parent and you need to have a difficult conversation with someone, then my advice is to do it in a very respectful way. Don't let it pass or linger. The second part is about being hands on, so if you're ever unsure of anything, just go and find out. My advice is not to leave anything up in the air when it comes to your kids. For example, don't leave the doctor's office if you're unsure of something or make sure you call the school back if you need to clarify anything. Stay involved and this will improve your chances of not getting unwanted surprises or something happening out of the blue or unexpected. Essentially, know the facts. If that means asking again, checking, confirming, following up or whatever, then my advice is to do just that – without feeling the need to apologize for doing so.

Goals. This may warrant more attention and a lot more focus but I at least want to look at/address goals. I think we all understand the importance of having goals in life and having something to strive for. When I hear people talk about goals it's commonly used in a professional setting like career goals and aspirations. Or it might be health goals or life/personal goals in general. Sure people may have a goal of spending more time with their family but what I'm saying here is to consider having very specific goals to parenting alone. Depending on the age of your child encourage them to set goals for themselves too. I also don't see anything wrong in you, as a parent, setting goals for your children. Of course they need to be realistic and without you pressurizing them, but when used correctly I think goals can be very useful. So my advice is to consider this as I'm not really sure if I have heard too much about specific parent goals, or specific goals set by parents for their children. I'm not saying no one does it or that it's never been discussed specifically related to parenting, but maybe it's just goals are more commonly talked about in different settings.

I'm no guru on goal setting so there will be a lot more advice out there on how to set goals. Goals being specific are obviously a key one or perhaps the main thing you come across. You don't need me to give examples, but I will give one anyway. The generic goal of spending more time with your family, in my view is not specific enough. So more of a specific goal might be to book a week or 2 week vacation together this year. It might not even need to be something big like that. It could be you just block out your weekends for the next month where it's dedicated to your family/children and it's almost marked as sacred. I think setting goals for your kids is also useful, particularly with younger children as I think parents play a key part in helping them achieve their goals. Thinking about it this is probably as important with older kids too, but all I'm saying is that younger ones are maybe a little more reliant. Or it might just be that some children don't automatically think about setting themselves a goal so the parent can introduce them to the concept. I think it's so useful when you have goals as I think a similar concept applies like I previously discussed with a "non-negotiable". This is where you're probably more inclined to get on with things and push on rather than let anything hold you back. Using one of the hypothetical examples earlier in the book, your child might have a goal of making varsity for their sport next year. Again nothing new and you won't be reinventing the wheel here; I just think that anything like this will help keep your child focused. This is because with this focus and if they really do want to make the team in this case, they will know the importance of doing some extra practice and working hard over a consistent period. It might even take the parent out of the equation having to ask/remind or nag them to do such a thing.

So my advice is to consider setting goals and try it - again it might help make you a better parent. I repeat, setting goals is nothing new and I think most know the importance of them being specific. Have parenting goals, but by just saying or thinking that you want to spend more time with your family won't get you too far in achieving it. I refer to this again and this is only a presumption, but I think this one may be relevant for a lot of real world parents. I think goals in relation to parenting all come back to scheduling, planning, time management and prioritizing. Staying with the example of spending more time with your family, all of these things become relevant if you determine you really do need more family time. Sometimes you might need to spell it out for yourself and again nothing new, break it down. Either way whatever is important to you as a parent and with your child, my advice is to consider setting goals to keep you all on track – or perhaps more simply to help ensure your priorities are consistently in check.

Conflicting emotions at the same time. I don't know how else to explain it, but sometimes it's as if you have conflicting emotions/feelings when reacting to something. For example my daughter may do something that frustrates me and part of me wants to shout and part of me wants to give her a big hug. I once heard an analogy which I think proves the point here, where hypothetically your child may run out in the street/road – they're ok, nothing happened. But what do you do? How do you react? In the moment you may just have those conflicting feelings/reactions where part of you may just want to shout or yell at your child. But at the same time the other part of you may just want to give them a big hug with the relief that they're ok and nothing happened. A funny one for me, looking back at the other day was where my daughter was playing some tennis games, introducing her to the concept of scoring. Now every time the ball would be going way out and in the air, she would try to hit it and so if you know tennis when that happens you lose the point. It's all done in an environment to learn, but the fact she kept doing it with continued help from coaches showed she was just not getting it. However, the fact she was doing it over and over at one point I'm not going to lie, I did want to shout: "What are you doing?" But again, in that very same moment that kind of confused/oblivious look she had did also make me want to just go over and give her a big hug. I'm just throwing this out there for another thing to think about as I think as parents we regularly face situations where we almost want to react to the same situation in two completely different ways. Maybe a real obvious one is something like your child spilling their drink or breaking something. The reality is that things like this will happen and as a parent it's easy to react one way or the other; where on the one hand you might shout and on the other you may sympathize as you know mistakes will just happen from time to time. Again without trying to over-complicate/over-think everyday occurrences, just consider or at least try sometimes to have a long-term outlook. In these examples whether it's learning to score at tennis, spilling a drink or breaking a glass think about whether you want your child to be brought up in an environment where mistakes are ok? I say this because the more and more things my child gets exposed to, I continue to understand the importance of children knowing that mistakes are ok and are actually key to learning/developing in anything. So when I mention environment, I mean it so that you're not getting to a point where your child fears making mistakes or starts to avoid things because mistakes are likely to happen. I think you will be amazed of how such subtle things can gradually creep in which I think can start from these type of everyday things. Look I'm not saying give your child a high five for spilling something or making some other mistake, but I think the point I'm really trying to get to is for you and them to really understand that mistakes are actually ok, because I really do think that this sort of outlook will help you all in the long-run.

Other parents, other children and comparing. My advice here is not to say "don't compare". For all the best advice in the world, I think that it's just within our nature to compare, whether we do it purposely or not. So whilst I'm acknowledging that it's hard not to, my advice is to try to, at least, reduce the tendency. I think the best way for this to be done is to be less concerned with what is going on in other people's lives, what other parents are doing, what other kids are doing etc. I have said it throughout that nothing is equal. Our lives are the combination of so many different variables and to paint an analogy where it's a puzzle of tiny pieces where each and everyone one is different/unique. I see a lot of people these days, not just parents, who are more interested in the timeline on their phone or looking up images/videos of what other people are doing with their lives. When you do something like this it's almost inevitable that you compare yourself, your situation or even what you're even doing right now. I don't want to come across cynical either, but you have to realize that what people upload to their profiles is not necessarily their reality – not too many people out there want to show off anything perceived to be negative. However I do know that some people like put their whole lives out there, so to speak.

Not just that, but many watch so called reality shows with celebrities and, again, it's only natural to compare. The irony with reality shows is the word reality as, in my view, when looking at it in real life it's a completely different world (far from reality). Think about it, wouldn't you act a little different if someone was filming you for the world to see? Rather than being real, would you be more concerned in how you're perceived? Your time and energy are so valuable as a parent, and I think that some waste theirs focusing on the lives of other people. In doing so you may not be intentionally comparing your life to theirs, but like I said I think on some level you most certainly or inevitably will. This book is about becoming a better parent so this is the focus throughout the book. So bear that in mind when I say all these things. This isn't saying that you shut out the outside world, it's not saying that at all. The point that I want you to at least consider is focusing less on what other people do whether it's in your neighborhood, phone or on TV. Don't lose focus with what's important to you, even if it's not the social norm. I say this because I feel that when we compare, we then have a tendency to try to emulate/better what the other person is doing or that sometimes it might just be about trying to fit in/keep up. The concept of "Keeping up with the Joneses". This is where we can end up copying someone else and not being ourselves. If you think about it, so many social norms are driven by social media whereby people are basically copying someone else. In doing so they're not being original at all. I want to make clear that this advice is just focused on comparing. So my advice is not to so get caught up in what other people are doing. Remember that we all live different lives and have different circumstances as well as resources – nothing is the same or equal. I think that if you do this you will be using your time much more valuably by concentrating on what your family is doing and keeping your focus on that rather than anything or anyone else. By doing this, I think you will have much less of a tendency to compare yourself to another because you're not focusing on others, rather just your family. Before I move on, I want to make clear this doesn't contradict the advice of making sure that you're not so deep in your own bubble that you forget others around you. This is about spending time comparing yourself to people online or on reality shows where you don't actually even know that person or socialize with them in person.

Don't wish your life away. An additional piece of advice for new parents which I will elaborate more on is to enjoy every moment. This advice sounds rather too generic or cliché. So to be more specific, don't get caught up or obsess over things which seem so important in the moment where you in effect sometimes wish your life away. Some examples here I see other parents do all the time and what we did ourselves in certain areas is getting frustrated when your child is not crawling, talking, walking, going to the pottie by themselves etc…There is an endless list and it's easy to get impatient particularly when you see other kids at a similar age to your child who may be doing something before them. As I said earlier, I suppose it's only normal to compare with other kids, but I think it's important not to get worked up about these type of things as everyone is unique in that sense. Or it may not even be impatience it's kind of more like onto the next thing. Like you want for your new born to roll over and then you might soon start thinking about crawling and then the next thinking which might be walking. Each time you're kind of your wishing for that next thing to come along. So back to my original advice of savor every moment, I don't mean it in some overly deep way. I mean it by advising you don't wish your or your child's life away just for them to finally do something or hit a certain milestone. My advice is don't get wrapped up in some of the things that will naturally happen and happen on their own. Or to put in another way in that in time it will all take care of itself. If you try and force the issue you will bring stress to something which should really be all about enjoyment. This may make you smile or even roll your eyes. To apply what I've just said in our life, my wife was keen for our son, Max, to start crawling – let's just say he was a little late to the game! But when he did she then made a comment along the lines of how it was a whole lot easier before he started to crawl. (I've just realized how long it's taken me to write this book as my son wasn't even born before I started writing this and now he is crawling)! I have referenced not wishing your life away specifically to new parents, letting certain things take their course, but the concept very much applies to all in my opinion. Our attention can quickly turn to the next thing once our child hits a certain milestone at any age. Whenever I hear advice like enjoy the journey, I do feel it sounds a little text book like. However, in this context, I believe it can be applied as I actually think it's good advice because you will cherish the moments you have with your children even more, instead of constantly turning your attention to something else or the next thing.

Life is unpredictable and sometimes you can't even make it up. Again no advice on this point, but I want to share something as this literally just happened only a few days ago whilst writing this book. We were having a lovely day, I had a day off work and we were just planning out the rest of the afternoon (I had just made myself a nice cup of coffee, literally going to take a few minutes to myself) when my daughter slipped on our tile floor and cut her chin open. So our afternoon was then spent at the ER instead. Don't ask me how she did it because I'm still trying to work it out as I'm not getting much from my daughter. My father in law often refers to the well-known saying of "you can't make this sh*t up." I think this applies to many everyday things with children. I suppose I'm trying to put a light spin on what happened to show our days can throw up many unexpected things like this. If anything I will try and link this back to following a really strict routine or some rigid schedule, as I just don't think it works because of the unpredictable nature of parenting. As you know, I place great importance on scheduling, but there are times like this where everything gets thrown out the window as something like a trip to the ER room takes over. I'm sure every parent has some sort of story where you couldn't even make it up if you tried.

Don't always let your child win. It has taken me a long time to complete this book and during that time we have gone through different phases particularly with our daughter. As I write this, a challenge we are dealing with right now is that my daughter hates to lose at anything - it could be as simple as a matching/board game. It's a weird one really because on the one hand someone might say it's good for a child to be competitive and that shouldn't be interfered with. But the issue we're having right now is that she's not being a good sport with things. In addition, I also think that she is starting to avoid certain situations where she might lose at something, so if that is the case there is certainly no benefit in that at all. She's still only 6 and I hope this is a short phase that we will work through, but I have to acknowledge that as a parent I have contributed to this current issue. Funnily enough I came across some advice in another parting book which encouraged parents to let their kids win at anything/everything to help build things like confidence. I took this advice on board and I'm sure as a parent you can relate to a time when you just let your child win at something. But I was doing this all the time and now I think I missed a trick by doing this. The way I feel right now is that I would much rather my child be a good sport, know that losing is part of playing games and what is really important is how your react to a loss – important things like not giving up and trying again. I think you can help teach your child important values in very simple things like playing a board game or a race or a free throw contest as some other basic examples to throw out there. Look I'm not saying you should beat your child every time and never let them win in something. I just took it to the one extreme and in my case it hasn't really worked out as I hoped. Again every case is different, but I'm just sharing my experience with using such an approach and my advice would be to not do it. I would now be much more inclined to say let a child experience defeat in something, but I would also say to not just leave it there. Think and relay important messages when they might lose in something. It could be things like saying good job, you got me this time and I will try again to try to get back you next time out. Encourage that willingness to not give up and that losing is a valuable learning experience to help in development. Obviously age/maturity is an important factor here as well as the activity, but even so, I do genuinely believe important messages can be passed on with the simplest types of things and even from a very early age.

Boy and girls are different. A final thought and perhaps a somewhat controversial one given that it seems the PC police/brigade are also trying to neutralize gender these days. But I did say that I will be honest throughout this book and I don't want to exclude something just to avoid any criticism. So at the risk of being shot down, I have to say that, in my experiences to date, boys and girls are very different. Of course this is such a general statement and ignores how all children are unique in their own sense. But I have to say I have just noticed similarities in how boys and girls (if I'm allowed to say that?) interact. I have a boy and a girl so there is certainly no favoritism on my part, but I will just share some of the things I regularly see. I notice a lot of the time that boys and girls naturally gravitate towards kids of the same gender, particularly with younger children. There is no segregation or anything like that, but I tend to find when left to their own devices, girls want to play or be on the same team as girls, and boys want to play and be on the same team as boys. Let me make it clear that I'm generalizing here, but nonetheless it's something that I actually observe, so arguably it's more objective/fact then subjective/opinion. I'm sure someone might counter this with something along the lines of how society conditions things like this to happen, but with first-hand experience I just don't see it that way.

Continuing with speaking generally, another similar trait I see is that, when girls are together they form an orderly line, play in turn, listen and follow directions better. I find boys are just more boisterous so to speak and I'm not saying that's a bad thing, just an observation. So although this may not always ring true all of the time, the advice here is to actually recognize where such differences are obvious, because it will no doubt alter your approach. Not that you purposely would treat boys or girls differently or favor one or the other, but common sense would say that your approach may need to somewhat alter with a group of boisterous/overexcited/energetic boys than a group of calm girls. I'm all for equality when it comes to gender and no more so the fact that I have a daughter of my own. The point that I'm trying to make or advice is not to ignore obvious things, because it might help you respond in the obvious way, particularly when in a group setting. I say this because I think these days it's got so far where we might be inclined to overthink something or try way too hard to be all politically correct when it might well be that simple common sense will do. Maybe what I've just said will rattle a few feathers, I don't know? But whenever I speak to parents on this topic they all seem to say the same thing and agree that generally speaking boys and girls just are different and we certainly don't need to start referring to them as Theybies, Itbies or Whateverbies.

Sex of your child. This is not advice but I just want to share my own experience with finding out the sex of my first child. I just want to share it as it has all been part of my experience of becoming and being a parent. Like with what I just said, I will maintain my honesty throughout and I won't leave something out with the fear of it being a little controversial. I do want to make clear that the most important thing for me, like most if not all, when finding out that you're becoming a parent is to have a healthy child. I have learned this more than anyone after losing our second child, Emily. But I'm human and I won't lie that I did have a preference of having a boy when we found out that my wife was expecting with our first. Again I stress the word "preference" and that I'm human in that sense. I think some admit it or are more open than others when it comes to what they want the sex of their child to be. I'm fully aware that some people are not fortunate enough to have children, so I'm certainly not looking to offend here as I said it's just about being honest. I do think that many parents (certainly not all) have a preference, but that's what it is, a preference, and not the be all and end all. So what I'm trying to say is that in the real world the reality is that I think the sex of a child is important to many expecting parents – period!

So again, without lying, when we found out that we were having a girl, I was a little disappointed at first but still obviously excited about having a baby. I wanted a boy. Now I can't really explain too specifically, but after our daughter was born, I can't even begin to give justice to describing how special it is to have a baby girl. What is ironic in this whole process is that after having a girl, my preference then completely shifted to wanting a girl in our following pregnancies. So the same scenario repeated itself in reverse where my preference was a girl in our third pregnancy and we now have a boy. The world is a funny place and I guess life works in mysterious ways! I don't really know why I wanted to share this but maybe some of you can relate to some of my feelings. It's strange how life works out sometimes. I suppose what you can take from this, certainly if you're an expecting parent, is that the original advice which you will hear all the time is true in that it really doesn't matter what the sex of your child will be. This is because once they're born you wouldn't change them for the world or anything about them!

As we draw to the end of the book, at this stage I want to acknowledge that, at times, I have given some cold and hard truths. But I think that, in writing something like this, it needed me to be completely honest and open otherwise my words would lose meaning and purpose. I have said throughout that this isn't about me using language to gain universal approval and being all politically correct. This isn't about you agreeing with everything I have to say either. So the main point that I'm trying to make here is not to be sensitive to any of the points I have made in the book. What I want you to consider is that much of the advice that I have given in this book has come from my own mistakes and experiences. I have also provided a lot of advice related to my observations. In these cases I have purposely tried not to be too judgmental, rather I just say it as I see it. Things I have seen first-hand which are truths rather than made up – again

I say what I've seen. I make these points because, as I said earlier in the book, parenting is so personal to us, so we can easily become offended. So whilst parenting is so personal, don't take anything written here personally. Sometimes you may need to be cruel to be kind and I say this because this type of saying may be relevant in some cases. I also want to make clear that my intention is for my advice not to insult in anyway. It all comes back to becoming a better parent. So I think the key is to consider the points, knowing or realizing my intention throughout has been to help you do just that. Essentially what I'm saying is put something to one side, certainly if it will help you indeed, become a better parent. Apply my advice directly to yourself, be honest with your reflections and then determine the right action for you. If you disagree with something I've said, then still consider the topic and draw your own conclusions. In many ways I think it will help you to think twice about certain things or by sometimes looking at something in a different way. I firmly believe that there is so much in this book that can help you become a better parent which is the reason why you're reading this. My aim all the way through has been to talk to you on the same level so I hope that has come across as you have read through. So before I officially closed out, I just wanted to say that and make all of this very clear. Everything has been focused on becoming a better parent, so if anything just remember that key point.

43 SUMMARY/CONCLUSION

With my closing remarks, I would like to bring it back to the start of the book as, after reading this, I hope that you have related to many of my thoughts/advice/suggestions on parenting. Even more, I sincerely hope that any advice I have shared can help you in some way to become a better parent. That is perhaps the main objective of this book. Ultimately I think that is all we can do, to try and become better parents and acknowledge that there is no such thing as the perfect parent. I think if we have this mind-set and approach then we will actively seek out ways to improve which, in turn, will positively impact the lives of our children, as well as our own as parents. Its sounds very cliché and I'm still in the early parts of the process, but parenting is very much a journey for which I have already experienced incredible highs and the lowest of lows. My advice is just that, advice, so I'm sure some of my thoughts shared will be more applicable than others and there may be areas in which you differ in opinion. I also thought it was important to share some of the mistakes that I have made from which you can hopefully learn from too.

My intention was to be completely open and honest throughout with my personal views. As I've said on several occasions you may not agree with everything I have had to say, but a positive by-product may be that you give some thought or extra consideration to an area that you may not have previously given much attention to. So in that sense I would still see it as a benefit even if you do it or look at something in another/different way. Again it's all about applying it to your own unique personal circumstances. I purposely didn't write this to gain universal approval and I certainly didn't try to make my advice sound all PC. We're real parents in the real world, so as I've said all along, I have tried to communicate in that way throughout. I hope this book has come across or has been presented to you in an everyday sort of way which you clearly/easily understand – no jargon, no ideologies, no fantasies, providing no-nonsense, simple, meaningful and real advice/suggestions.

With over 40 chapters in this book there is a lot of advice and if you just picked one thing and improved in a certain area as a parent then I think it's worth it. But I will be the first to admit that one thing won't necessarily have a drastic impact on your life as a parent. To see more of that drastic impact I think would be the result of the culmination of many different things which is why I looked at so many different areas/topics in relation to parenting. In addition that big/vast improvement can only be realized over time and that can be a considerable amount of time. The challenge these days is that we want more of that huge impact now or in an instant. However, the reality is there is no magic pill/formula here and let's be honest; if you really want to get good at something/anything (like parenting) you have to put in the work day after day. So I wanted to make that clear in that to really see the effect or benefit in all this really does require your long-term commitment over an extended period so that you can really feel the impact it will have on you and your children/family. If you understand that the purpose/goal is to become a better parent for your children, then I think the more inclined you will be to commit overtime.

As for parenting style, personally I don't think you can give or describe yourself with some form of generic label. For those new parents, I will share some advice from my old profession when I used to work in the professional soccer industry with head coaches/managers. The experienced coaches were always asked what advice they would give to someone starting out. I always came across the same type of response which essentially said: "Do it your way!" I think this advice is so relevant when it comes to parenting. Do it your way and be your own person/parent. Don't try and emulate your neighbor or friend or the reality TV star or even necessarily how your parents raised you. That isn't to say completely disregard everything – do take advice and if you see something someone else does with success then, sure, try and make it work for you. In the end I'm saying that I think you can't look to exactly copy anyone else or another family as all things are not equal. All of our individual circumstances in life differ to get to where we are today. I personally see nothing wrong in learning from others, but essentially from the beginning you are, in a sense, learning as you go, or learning on the job. I have said it throughout that parenting is so complex that it's somewhat useless to try and emulate another. We all have a unique path which has so many variables. It's almost like we have our own tailored jigsaw puzzle with the tiniest of pieces, all of which are different to each and every one of us. That is why I highlight the importance of doing it your own way. If you think about it children living in the same street, going to the same school, in the same class can have those things in common, but can live completely different lives. Does a child have siblings, if so how many? What are the ages of the children? Are they boys or girls? Again I just want to paint a picture with a few obvious variables which make each and every life different. But the list is endless, which again makes the case for doing it your way.

Ultimately you do have to put your family first and do what is right for you and your family. But this is a slogan/affirmation of some sorts, so make sure your actions back up such statements. Be open to advice such as what is given in this book, but apply it to your own situation and try things that might positively work for you. But you're the one to make the call. Again it's all with the purpose of becoming a better parent. This book gives advice – it's not telling you how to raise your kids by outlining some form of new parenting style. This book provides advice/ideas which hopefully you can incorporate in a positive way to your own unique situation and unique way of raising your children. As I said in other areas hopefully some of my views can at least provoke thought to then help you in some way, shape or form. On the other hand, hopefully it can help you in a big way or get you thinking about things you may have never even thought of.

I'm conscious that I'm using the word "hope" a lot, but I do genuinely hope you can relate to so many things that I have shared. With that I do really believe the advice offered can help you become a better parent. I simply wanted to share views from an ordinary/normal guy living in the real world who has the same real world issues/challenges shared by so many other parents. I acknowledge the many challenges we face day-to-day which test our resources as well as resolve. When I say resources there are many like financial, but I think the biggest is time. We all have 24 hours in a day and this easily gets consumed as a parent and the energy/life can be sucked out of us very quickly. With that, it's so important for you to look to utilize your time with your children as efficiently and effectively as possible. When I review this book, and if I was asked to give one key takeaway which is so important to parenting and improving parenting, it would simply be making better use of time. In essence time management, but with the core focus of how you as the parent and your children use it. I think the core focus of parenting is about ensuring the time you and your children spend each day is fully utilized – certainly when with each other! If I'm being honest I just don't think enough parents do this these days and take time with their children somewhat for granted or perhaps don't really fully appreciate its value day-to-day. I mean this more on being truly present in the moment when with your child or family which I have continued to stress/reference throughout, because I believe it's so important, but sometimes it's something which is possibly overlooked. I will briefly share some advice of relevance to this that I previously came across in another book which wasn't actually focused on parenting. The advice was to be as prudent with your time as you are with your money. Think about it, so many parents in the real world have to watch every penny they spend and budget every expense they have. So to bring this concept specifically to parenting, if you place high importance on where your money goes each week or month, place the same level of importance on your time and again that time specifically when you're with your children. I could give many analogies here to paint the picture. But perhaps the most obvious one is that you wouldn't just throw money away or waste it by flushing it down the toilet/drain. So apply this same notion to you and your child's time.

All of our lives have been impacted with technology. But I see so many, choosing time on their cell-phone over time with their kids when they're together. I admit I'm generalizing here and I know, I know I have referenced this so many times in the book that you may be sick and tired of me talking about it. But the way I see it, being distracted when you're in your child's presence is a complete waste of time and, in a way, means you're not really present at all. However, I'm sure that every parent wants their child to succeed and fulfil all of their potential. So that comes in making each day count which is the bold way of just saying, make best use of your time. This includes ensuring that your child will be also be making best use of their time every day. Be extra mindful of this, because when you break it down you may well find that you're not together for the best part of it. But that doesn't decrease your responsibility for what they will be doing in that time. Me saying to you make each day count is another thing that sounds a bit blasé, so again it's really about simplifying it to say that ensure your time, being you and your child's time, is used very wisely. You might think I repeated the same point there, but there is a difference. The first element was in relation to being truly present when together with your child, but outside of that your and your child's time is equally precious, so I will say it one more time – ensure it's all used to full effect!

As the saying goes, time is precious. I don't know about you, but this message becomes so clear as I get a little older and as I see loved ones like my parents getting older too. Time in general is precious and so the time we have with our children and the impact we as parents can have on their life is even more valuable. We all do it and it's easy to take things or time for granted from time to time, not truly appreciating its value. But the more you understand the importance of time, the more likely you will cherish moments with your children and ensure you make best use of the time you have with them. People often say how scary it is how fast time flies. For me, the scary element is that when time is gone, it's gone and gone forever; you can't get it back. Time eventually runs out for us all. So I constantly try not to take anything for granted with my children which is why I don't want to miss out on anything. I want to give them all the opportunities that I can provide with the resources available to me. I don't want to ask or say to myself "where did the last 5 years go?" Or "I wish I would have done this" or "I wish I would have done that". I want to try and take more control of my time where I live with purpose which can provide such opportunities for my children. Even though I say all this, I would be the first to acknowledge that this is still easier said than done. Like any parent, I still have days when things get the best of me, the day runs/gets away where it's a struggle just to keep up or I'm a little snappy/moody because I'm simply tired/stressed. But what I would say is that my intentions are very clear, so such days are more few and far between. At the same time, I will not pretend that I now have it all figured out and that I have all the answers, because I don't. I'm still in the relatively early stages as a parent, still learning, still making mistakes, so all I can do is try and keep improving at it as best I can.

When people are asked what is the most important thing in their lives, I would say the overwhelming number one response would be family (although this is an assumption, I don't have any hard evidence to back this up). If this is the case for you, then make sure you back your words up with your actions, big and small. It's somewhat easier to be there for a family member in their hour of need, but I think the so called small things should be given equal importance. So if your child is the most important part of your life then, when you arrive home, greet your child that way. If your child is talking to you or showing you a picture they made, give them your undivided attention. If you're eating dinner with them then eat with no distractions. If they're telling you a story about their day, listen and I mean listen to it. Make eye contact with them and show your raw emotion. This is what I mean by the small things which I think will show your love as much as anything else. Let your actions not words show that you put family first and that family is the most important part of your life. If anything continue to be mindful. The reality is we're not always going to be that perfect parent, but I think the more you think about such things and how you should/want to act, it will no doubt help you improve by making better choices, thereby making you a better parent!

I have referred to well-known and timeless sayings throughout the book such as "going above and beyond" or "going the extra mile" as a parent. Sometimes it might be as simple as asking yourself whether you're doing just that? Are you going the extra mile for your kid? Are you going above and beyond? It's easy to say you will, but again do your actions reflect such big and bold statements? Sometimes in life you really do get what you give. Again timeless bits of advice like "you get what you give" or "you get out what you put in", I believe can really be applied to parenting. Of course our children are their own individuals and as they become older, it's only natural for them to become more and more independent, assuming more responsibility. At the same time, I don't think that the role of a parent can be underestimated in anyway in shaping the life of someone – good or bad. So when you consider something like "getting what you give" consider this with your parent/child relationship. When I think of giving, I think more in a sense of the love and attention that you give to your child. Or it could be opportunities, things like that. Consider this because if you want your child to be successful (get), then I believe you have to do all you can as parent (give). If you do really give all you've got to your children then ultimately you can do no more. If this is true then you won't have the pain of regret at some point down the line.

Without being all philosophical there comes a time when we're asked those deep and meaningful questions like: "What's your Why?" "What is your life's purpose?" "What do you want to be remembered for?" I think these questions are sometimes challenging as some cannot give an immediate answer or are still unsure. I think that I'm fortunate in that I do know my why/purpose, I know what I want to be remembered for and I know why I'm getting out of my bed each day. My goal/purpose is to be the very best dad I can be, to provide every opportunity for my children in life and at the same time trying to making each and every day count with them in some way. Way down the line I want to be remembered as a family man who always put his family first, who did anything for his kids and was always there for them. Essentially I intend to always back up my intentions/words with my actions. I have to be honest with myself when considering things like this, but ultimately my children will determine this on their own at some point later in their life. I think that is something else for you to consider in that your own children will make such a determination for themselves when they're older on the role that you played as their parent. However, as I say that, ultimately you will also know the answer to such a question, on the impact you had on their life without having to ask anyone else, but you. So when I say I'm fortunate to know the answer to such deep questions is because ultimately I know "My Why." I have such a strong purpose so I know why I work so hard for my family and as a result my wife/children are front and center with everything.

I will sign off with a sincere thank you for reading this. If you're reading a parenting book you obviously have your child's best interests at heart. As parents we play such a major part in their lives and can have such a huge impact – positive or potentially negative. I believe that by constantly looking to improve as a parent we're doing our part and all we can as part of the extremely complex process it is in trying to raise a child. I really hope that you can use some, if not much, of my advice shared to benefit you as a parent. I hope as a result of reading this and the actions you take that you do become a better parent. If this happens you, your children and your family will feel the benefit in so many ways. I wish you the very best in your role as a parent and every success in the future for your child/children.

ABOUT THE AUTHOR

My name is Matthew Amos. This is my first ever book and I'm so proud to have completed it. Ever since I became a parent, the thought always crossed my mind to put down my thoughts, to share advice and all of my experiences of being a parent in the real world which I think so many other parents out there can relate to. It wasn't until, by chance really, through a conversation with a work colleague, that I understood how to make the publishing of a book of my own a reality. Now that I have made it a reality, I hope I can positively impact the lives of many other parents and I believe by publishing this provides me with the opportunity to do just that. I currently live in Melbourne, Florida although I was born and raised in Birmingham, England. I'm such a proud husband to my wife Gina and a proud father to our daughter, Isla, and our son, Max, as well as our other daughter, Emily, who is no longer with us. It sounds very cliché, but as a proud father and husband, I would describe myself very much as a family man. I really do try and live by the saying of "family first" through my daily actions and choices.

www.ingramcontent.com/pod-product-compliance
Lightning Source LLC
Chambersburg PA
CBHW072002060426
42446CB00042B/1353